D1554421

Breaking Boundaries with the Goddess

New Directions in the Study of Śāktism

Narendra Nath Bhattacharyya, Chinsurah, 8 December 2000.
Photograph by Rachel Fell McDermott

Breaking Boundaries with the Goddess

New Directions in the Study of Śāktism

Essays in Honor of Narendra Nath Bhattacharyya

Edited by

CYNTHIA ANN HUMES
RACHEL FELL McDERMOTT

MANOHAR
2009

First published 2009

ISBN 978-81-7304-760-2

Published by
Ajay Kumar Jain *for*
Manohar Publishers & Distributors
4753/23 Ansari Road, Daryaganj
New Delhi 110002

Printed at
Salasar Imaging Systems
Delhi 110035

For

Naren-da

Contents

PART III: THE CONTRIBUTIONS OF ART HISTORY

PART IV: EXPERIENCING ŚĀKTA POWER

Illustrations and Maps

FIGURES

MAPS

Acknowledgments

Chief among those whom we would like to thank for the completion of this project is Narendra Nath Bhattacharyya (1934–2001). Narendra Nath, Narendra, Narendra-ji, Naren-da, or NNB, as he is referred to variously and affectionately throughout this book. It was he who gave Rachel McDermott the honor of editing his felicitation volume, as it was to have been then, in 1990. That various interruptions and obstacles intervened in the subsequent years to cost us the privilege of putting the book in his own hands is a sadness for us, and it is made less painful only because of the fact that we shall be able to present it to his beloved wife and daughter, Manjula Bhattacharyya and Parnasabari Bhattacharyya. Naren-da was a champion and patron of fledgling scholars in his field of study. He thought, selflessly, that by gifting the project to a graduate student he would help advance a scholarly career.

We also owe a debt of gratitude to the various contributors, who have endured an unusually long gestation period; to Ramesh Jain of Manohar Publishers, who has patiently waited fifteen years for this book, and to his editorial staff, particularly Siddharth Chowdhury; to Kristin Miller, Ben Royas, and Linda Tuthill, the several technological experts at Claremont McKenna College who helped prepare the manuscript for submission; and to Peter Dreyer, our superb copy editor.

Finally, I, Rachel McDermott, would like publicly to thank Cynthia Humes for coming to my rescue in the late 1990s to help bring this book to fruition. Despite the long wait, both of us feel proud of the work represented by the range of scholars who have joined us in honoring NNB, and we thank them for their work and him for inspiring it.

Claremont, California CYNTHIA ANN HUMES
New York, New York RACHEL FELL MCDERMOTT

Notes on Transliteration

In keeping with NNB's own meticulous scholarly writing style, the essays in *Breaking Boundaries with the Goddess* are presented with diacritics. Our contributors use Sanskrit, Hindi, Bengali, Tamil, and tribal languages, and for the most part we have tried to follow the transliteration conventions appropriate for each language. In general, deities' names are capitalized, with diacritics; the names of genres and their anglicized adjectival derivatives (e.g., Vedas, Purāṇas, Upaniṣadic) are romanized, capitalized, and given diacritics; all foreign terms are italicized, in lower case, with diacritics, except for a select few that have entered the English language (e.g., raja, maharaja, ashram, guru); and all proper names, including caste and tribal groupings (e.g., Brāhmaṇa, Vaiśya, Ḍom, Śabara), are capitalized, romanized, and given diacritics, according to local custom. The exception concerns famous people who have anglicized their names (e.g., Narendra Nath Bhattacharyya) or who are known principally by such English spellings. Where there is an accepted English spelling, place names are given in that form, without diacritics (e.g., Kolkata, Varanasi); smaller towns and villages are spelled according to the wishes of each author—some with diacritics and others without.

We use 'Tantra' to refer to the system, 'Tantras' for the texts, 'Tantric' as an adjective, and 'Tāntrika' for the human practitioner. 'Goddess' is capitalized when indicating the Great Goddess and lower cased when referring to a specific goddess (e.g., the goddess Vindyavāsinī), an unnamed goddess, or a class of goddesses.

Introduction

CYNTHIA ANN HUMES and RACHEL FELL McDERMOTT

A SCHOLAR'S INTELLECTUAL JOURNEYS

This book was intended to be a felicitation volume; sadly, it has become a commemoration. The fault for this lies mostly with us, the editors, who took an inordinate amount of time to collect, edit, and prepare the essays for publication; Kāla, or Time, is responsible for the rest, taking Naren-da away from us too early. The contributors to this volume represent only a fraction of the many scholars whom Naren-da touched professionally and personally during his academic life; he had a large network of colleagues at the University of Calcutta, where he taught from 1966 to 1999; at Rabindra Bharati University, where he worked as a Visiting Fellow at the School of Vedic Studies from 1992; at the various museums and art institutes in Calcutta; in the colleges and schools in his native Hooghly district; and at institutions of higher learning across India, where he lectured and mentored promising scholars. Those of us assembled here—many of us Westerners, whom Naren-da aided in our research; others Indian colleagues, with whom he worked closely—in our own ways feel that our lives have been changed because of his kindness and example and that the course of our present and future research has been set in a fruitful direction because of his comments, suggestions, and scholarly publications.

Narendra Nath Bhattacharyya was a man of prodigious output, mental flexibility, and personal humility. Of his many published Bengali and English books, seven were revised and updated, with the author publicly acknowledging that he had changed his ideas in light of new research or new theoretical approaches to old material. He was preparing manuscripts nearly until the day he died.

Bhattacharyya always loved the study of history. He received a BA in the subject from Hooghly College and was in the middle of an MA program in Modern History at the University of Calcutta when he suddenly withdrew to join Motilal Roy, the founder of Prabartak Sangha, a constructivist society that worked for the uplift of the poor in Chandannagar. 'Whatever you want to do, you should know your own culture,' Roy apparently told Bhattacharyya. Under the influence of Roy and another member of the society, Nalin Chandra Datta, Bhattacharyya became interested in Indology, and later in 1958, he obtained his MA in Ancient Indian History and Culture from the University of Calcutta. In 1964, he was awarded the Griffith Memorial Prize for his essay 'Indian Puberty Rites' (published in 1968); and in 1965, he received his PhD, also from the same department at the University of Calcutta. His dissertation, written under the supervision of the renowned historian D.C. Sircar, was published in 1970 as *The Indian Mother Goddess*. Once set upon this trajectory of interest and output, Bhattacharyya traveled ahead with purpose and speed: by the time of his death in 2001, he had published thirty-seven books, twelve in Bengali and twenty-five in English, in addition to forty-seven articles in English alone. Four additional English book manuscripts were on his desk at the time of his death and are to be published posthumously.

Several intellectual themes and commitments run like strong threads through his various literary creations. Perhaps the most important, that which ties all of the rest together, is his insistence that one attend to the social embeddedness of religious rituals and beliefs: 'In all my works, which are mainly concerned with the religious history of India, I have always tried to assert that the study of any ritual or cult in itself is of no value unless it is used as a means to understand the vast and enormously complicated problems of Indian social history.'[1] It was, in fact, this introduction of anthropological resources—in addition to texts, the traditional stock-in-trade of ancient Indian historians—that won him the Griffith Memorial Prize for 'Indian Puberty Rites'; as he claimed in the published preface to that work, 'the precise nature of the social institutions of ancient India is a question which the literary evidence is in itself too fragmentary to solve'.[2] The new data on which he drew, in this early work as well as in most of his later books, were accounts of surviving tribal and popular customs and institutions. For instance, in *Ancient Indian Rituals and Their Social Contents*, a survey of the conceptual and historical development of rituals associated with kingship, initiation and puberty, menstruation, fertility, and death and resurrection, he argued that the investigation of contemporary Indian tribal societies could demonstrate how the earliest forms of Indian rituals probably derived from a tribal milieu, before class and kingship were imposed upon them. Again, in *The Indian Mother Goddess*, he made claims about the linkages between early agricultural rites and beliefs connected with fertility goddesses, claims he based on several types of nontextual evidence: in addition to coins and inscriptions,[3] information on the practices of modern tribal agriculturists and reports of women's rites and customs. He plumbed mythic accounts of gods and demons from the more than three hundred tribes in the Indian subcontinent as source material for his book on Indian demonology.[4] Overall, these methodological principles of refusing to admit a great difference between tribal and modern forms of religion and of trying to honor tribal culture, rather than labeling it mere superstition or magic, are eloquently stated in his book, *Religious Culture of North-Eastern India*: 'Human psychology is one and the same everywhere, whether in Āryāvarta or in Nagaland or in West Asia.'[5]

Integral to Bhattacharyya's interest in uncovering submerged meanings, in championing the cause of repressed peoples or elements in history, is his critique of hierarchy and privilege. He detected behind the development of ideas in India evidence for the loss of tribal democracy and autonomy, suppression of a women-centered culture, and the concomitant self-elevation of a patriarchal, kingly and priestly ethos in society. In fact, the entire 'Indian way of life' was, for Bhattacharyya, 'essentially the affair of the dominant class, the higher castes, which has nothing to do with the greater section of the people'.[6] Many of his books contain examples of this interpretive lens. How, for instance, did the agricultural goddess Durgā get transformed into a war goddess? Maybe, he speculated in *The Indian Mother Goddess*, she represented the feelings of the peasants, who had to contend with oppressive landlords and ruling classes and who caricatured their overlords as demons.[7] In his later years, he even counseled visiting scholars to stay away from Calcutta during the Durgā Pūjā season, as the festival had been so commercialized and corrupted by priestly interests.[8] Again, in surmising about the 'original and sophisticated forms of the Vedic sacrifices or *Yajñas*,' he suggested that while they had their 'genesis in primitive magical beliefs and practices, [they probably got] ensnared by the logic of pure society, and [finally culminated in] a meaningless but profitable affair of the priests, kept shrouded in deep mystery and jealously guarded.'[9] Finally, he dedicated his first book on the Jains to the holy name of Lord Mahāvīra, 'who inspired men to fight against oppression and exploitation, disease and death, cruelty and caste, anger and pride, deceit and greed'.[10] It was partly because of this theory of history that he evinced such a distrust of the Brāhmaṇical textual tradition.[11]

As is evident from these intellectual convictions, Bhattacharyya was a keen student of classical Marxism and fond of its idealistic and deterministic aspects. However, he had an uneasy relation with Bengali communism and claimed at the end of his life that he bore a hatred for Indian communists because of their antinational activities and their denunciation of Indian culture. In this he was a follower of M.N. Roy, who was critical of Marxism for what he perceived to be its total disregard of the individual. In the 1990s, when he was revising several of his successful books for new editions, Bhattacharyya toned down the Marxist flavor of his interpretations; in the preface to the second edition of his *Jain Philosophy,* for example, he observed that to 'stigmatize the Brāhmaṇas as social and intellectual villains' was 'unhistorical and prejudiced'.[12]

Aside from his socially conscious approach to intellectual history, Bhattacharyya was faithful to several other methodological commitments as well, three of which we wish to mention here. The first was his open, accepting, and even forgiving attitude toward

Western scholarship. Although he chose not to write in an overtly postcolonial fashion, he was well aware of the failings of Orientalist scholarship and cited the arrogance of imperialist interpreters in several of his books, English and Bengali. 'The Western Indologists and their Indian counterparts undoubtedly rendered commendable service by editing, translating and interpreting the ancient religious texts as a result of which new horizons have been opened in the field of religious studies. But at the same time one should admit that, notwithstanding their sincere attempts, their vision was circumscribed by the outlook they inherited from their own culture and tradition. In most cases they interpreted the Indian religio-philosophical terms in close dependence on those of the West. But it will be wrong to say that they were indifferent to such problems. . . . Still in many cases some kind of superficial rendering could not be avoided, and it is not possible even now.'[13] Indeed, one could characterize the whole of Bhattacharyya's academic career as an attempt to undermine 'the impact of Western education [that] has made everyone so accustomed to Western terms and concepts that it has now almost become impossible to stand squarely on pure Indian tradition'.[14] His Bengali writings, in particular, are aimed at acquainting students with Indian history; his book on the Indian freedom movement (*Bhārater Svādhīnatā Saṁgrāmer Itihās*) is still regarded as authoritative, and it has been reprinted many times. Furthermore, because he was regarded as a historical authority on Hooghly district and Chinsurah town, where he lived all his life, he was entrusted by the state government's Ministry of Information and Culture with preparing a comprehensive account of the *Antiquities of the Hooghly District*.[15] Conversant with world history, Bhattacharyya nevertheless defended the local.

In spite of his incisive critiques of Western bias, he was extremely appreciative of many Western thinkers—his books are full of references to Western anthropologists, sociologists, and historians of religion—and those of us from Europe or America who came into contact with him were all touched by his gentle, humane, and helpful attitude toward our research projects. One might, in fact, aver that it was his Marxist tendency to place people's ideas in their socially deterministic environments that gave him the grace to be able to forgive Western Orientalism; as for those of us writing and researching at present, Bhattacharyya cautioned against an overzealous, unselfconscious, and totalizing hermeneutic.

Another of Bhattacharyya's methodological concerns was the erasure of inappropriate academic boundaries. For him, the study of ancient India necessitated a facility in the full range of religious and philosophical trends, which included the Buddhists and the Jains, who, he felt, had much in common with those who came to be called Hindus. Buddhist and Jain materials are woven into many of his thematic books—*The Indian Mother Goddess* (1970, 1977, 1999), *A Glossary of Indian Religious Terms and Concepts* (1990), *The Geographical Dictionary* (1991), *Religious Culture of North-Eastern India* (1995), *Indian Religious Historiography*, vol. I (1996), *Indian Demonology* (2000), and *Dictionary of Indian Mythology* (2001)—and he devoted a total of seven English books to one or the other tradition: *Jain Philosophy: Historical Outline* (1976, 1999), *History of Researches on Indian Buddhism* (1981), *Buddhism in the History of Indian Ideas* (1993), *Jainism and Prakrit in Ancient and Medieval India: Essays for Prof. Jagdish Chandra Jain* (1994), *Tantric Buddhism: Centennial Tribute to Dr. Benoytosh Bhattacharyya* (1999), *Tantrābhidhāna: A Tantric Lexicon* (2002), and *Encyclopaedia of Jainism* (forthcoming).

Pushing his scholarly frontiers even further, Bhattacharyya believed that insights derived from the comparative study of religion could be immensely beneficial in the historian's interpretive task. During the 1960s, he wrote serially in a Bengali weekly on reputed ancient and medieval texts, covering Gilgamesh, the Zend Avesta, the Talmud and Midrash, Greek, Latin, and Chinese classics, the Teutonic Edda, European romances and chansons, and Norse legends. In various of his monographs he compared Indian religio-philosophical conceptions with those of the Greeks, Babylonians, Romans, Egyptians, Arabs, Persians, and Chinese. Sometimes this served to indicate historical influence or similarity; at other times it proved the distinctiveness of the Indian data. An example of the latter is his conclusion to a chapter devoted to the comparison of the 'Indian Mother Goddess and Advanced Religious Streams': 'Nowhere in the religious history of the world do we come across such a completely female-oriented system as Śāktism.'[16]

This provides an appropriate transition to the main thematic study of our book, *Breaking Boundaries with the Goddess*. For we have chosen to emphasize one of Bhattacharyya's favorite subjects, one to which he returned again and again in his academic writings: the Goddess. He grew up in a mixed religious household, with a Śākta father and a Vaiṣṇava mother, but seemed to find the Goddess tradition more intellectually interesting. His formal passion for the topic derived from his college days, when he read Frazer's *The Golden Bough* and Briffault's *The Mothers*,[17] books that introduced him to the ideas of matriarchy and matrilineality, magical fertility rites, and beliefs leading to the development of the universal Mother Goddess cult. He found a compatible fit between the writings of these Western goddess specialists, most of whom were evolutionary anthropologists, and the Marxist approach of his early intellectual guru, Debiprasad Chattopadhyay.

His main works on Śākta history and religiosity—*History of the Śākta Religion* (1974, 1996), *The Indian Mother Goddess* (1970, 1977, 1999), a chapter on 'Śāktism' in *Indian Religious Historiography*, vol. 1 (1996), and 'Śāktism and Mother Right' in *The Śakti Cult and Tārā*, edited by D.C. Sircar (1967)—are chronological surveys of Śākta ideas, cults, rituals, and social groups, from prehistoric times to the modern period. His chief interpretive lens was the study of process and change; he argued that primitive conceptions of fertility and regeneration emerged from the 'simple analogical associations of earth and woman in terms of the magical principles of similarity and contiguity' and then 'acquired new conceptual dimensions in subsequent ages'.[18] In its present form, then, 'Śāktism is essentially a medieval religion, but it is a direct offshoot of the primitive Mother Goddess cult which was so prominent a feature of the religion of the agricultural peoples who based their social system on the principle of mother-right.'[19] In his earlier works, Bhattacharyya agreed with Frazer regarding the theory of an ancient matriarchy; in later or in new editions of earlier works, he seemed more cautious.[20] However, he never ceased to idealize the early—and, to him, 'purer'—strands of the Śākta tradition.

Closely linked with Śāktism is Tantra, another topic of perennial interest to Bhattacharyya and his readers. In his popular *History of the Tantric Religion: A Historical, Ritualistic, and Philosophical Study* (1982, 1999), in his characteristically wide-ranging manner, he covered a multitude of subjects: what he called Tantra's 'primitive substratum,' Tantric literature, the question of influences (was the tradition indigenous to India?), the relationship between Buddhist and Hindu Tantra, Tantric practices, Śākta Tantra, and Tantric Art. Just as in his *History of Indian Erotic Literature* (1975), where he claimed that his goal was to 'sweep away the fog of exaggerated notions which have so long characterized the study of this subject',[21] so also in his study of Tantra. He wanted to encourage scholarship on a religious strand whose roots lay in a repressed, vilified, and often misunderstood part of the ancient Indian past: a society dominated by female-centered rites and sexual cults. In keeping with his Marxist skepticism, however, he was not himself persuaded by the Tāntrikas whom he met during the course of his research. While he stoutly defended the contributions of Tantra to Indian material arts, medicine, alchemy, and fine arts, and affirmed Tantra's ethical and liberative 'science', he accorded no validity whatsoever to its ritualistic aspects. Indeed, he had met many Tāntrikas throughout his life, but none of them convinced him that they were true adepts or powerful beings.[22]

By the time of Bhattacharyya's death, he had proven that a man who had never traveled outside India, who never lived anywhere but the house in which he and his father had been born, and who spent more than thirty years in an academic department without a private office, a computer, a fax machine, a private phone, or a funded research library, could be an internationally recognized master interpreter and an encyclopedic expert in the field of ancient Indian history. Those of us who have contributed essays to this volume do so with pride to be associated with his memory.

IN STEP WITH A PIONEER: COLLEGIAL ESTEEM AND THE PRESENT VOLUME

Many of us work in fields defined or nuanced by the contributions of Narenda Nath Bhattacharyya. Part I of *Breaking Boundaries with the Goddess* is devoted to research that reexamines familiar texts or familiar figures, not only to further scholarly inquiry but also to tap hitherto unutilized resources. For example, in 'Engendering Alternative Power Relations: The *Virāj* in the Vedic Tradition,' Kumkum Roy reaches back into Vedic texts for cosmogonic conceptions that might differ from the male myths of Puruṣa and Prajāpati. What she finds is a minor tradition that is nonhierarchical and little touched by patriarchal values: the creative force of the *virāj*. Although speculation focused on the *virāj* eventually ceased to provide a viable alternative to the masculine Brāhamaṇical norm, the fact that it was accommodated and not obliterated in the late Vedic tradition signals to Roy the acknowledgment of its significance. Likewise, Sanjukta Gupta surveys the long history of the Pāñcarātra/Śrī-Vaiṣṇava tradition—examining Pāñcarātra theological principles, a Pāñcarātra meditational icon of Śakti from the Kuṣāṇa period, and medieval debates about the ontological status of Lakṣmī—to show that philosophically, ritually, and theologically Śrī or Lakṣmī was far more important to the early tradition than she later became. Hence in 'Once Upon a Time the Supreme Power: The Theological Rise and Fall of Lakṣmī in Pāñcarātra Scriptures,' Gupta demonstrates both what the past held and why it came under attack. A third example in this vein is the essay by Thomas B. Coburn, 'Sītā Fights While Rāma Swoons: A Śākta Perspective on the *Rāmāyaṇa*,' which examines the *Adbhuta Rāmāyaṇa*'s presentation of Sītā as a strong, powerful deity who outstrips Rāma in the demon-slaying capacity, killing not simply the ten-headed Rāvaṇa but his thousand-headed multiform. Coburn discusses the implications of this Sītā, the inverse of the demure and victimized heroine of Vālmīki's version, and concludes that 'the *Adbhuta Rāmāyaṇa* invites us, both scholars and inhabitants of India, to think about who Sītā is in new ways'.

Each of these three contributors shares with Bhattacharyya an interest in the past and a conviction about its relevance. Moreover, Roy, Gupta, and Coburn all argue that the diversity of Indian religio-philosophical strands is rarely suppressed; the *virāj* and the ultimately powerful Lakṣmī and Sītā are not erased but pressed down into subterranean layers of the tradition, where they may, when needed or rediscovered in particular historical situations, rise to importance again. What further intrigued Bhattacharyya about these scholars' essays when he heard about them before his death was their implicit recovery of a woman-centric perspective. The Vedic tradition, with its male priests, male sacrificers, and male creators, and the Vaiṣṇava communities focused on the dominant figures of Viṣṇu and Rāma may look patriarchal, but gender-neutral or gender-equal features lie hidden within them, waiting for notice.

A second set of essays, grouped together in Part II under the heading 'Rethinking Blood, Cadavers, and Death,' presents new perspectives—historical, field-oriented, and textual—on sacrifice. The three authors, Francesco Brighenti, June McDaniel, and David Kinsley, all consulted with Narendra Nath Bhattacharyya on the subjects of their research, and he helped them either with their fieldwork or with their thinking or both.

Brighenti illumines the practice of animal sacrifice in the Śākta tradition by looking back and around: first at what we can glean about sacrificial customs involving animals and perhaps humans in the ancient Indus culture; and then at ethnographic reports, British and modern, on continuing sacrificial practices among tribal societies in the Indian subcontinent. His 'Traditions of Human Sacrifice in Ancient and Tribal India and Their Relation to Śāktism,' perhaps more than any other essay in the present volume, follows Bhattacharyya's lead in attempting to construct a theory of evolution and development in which data from tribal and other nonprivileged groups are brought into the interpretive project for consideration. Also like his mentor, Brighenti explores the implications of early ideas of agriculture, fertility, sacrifice, and violence, and links them to similar conceptions prevalent in other parts of the world where religiously interpreted sacrifice is valued.

June McDaniel's essay, 'Sitting on the Corpse's Chest: The Tantric Ritual of *Śava sādhana* and its Variations in Modern Bengal', focuses on living Tāntrikas in West Bengal whom McDaniel interviewed in the 1980s and 1990s. She describes contemporary Tantric attitudes toward and practices involving corpse rituals, commenting that these can be categorized according to shamanistic, yogic, and devotional viewpoints. In addition, she situates the practitioners and their rituals in the current communist political environment in West Bengal and defends her Tantric informants from charges of immorality. In this last sense, although she is more sympathetic than Bhattacharyya to actual living Tāntrikas, she shares with him a dedication to the recovery, elucidation, and vindication of an important but often maligned strand of the Indian religious tradition. The same is true, from a more theological and psychological perspective, of David R. Kinsley, who, in his 'Corpses, Severed Heads, and Sex: Reflections on the Daśamahāvidyās,' attempts to understand what it is that is transformative and wisdom-producing about the ten goddesses of great wisdom (*mahāvidyās*). In this essay, originally written as the prototype for his later book on the subject, *Tantric Visions of the Divine Feminine: The Ten Mahāvidyās*,[23] Kinsley proposes a theological perspective from which the emphasis on decapitation, blood, and sacrifice in the worship of the ten Mahāvidyās is liberating for the spiritual aspirant, whether committed Tāntrika or devotional householder.

From texts and sacrifice we turn, in Part III, to art history. Both Bratindra Nath Mukherjee and Gautam Sengupta start with a goddess image whose name, provenance, and context they essay to identify. Mukherjee's is a wall painting in Central Asia, in western Tadzhikistan, in a town called Pendzhikent, seventy kilometers east of Samarkand, whereas Sengupta's is a black stone sculpture found in Raigunj in the district of North Dinajpur in West Bengal. Despite their differing media and geographic locations, both goddess depictions present their interpreters with similar difficulties: what tools can one use to identify them, and how does one know when one has reached the limits of understanding? Mukherjee, in 'The Northernmost Representation of an Indian Goddess of Power,' and

Sengupta, in 'An Unnoticed Form of Devī from Bengal and the Challenges of Art Historical Analysis,' provide an instructive contrast in this regard. Both use common art historical techniques, such as consulting texts, comparing the image in question with other, similar images from the region, and examining historical and archaeological data to determine whether the relevant sociopolitical environment could hold any clues. However, Mukherjee feels able to conclude definitively on the identity of his wall painting, whereas Sengupta, having considered all aspects of his stone image, does not. There is wisdom in both conclusions. Also, though focusing on opposite ends of South Asia, Mukherjee and Sengupta appeal to principles dear to Bhattacharyya's academic life, Mukherjee insisting that we look outside the Indian subcontinent to Central Asia for clues to what became known as 'Indian' goddess worship, and Sengupta offering a close regional 'reading' of one district in Bhattacharyya's home state.

Our final essays in Part IV share a common interest in power: the transformations possible through *śakti*, and through the Goddess as Śakti, in the experiences of Hindu men and women. In 'A Festival for Jagaddhātrī and the Power of Localized Religion in West Bengal,' Rachel Fell McDermott focuses on Jagaddhātrī, a goddess of immense importance to several towns and small cities in Hooghly, Howrah, and Nadia districts, where her annual festival, modeled on that of Durgā, but occurring exactly one month later, is the height of the religious calendar. A deity of the 'high' Sanskritic and Purāṇic tradition who was localized in the eighteenth century by a wealthy Śākta zamindar (landowner), Jagaddhātrī is now worshipped in carnivalesque public displays that rival Durgā's festivals in opulence and, her votaries claim, in power. The power she bestows is situated in the realms of devotion, blood sacrifice, and political clout; recently, it has extended even further, to localities in the diaspora where Bengalis turn to her for aid in identity-formation.

The power that informs the topic of Jeffrey Kripal's essay, by contrast, is Tantra. In 'Shashibhushan Dasgupta's Lotus: Realizing the Sublime in Contemporary Tantric Studies,' Kripal employs the lens of 'sublimation' to provide a bridge of understanding between psychoanalysis and Tantra. He argues that both systems prescribe the creative transformation of sexual energy and that 'psychoanalysis can poetically be described as a kind of Western Tantra, as a century-long meditation on the powers of sexuality, the body, life, death, and religion'. This proposal is part of Kripal's ongoing project to bring the insights of Śākta Tantra and psychoanalysis into fruitful and mutually illuminating conversation, and although this essay will not be uncontroversial, it is consonant with Bhattacharyya's own conviction that eroticism and sexuality are closely entwined in Indian religiosity.

The last two essays in many ways belong together. Miranda Shaw and Cynthia Ann Humes both examine the implications of South Asian conceptions of divine females in the lives of South Asian women—and arrive at radically different conclusions. In 'Magical Lovers, Sisters, and Mothers: *Yakṣiṇī sādhana* in Tantric Buddhism,' Shaw investigates Buddhist Tantric texts and introduces us to the subject of *yakṣiṇī sādhana*, or the invocation in Tantric meditation of a class of powerful, alluring, fertile, and potentially dangerous female spirits who are said to act as the aspirants' wives or lovers. She then postulates that positive conceptions about the *yakṣiṇī* may have influenced attitudes toward the Tāntrika's actual female ritual partner, or *ḍākinī*, the vehicle for his spiritual transformation. This essay builds upon Shaw's prior work on accomplished women in the Buddhist Tantric tradition and aims to recover women's agency in a hitherto—and wrongly—assumed patriarchal context. Humes's findings are not so idealistic. Drawing on fieldwork conducted among patrons of the goddess temple at Vindhyachal in North India, in 'The Power of Creation: *Śakti*, Women, and the Goddess,' she notes that the conception and adoration of divine females such as the goddess Vindhyavāsinī worshipped there do not necessarily translate to the extension of positive conceptions of female empowerment in the lives of most South Asian women. Her study is a fitting conclusion to the volume, for it is intentionally informed by and engaging of Narendra Nath's writings. She considers his many statements about agricultural metaphors in early Hindu texts that draw comparisons between soil and women, and link procreative power with social power; his theories of 'dependent' and 'independent' Śāktism; his distinctions between virgin goddesses; as well as conversations she held with him during her times in India conducting fieldwork.

Apart from the four broad topics, or parts, into which these essays are divided, there are at least six other cross-cutting themes characterizing the work of the volume's twelve contributors: (1) Brighenti, Humes, and McDaniel echo Bhattacharyya's advocacy on behalf of the politically or ritually disadvantaged, whether these be tribals, low-caste women, or Tāntrikas; (2) Coburn, Gupta, Humes, Roy, and Shaw all challenge received wisdom about gender hierarchies, even if they do not come to the same conclusions about the usefulness of feminist analysis; (3) Brighenti, Kinsley, Kripal, McDaniel, and Shaw discuss Tantra and sexuality, Brighenti highlighting its connection to ritual violence and the other four arguing that the erotic aspects of the Śākta tradition should be valorized, not vilified; (4) Bhattacharyya's commitment to the inclusion of Buddhist and Jain materials in surveys of Indian history is shared by Coburn, who sees parallels in Buddhist and Jain stories about Sītā with that preserved in the *Adbhuta Rāmāyaṇa*, Sengupta, who looks to Jain goddesses as possible clues for the identification of his Raiganj image, and Shaw, whose area of expertise is the Buddhist goddess tradition; (5) McDaniel, McDermott, and Sengupta have chosen field sites to the west of the Hooghly River in West Bengal and hence contribute to the elucidation of a local history that was dear to Bhattacharyya's own heart; and (6) although all of our contributors are conversant with Western theory, Humes and Kripal in particular have written essays which attempt to link their Indian data with Western hermeneutical ideologies. Bhattacharyya, we hope, would be gratified by the many ways in which his intellectual heirs have charted paths along routes similar to his own.

BREAKING BOUNDARIES WITH THE GODDESS: FUTURE STUDY OF ŚĀKTISM

As we have seen, each of the essayists in this volume urges those of us engaged in the study of Śāktism to push out in new directions:

to examine familiar texts for new meanings, even if these conflict with cultural or sectarian 'truths' as defined in dominant Brāhmaṇical categories; to utilize ancient Indian materials, archaeological and linguistic, to clarify modern phenomena; to listen in fieldwork to the politically disenfranchised and argue for the importance of their perspectives, if necessary criticizing Western and Indian prejudice; to employ a hermeneutic of empathy, validating Śākta and/or Tantric beliefs and rites; to seek fearlessly to understand the relationship between goddesses and women, no matter what one's hypothesis; to make bridges between Eastern and Western analytic categories; to break out of geographic narrowness to embrace a global perspective beyond the Indic subcontinent; and to be humble enough to conclude, when appropriate, that one cannot answer all questions.

As volume editors, we would like to propose some even broader changes or improvements to our field of interest, changes that may require too much money or time to be immediately feasible but that are nevertheless worth wishing for.

First, we could all benefit tremendously from the editing, printing, and translating of more Śākta texts. These could be published in paper form, but just as useful would be the development of a collaborative, centralized, and computerized database of ongoing translation projects. The same is true of images, and we commend the American Institute of Indian Studies for its mammoth image-bank project in India. Imagine the usefulness of such a resource to an art historian like Sengupta, endeavoring to chart the iconographic development of a particular South Asian deity.

Continuing the emphasis upon fieldwork is a second clear priority: close studies of sectarian communities, temples, pilgrimage sites, or political groups for whom the Goddess in some form is a rallying cry. Such research adds depth to scholarly understanding and, perhaps most significantly, reduces the risk of naive theoretical or textually grounded postulations. Given the heightened reliance by current nationalist Hindu political parties on the figure of Bhārat Mātā, or Mother India, as a means to stir patriotic fervor, we expect that Śākta symbolism will play an increasingly visible role in public debates on the nation.

Collaborative research is a third prime desideratum. This could occur between scholars who, though working in different geographic areas of the subcontinent and with different linguistic skills, are already concentrating on the same goddess or the same interpretive question. They could come together for a year to form a 'think tank' on a particular theme or issue that required the expertise of all of them. How, for example, is the Kālī of Bengal related historically to the Kālī of Kerala or the Kālī of Kashmiri Śaivism? Or, how might we erase strict lines between Buddhist, Jain, and Hindu categories in order to understand early goddess worship in South India? No one scholar can easily answer such questions. Indeed, joint projects—even though they are not rewarded in the current university system, which values single-authored works—are terribly important for the advancement of knowledge in the field of Śāktism, as its boundaries are so porous and its historical trajectories still so unknown. The field of religion as a discipline already draws upon the methodologies of anthropology, art history, folklore, history, psychology, and sociology; such linkages need to be made more explicit through active collaboration and interchange. The same can be said of dialogue on an international scale; we need more conferences where scholars from India, Europe, Japan, and the Americas are involved, and more granting agencies willing to fund them. In terms of access to published research, the English-speaking world is unfairly privileged, yet the inability of most scholars of South Asia to read Russian or Japanese, for instance, means that much excellent work in our fields remains inaccessible.

Our final suggestion for future work is the inclusion of the South Asian diaspora in the consideration of Śākta history and religiosity. And here we intend not only diasporic sites—such as, for example, the Lakṣmī temple in Ashland outside of Boston, the Kālī temple in Toronto, or the Durgā Pūjā celebrations in Tokyo—but also the South Asians who frequent them. Most of us outside the subcontinent who teach about Śākta goddess traditions find our classes increasingly populated with first-, second-, and third-generation South Asians: their hybrid perspectives on the 'home' culture, as well as their participation in recreations of that culture in the diasporic setting, can teach scholars much about the flexibility and malleability of goddess-centered communities. Perhaps more such students will themselves join other diaspora scholars in the field, enriching the conversation even further.

In sum, the best way to honor the multifarious, ever-creative, and transformative Goddess and her traditions in the subcontinent is to be receptive to new perspectives, new research techniques, and the insights derived from new collaborations. This is also the best way to pay affectionate tribute to Narendra Nath Bhattacharyya, whose academic career was characterized by openness: in his intellectual curiosity, in his advocacy for the vilified or neglected, and in his affable collegiality.

NOTES

1. Narendra Nath Bhattacharyya [henceforth NNB], preface to *Ancient Indian Rituals and Their Social Contents*, 1st edn. (1975; 2nd edn., New Delhi: Manohar, 1996), xviii. NNB repeated this phrase often; see also, e.g., his *History of Indian Erotic Literature* (New Delhi: Munshiram Manoharlal, 1975), ix.
2. NNB, *Indian Puberty Rites* (1968; 2nd edn., New Delhi: Munshiram Manoharlal, 1980), vii.
3. Other books by NNB in which numismatic and epigraphic evidence is used include *Ancient Indian History and Civilization: Trends and Perspectives* (New Delhi: Manohar, 1988); *The Geographical Dictionary: Ancient and Early Medieval India* (New Delhi: Munshiram Manoharlal, 1991); and *Religious Culture of North-Eastern India* (New Delhi: Manohar, 1995).
4. NNB, *Indian Demonology: The Inverted Pantheon* (New Delhi: Manohar, 2000).
5. NNB, *Religious Culture of North-Eastern India*, 31. This book was the published form of the H.K. Barpujari Lectures that Bhattacharyya delivered at North Eastern Hill University, Shillong, in 1994.
6. NNB, *History of Indian Erotic Literature*, 2.
7. NNB, *The Indian Mother Goddess* (1970; 3rd edn., New Delhi: Manohar, 1999), 61.
8. NNB, personal communication in Calcutta to Rachel Fell McDermott, October 1988.
9. NNB, 'Appendix III: Fertility Rites as the Basis of Tantricism,' in *Indian Mother Goddess*, 283.
10. NNB, *Jain Philosophy: Historical Outline* (1976; 2nd edn., New Delhi: Munshiram Manoharlal, 1999).

11. Representative statements by NNB against an elite intellectual stance can be found in his *Ancient Indian History and Civilization*, v–xv, and *Ancient Indian Rituals*, xv.
12. NNB, *Jain Philosophy*, ix.
13. From the preface to NNB, *A Glossary of Indian Religious Terms and Concepts* (New Delhi: Manohar, 1990), ix. For other, similar comments, see NNB, *Ancient Indian History and Civilization* and *Indian Religious Historiography*, vol. 1 (New Delhi: Munshiram Manoharlal, 1996).
14. NNB, *Glossary of Indian Religious Terms and Concepts*, ix.
15. NNB, *Huglī Jelār Purāṇkīrti* (Calcutta: Directorate of Archaeology, Government of West Bengal, 1991).
16. NNB, *Indian Mother Goddess*, 222. See also NNB, *Geographical Dictionary* and *Indian Demonology*.
17. Sir James George Frazer, *The Golden Bough: A Study in Magic and Religion* (1890; 3rd ed., London: Macmillan, 1912–1930), and Robert Briffault, *The Mothers: A Study of the Origins of Sentiments and Institutions* (New York: Macmillan, 1927).
18. See NNB's own summary of *History of the Śākta Religion* in *Indian Religious Historiography*, 321.
19. NNB, *Indian Mother Goddess*, 222.
20. For a statement in support of the matriarchy theory, see ibid., 23–29. In Appendix II in NNB, *Indian Mother Goddess*, 3rd edn., however, NNB described the history of the controversy surrounding an ancient woman-centered culture and concluded by favoring matrilineality over matriarchy. The same is true of his stance in *Indian Religious Historiography*.
21. NNB, *History of Indian Erotic Literature*, ix.
22. NNB, personal communication at Chinsurah to Rachel Fell McDermott, Tuesday, 26 September 2000.
23. David R. Kinsley, *Tantric Visions of the Divine Feminine: The Ten Mahāvidyās* (Berkeley: University of California Press, 1997).

PART I

Surprising Finds in Familiar Texts

1

Engendering Alternative Power Relations

The *Virāj* in the Vedic Tradition

KUMKUM ROY

I first met Naren-da at a seminar. I was prepared to be overawed by a scholar whose writings were remarkable for their range and commitment. What I had not anticipated was a man who wore his profound learning lightly, a man of warmth, understanding, vision, and humor. I learned to respect him for his humane perspective on life, a perspective we tend to lose sight of in an academic milieu that is often distorted by dazzling displays of erudition.

Naren-da's abiding interest in the female/feminine elements of early Indian culture and his quest for alternatives to the dominant Brāhmaṇical models have opened up the possibility of asking fresh questions and exploring our past with greater sensitivity. These perspectives are, moreover, interrelated, as alternatives to the Brāhmaṇical order are very often embedded in female/feminine frameworks of understanding. This is not surprising, given the masculinist thrust that underlies the Brāhmaṇical tradition. Yet the tradition was by no means monolithic—in fact, located within its interstices, we find often covertly or overtly opposed ideas that seem to have been incorporated but not assimilated. The conceptualization of the *virāj* in the Vedic tradition provides an example of this, and in focusing on it, I would like to take the opportunity to acknowledge our debt to Naren-da for his imaginative insights, for his passionate involvement in the discipline, and for his faith in the relevance of the past.

At its simplest level, *virāj* has connotations of a unique luster, an ability to illuminate. As a concept, it is marginal within the

Vedic tradition. In fact, if one considers the second to the seventh *maṇḍala* of the *Ṛg Veda* to be early, it is virtually nonexistent in the early Vedic context. And yet, although the *virāj* is not referred to very frequently, the Vedic discussion of the term, where available, has a certain richness and complexity that merits attention.

On the mythical plane, the *virāj* is conceptualized in androgynous terms. Thus, it is associated with both typically masculine deities such as Indra (*Śāṅkhāyana Śrauta Sūtra* 8.17.2), Agni (*Āpastamba Śrauta Sūtra* 5.15.2), and Soma (*Śatapatha Brāhmaṇa* 3.3.2.17), amongst others, as well as goddesses such as Aditi (*Śatapatha Brāhmaṇa* 2.2.1.20), Vāc (*Śatapatha Brāhmaṇa* 3.5.1.3), and Śrī (*Śatapatha Brāhmaṇa* 11.4.3.18).[1] In other words, one could conceive of both gods and goddesses as endowed with the qualities considered typical of the *virāj*.

More important, the *virāj* was not simply a divine attribute; it could serve as a conduit between the divine and the mundane world. *Virāj* was also interpreted as the name of a meter (*chandas*, feminine) that was regarded as particularly sacred and employed frequently in rituals. The meter was used to invoke, transfer, and confer *virāj*-like attributes on those who either participated in or undertook the performance of the sacrifice.

At another level, the *Aitareya Brāhmaṇa* (8.38.3) refers to the Uttara Madras and the Uttara Kurus, rulers of the semi-mythical land to the north of the Himalayas, as *virājs*. The other categories of rulers mentioned in the same context are *samrāṭ, bhoja, svarāṭ,* and *rājā.* The list occurs in the context of a ritual known as the *aindramahābhiṣeka* (literally, the great *abhiṣeka*, sprinkling or bathing of Indra, the typical warrior or chief deity in the Vedic pantheon), a ritual meant to legitimize access to power. Within this, we are told that in the central realms, the ruler is known as *rājā* (a term used for the chief and in later contexts for the king); in the east, as *samrāṭ* (the most complete *rājā*, and by extension, in later contexts, emperor); in the south, as *bhoja* (one who enjoys, in this case political power, and possibly resources); in the west, as *svarāṭ* (self-ruler, suggestive of untrammeled power); and in the north, as *virāṭ.* As I have argued elsewhere,[2] all these terms encapsulate distinct as well as overlapping relations of power, and it is in this context that the characteristics of the *virāj* acquire significance.

We have seen that the *virāj* was considered representative of luminosity. Possibly derived from this, it acquired connotations of universality, creativity, and generation.[3] It is likely that such 'meanings' rested on the all-pervasive qualities of light; it is through light that we are aware and we perceive, for light is synonymous with knowing. Light is thus in a sense power, but it is distinct from other kinds of power in that it strengthens both those who possess it and those who experience it. As such, it presents a contrast to other forms of power that posit a hierarchy between the powerful and the powerless, the dominant and the subordinate.

Most other notions of power/rulership acquire specificity and are delimited in terms of finite categories, whether spatial or social. They are thus bounded—*rājās*, for instance, are commonly related to or defined in terms of specific peoples. At the same time, such definitions focus on the differential allocation of power—the *rājā* is clearly distinguished or differentiated from his subjects. In this respect, too, *vairājya* (the abstract power attributed to or exercised by the *virāj*) presents a striking contrast, as the *virāj* is not conceived of as distinct from those over whom *vairājya* is exercised. In fact, the *virāj* is visualized as power that is assimilated or absorbed rather than as power that is endured, willingly or otherwise.

The power of the *virāj* is construed as manifest in the process of creation. Once again, the role of the *virāj* in this context is presented as somewhat unique. The *virāj* figures in the complex cosmogony of the *Puruṣa Sūkta* (*Ṛg Veda* 10.90. 5), where she is thought to be produced by the *puruṣa,* or primeval man, and is conceptualized as producing him in turn. This mythological episode, which is marginalized within the dominant Brāhmaṇical cosmogonies in the later Vedic tradition, encapsulates certain significant perceptions. It implies a view of creation stemming from a primeval heterosexual pair. In other words, it suggests that basic human activities could provide an analogy for comprehending and interpreting the cosmos.

Moreover, both partners in the cosmic drama are envisaged as equally important; the distinction between creator and created is deliberately blurred, merged, and reversed to produce an understanding of a flow of creative power, a flow that is not linear, but where, once again, power is transmitted between participants. This conceptualization of the relationship between male and female partners has few parallels in other myths and is virtually negated in later Vedic rituals, which constantly construct and reconstruct the relationship between the sexes in asymmetrical terms.

The negation of the egalitarian model manifests itself in later Vedic rituals focused routinely and systematically on the role of Prajāpati (literally, the lord of all beings) in creation. Prajāpati was a deity who was relatively marginal in the early Vedic tradition but was accorded centrality in the later Vedic context, where ritual speculation justified the performance of a range of sacrifices by suggesting that these were the means whereby Prajāpati had created the world (see *Pañcaviṁśa Brāhmaṇa* 6.1.1). This perspective is then deliberately extended to provide men with access to what is defined as a cosmogonic role. The logic is simple: if Prajāpati creates through the sacrifice, then men who can perform such rituals or get them performed have an opportunity to emulate the god. They implicitly become godlike and can be distinguished from others, such as men who do not or cannot perform identical rituals, and women, whose role in such rituals is clearly subordinate. In terms of power relations, then, the cosmogonic speculation portrayed as most valid and legitimate rested on an understanding of a single male creator god, whose creative powers were derived from nonphysical spiritual and ritual means. Moreover, the creator, Prajāpati, was literally asserted to be lord (*pati*) of his creation (*prajā*).

Thus, the relationship between creator and created was one of difference, not of identity. Men who aspired to take on the role of creator through rituals could hence differentiate themselves from others and could proclaim their power in no uncertain terms. This was, moreover, power that was centered on the creator; the traffic in power was thus one-way.

While the Prajāpati-centered cosmogonic speculation was not explicitly projected as an alternative to or substitute for the *virāj-puruṣa* myth, it is obvious that the implications of the two myths were inherently contradictory. Accepting one or the other would thus have implied subscribing to either of two available definitions of power relations that were logically mutually exclusive. Yet this logical distinction was very often and somewhat deliberately blurred. The peculiar and specific device through which this was achieved was the naming and deployment of the *virāj* as a meter, especially in the sacrificial context, as mentioned earlier.

The meanings attributed to the use of the meter in ritual situations were somewhat complex, to say the least. They rested on a recognition of the bond between *vairājya* and sacrality, however generally formulated. Thus, at one level the *virāj* meter was envisioned as identical with the sacrifice (*Śatapatha Brāhmaṇa* 2.3.1.18), while at another level it was viewed as a means of sacral communication—a mechanism for conveying the ritual to the gods and bringing it back to men (*Śatapatha Brāhmaṇa* 3.3.2.16). The underlying assumption then seems to be that the *virāj* was intrinsic to any kind of sacred activity. However, the very fact that the meter was thus invoked within and for the sacrifice meant that the *virāj* was appropriated by those who were asserting control over the ritual, namely, an increasingly well defined corps of specialized priests and their powerful patrons. Thus, the lines along which sacral power was to be transmitted were laid down with increasing care.

The *virāj* was also identified with food, *anna* (see *Śatapatha Brāhmaṇa* 12.2.4.5). Occasionally, the ten units of the meter were homologized with what were probably the ten most important edible resources—cow, horse, mule, ass, goat, sheep, rice, barley, sesamum, and beans (*Pañcaviṁśa Brāhmaṇa* 16.1.10). While such linkages were by no means unique to the *virāj*, this was then extended to suggest that the use of the meter in the ritual context would enable the sacrificer to become an eater of food or even a master of food, *annāda*, *annapati* (*Aitareya Brāhmaṇa* 1.1.6).

Two elements of this identification appear significant—first, the equation of the meter with food, one of the most basic prerequisites for human existence, and the almost simultaneous cognizance of this resource as something to be distributed, transferred, and disseminated. If the meter was homologous with the designation of a powerful person (as in the case of the Uttara Kurus referred to earlier), one can probably push the argument further to suggest that what was unique to this definition of power was the sharing rather than the hoarding of resources. In other words, persons who were identified as *virājs* in the human context would probably be expected to demonstrate benevolence; their power would rest on the dissemination rather than on the retention of material goods.

At the same time, the use of the meter in the sacrifice meant that the definition of benevolence was incorporated within a context that was not open to all. As such, a universalistic definition of power was paradoxically included within rituals that legitimized socioeconomic differences and hence robbed it of some of its strength. It is likely that the employment of the *virāj* in the sacrifice marked the symbolic acknowledgment of the popularity and attractiveness of its connotations. Nevertheless, the very incorporation of such connotations within a context that was carefully structured in terms of participants and roles would have detracted from the universality associated with it. Its precise significance was thus subject to contrary pulls.

Although the meter was appropriated within the ritual context, its usage was somewhat unique. Some equally popular meters, such as *gāyatrī*, *triṣṭubh*, and *jagatī* (consisting of eight, eleven, and twelve syllables, respectively) were used to express differences amongst the *varṇas* (castes). These meters were considered symbolic of the Brāhmaṇa (priestly category), Kṣatriya (warrior category), and Vaiśya (common people), respectively, and were employed to render hierarchical relations amongst or between *varṇas* visible (or, more accurately, audible) in the ritual situation. The fact that the *virāj* was not pressed into such symbolism would suggest that it was not very easily associated with specific forms of social differentiation. In other words, the understanding of the *virāj* as universal and undifferentiated was rather strongly entrenched and was not amenable to ritual manipulation beyond a point.

The implicit universality of *vairājya* is also apparent in the location of the *virāj* in terms of gender categories. While both divine and human worlds were envisaged as stratified on the basis of gender, *vairājya* was an attribute of both gods and goddesses, as mentioned earlier. In other words, just as *vairājya* was not understood as specific to a particular *varṇa* and could not be claimed as an exclusive attribute of any single social category, so also it was regarded as potentially accessible to both men and women.

It is difficult to specify how such accessibility was translated in concrete terms. We have, for instance, the possibility of praying during the fortnightly new and full moon sacrifice so as to ensure that the son of the sacrificer would become a destroyer of enemies, while the daughter would become a *virāj* (see *Baudhāyana Śrauta Sūtra* 1.12). There is no means of ascertaining how often such prayers were actually offered, but the fact that the desire for a powerful daughter was provided for is in itself significant. The power attributed to the daughter was, nevertheless, carefully circumscribed—the woman in question was not expected to pray directly for her own empowerment, and such an endeavor would probably have been judged illegitimate. Besides, *vairājya* was envisioned within a context that was explicitly domestic. Thus, the universalistic connotations implicit in the definition of the term would have been at once marginalized and contained.

While *vairājya* was thus recognized within or relegated to the domestic context, it was also occasionally portrayed as a goal to be attained through the performance of more public (and large-scale) sacrifices. However, *vairājya* was rarely imagined as the chief objective of such rituals. In fact, perhaps the closest approximation to such a possibility occurs in the context of a relatively obscure ritual known as the *virāṭ-svarājya*, recommended for men who wished to acquire both the attributes associated with the *virāj* and the untrammeled power of the *svarāṭ* (mentioned above). On the mythical plane, the performance of this sacrifice was supposed to enable the god Mitra to acquire *vairājya*, while Varuṇa acquired *svārājya* (*Śāṅkhāyana Śrauta Sūtra* 14.30.1); both attributes were supposed to accrue to men who followed their example.

The relative paucity of references to *vairājya* as a goal to be attained by the sacrificer contrasts with the frequent occurrence of the term *rājya*. As is well known, one of the major concerns of the later Vedic tradition seems to have been codifying or systematizing complex rituals such as the *rājasūya*, *aśvamedha*, and *vājapeya*, which were viewed as occasions for proclaiming the royalty of the *rājā*.[4] While the *rājā* was occasionally referred to as a *virāj* on such occasions, this was not perceived or portrayed as central or crucial to his change of status and its socio-ritual recognition.

How does one explain the fact that the *virāj/vairājya* was both considered significant enough to merit mythico-ritual speculation and at the same time marginalized? I would suggest the following possibility. If one envisions the human *virāj*, either a man or a woman, as exercising benevolent power, characterized by the sharing or distribution of resources, it is likely that such a person would be conceived of as performing sacrifices or invoking the sacred for general well-being. This could then be extended to identifying the person with the sacral process, a fairly frequent device for creating and sanctifying meanings in the Brāhmaṇical tradition.

Simultaneously, however, the sacrifice was increasingly being systematically appropriated within a context of social differentiation. This appropriation is evident in the detailed discussion on the nature and function of the priesthood, for instance, whereby a specific social category, the Brāhmaṇas, acquired importance as mediators between gods and men. Furthermore, the sacrifice was also being used as an occasion for rendering social differences visible, and for sanctifying such differences, including defining and justifying relations amongst *varṇa*s and between genders. From the perspective of those interested in maintaining social differences, the universalistic, undifferentiated benevolence associated with the notion of *vairājya* would have appeared to be implicitly, if not explicitly, threatening. In such a situation, the molders of the tradition seem to have adopted a strategy of accepting *vairājya*, probably as a concession to those who valued the ideals implicit in it. However, such acceptance was not converted into a more positive endeavor to enforce or propagate *vairājya* as desirable. In fact, while the notions associated with *rājya* were elaborated at length in a variety of ritual contexts, *vairājya* was recognized but marginalized.

This process was accompanied by shifts within mythical

speculation as well, evident, for example, in the *Paryāya Sūkta* (a hymn focusing on a range of cosmogonic and social possibilities) of the *Atharva Veda* (8.10). While I have explored this hymn at some length elsewhere,[5] I shall touch briefly here on the features that are significant for the present discussion. In the first place, the *virāj* is personified and claimed as explicitly (and exclusively) feminine, a powerful gendered subject, and is consequently slightly problematic in a situation of gender stratification. The problem of the power of the *virāj* and what to do with it is resolved along a number of lines of speculation.

Each of these resolutions envisages ways and means of appropriating this typically feminine power. For instance, the power of the *virāj* is portrayed as descending into the sacrificial fires, including the *gārhapatya* fire, one of the three sacred fires, to be maintained in perpetuity by the householder, from which the fires for specific sacrifices are kindled. *Virāj* is thus obtainable by the knowledgeable sacrificer, who would then be regarded as a *virāj*. However, he would use his newfound power to assert his control over the household or *gṛha*. He would become a *gṛhamedhin* (literally, a householder who was also a sacrificer, i.e., a participant in both social and sacral realms) and a *gṛhapati* (male head of the household, also used for a performer of domestic and other rituals [*Atharva Veda* 8.10.1.3]). Thus, feminine power was transmuted in the process of being transferred, and it supported the patriarchal model of the Vedic household.

Other resolutions presented the process of transfer in more violent terms. This included the 'killing' of the *virāj* by gods, men, and patrilineal ancestors, amongst others (*Atharva Veda* 8.10.3). While the *virāj* was thought to revive after each death, this revival was interpreted as beneficial to those who destroyed her. Once again, the underlying notion seems to be one of feminine power that is appropriated for the benefit of masculine categories.

A similar though less violent appropriation is evident in the conceptualization of the *virāj* as a cow, which produces a calf and milk for the benefit of various categories of beings (*Atharva Veda* 8.10.4). The calves are usually portrayed as powerful and masculine. For example, Indra was regarded as the calf of the gods, Yama of the *pitṛs* (patrilineal ancestors), and Manu Vaivasvata of men, while the means of sustenance considered typical of each category was designated as milk. Thus the 'milk' for men consisted of *kṛṣi*, cultivation, or *sasya*, grain. Although both calf and milk represent the feminine procreative and generative powers, what is foregrounded in such mythic formulations is not the inherent feminine principle(s) but the manifestations, which are integral to a masculine domain. In other words, the *virāj* was visualized in terms of power that was to be appropriated, absorbed, transformed, and transmuted.

It is evident that the notion of the *virāj* as feminine and powerful was regarded as somewhat problematic, especially in the context of large-scale public rituals and in priestly speculation. As I have suggested, the problem stemmed from two interrelated elements of *vairājya*. The first was its androgynous or even feminine nature, which was regarded as increasingly anomalous in a context where gender stratification was valorized. Second, the definition of power in terms of sharing, transmission, and benevolence was so closely interwoven with the formulation of the *virāj* that this was probably perceived as threatening or even disruptive to an order that rested increasingly on asymmetrical relations of power, where power was ideally to be concentrated in the hands of a few.

In spite of such considerations, the fact remains that the *virāj* was not obliterated from the 'high' canonical tradition. That it was accommodated typifies a tacit though reluctant acknowledgment of its significance. The definition of the *virāj* as benevolent, and as the wielder of diffuse rather than concentrated power, probably emanated from men and women who cherished relatively egalitarian norms and values, which they sought to formulate through myths and rituals. Unfortunately, but perhaps understandably, they remain anonymous within the tradition. Yet the priesthood, whose very existence was predicated on notions of hierarchy and social difference, was compelled to concede a certain space for such alternatives and had to exercise considerable ingenuity to rework their implications. What is also obvious is that the Brāhmaṇical masculinist norm did not go unchallenged.

NOTES

1. The following Vedic texts, in Sanskrit and English, were consulted for the purposes of this essay: *Aitareya Brāhmaṇa*, ed. Kasinatha Sastri Agase (Poona: Hari Narayana Apte, 1986); *Aitareya Brāhmaṇa*, ed. Satyavrata Samasrami (Calcutta: Bibliotheca Indica, 1895–98); *Āpastamba Śrauta Sūtra*, eds. Richard Garbe and Chintaman Ganesh Kashikar (Calcutta: Bibliotheca Indica, 1882, 1885, 1902); *Atharva Veda*, ed. and trans. Devi Chand (New Delhi: Munshiram Manoharlal, 1982); *Atharva Veda Samhitā*, trans. W. D. Whitney (Cambridge, Mass.: Harvard University Press, 1905); *Baudhāyana Śrauta Sūtra*, ed. Willem Caland (Calcutta: Asiatic Society, 1904, 1907, 1913); *The Hymns of the Ṛgveda*, trans. Ralph Griffith, 4th edn. (1889; Varanasi: Caukhamba Sanskrit Series Office, 1963); *The Hymns of the Rig Veda*, ed. F. Max Miiller, 2nd edn. (1877; Varanasi: Caukhamba Sanskrit Series Office, 1965); *Pañcaviṁśa Brāhmaṇa*, trans. Willem Caland (Calcutta: Asiatic Society, 1913); *Pañcaviṁśa Brāhmaṇa*, ed. Ananda Candra Vedantavagisa (Calcutta: Bibliotheca Indica, 1870, 1874); *Rig Veda Brāhmaṇas*, trans. Arthur Berriedale Keith, vol. 25 of the Harvard Oriental Series (Cambridge, Mass.: Harvard University Press, 1920); *Śāṅkhāyana Śrauta Sūtra*, trans. Willem Caland, ed. with an introduction by Lokesh Chandra (Delhi: Motilal Banarsidass, 1980); *Śāṅkhāyana Śrauta Sūtra*, ed. A. Hillebrandt together with the commentary of Varadattasuta Ānartīya and Govinda (1888–89; reprint, New Delhi: Meharchand Lachhmandas Publications, 1981); *The Śatapatha Brāhmaṇa: According to the Text of the Mādhyandina School*, trans. Julius Eggeling, reprint of *The Sacred Books of the East*, vols. 12, 26, 41, 43, 44 (Delhi: Motilal Banarsidass, 1963–78); *The Śatapatha Brāhmaṇa*, ed. Albrecht Weber (Varanasi: Caukhamba Sanskrit Series Office, 1964); and *The Tāṇḍyamahā Brāhmaṇa According to the Sāmaveda*, ed. A. Cinnasvami Sastri (Banaras: Caukhamba Sanskrit Series Office, 1935, 1936).
2. Kumkum Roy, *The Emergence of Monarchy in North India, Eighth–Fourth Centuries B.C., as Reflected in the Brāhmaṇical Tradition* (New Delhi: Oxford University Press, 1994).
3. Jan Gonda, *Ancient Indian Kingship from the Religious Point of View* (Leiden: E.J. Brill, 1969), 118.
4. The *rājasūya* marked the symbolic birth of the *rājā* into his new role. The sacrifice was composite, incorporating a range of rituals, such as annual rites associated with the agricultural cycle, and a public proclamation of the *rājā*'s change of status. The *aśvamedha,* or horse sacrifice, was recommended for the *rājā* who wished to assert supremacy over others. Its central element was the ritual slaughter of a horse after it had been left free to wander for a year, it being understood that all those who let the horse pass unchallenged through their realms during its wanderings accepted the supremacy of the horse's owner. The *vājapeya*, literally, food and drink, was marked by a ritual chariot

race in which the *rājā* was declared to be victorious, and was characterized by claims to resources. Each of these rituals legitimized relations of power, based to a greater or lesser degree on claims to status, military prowess, and resources. As such, the notion of power that was accorded centrality was very different from that associated with the *virāj*.

5. Kumkum Roy, 'Perceptions of Power: An Analysis of the *Paryāya Sūkta* (8.10) of the *Atharva Veda*,' in *Proceedings of the Indian History Congress* (1992): 56–62.

2

Once Upon a Time the Supreme Power

The Theological Rise and Fall of Lakṣmī in Pāñcarātra Scriptures

SANJUKTA GUPTA

The principle of *śakti*—divine power and dynamism—has been used by Indian theologians to explain the concept of the supreme divine, the creator and the savior. Indeed, late Upaniṣadic thinkers resorted to *śakti* as a constellation of cosmological and soteriological ideas to help them redefine the ancient monistic theology of Brahman, the unique, eternal, and transcendent reality, or supreme God, totally identified with *ātman,* the self. In needing to explain the relationship between the creating God, his physical creation, and sentient creatures, while also preserving claims to Brahman's unique, immutable, and unconditional nature, Upaniṣadic theologians encountered soteriological problems, for the very transcendence of Brahman can lead to the charge that Brahman is disconnected from everything. Some theologians tackled this problem by introducing the concept of *śakti*. In the *Śvetāśvatāra Upaniṣad* (4.1), the One, the God (*deva*), is said to create the diversified universe through his multifaceted *śakti*.[1] In a theistic cosmogony, *śakti* has dual functions. It both evolves as the ultimate source of the universe, or *prakṛti*, and obscures the true identity of individual selves, thereby keeping them fettered to the chain of continuous death and rebirth (4.9–10). As an obscurer of the real, *prakṛti* is called *māyā*, which is both delusion and divine creative power.

In a methodological move similar to that of the *Śvetāśvatāra Upaniṣad*, an important early Vaiṣṇava sect called the Pāñcarātras also used the concept of *śakti* to resolve soteriological issues introduced in monistic Vedāntic thought.[2] In this essay, I trace the history of such Pāñcarātra speculation on *śakti*. I first demonstrate how in the early period *śakti* occupied a central position as the divine personality, as well as the essential source of conscious individuals, explaining the relationship between the supreme *śakti* and the various divine *śaktis*, their roles in Pāñcarātra soteriological practice (*sādhanā*), their place in the cosmology and ontology of that system, and the ways in which they are conceived iconographically.[3] Second, I discuss how over several centuries *śakti*'s centrality gradually became obscure. In the fourteenth century CE, the interpretation of *śakti* was at the root of a major controversy in the theology of Pāñcarātrin adherents, who called themselves Śrī-Vaiṣṇavas. The resulting schism divided Śrī-Vaiṣṇavas into northern and southern groups.[4] Another way of viewing this diminished theological role of the feminine principle in Pāñcarātra and Śrī-Vaiṣṇava contexts is to focus on the fate of Śrī/Lakṣmī, the innate power and energy of God, hypostatized as a goddess and mythologized as the supreme God's divine spouse. As we shall see, the diminution of *śakti* occurred during a maturation of theological strategies, reflecting shifting priorities: as the need to provide a single, undifferentiated theistic deity emerged, rather than the preservation of a coherent ritualistic religious practice, the status of *śakti* decreased.

Examining the earliest evidence within the Pāñcarātra system of theology reveals how important *śakti* has been in its soteriology.[5] Pāñcarātrins followed a gnostic approach very close to that of Vedānta: one reaches salvation through the realization of one's self as essentially not different from God's *śakti*. This soteriology follows the yogic method of analyzing human nature in the quest for the essential person, eliminating in the process the grossness, diversity, and opacity that obscures that essence. This is achieved by understanding the process of creation that evolves from and through *śakti*, which is innate in God, coexistent and consubstantial with him. Creation begins with a differentiation in the unity of God—in other words, with the appearance of speech, or *vāc*, also considered to be divine cognition or awareness, *jñātva*, the vehicle of reflection.[6] The reflexive awareness of the Unique One initiates a cognitive activity toward its object, the Unique One's own self, *ātman*. Such cognition needs speech to illuminate its nature, to indicate name and content. Thus the very first moment of disturbance in the unity of the Supreme Being is an act of cognition that requires speech (*vāc*).[7] From this self-reflection develops both the divine will (*icchā*) to create and the divine power to create, which is eternal and immutable (*acyutā śakti*). In the Pāñcarātra system, such *śakti* is also identified with the supreme Person's 'I-ness' (*ahaṃtā*), or divine personality responsible for projecting embodied beings; an additional theological label for this *śakti* is active consciousness, or *saṃvit*.[8] *Saṃvit* is thus the primal moment of self-consciousness on the part of the supreme Person—who is, in this school, Nārāyaṇa or Vāsudeva[9]—the end of his indeterminate and quiescent state, heralding his creative will and agency. Awareness of himself starts the phenomenon of subject-object cognitive polarization—although at this point both subject and object are the same. This creative power or *śakti* is also called knowledge (*vidyā*), nature (*prakṛti*), and illusion (*māyā*), and is subdivided into five additional parts, or *kalās*:[10] time (*kāla*), divine omnipotence (*kriyā*), omniscience (*jñāna*), will (*icchā*), and primal dynamic flux (*prāṇa*).[11] Because each individual's personality emanates from the divine personality, to know one's own true self is to know one's identity with *śakti* and its qualities; the transcendent divine *śakti* inheres in every phenomenon as its essence. In other words, in the early Pāñcarātra system, the spiritual goal is to concentrate on *saṃvit* as the self (*ādhyātmika*).[12]

The cosmos, as a Pāñcarātra yogin learns about it, is refracted in six trajectories, the first two of which—(1) speech (*vāc*), and (2) *śaktis*, understood as real world ingredients or building bricks (*kalās*)—we have already introduced. The last four graded stages of manifestation are (3) the multiple emanations of the four cosmic realities (*tattvas*) or diversifications (*vyūhas*), Vāsudeva, Saṃkarṣaṇa, Pradyumna, and Aniruddha, who embody the cosmic process of the emergence of the universe, (4) mantras and their deities, (5) the way of the individual (*pada*), characterized by the four states of waking, dream, dreamless sleep, and transcendence, and (6) the way of the empirical world (*bhuvana*). The final two of these six are subjects; the content of their experience is registered as names and their corresponding forms (*nāma* and *rūpa*). The highly accomplished yogin starts from stage three, the *tattvas*, and then finally arrives back at the *kalā* level, the ultimate stage of soteriological practice in which he realizes his identity with the primal *śakti*, *saṃvit* and *vāc*, the aggregate of these *kalās*.[13]

The centrality to early Pāñcarātra soteriology of the concept of *saṃvit śakti* is demonstrated by the description of this final phase of yogic practice leading to emancipation. To achieve success in the yoga of *tattvajaya*, or the removal of the yogin's association with the empirical categories that created his individual identity and differentiated it from the supreme being,[14] he identifies himself with the primal group of *śakti*s who emanated successively from the original *saṃvit śakti*, fixing his mind on the mantra of each, in reverse order.

Yogic meditation, both in its differentiated (*savikalpa*) and nondifferentiated (*nirvikalpa*) states, uses a threefold system of meditation—concentration (*dhyāna*), meditation (*dhāraṇā*), and stasis (*samādhi*).[15] Regarding the first, Mircea Eliade remarked, 'In Tantric *sādhana*, iconography plays a role that, though of the greatest importance, is difficult to define in a few words.'[16] Further, 'Tantric iconography represents a 'religious' universe that must be entered and assimilated. This 'entrance' and 'assimilation' are to be understood in the direct meaning of the terms: in meditating on an icon, one must first 'transport' oneself to the cosmic plane ruled by the respective divinity, and then assimilate it, incorporate into oneself the sacred force by which that particular plane is 'sustained' or, as it were, 'created.''[17] Eliade's observations show his deep understanding of the system of meditation involved. He further remarks, 'When a Tantric text describes the way to construct a mental image of a divinity, we seem to be reading a treatise on iconography.'[18] Here he is referring to what is known as *dhyāna*, or the concentration on prescriptive meditational images of gods and goddesses on which the whole of Tantric iconography is based. Tantric yogins of all types, including those following the Pāñcarātra system, are exhorted—as the first of three stages in the spiritual life—to assimilate and absorb such divine forms within their individual selves, thereby achieving stasis of their naturally dynamic thought processes. The sacred texts of the Pāñcarātra describe these *dhyānas* as the divine forms of mantras, which are their sonic counterparts.

In theistic systems, God is responsible for creating not only the empirical world but also the world of mantras and their deities, which are the means to escape from transient existence. Both of these activities, creating and liberating, are expressions of the same *śakti*.[19] When the yogin achieves the knowledge that is truth in itself (*ṛtambharā prajñā*), discriminating knowledge (*viveka buddhi*), and the idea that he is totally unrelated to any form of diversity (*kaivalya*), he finally realizes the nature and functions of the divine *śakti*. Her various aspects, also known as *śakti*s, are, as mentioned above, time (*kāla*), divine omnipotence (*kriyā*), omniscience (*jñāna*), will (*icchā*), and primal dynamic flux (*prāṇa*), the last four of which, in ascending order, are the pure *śakti* forms of the four *vyūha* deities Aniruddha (*kriyā*), Pradyumna (*jñāna*), Saṃkarṣaṇa (*icchā*), and Vāsudeva (*prāṇa*).[20] Hence in the Pāñcarātra salvific schema the effect of time disappears through practice of *savikalpa samādhi* and the awakening of *viveka buddhi*, and the yogin practicing *nirvikalpa* meditation identifies himself with the relevant *śakti* at each step, realizing his identification consecutively with the remaining four *śakti*s and ending with *prāṇa*, the pure dynamism of Vāsudeva.[21] But all the time he also is aware of the fact that all four *śakti*s are present simultaneously through each step; the active divine consciousness, or *saṃvit*, symbolizes the unity of all *śakti*s. Now these meditations are conducted by utilizing all three components of the process of stasis, namely, *dhyāna, dhāraṇa,* and *samādhi*. Therefore, as the mantra texts explain, each *śakti* has a *dhyāna* form for fixing the yogin's mind—and hence we turn to a brief exposition of the complex system of Pāñcarātra iconography.

In Pāñcarātra Vaiṣṇava religion, images and icons acquired an important position at a very early stage. As the mantras became the focal point of meditation, their visual forms were believed to manifest their mantric power.[22] During the period between second century BCE and the fifth century CE, a great number of icons and images of Brāhmaṇical deities were in existence, many of them Vaiṣṇava.[23] For private worship and meditation, a practitioner needed a quiet and secluded place. These private icons were in the round, showing the deity from all four sides.

I deal now with two Pāñcarātra images, one of which depicts these primordial *śaktis*. It is small but completely in the round, and preserves enough features to identify it as a *dhāraṇī*, or support for the yogin's meditation. An investigation of this image will provide an example of the manner in which early Pāñcarātra yogins meditated on the primordial *śakti*/*śaktis* to attain salvation. In his book *Viśvarūpa*, T.S. Maxwell presents two diagrams of very important and rare Pāñcarātra cosmogonic icons of composite figures, preserved in the Mathura Museum.[24] They belong to the Kuṣāṇa period, *c.* first or second century CE. The first (his fig. 1.2 and pl. 14) is a composite figure containing a central columnal goddess who is surrounded by five other goddesses (see figs. 1 and 2).[25] One of these emerges from behind the central figure's head, vertically positioned. The other four appear two on each side of the central goddess, growing somewhat obliquely from behind her shoulders and the sides of her head. The central columnal figure is the largest of the group. On the rear of the icon a tree is sculpted. The similarity of this image to his other diagram (fig. 1.1), a Caturvyūha image (depiction of the four [*catur*] *vyūhas* together), is striking.[26] The only difference is in the number of figures: six as opposed to four. Maxwell has discussed the interpretive problems associated with these images quite extensively, claiming that since the curved tree behind the multiple-imaged Caturvyūha icon proves its—and hence Viṣṇu/Nārāyaṇa's—cosmogonic nature,[27] the same cosmogonic aspect can be asserted of the multiple-imaged form of the goddess, with its background tree-icon. Here I go further and suggest that this composite six-goddess image must have been used as a *dhāraṇī* for the *tattvajaya* meditation, which aimed to help the aspirant reach unconditional yogic stasis (*nirvikalpa samādhi*).[28]

The group of five *śaktis* (*kāla*, *kriyā*, *jñāna*, *icchā*, and *prāṇa*) is designated as the *bhavopakaraṇa*, the ingredients for the making of creation,[29] and in addition they represent the evolution of creation.

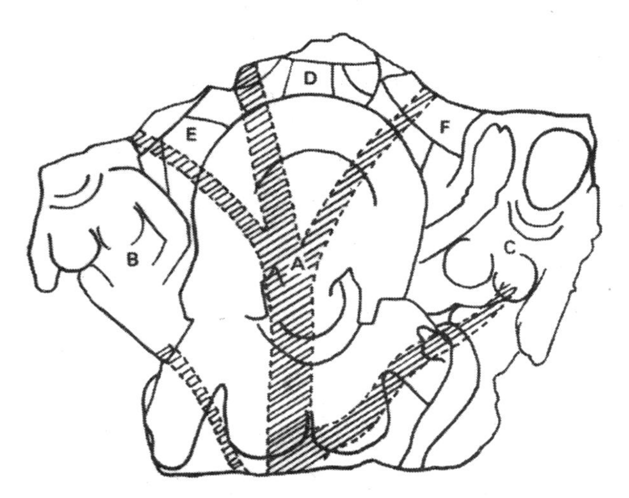

Fig. 1: A diagram of a rare Pāñcarātra cosmogonic icon, depicting a central columnal goddess surrounded by five other goddesses. Kuṣāṇa period, *c.* first or second century CE. Mathura Museum. From T.S. Maxwell, *Viśvarūpa* (Bombay: Oxford University Press, 1988), fig. 1.2, p. 36.

Fig. 2: Photograph of the image in Figure 1. From T.S. Maxwell, *Viśvarūpa* (Bombay: Oxford University Press, 1988), pl. 14.

I relate these *śaktis* to the image in Maxwell's book (fig. 1.2 and pls, 14–16).[30] I totally agree with him in regarding this multiple goddess image 'as the intelligent expression of complex and coherent religious philosophy.'[31] The figure is in the round and on its own, unconnected to any male deity, and I strongly believe that this figure was used by the Pāñcarātra yogins to practice *tattvajaya* meditation. The icon is very damaged and almost all the faces are broken, yet it still retains enough distinctive marks to show its religious affinity to the other image of the fourfold cosmic emanations (Caturvyūha *mūrti*) of transcendental Vāsudeva, the supreme godhead of the Pāñcarātra Vaiṣṇava sect. From Maxwell's description it is clear that the central figure is the main object of concentration, which is the supreme *śakti* manifest as *vāc*. This is *saṃvit*, the first emergence of divine awareness, the first moment of polarity within the Supreme Being who becomes aware of himself.[32] Once we see the composition of this primary creation, we can appreciate the skillful location of the five *śakti* images. Of these, *prāṇa* and *icchā* are depicted closer to the main deity, both being integral to the Unique One's self-awareness and the cognitive process involved. *Jñāna*, *kriyā*, and *kāla* are positioned farther away. All five are clustered together to underscore the fact that they all are equally primary cosmogonic *śaktis* and incorporate definitive processes of creative action.[33]

According to the *Pauṣkara Saṃhitā*,[34] when the yogin starts on the practice of *nirvikalpa samādhi* he has already moved beyond the range of *kāla* and hence deals, in ascending order, only with the four *śaktis kriyā*, *jñāna*, *icchā*, and *prāṇa*. Although God as Brahman is unconditionally transcendent and immutable, his *śakti*, which is intrinsic in and inseparable from him, paradoxically can and does change, evolving into multitudinous phenomena, active and ever vibrating. Here the *Saṃhitā* hastens to assert that *śakti* is also immutable, *acyutā*. This may seem paradoxical: *śakti* is immutable, yet she evolves; she is pure consciousness (*saṃvit*), yet she deludes individuals. When these theological and cosmogonic truths are depicted in Pāñcārātra imagery, the simultaneity of *saṃvit*, the clear light of consciousness, and its emanations *kriyā*, *jñāna*, *icchā*, and *prāṇa*, is envisaged as a central mass of illumination or sun, with surrounding rays.[35] Before entering and being assimilated into the central light, *saṃvit śakti*, the yogin is aware of his individual self, which consists of his mind, intelligence, and ego, all of which are intrinsic parts of his personality. In yoga, he identifies this group of inner categories with the *vyūhas* Saṃkarṣaṇa, Pradyumna, and Aniruddha. This idea is expressed in the *Mahābhārata*, and Śankara mentions it in his refutation of the Pāñcarātra position in his commentary on the *Brahmasūtra*.[36] The four *vyūhas* are related to each other in the mythology of Kṛṣṇa/Vāsudeva and are separate personalities. But in the context of Pāñcarātra soteriology the images show minimal iconographic difference, which emphasizes their closeness to their source. Thus the yogin starts by using mythology and iconography to focus on their relatedness. Then, rising to the metaphysical level, he plunges in deep meditation on them, concentrating on their essential nature as parts (*kalās*) of the supreme *saṃvit śakti*.

Returning to the icon under discussion, we note that it contains six figures, at least three of whom are definitely female. In Pāñcarātra meditation prescriptions, the yogin is instructed to concentrate on the lowest, or *kāla-śakti* first, merging it through his efforts into the next higher, *kriyā-śakti*, and so on. Thus it makes sense to interpret the farthest of the six figures as the relatively gross *kāla-śakti* and the main goddess as *saṃvit-śakti*[37]—the whole statue a symbolic aid in *tattvajaya* meditation. If we accept with Maxwell that both of his images were utilized for the same *tattvajaya* meditation, then we can speculate that they were meant to represent two steps of that yogic process: first, meditating on the Caturvyūha image, where the distinct diversification of *śakti* is emphasized; and second, turning to the goddess image, concentrating on the *saṃvit-śakti* together with its derivative *śaktis*. If this is a feasible interpretation of the two icons, we have material evidence of a highly unusual type to confirm not only the importance of *śakti* in early Pāñcarātra thought but also the visualization techniques by which adepts were trained to meditate on reversing the process of creation within their own bodies.

Thus far I have talked about the divine *śakti* of Nārāyaṇa, the Supreme Godhead of the Pāñcarātra canon. When conceived as a goddess, however, this female power is called Lakṣmī or Śrī. Śrī is prominent in early Indian religions. Symbolizing wealth and prosperity as well as fertility in her identity with Lakṣmī, this goddess dominates early female divinities represented in sculpture. She is highly eulogized in the apocryphal *Ṛg Vedic* hymn the *Śrī-sūkta*. The *Mahābhārata* records a legend of her abandoning the demon monarch Bali in favor of Indra. She also deserts Indra due to the curse of the sage Durvāsas and hides herself under the sea until the famous cosmic event of the churning of the ocean. She emerges from the waters and unhesitatingly flies into Viṣṇu's arms.

Both the *Mantramahodadhiḥ* and the *Śāradātilakam* describe the combined icon of Lakṣmī and Vāsudeva as the primal two-in-one divinity.[38] In early Pāñcarātra texts, too, Nārāyaṇa/Vāsudeva is associated with Lakṣmī.[39] The *Lakṣmī Tantra* clearly says that all divine *śaktis* are emanated from her.[40]

Since Lakṣmī is the goddess of beauty, prosperity, and royal fortune, it is not surprising that she is associated with divine kings such as Indra and Viṣṇu. When the latter was revered as the supreme sovereign divinity, Lakṣmī naturally became his spouse.[41] Both Hemchandra Raychaudhuri and Jitendra Nath Banerjea record that during the early centuries of the common era until the decline of the Gupta dynasty,[42] Bhāgavata religion drew a lot of attention and appreciation from the imperial Guptas.[43] Not only do inscriptions of the period refer to Viṣṇu, but quite a few Gupta coins also bear the images of both Viṣṇu and Lakṣmī.[44] Although either Bhūmi, the earth goddess, or Sarasvatī, the goddess of learning, is sometimes regarded as Viṣṇu's second wife, shown iconographically at his left side, Lakṣmī always remains on his right side as his main wife. Banerjea believed that the huge image found at Besnagar belonging to the third or second century BCE represents goddess Śrī, who was already worshipped by the Pāñcarātra cult as the active principle, the chief consort of the supreme Vāsudeva.[45]

So why was it that in late medieval south India Lakṣmī's divinity was seriously questioned? P. Pratap Kumar has quite exhaustively investigated the position of Lakṣmī in south India;[46] here, therefore, I discuss just a few points. Firstly, both Yāmunācārya (tenth century) and Rāmānuja (1017–1137)—the founding teachers of the Śrī-

Vaiṣṇava sect, which 'drew its ritual tradition quite openly from the Pāñcarātra tradition'[47]—adopted the Pāñcarātra concept of Lakṣmī: that as Vāsudeva's *śakti* she was essentially homogeneous (*sāmarasya*) with the godhead.[48] Rāmānuja acknowledged Lakṣmī's coexistence with Viṣṇu in the *Vedārtha-saṃgraha* 5.217: 'O great Brahmin, just as Viṣṇu pervades every phenomenon, so also does she. She is the essence of the gods, and also of human beings.'[49] Moreover, he calls her nontransient (*anapāyinī*), an epithet often used to qualify Lakṣmī in the *Lakṣmī Tantra*. Parāśara Bhaṭṭar (1017–1137), a disciple of Rāmānuja, speaks of Lakṣmī as Viṣṇu's *śakti*. He also refers to her as the source of mantras as well as of the universe; all *śakti*s emanate from Lakṣmī, and she is the life-breath (*prāṇa*) of Viṣṇu.[50] Obviously Bhaṭṭar was aware of the Pāñcarātra idea of the primary polarization of *śakti* as *saṃvit*, *vāc*, and *prāṇa*.

Lakṣmī's exalted position, as taught by early Śrī-Vaiṣṇava teachers, posed problems for later interpreters, who began to accord her a superior but non-divine identity. After the time of Yāmuna, Rāmānuja, and Parāśara Bhaṭṭar, theologians of the sect started developing the concept of Śrī/Lakṣmī as the supreme intercessor (*puruṣakāra*). This was linked with the ideal of surrender (*prapatti*) to the will of God (Īśvara), where God was conceived as paramount over all sentient (*cit*) and insentient (*acit*) things. Teachers who developed Śri-Vaiṣṇava theology wrote extensively on the nature of *cit*, *acit*, and God.[51] As S.N. Dasgupta puts it, 'there are, on the one side, the self-conscious souls, and, on the other, the omniscient and all powerful Īśvara and the manifold external world. These three categories are real.'[52] In spite of the fact that Lakṣmī was accepted as Nārāyaṇa's inseparable divine power, later teachers encountered difficulty in placing her in either of the sentient categories, *cit* or Īśvara. Theories inherited from Rāmānuja concerning God's relationship with individuals—*śeṣa-śeṣī-bhāva* and *śarīra-śarīrī-bhāva*—posed additional problems for the categorization of Lakṣmī. The first establishes that individuals belong to God, the final authority. They are entirely under the control of God and God alone. Self-conscious selves exist only for him. The latter idea posits that the creation, both sentient and insentient, forms God's body and hence is external to him who is the essence of all. As our inner self controls our body's functioning, so God controls all individuals and objects.

In light of these theological tenets, later sectarian interpreters had to explain whether Lakṣmī was external or internal to God (Nārāyaṇa). Rāmānuja had made her a special mode (*prakāra*) of God in which he enacts her function of being the source *(prakṛti)* of all. However, the more conservative adherents of the sect, uncompromisingly *ekāntin* (following only one God), did not include Lakṣmī within the category of Īśvara and hence had to incorporate her into the category of *cit*, or individual selves, even though they granted her, as God's spouse and most beloved and charming companion, the status of the supreme self. According to this view, because of her great beauty, supreme wisdom, and compassion, she cleverly and wisely influences God to pardon his true devotees even when they commit sins. Two great Śrī-Vaiṣṇava philosophers and theologians, Vedānta Deśika (1268–1369) and Piḷḷai Lokācārya (1264–1327),[53] finally brought these competing views into the open and addressed the 'Lakṣmī problem' in debate.[54] Vedānta Deśika regarded Lakṣmī as an inseparable part of the category of God, and hence eternal and all-pervasive: a divinity integral to Nārāyaṇa who voluntarily, as his spouse, accepts dependence upon him. But Piḷḷai Lokācārya took the opposite view, regarding her within the category of sentient individuals, totally different from God and therefore neither pervasive nor eternal; she was chosen by Nārāyaṇa as his spouse because of her countless excellent qualities and her wisdom, devotion, and beauty. Even when she has the power to punish a sinner she lets God do it. In fact, opines Lokācārya, she influences God only when she wants him to exercise his grace in pardoning sinners, and it is only through her motherly, intercessory activities that a mere mortal can aspire to divine blessings.[55] Therefore, Lakṣmī can intercede, but she cannot grant grace herself. She is the epitome of wifely virtue and motherly love. But divine she is not.

Even the method of devotional worship (*bhakti-upāsanā*) that had been advocated by Rāmānuja and Vedānta Deśika as another means to salvation was rejected in this conservative tradition of

Piḷḷai Lokācārya and relegated to the position of a mere self-purificatory preparatory discipline. For him, liberation could come only through the practice of *prapatti*—unconditional surrender to God's authority as the total controller, *śeṣa*—and by no other means. Unflinching faith in God's protection was ranked above meditation on God and his creative and redemptive powers.

The northern school, following the tradition of Vedānta Deśika, has continued to hold the position that Lakṣmī is not only inseparable from but also equal to Viṣṇu (the southern school could accept the former of these relations but not the latter). In terms of temple worship, the rituals performed for Viṣṇu and his consort are more or less the same in both communities; what differs is devotees' theological interpretations of those rituals. But temple worship itself is an indicator of Viṣṇu's typical dominance, even among followers of Vedānta Deśika. For although there is a 'rough equality in the number and type of rituals conducted for Viṣṇu and Śrī', festivals dedicated to Śrī tend to be confined within the temple walls, whereas those for Viṣṇu have a wider, more public scope. 'This cloistered atmosphere [of Śrī's processions] may reflect male attitudes toward women that form part of Hindu tradition—attitudes that prescribe certain restrictions for women.'[56]

Thus it is that Śrī/Lakṣmī, who began as an independent goddess of wealth, prosperity, beauty, and fertility, worshipped on her own or in conjunction with Kubera, Indra, and finally Viṣṇu, progressed in the Pāñcarātra religion to become the supreme power of Viṣṇu/Nārāyaṇa and the source of all creation, the divine potency, potentiality, and energy, then mythicized as his spouse.[57] In the early Pāñcarātra tradition, the primary manifestation of the creative urge of the divine is equated with the goddess Vāc and her primary manifestations, *kāla, kriyā, jñāna, icchā*, and *prāṇa*. Vāc and these five emanations form the primal group, where *vāc* is the active divine awareness, *saṃvit* is the central power, and the realization of them through one-pointed meditation as one's self-identity is releasing knowledge or gnosis. To facilitate this meditation, early practitioners used images, a few fragments of which have come down to our time. Two clear examples of such meditational icons are the images discussed above, which date from the second to first centuries BCE, when Pāñcarātra soteriology was thriving. From the depiction of the six powers, with the sun-like *saṃvit* in the middle, we can infer that they were used as objects of mental fixation by yogins desirous of release from the bondage of transient existence. It is possible that the paramount power of Nārāyaṇa was by then identified with Lakṣmī. Her position rose steadily, and other cults devoted to her grew up alongside the Pāñcarātra. But for the later southern school of Śrī-Vaiṣṇavism, following the lead of Piḷḷai Lokācārya, Lakṣmī lost her divinity, a compromise deemed necessary in order to safeguard the oneness of God.

NOTES

1. See also *Śvetāśvatāra Upaniṣad* 6.8: *Parāsya śaktir vividhaiva śrūyate svābhāvikī jñāna kriyābalāni ca* |; 'One hears about his highest and truly diverse power, which is part of his very nature and is the working of his knowledge and strength.' The translation is Patrick Olivelle's: *Upaniṣads: A New Translation* (New York: Oxford University Press, 1996), 264.
2. Dating the rise of the Pāñcarātrin sect as a clearly defined group with established philosophical beliefs and ritual practices is not easy. We know that the system is fairly old, as Pāñcarātra soteriology and ritual practices were thriving at least by the second century BCE, causing Bādarāyaṇa in that same era to comment on (or refute?) their doctrines in his *Brahmasūtras*. Furthermore, by the time of Śaṅkara in the eighth century, the Bhāgavatas possessed the *Pāñcarātra Saṃhitās* as their canonical scriptures; as a community they too date at least as far back as the second century BCE. Firm textual evidence for the detailed exposition of the Pāñcarātra doctrines cannot be found earlier than the *Mahābhārata*, however, where the *Nārāyaṇīya* section (dated to the early fifth century?) expounds ideas that receive more detailed treatment in the earliest *Saṃhitās*, the *Pauṣkara*, *Jayākhya*, and *Sāttvata*, probably dating from the late fifth to early sixth centuries. After the Pāñcarātra was enfolded into the emerging Śrī-Vaiṣṇava tradition in South India after the eleventh century, the theological aspects of the former tradition were sidelined; thereafter, the prime concerns of the Pāñcarātra were directed to practical liturgy alone, in other words, to the construction of temples and images, and rituals such as spiritual initiation (*dīkṣā*) and the various types of image worship. See Mitsunori Matsubara, *Pāñcarātra Saṃhitās and Early Vaiṣṇava Theology: A Translation and Critical Notes from Chapters on Theology in the Ahirbudhnya Saṃhitā* (Delhi: Motilal Banarsidass, 1994), 1–49.
3. For a discussion of some of the same material, but without the focus on *śakti*, see Sanjukta Gupta, 'Yoga and *Antaryāga* in Pāñcarātra,' in *Ritual*

and Speculation in Early Tantrism: Studies in Honor of André Padoux, ed. Teun Goudriaan (Albany: State University of New York Press, 1992), 184–87. There I focused on a yogic practice described in the three early Pāñcarātra Saṃhitās, the *Sāttvata*, the *Jayākhya*, and the *Pauṣkara*, as well as in two late texts of the school, the *Lakṣmī Tantra* and the *Ahirbudhnya Saṃhitā*, a practice in which one meditates on the basic Pāñcarātra four-fold divinity, Vyuha-Vāsudeva. The lateness of the *Lakṣmī Tantra* (ninth to twelfth centuries) does not diminish its authority since a well-known Śrī-Vaiṣṇava commentator on Pāñcarātra scriptures, Alaśiṃha Bhaṭṭa (early nineteenth century CE), refers to it extensively as authoritative. Its special feature is its close following of the early Pāñcarātra concept of transcendent consciousness, *saṃvit*, in the process quoting a chapter of the *Saṃvitprakāśa* by Vāmanadatta, who himself had quoted early Pāñcarātra scriptures in his exposition. Since the *Kāśmīrāgama-prāmāṇya* by Yāmuṇācārya is lost, we do not know whether or not the northern development of the Pāñcarātra theology was widely known in the south. However, as a representative of that northern tradition and its concept of supreme *saṃvit śakti*, the *Lakṣmī Tantra* is of unique interest. See Yāmunācārya, *Āgamaprāmāṇyam*, ed. M. Narasimhachary (Baroda: Oriental Institute, 1976), 4.

4. See K.K.A. Venkatachari, *The Maṇipravāḷa Literature of the Śrīvaiṣṇava Ācāryas, 12th to 15th Century A.D.* (Bombay: Ananthacharya Research Institute, 1978), 133–55.
5. The relation between Brahman and the word or speech is very clearly put forward by Bhartṛhari (*c.* sixth century CE); see Wilhelm Halbfass, *Tradition and Reflection: Explorations in Indian Thought* (Albany: State University of New York Press, 1991), 4–5 and 37–38.
6. In Kashmir Śaivism, this is known as *vimarśa* and is identified with the supreme Goddess.
7. *Sāttvata Saṃhitā* 3.3–4; see *Sāttvata Saṃhitā, with a Commentary by Alaśiṃha Bhaṭṭa*, ed. Vraja Vallabha Dviveda (Varanasi: Sampurnanand Sanskrit University, 1982), 34. Also consult Gupta, 'Yoga and *Antaryāga* in Pāñcarātra.'
8. The Kashmiri philosopher, Vāmanadatta, who wrote a clear exposition of the position of *saṃvit* in Pāñcarātra soteriology and cosmogony, also supported the early Pāñcarātra idea that speech, *vāc*, was identified with *saṃvit śakti* and was thus the active principle in the act of creation; see his *Saṃvitprakāśa*, the first chapter of which (137 verses) is quoted in its entirety in the first chapter of the *Lakṣmī Tantra*. *Saṃvit-Prakāśa by Vāmanadatta*, ed. Mark S.G. Dyczkowski (Varanasi: Ratna Printing Works, 1990).
9. *Lakṣmī Tantra* 1.1–29; see *Lakṣmī Tantra: A Pāñcarātra Text*, trans. and ed. Sanjukta Gupta (1972; 2nd ed., Delhi: Motilal Banarsidass, 2000), 1–4.
10. *Śvetāśvatāra Upaniṣad* 5.14 calls the primary creation made of parts *kalā-sarga*: 'Who is to be grasped with one's heart, who is called 'Without-a-Lord,' who brings about existence and non-existence, who is the Benign

One, and who produces both the creation and its constituent parts—those who know him as God have cast aside their bodies' (*Upaniṣads,* trans. Olivelle, 262–63). This conception of the whole of creation can be equated with the abovementioned *śaktis*, or parts (*kalā*), emanating from the supreme *śakti*. *Jayākhya Saṃhitā* 10.58–59 (p. 90) explains that mantra yoga leads to the total identification of the yogin with *icchāśakti*, the bliss-filled, primordial emanation of the divine *śakti*; see verse translated below, n. 20. The same text in another context, 4.117 (p. 37) explains that the supreme unconditioned divine Nārāyaṇa subsumes all *śakti* manifestations.

11. *Jñāna*, or consciousness, itself has five refractions—*aiśvarya* (glory), *śakti* (power), *bala* (strength), *vīrya* (heroism), and *tejas* (splendor), all of which are integral for the concept of a personal godhead; see *Lakṣmī Tantra* 2.23–48 (pp. 9–12 of *Lakṣmī Tantra,* trans. and ed. Gupta), and Sanjukta Gupta, 'The Caturvyūha and the Viśākha-yūpa in the Pāñcarātra,' *Adyar Library Bulletin* 35, pts. 3–4 (1971): 189–204. For discussion of the specific meanings of *prāṇa* in this philosophical system, see Peter Connolly, *Vitalistic Thought in India: A Study of the 'prāṇa' Concept in Vedic literature and Its Development in the Vedānta, Sāṃkhya and Pāñcarātra Traditions* (Delhi: Sri Satguru, 1992), 169–83.
12. *Jayākhya Saṃhitā* 4.51cd–52ab, 60–81; 6.82, 211–12. See the version edited by Embar Krishnamachaya (Baroda: Oriental Institute, 1967), 32, 33–34, 43, and 58–59.
13. See Gupta, 'Yoga and *Antaryāga* in Pāñcarātra,' 184–87.
14. *Pauṣkara Saṃhitā*, ed. His Holiness Sree Yatiraja Sampathkumara Ramanuja Muni of Melkote (Bangalore: A. Srinivasa Aiyangar and M.C. Thirumalachariar, 1934), 33: 90. I have drawn extensively upon this text, even though it is not properly edited and some parts are clearly late. However, the yogic system it teaches is certainly old.
15. Mircea Eliade, *Yoga: Immortality and Freedom*, trans. Willard R. Trask, 2nd ed. (London: Routledge and Kegan Paul, 1969), 76.
16. Ibid., 207.
17. Ibid.
18. Ibid., 208.
19. *Jayākhya Saṃhitā* 4.30–33 (p. 30).
20. See *Lakṣmī Tantra*, trans. and ed. Gupta, xxviii–xxx, and 'Yoga and *Antaryāga* in Pāñcarātra,' 181–87. The *Jayākhya Saṃhitā,* 10.58–59 (p. 90), refers to these five *śaktis* in connection with the yoga system a Pāñcarātra practitioner should follow as part of his religious practice aiming at salvation, described as the release from rebirth: '*Caitanyam jīvabhūtaṃ yatprasphurattārakopamam* I *bhāvanīyaṃ tu viśrāntaṃ nissṛtaṃ bhūtapañjarāt* I *niṣprapañce pare mantre pañcaśaktyākhyavigrahe* II' (Consciousness that has become individual should be envisaged as a glowing star that, having been released from the cage of five elements, has become quiescent in the

supreme mantra, in the form called the five *śaktis* who are beyond the multitudinous creation). In a recent paper, Joanna Jurewicz, interpreting *Ṛg Veda* 10.129, the *Nāsadīya Sūkta*, points out that the first creative act of the single creator was a cognitive act; Jurewicz, 'Playing with Fire: The *Pratītyasamutpāda* from the Perspective of Vedic Thought,' *Journal of the Pali Text Society* 26 (2000): 77–103. See also *Jayākhya Saṃhitā* 4. 61–62 (p. 33). The passage from a total lack of cognition to the awareness of the creator's own self is depicted through the metaphor of his breathing without air through his power (*svadhā*). This hymn mentions the divine power, manifest as breathing (*prāṇa*) and as desire (*icchā*), which is described as the first seed of mind: cognition, or *jñāna*. I suggest that although they are not mentioned in the Vedic hymn, the next two emanations of *śakti* in the Pāñcarātra sequence—divine omnipotence (*kriyā*) and time (*kāla*)—might appear to be implied; if so, one can trace the Pāñcarātra cosmogony back to that of the Vedas.

21. *Sāttvata Saṃhitā* 3.3, 12–13, 15–16 (pp. 34–35). The supreme *vyūha* state is stated to be identical with *śakti*, who is both grounded in her own bliss (*svānanda*) and composed of dynamic flux (*spanda*).
22. *Sāttvata Saṃhitā*, pp. 393–95, 407–10.
23. Jitendra Nath Banerjea, *The Development of Hindu Iconography*, 4th edn. (1956: New Delhi: Munshiram Manoharlal, 1985), chaps. 3–5.
24. T.S. Maxwell, *Viśvarūpa* (Bombay: Oxford University Press, 1988), p. 18, fig. 1.1, and p. 36, fig. 1.2; pls. 10–16.
25. Ibid., 35–36.
26. Ibid., 18.
27. Ibid., 17–46. See also Gupta, 'Caturvyūha and the Viśākha-yūpa in the Pāñcarātra.'
28. Maxwell offers a different interpretation of the goddess-image than I do. He proposes that the six figures represent the female forms of the four *vyūhas*: Śānti (Vāsudeva), Śrī (Saṃkarṣaṇa), Sarasvatī (Pradyumna), Rati or Mahālakṣmī (Aniruddha), Mahākālī and Mahāvidyā (two powers emblematic of Mahālakṣmī). See Maxwell, *Viśvarūpa*, 42–46.
29. *Pauṣkara Saṃhitā* 33.139–40.
30. Maxwell, *Viśvarūpa*, 36–46.
31. Ibid., 46.
32. *Jayākhya Saṃhitā* 4.60–61 (p. 33).
33. *Pauṣkara Saṃhitā* 33.133–70.
34. *Pauṣkara Saṃhitā* 33.113.
35. See *Jayākhya Saṃhitā* 6.73–90 (pp. 46–48).
36. *Mahābhārata* 12.218.11–12 and 334–51 (the *Nārāyaṇīya* book of the *Śāntiparvan*); and Śankara's commentary on *Brahmasūtra* 2.2.42–45, which, according to the commentarial tradition, deals with the doctrine of the Pāñcarātra. For a discussion of Śankara's interpretation, see *Yāmuna's Āgama*

Prāmāṇyam; or, Treatise on the Validity of Pāñcarātra, trans. J.A.B. van Buitenen (Madras: Ramanuja Research Society, 1971), 16–26.

37. *Jayākhya Saṃhitā* 6.221–36 (pp. 58–59).
38. Mahīdhara, *Mantramahodadhiḥ* 21.103–104; see the translation 'by a board of scholars,' Sri Garib Dass Oriental Series, no. 12 (Delhi: Sri Satguru, 1985), 418. Also refer to 6.42–44 of Lakṣmaṇa Deśika, *Śāradātilakam*, with the commentary of Śrī Rāghava Bhaṭṭa, ed. Ācārya Karuṇāpati Tripāṭhī (Varanasi: Sampurnanand Sanskrit University, 1997), 1: 258. Both of these texts are discussed at length in Gudrun Bühnemann, *The Iconography of Hindu Tantric Deities* (Groningen: Egbert Forsten, 2000).
39. *Sāttvata Saṃhitā* 12.192, 206 (pp. 253, 254); *Jayākhya Saṃhitā* 6.77–78 (p. 47).
40. *Lakṣmī Tantra* 8.1–50; 9.1–59; 10.1–7; see *Lakṣmī Tantra*, trans. and ed. Gupta, 44–54.
41. Hemchandra Raychaudhuri mentions an inscription from Junagadh saying that Viṣṇu 'for the sake of the happiness of the lord of the gods, seized back from Bali the goddess of wealth and splendour.' Obviously, the author is referring to the story of Viṣṇu's Vāmaṇa incarnation, where the Lord restored Indra's sovereignty by banishing Bali to the lower region (*pātāla*). See id., *Materials for the Study of the Early History of the Vaishnava Sect* (Calcutta: University of Calcutta, 1936), 102. It is clear then that Lakṣmī represented royal fortune and prosperity. Consult also Jan Gonda, *Aspects of Early Viṣṇuism* (Utrecht: A. Oosthoek, 1954), 100, 164, 166, 172, 176, 188, 192, 197, 208–9, 211, 217–18, and 224–25.
42. Banerjea, *Development of Hindu Iconography*, 189--98, 384–427; Raychaudhuri, *Materials for the Study of the Vaishnava Sect*, 98–109.
43. The Bhāgavatas (lit., those who worship Bhagavan, or Vāsudeva/Kṛṣṇa) were a coherent Kṛṣṇa-centered community from at least the first century BCE or even earlier. They had a consistent ritual and theological tradition and were devotional monotheists, conceiving of the supreme being as a personal god.
44. Parmeshwari Lal Gupta, *Coins*, 3rd edn. (Delhi: National Book Trust, 1969), 53, 55.
45. Banerjea, *Development of Hindu Iconography*, 104–5. Banerjea explains that the Besnagar image is an important exception to the general rule that Lakṣmī or Śrī was rarely the central image in a Pāñcarātra shrine.
46. P. Pratap Kumar, *The Goddess Lakṣmī: The Divine Consort in South Indian Vaiṣṇava Tradition* (Atlanta: Scholars Press, 1997).
47. Ibid., 5.
48. M. Narasimhachary, *Contribution of Yāmunācārya to Viśiṣṭādvaita* (Hyderabad: Sri Jayalakshmi, 1998), 31–32.
49. Rāmānuja, *Vedārthasaṃgraha*, trans. S.S. Raghavachar (Mysore: Sri Ramakrishna Ashrama, 1968), 170–71.

50. For example, see Parāśara Bhaṭṭar, *Guṇaratnakośa* 34, as cited in Kumar, *Goddess Lakṣmī*, 122n45.
51. Surendranath Dasgupta, *History of Indian Philosophy* (Cambridge: Cambridge University Press, 1940), 3: 89–93, 159–64.
52. Dasgupta, *History of Indian Philosophy,* 3: 154.
53. Venkatachari, *Maṇipravāḷa Literature*, 95–108; Dasgupta, *History of Indian Philosophy*, 3: 159–62; Narasimhachary, *Contribution of Yāmunācārya to Viśiṣṭādvaita*, 32–49.
54. For explications in greater depth, see Kumar, *Goddess Lakṣmī*, esp. 96–131.
55. *Śrīvacana Bhūṣaṇa of Pillai Lokācārya*, trans. and ed. Robert C. Lester (Madras: Kuppuswamy Sastri Research Institute, 1979), aphorisms 8–22 (pp. 16–20).
56. Vasudha Narayanan, 'Śrī: Giver of Fortune, Bestower of Grace,' in *Devī: Goddesses of India*, eds. John Stratton Hawley and Donna Marie Wulff (Berkeley: University of California Press, 1996), 103–4.
57. *Taittirīya Āraṇyaka* 3.13.6: 'hrīśca te lakṣmīśca patnau' (Hrī and Lakṣmī are your two wives). Hrī is a manifestation of Lakṣmī. See the version with a commentary by Bhaṭṭa Bhāskara Miśra, ed. A. Mahadeva Sastri and K. Rangacarya (Delhi: Motilal Banarsidass, n.d.), 306.

3

Sītā Fights while Rāma Swoons

A Śākta Perspective on the *Rāmāyaṇa*

THOMAS B. COBURN

In India and Southeast Asia, no one ever reads the *Rāmāyaṇa* or the *Mahābhārata* for the first time. The stories are there, always already.

A.K. Ramanujan

The only reason I have not reduced you to ashes with my incendiary potential is because Rāma has not commanded it and I have held my ascetic power [*tapas*] in check. My abduction from the illustrious Rāma was possible only because it had been ordained as the means for your death.

Sītā addressing Rāvaṇa in Laṅka

You should never assign a meaning to a myth because if you assign a meaning, the mind clamps onto just that one meaning. Then it's no longer active, because when a story is active it allows for new beginnings all the time. Don't give meanings to anything . . . [for] it doesn't ever mean just one thing.

Swamiji, a contemporary storyteller

Sudhir Kakar has reported that when Indian adolescents were asked to select their ideal woman from a list of twenty-four gods, goddesses, heroes, and heroines, 'Sītā was seen as the ideal woman by an overwhelming number of respondents: there were no age or sex differences.'[1] Elsewhere Kakar claims that 'the hegemonic narrative' of Hindu culture as far as male development is concerned . . . is that of Devī, the great goddess, especially in her manifold expressions as mother in the inner world of the Hindu son'.[2] One need not follow Kakar into psychoanalytic interpretation to sense that there are important issues here. When there has been so much recent scholarship that calls our attention to the breadth and diversity of the *Rāmāyaṇa* tradition,[3] and when politicized interpretations of that epic have so rent the fabric of contemporary India, which Sītā, one might ask, is the Sītā so idealized by young Indians? How does the multiplicity inherent in the *Rāmāyaṇa* tradition bear on understanding Sītā as a role model? Similarly, since it is now a commonplace that the Great Goddess as mother is not merely a benign nurturer but also a horrific destroyer, we might also ask: how is this Devī, who is often *anything but* a model wife, related to the exemplary Sītā?[4] These questions, of course, are very much akin to those that Narendra Nath Bhattacharyya asked throughout his scholarly career, for, as he himself notes, 'I am in the habit of saying in all my books that the study of any aspect of Indology in itself is of no value unless it is used as a means to understand the vast and enormously complicated problems of India's social history.'[5] To pursue these questions here is to acknowledge with deep gratitude the scholarly debt in which he has placed so many of us.

In this essay I explore questions such as those noted above with primary reference to a little-studied Śākta version of the *Rāmāyaṇa*, the *Adbhuta Rāmāyaṇa*, 'The *Rāmāyaṇa* of Wonders,' or 'The Astonishing *Rāmāyaṇa*.' The Sanskrit text appears to date from the late sixteenth century and to have originated in northeastern India, though there are also resemblances to Tamil materials.[6] It runs to some 1,350 verses, mostly sixteen-syllable verses or *ślokas*, in twenty-seven chapters. The fact that it has drawn little scholarly attention is not surprising, since it is stylistically undistinguished, repetitious, and occasionally simply lapses into lists—of demons and their weaponry, of battles, of divine Mothers (*mātāraḥ*), of Sītā's names. As we shall see, the *Adbhuta Rāmāyaṇa* is better understood as a folk tradition, with a coherence of its own, rather than as a polished 'text'. This particular telling of the *Rāmāyaṇa*, however, is not just an antiquarian curiosity. The Sanskrit text has been published within the past few years and remains in print with

Hindi translation, not just in one but in four separate editions.[7] It may therefore appropriately serve as a point of entry into thinking about larger issues of gender identity and contemporary resonances within the *Rāmāyaṇa* tradition.

THE 'WONDROUSNESS' OF SĪTĀ KILLING RĀVAṆA

As a first approach to our '*Rāmāyaṇa* of Wonders,' we need to take note of an apparent anomaly. How is it possible to consider Śākta materials and the Rāma tradition in the same breath? Received scholarly tradition suggests that the ethos of Śāktism, particularly as it converges with the esotericism and eroticism of Tantra, is qualitatively different from that of puritanical mainstream Vaiṣṇavism. Representative of this view is Kathleen Erndl's observation that 'the mythologies of Śiva and of Kṛṣṇa allow a free interplay between eroticism and asceticism: though the two are in tension, full expression is given to both. In the character of Rāma, however, sexuality appears to be almost completely suppressed'.[8] Similarly, Frank Whaling, in discussing the views of Rāma and Śiva in the *Adhyātma Rāmāyaṇa*, notes:

> [T]here is a deep difference between the creative Sītā and the Goddess of Tantra. In the Śākta movement the Goddess often assumes not merely a creative role but also a dominant role over against the male God, and stress is placed upon a 'female theology.' This is also carried over into the Kṛṣṇa movement wherein Rādhā sometimes assumes an equal or dominant role. . . . Although Sītā is sometimes seen in terms of Śakti there is rarely any suggestion that she is dominant over Rāma or even equal to Him. This is a difference between the Rāma and Kṛṣṇa movements.[9]

John Carman, too, observes that the Śrī-Vaiṣṇava tradition remained faithful to the teaching of Yāmuna and Rāmānuja, for it 'never accepted the Tantric view that the Consort of Nārāyaṇa was the active creative principle in Her own right, the Śakti'.[10]

My first reading of the *Adbhuta Rāmāyaṇa* did indeed produce the astonishment its title promised. Not only was the familiar storyline of the *Rāmāyaṇa* condensed almost to extinction and unfamiliar episodes inserted, but the last half of the text was devoted to recounting how Sītā vanquished the Thousand-Headed Rāvaṇa, and to glorifying her as Devī, the nurturing and destroying Great Goddess. The most abrupt reversal of expectation occurs in chapter 23. Sītā has declined to join in the festivities upon the triumphal return to Ayodhya, after Rāma has slain the ten-headed Rāvaṇa, because she has known since childhood of his thousand-headed older brother, also called Rāvaṇa (chap. 17). Indeed, she laughs derisively at those who think Rāma has done something worth celebrating (17.17, 18.6). Setting out to vanquish this bigger and badder Rāvaṇa,[11] most of Rāma's supporters find themselves blown back to their starting point by Rāvaṇa's hurricane-blast arrow (21.6). Rāma himself loses consciousness when his chest is pierced by a razor-edged arrow that continues on into the nether regions (22.47–49). Chastised by the attendant sages for having involved Rāma in this debacle, Sītā picks up Rāma's bow and arrow from his chest:

Bellowing at the mighty, valorous demon,
Laughing boisterously and loudly, Sītā, daughter of Janaka,
The goddess, who has many hideous forms, abandoned her own form [*svarūpa*]
(And took on a form) fit for killing. . . .
Gaunt, with sunken eyes that whirled in circles,
Long of leg, bellowing aloud, garlanded with skulls,
With anklets made of bone, fearsome, invincible in valor and speed,
Harsh-voiced . . . with lolling-tongue . . . ,
She was as black as the ocean at the time of *pralaya*.
Carrying bell and noose, sword and shield,
She jumped down quickly from her chariot
And fell on Rāvaṇa's chariot like a hawk.
In a flash she playfully lopped off Rāvaṇa's
Thousand heads with her sword. (23.7–13)

We recognize this figure, of course, as Kālī. But in the immediate sequel, as she continues the carnage, she is explicitly called 'Sītā' and 'Jānakī' (23.15, 18, 20, 22). What has here become of the sweet, mild maid of Mithila?

Rather than address this anomaly head-on, I propose to approach it obliquely. What appears from one angle to be an impasse may, from another, turn out to be part of a familiar logic of popular Hinduism. It may also tell us something about the question of role models and archetypes with which we began.

THE *ADBHUTA RĀMĀYAṆA* AS A 'PURĀṆICIZED' *RĀMĀYAṆA*

Let us note, first, that the *Adbhuta Rāmāyaṇa* is in many respects more like the Purāṇas than the classical epic tradition. It is filled with tales of powerful sages, who often unleash powerful curses. It contains didactic dialogues between interlocutors, both divine and human, often dealing with cosmogony and reworking the familiar concepts of Sāṃkhya-Yoga (chaps. 11–14). Its sometimes tedious battle scenes stupefy the reader, as they would those who hear such tales orally. The importance of devotion to a personal deity is pervasive. The theology of the *Bhagavad Gītā* looms in the background throughout. Sometimes it comes to the fore. At the very beginning of the text, Vālmīki promises to recount the essence of the *Sītā Māhātmya*, identifies Sītā with material nature (*prakṛti*), and then quotes *Bhagavad Gītā* 4.7, appropriately modifying the last quarter: 'Whenever there comes to be a decline in dharma, O truthful one, and an uprising of unrighteousness, then *prakṛti* comes into existence' (1.18). Elsewhere (chaps. 10 and 25), the granting of a divine eye to Hanumān and Rāma, respectively, recalls Arjuna's vision in *Bhagavad Gītā* 11. The text's account of itself is reminiscent of Purāṇic self-reflexiveness on the question of origins. At the outset of the *Adbhuta,* Vālmīki is said to have composed two *Rāmāyaṇa*s, one in a thousand million verses for the use of gods and seers and another in twenty-five thousand verses for humans on earth; the about-to-be recited *Adbhuta* is said to consist of excerpts from the former (1.35).

This resemblance should prepare us for the appearance of popular or folk Purāṇic mainstays, in postclassical tellings of the *Rāmāyaṇa*, where they appear side by side with increased emphasis on devotionalism. Once we grant this, other developments in later tellings of the *Rāmāyaṇa* become intelligible. Though reflecting primarily on Tamil materials, Kamil Zvelebil's synopsis of historical developments within the folk tradition is provocative:

> After the accomplished deification of Rāma, when Rāma the hero became Sri Rāmaswami, the Supreme Lord . . . , a new hero of superhuman proportions yet not of . . . too distant and utterly divine proportions was needed. . . . Since the

struggle of gods against demons . . . is eternal, being the one basic and archetypal phenomenon of Hindu mythology, the more the god Rāmaswami . . . becomes divinely passive (inactive divine principle) and distantly lofty, the more active, the more dynamic become two other characters of the *Rāmāyaṇa* saga in its folk versions: Sītā and Hanumān. Sītā is the expression of Śakti tendencies of medieval South Indian and Bengali Hinduism, whereas Hanumān becomes the ideal expression of the valour, skills and shrewdness of the medieval South India warrior class who have to keep up the struggle against a terrible foe—the Muslim invader.[12]

David Shulman offers a somewhat different slant on similar material, noting how a Tamil folk *Rāmāyaṇa* strives to stay in touch with the struggles of daily life—portraying Sītā 'as a bold and active woman quite prepared to argue with her husband for her beliefs'[13]—while also acknowledging the enhanced divinity of the main characters. Though this Tamil telling of the *Rāmāyaṇa* appears to have greater narrative unity than our text, it resembles the *Adbhuta* in many ways as Sītā kills a new Rāvaṇa, now with 100 heads. In Shulman's telling, however, Sītā earns the right to kill Rāvaṇa as a boon from Śiva, Rāma watches her battle from the palace rather than being struck senseless as in the *Adbhuta*, and Sītā sends Hanumān to help force *satī* on all the demon widows. Shulman links this search for ever new antagonists to the structure of South Indian religion:

Sītā's battle reflects an enduring struggle which one sees expressed in many South India village cults, especially those focused on the goddess. On the one hand, her defeat of the monstrous Śatakaṇṭha [Hundred-Heads] leaves the world devoid of evil. . . . On the other hand, the very fact that the text finds it necessary to embark on this wholly new narrative of battle . . . suggests that even this victory will be only temporary. Some day yet another threat to order will arise, and the battle will be resumed.[14]

While we cannot link our text, the *Adbhuta Rāmāyaṇa*, to South Indian villages, we can agree with Shulman on the transformation of Vālmīki's characters when infused with either new theological or new folk sensibilities:

Vālmīki, who has the most completely human hero, also offers the most idealized portrait of his characters—as . . . in his chaste and gentle Sītā. . . . [Folk versions show] us a definitely divine heroine acting in a manner which cuts across the human ideal of restrained womanhood. The force of normative idealism appears to diminish as one ascends the scale from human hero to divine, or as one 'descends' from classical to folk context; and it is the folk source which offers perhaps the most passionate and powerful vision.[15]

Our first conclusion, therefore, is that in the *Adbhuta Rāmāyaṇa* we have to do with a telling of the Rāma story which, though written in the symbolically important, refined language of Sanskrit, bears resemblance to folk *Rāmāyaṇas* told in various vernaculars. It is therefore more like the women's Telugu songs studied by Narayana Rao than the *kāvya* of Vālmīki.[16] It is a Purāṇicized kind of *Rāmāyaṇa*.

OF GODDESSES AND KINGS

There is a second helpful line of thought for approaching our text. That is the relationship between goddesses and kings. Surely no one who has lived in North India through the overlapping autumnal celebrations of Durgā Pūjā (Navarātra), Dasarā, and Rām Līlā can have failed to muse on the logic of their coincidence. Elsewhere I have noted how the association between goddesses and kingship tellingly recurs at many moments in the emergence of an autonomous Goddess tradition into Sanskrit.[17] In addition, when one finds that the textual 'triumph' of the Great Goddess, the *Devī Bhāgavata Purāṇa*, includes a synopsis of the Rāma story that attributes Rāma's success to his performance of a Navarātra ceremony—just as Kṛṣṇa counsels Arjuna to recite the *Durgā Stotra* in an insertion into the *Mahābhārata* just prior to the *Bhagavad Gītā*—the matter clearly calls for further investigation.[18]

Madeleine Biardeau can serve as our guide here, via her analysis of the *śamī* tree and the sacrificial buffalo, even though her emphasis is on the *Mahābhārata*, rather than the *Rāmāyaṇa*.[19] She starts with a desire to discern two things: first, a link between the autumnal festivals just noted—Navarātra and Rām Līlā—and, second, a logic for the placement of the two Durgā hymns in the *Mahābhārata*. The first such hymn occurs as the Pāṇḍavas begin their year in exile and put their weapons in a *śamī* tree, and the second, as we have noted, occurs just prior to the *Gītā* and final battle. Biardeau cites an unspecified telling of the *Rāmāyaṇa* that has Rāma receiving the favor of killing Rāvaṇa from Durgā on the eighth day of Durgā Pūjā, the traditional day of buffalo sacrifice, and then offering a *pūjā* to the *śamī* tree on the tenth day (Dasarā) in order to remove the rust from his weapons and restore their fire after the monsoon. She discerns a structural parallel here with the Pāndavas, putting their weapons in the thickest part of the *śamī* tree to keep them dry, so that their potency will remain latent during the rains and exile.[20] The symbolic logic of choosing the *śamī* tree derives, Biardeau argues, from the kindling sticks (*araṇi*) of Vedic ritual, where *śamī* wood is seen as female and *aśvattha* as male. 'Śamī is thus the womb of fire, in which fire dwells in a state of calm . . . when extinguished. It is the rubbing of the two *araṇi* which inflames it.'[21] There is also apparently a deeper debt to Vedic ritual. 'In Vedic sacrifice, the victim is seen as a substitute for the sacrificer. . . . The victim must therefore be something of the sacrificer's, a possession or creature which he has bought, which belongs to him, which costs him something.' This logic is continued in the sacrifice of battle that is the *Mahābhārata*, where the sacrificial victims are one's own relatives. It is also apparent, Biardeau claims, in the Goddess's battle with the buffalo demon, Mahiṣa, who is variously represented both as her victim and as the reincarnation of her consort: Śiva lies prostrate beneath her, begging the favor 'of remaining eternally beneath her feet' and so is reborn as Mahiṣa.[22] Kingly competence, like all worldly success, is thus contingent on submission to the power that is the Goddess. In this organically interrelated vision—this 'universe of bhakti'—'the tasks of this world are no longer opposed to the work of deliverance, they lead to it'.[23] Regarding the *Mahābhārata*, Biardeau can then conclude, surface appearances (and the critically edited text) notwithstanding: 'The presence of the Goddess appears like a watermark at every crucial turning point in the epic story; at once submissive, bellicose and finally victorious.'[24] That something similar might be said of the Rāma cycle is a matter that the *Adbhuta Rāmāyaṇa* invites us to contemplate—as we shall now see.

SĪTĀ'S IDENTITY IN THE *ADBHUTA RĀMĀYAṆA*

It has often been remarked that Vālmīki's Sītā, for all of her demure chasteness and uncritical submissiveness to her husband, is central to the action of the *Rāmāyaṇa*: not only does she foolishly covet the golden deer in the forest, permitting her abduction by Rāvaṇa, but all subsequent events are ramifications of that abduction. Furthermore, it is scarcely conventional wifely behavior for Sītā to insist on accompanying Rāma to the forest or, in penetrating the illusion of the jewelled deer, to direct Lakṣmaṇa to leave her and help Rāma. Beyond this, certain passages in the text imply a deliberate restraint on Sītā's part, a potential to take matters into her own hands that she refuses to indulge, so that Rāma might fulfil his dharma of rescuing her. The citation that forms one of the epigraphs to this essay is one such passage. Such intimations lend themselves to analysis that reveals a Sītā far more complex and far more powerful than is often realized. In a close examination of Vālmīki's text, for instance, Cornelia Dimmitt has shown how Sītā 'can be seen to display the qualities of a goddess in two different modes: as mistress of the plants and animals she is intimately related to the fertility of the earth, and as Śakti, the energy that inspires the hero Rāma to action, she is the source of his power as king'.[25]

As we have seen, and as recent scholarship has vividly demonstrated, later retellings of the Rāma story often develop such latent points in Vālmīki's telling by providing dramatic revisionings of characters, particular episodes, and even the entire narrative. It is very tempting to dismiss such retellings as the *Adbhuta Rāmāyaṇa* because of their mediocrity as literature, their almost outlandish abbreviation of the familiar story and insertion of sometimes bizarre new episodes, their flirtation with incoherence.[26] For instance, in the only substantial study of the *Adbhuta* that I have encountered, done by George Grierson many years ago, the author disdainfully notes that 'the building of the causeway, the taking of Laṅka, and the destruction of Rāvaṇa . . . are all dismissed in a single śloka' and affirms that the text's 'chief value is as a storehouse of folklegends'.[27] More recently, W.L. Smith says of the *Adbhuta*: 'This modestly sized work contains a summary of the *Rāmāyaṇa* sandwiched by two apocryphal episodes', the birth of Sītā and her slaying of the thousand-headed Rāvaṇa, between which 'there is no intrinsic connection'.[28] Close analysis of what the *Adbhuta* has to say about Sītā, however, provides both 'wonderment' and fresh insight into her broader identity in the Indian context. Let us look, then, at what the text says about Sītā.

We should note, first, that Sītā's identity is developed discursively, in narrative form, while Rāma's is presented didactically and philosophically. In the first chapter, for instance, Vālmīki, immediately after noting the existence of the two versions of the *Rāmāyaṇa* and promising to tell the *Sītā Māhātmya*, says of Sītā: 'Sītā is *prakṛti*, the beginning of creation . . . , the perfection of tapas, the acquisition of heaven. . . . She is praised as knowledge and ignorance, . . . consisting of the *guṇas*, beyond the *guṇas*, having the *guṇas* as her very soul. She is Brahmā and the egg of Brahmā, the cause of all actions, consisting of thought [*cit*], . . . the great *kuṇḍalinī*, . . . by whom all this moving and unmoving universe becomes manifest' (1.13–16). Immediately, he then turns to Rāma, of whom he says: 'Rāma is the highest light manifest, supreme support, highest person. In form (*akṛti*) there is no difference at all between Sītā and Rāma. Rāma is Sītā, Jānakī is beloved of Rāma, there is not the slightest difference between them. . . . Rāma is unthinkable, seeing everything through his eternal consciousness, abiding within all, the one agent in all worlds, the supporter, the destroyer . . . , known by yogis through his union with Sītā' (1.19–21). The text, it would appear, is not interested in a separate, overtly conceptual and philosophized Sītā. When the subject matter inclines in such a direction, it is to Rāma that it turns. The major evidence for this distinction is the extended philosophical self-disclosure that Rāma gives to Hanumān in chapters 10–15, to which the text applies the label *upaniṣad*. By contrast, when extended attention is given to Sītā, it is in the form of the compounding of her names, found in chapter 25. If we would know more of who Sītā is, we must attend to the logic that is unobtrusively woven into the narrative portions of the text.

There are three key episodes in developing Sītā's identity. We shall look briefly at each of them.

First, there is a story that connects Sītā with her later birth into Janaka's lineage. This is the story of Ambarīṣa (chaps. 2–4). This pious king, an unswerving devotee of Nārāyaṇa, has a lovely daughter, Śrīmatī. The sages Nārada and Parvata both seek her hand in marriage, and her father agrees to allow her to choose one of them. Both saints appeal to Viṣṇu to sully the appearance of the other and, responsive god that he is, he agrees, placing a monkey's face on Parvata and the face of a cow-tailed monkey on Nārada (chap. 3). The faces, however, are only visible to young Śrīmatī.[29] Confused by their appearance, she instead chooses a beautiful youth who has mysteriously appeared, and who then carries her off. He is, in fact, Viṣṇu in disguise. The two saints, each humiliated by the other, complain to Viṣṇu. He replies that because he is unable to resist responding to fervent devotees, he had to respond to their respective requests. He denies absconding with Śrīmatī. The sages immediately suspect Ambarīṣa, on whom they throw a curse of darkness. When Ambarīṣa flees to Viṣṇu, taking refuge from the curse, the sages see that the whole charade has been an example of Viṣṇu's *māyā*. In wrath they then cast curses both on Viṣṇu himself and on the innocent Śrīmatī. Viṣṇu is cursed to be born as the son of Daśaratha, that is, Rāma, in the lineage of Ambarīṣa. Śrīmatī will be born from the earth and taken by Janaka as his daughter, that is, Sītā. The curse goes on: through the misdeeds of a demon, Janaka's daughter will be abducted. Just as Śrīmatī in this lifetime has been demonically spirited away by Viṣṇu, so will Sītā then be spirited away by a demon. Just as Nārada and Parvata were made miserable on Śrīmatī's account, so will Rāma weep and grieve on Sītā's account. Viṣṇu then accepts this destiny for the two of them, saying that the curse of a sage can never be undone (4.62–66).

The second episode that shapes Sītā's identity also involves a sage's curse. It is part of a larger, very peculiar story that revolves around music and singing, where the most gripping image is of the sage Nārada in a crowd of maimed men and women—who turn out to be the various *rāgas* and *rāgiṇīs* who have been mangled by his dreadful singing (7.26)! The crucial interaction is this. A great festival in honor of Kauśika features the Gandharva singer Tumburu. Sweeping regally into the hall, Lakṣmī has her courtiers shove the assembled gods and sages to one side with their staves, and Viṣṇu proceeds to reward Tumburu lavishly. Nārada, seething with rage and bitterness, blurts out a curse in anger: 'Since I have here been treated like a demon by Lakṣmī, surrounded by her retinue, harshly beaten with blows from their sticks, may Lakṣmī be reborn in the womb of a demoness (*rākṣasī*). Since I was scornfully cast out by her servants, may that *rākṣasī* contemptuously cast you [Lakṣmī] away upon the ground' (6.16–17). Everyone, including Nārada, immediately realizes the enormity of this curse, but there is no undoing of the words, once uttered. Lakṣmī accepts the curse, but asks to set a condition on it: she will be reborn in the womb of a *rākṣasī* only after that demoness has voluntarily drunk a jar filled with the blood of forest sages, which has been put into the jar drop by drop. Nārada consents to this condition (6.23–26).

The third episode brings the first two together in a clever synthesis and adds important details of its own. It begins with the ten-headed Rāvaṇa. He has practiced *tapas* for many years, scorching the earth and winning a boon from Brahmā (8.2–6). Rāvaṇa asks for invincibility from enemies of all sorts, but Brahmā replies that this cannot be. He should pick another boon, more limited in scope. Rāvaṇa agrees, but, in good bartering fashion, adds that he then wants a second boon as well. Calculating that he has nothing to fear from human beings, Rāvaṇa omits them from his first request, asking that he be invulnerable to all assaults by nonhuman creatures. His second request is brief and simple—and redolent with associations from throughout the Hindu tradition. He asks that in the event he should deludedly become overcome with desire for his own daughter and she should refuse him, he will die. Fatefully, Brahmā grants Rāvaṇa both boons (8.8–12).

The scene then shifts quickly to Rāvaṇa's ensuing depredations. In the course of his conquests, he comes to Daṇḍaka wood, where he finds a group of sages piously attending their fires. He poses himself a question: 'How can I be the ruler of the three worlds without conquering these beings? But isn't it wrong for anyone to kill pious sages?' (8.16) The solution he devises requires each of the sages to draw a little blood with the tip of Rāvaṇa's arrow, which he collects in a jar. Unbeknownst to him, however, the sage Gṛtsamada has been using that jar for another purpose. That sage, already having a hundred sons, has been importuned by his wife for a daughter: 'May my daughter be Lakṣmī herself.' Accordingly, Gṛtsamada has daily been putting milk from a blade of *kuśa* grass into the jar, accompanied by mantras, to conjure up Lakṣmī's presence. When Rāvaṇa takes the jar of sages' blood home, he says to his wife Mandodarī: 'Protect this jar, O fair one, knowing that the blood in the jar is more powerful than poison. Do not give it away and do not drink it' (8.23–24). Rāvaṇa then continues his conquests and his ravishing of women in earthly and celestial realms. On seeing the latter, Mandodarī, much in love with her husband, becomes despondent and decides to kill herself. She guzzles down the blood of the sages, but instead of dying, she becomes pregnant—with, of course, Lakṣmī. The embryo begins to glow and Mandodarī is filled with wonder. She concludes that it was the sages' blood that has impregnated her, but she is then immediately overcome with horror: 'My husband Rāvaṇa is filled with desire for equally lustful women, and it is a year since he has lived with me. What am I, a good woman who has become pregnant, to say when I see my husband again?' (8.32–33). Mandodarī's solution is to go away. Under pretext of performing a pilgrimage, she journeys to Kurukṣetra, where she tears out the fetus and buries it in the earth. Purifying herself with a bath, she goes home and tells no one of the affair. Shortly thereafter, Janaka comes to Kurukṣetra to perform a sacrifice and, in the course of preparing the field, ploughs up a beautiful young girl. This episode then concludes in conventional fashion, with Janaka taking the girl home as his daughter Sītā.

From here on the text assumes familiarity with the more normative Rāma story. It says nothing of Rāma's childhood, marriage, Kaikeyī's plot, or the departure from Ayodhya. Chapter 10 says laconically that Rāma, Sītā, and Lakṣmaṇa went to the woods 'for some reason' (*kenāpi hetuna*). The text treats Sītā's abduction summarily and simply assumes Rāvaṇa's lust for her, without reminding us that this is a father's lust for his daughter. The *Adbhuta's* chief concern through the middle chapters is, as noted earlier, to convey the secret teaching about who Rāma is. When Rāma solicits Hanumān's help, Hanumān explains to him that the abducted Sītā was not the real Sītā, but an illusory form—a motif that is also found in the *Adhyātma* and Tulsidas' *Rāmāyaṇa*s, but that is here without any narrative or philosophical force. When the text turns, from chapter 17 onward, to the story of the thousand-headed Rāvaṇa, it tells us little more about who Sītā is than what we have noted earlier, that is, she laughs at those who think Rāma's killing of the ten-headed Rāvaṇa is a deed worth celebrating, and she metamorphoses into a Kālī-like form to kill Rāvaṇa when Rāma is wounded and passes out. We may briefly note the aftermath of that killing. Sītā goes on a rampage, slaying the remaining demons. Mātṛkās ooze from her pores to help in the slaughter. Headless corpses dance, and Sītā and her companions play ball with Rāvaṇa's thousand heads. Fearing that the universal dissolution (*pralaya*) is upon them, the gods ask Śiva for help: he throws himself as a corpse under the feet of the Kālī-like Sītā, but still the carnage continues (chap. 23). The gods then praise Sītā as the sole Śakti of Viṣṇu, the one through whom he attains his highest bliss and who under the spell of *māyā* causes the world to whirl around. Rāma is the thinker, Sītā the thought (24.3–22). Sītā, however, replies: 'While my husband Rāma lies, as if dead, with a razor-arrow through his heart, what benefaction can I wish for the world?' (24.24). The gods then seek to revive Rāma, splashing him with water, and he regains consciousness. But on seeing, not Sītā, but this Kālī-like figure in front of him, he thinks that the battle is still going on and takes up his weapons. The gods explain to him what has happened, and he approaches the Goddess, asking who she is. She replies that she is the highest *śakti* and, as Kṛṣṇa does for Arjuna in the *Gita*, she gives him the divine eye, so that he may see her in her heavenly form (25.5–7). Rāma then praises her with 1,008 names (chap. 25), at the end of which, terrified, he asks her to resume her other, gracious (*saumya*) benign form, which she does (26.3). Rāma asks for the return of his brothers and army. Sītā assents (26.47), they all return to Ayodhya, and Rāma reigns happily, in the company of Sītā and his brothers, for eleven thousand years (27.9).

SĪTĀ AS PAN-INDIAN GODDESS / ROLE MODEL, PAST AND PRESENT

What, then, can we conclude about the *Adbhuta Rāmāyaṇa*'s understanding of Sītā? What does it tell us about the relationship of goddesses and kings, and about Sītā as role model in contemporary India? Much could obviously be said about this tantalizing tale, and I shall limit myself here to four comments.

First, the evidence we have considered clearly indicates the necessity of thinking of the *Rāmāyaṇa*, not as a text, but as a tradition encompassing multiple and diverse voices. Such a conclusion clearly places us on one side of the ongoing debate over whether it is appropriate to privilege Vālmīki's Sanskrit *Rāmāyaṇa* over other tellings of the tale.[30] The *Adbhuta*'s voice has been little heard in scholarly circles, and listening to it would appear to have considerable potential for shedding light on the overall nature of the *Rāmāyaṇa* tradition. Whether Hindus have heard this voice more acutely than scholars is a difficult, important matter. How well-known is the *Adbhuta Rāmāyaṇa*? Or, acknowledging that the story is the important thing, not this particular text, how well-known is this story today? We cannot answer this question at present, although there is isolated, tantalizing evidence.[31] Assuming that the story is not an utter anomaly, that it is part of the *Rāmāyaṇa* that A.K. Ramanujan says is 'always there' in Hindu consciousness, its significance is still not entirely clear.[32] Does it represent a 'counter system,' such as Ramanujan argues may be found in women's tales?[33] It is hard to argue that this is the case here. The discontinuities within the text—the fact that the narrative is interrupted and episodes are unevenly modulated—make it difficult to discern any single, self-conscious authorial or editorial stance. Such eclecticism is, of course, familiar to those who work in Purāṇic materials.

On the other hand, we can surely hear from time to time what seems to be a woman's point of view. This is most apparent, perhaps, in Mandodarī's grief over Rāvaṇa's womanizing and in her quandary over an unwanted and untimely pregnancy. Such a perspective might be seen more broadly in the striking inversion at the heart of the tale: in Rāma's martial impotence at the head of battle, and in the benign Sītā's transformation into the horrific Devī. But rather than seeing such episodes simply as contrary and counter to a Vālmīkian *Rāmāyaṇa*, as glimmers of female subjectivity, I think we should also see them as deliberate inversions of the conventional storyline. What the festival of Holi does for the rest of the Hindu calendar year, the *Adbhuta* does for the *Rāmāyaṇa* tradition: it stands it on its head, acknowledges the *māyā*-like quality of all norms, and celebrates the reversal. Since Devī is herself the coincidence of opposites—both knowledge and ignorance, the cause of both bondage and release—she is a particularly apt cause of and subject for such celebration (see fig. 3).

Fig. 3: A contemporary poster of the Great Goddess (Devī), in whom all other deities reside.

In offering such an interpretation, the notion of 'intertextuality', which has become so useful in the study of Indian folklore and the Purāṇas, offers a promising theoretical stance.[34] The problem, of course, is that, unlike Narayana Rao in his study of women's oral Telugu *Rāmāyaṇas*[35] and Ramanujan in his study of women's tales in Karnataka,[36] we here lack a specific linguistic or social context for our story. I shall say more about our text's affinities with other accounts in a moment. However, as a general principle for assessing the status of this tale in Hindu consciousness, we would do well to bear in mind what Narayana Rao says about his informants: 'Like most of the participants in the tradition, these women believe the *Rāmāyaṇa* to be fact and not fiction, and its many different versions are precisely in keeping with this belief. Contrary to the usual opinion, it is fiction that has only one version; a factual event will inevitably have various versions, depending on the attitude, intent, and social position of the teller.'[37]

My second comment pertains to the remarkable lineage that is ascribed to Sītā in our text. As we have seen, she is Lakṣmī, but she is, by her own wish, born in the womb of a demoness. As one who is born from Rāvaṇa's wife, Mandodarī, she is, by implication, born in Rāvaṇa's lineage and may be seen as his daughter. Although it is Rāma who kills the ten-headed Rāvaṇa, it is Sītā who kills his elder brother, the thousand-headed Rāvaṇa, who is technically Sītā's uncle but who is clearly a doublet of her father, even sharing his name. Thus, Sītā avenges herself on the very family into which, and on the father to which, she was born. W.L. Smith has done valuable work on the interrelationship between the *Rāmāyaṇas* of eastern and greater India, and I here quote his treatment of this episode as an oral tradition that variously finds its way into the written record: 'As early as the third century *Vasudeva-hiṇḍī* by the Jain Sanghadāsa, Sītā is known as the daughter of Rāvaṇa and placed in a box that is buried in the field where Janaka's plow later turns it up. In the ninth century the story is used in the Jaina *Rāmāyaṇa* of Guṇabhadra. Around the same period it appears in the Khotanese and Tibetan versions but here the box containing the baby girl is cast into a river rather than buried. The tale is also found in most of the Southeast Asian *Rāmāyaṇas*: in the Malay ... Lao . . . Thai . . . [and] Burmese.'[38]

It is subsequent to all of this that the story finally finds its way into a Hindu *Rāmāyaṇa*, and that is in the very text we have been considering, the *Adbhuta Rāmāyaṇa*. Smith offers the following reflection on this evidence.

> The variant [of Sītā being Rāvaṇa's daughter] was thus known in India for at least a thousand years before a Hindu poet chose to use it. At the same time the story is found almost everywhere in the Buddhist and formerly Buddhist countries of Central and Southeast Asia. . . . The story seems to have no intrinsic sectarian connections whether Jaina, Buddhist, or *Śākta* Hindu, rather it shares many features with the much more ancient and well-known 'myth of the hero' which appears in a number of Indo-European languages; according to it while his mother is pregnant with him, it is prophesied that the hero will be a danger to his father. The father attempts to do away with the hero . . . the baby is saved . . . then finally the hero returns to take revenge upon his father thus fulfilling the prophecy. Though Sītā is a daughter and does not kill Rāvaṇa [except in the Adbhuta Rāmāyaṇa!], the story corresponds rather well with these schemata and in most versions of the epic it is repeatedly pointed out that she is the direct cause of Rāvaṇa's death.[39]

This evidence suggests that many audiences have known for nearly two thousand years that Sītā may be understood as Rāvaṇa's daughter, regardless of what any particular text or story says. Why within India the story took so long to find Hindu attestation, when it had long received Jain and Buddhist recognition, is a matter that must be left for future inquiry. Such an inquiry might be part of further exploration into the history of sectarian polemics in India, where the *Adbhuta Rāmāyaṇa* can be seen as a Hindu effort finally to undercut the long-standing Jain and Buddhist claim that Sītā was Rāvaṇa's daughter by demonstrating that she is actually Lakṣmī and the daughter of Hindu sages. Such an inquiry might also explore different attitudes toward women, past and present, in Jain, Buddhist, and Hindu circles, noting, for instance, that, in striking contrast to the dominant Hindu ethos of India, in the Buddhist countries of Southeast Asia 'women are among the world's most liberated females, and in Burma, particularly, they hold a power that is awesome to behold.'[40]

This, in turn, might prompt questions about Southeast Asian *Rāmāyaṇas* as both appropriations of, and resistance to, Indian understandings both of religion and of gender roles. Such an inquiry, finally, might seek comparative historical leverage on all these issues by asking how it is that the *Adbhuta Rāmāyaṇa*, a sixteenth-century text that is remarkable for its content and undistinguished for its style, remains in print in India today in four separate editions. Who is the audience for these modern publications? Why has the text been published so often lately, and how can this help us understand contemporary Indian reverence for and idealization of Sītā?

The remarkable lineage ascribed to Sītā in our text also has a deep, but more symbolic resonance specifically within the Hindu tradition. This is my third conclusion. We saw earlier that Biardeau's analysis of the *Mahābhārata* invites us to see its central battle as an extension of the logic of Vedic sacrifice, where the sacrificial victims must be a part of one's own self, one's own relatives. She also argued there that the Goddess's battle with the buffalo demon Mahiṣa may likewise be seen in these terms, with Śiva as both the Goddess's consort and reborn as her victim-devotee, Mahiṣa. The *Adbhuta* suggests a similar logic at work in the *Rāmāyaṇa*. Now, however, it is the Goddess herself, rather than her antagonist-lover, who undergoes rebirth. It is Lakṣmī's birth in the womb of Mandodarī that enables her to claim Rāvaṇa as her own lineage and therefore as her own proper victim. The *Rāmāyaṇa* tradition, from this angle, is just as much about the Goddess and her importance to proper kingship and world-maintenance as is the *Mahābhārata*. Both, in turn, are rooted in the older Vedic view that all sacrifice is fundamentally self-sacrifice, so vividly described in the *Puruṣa Sūkta* (*Ṛg Veda* 10.90)[41] and so vividly alluded to by Rāvaṇa in our text when he cites the destructive consequences of incest.[42] As Alf Hiltebeitel has noted, there is virtual unanimity in studies of martial oral epics that 'females are the primary instigators of destruction'. The same, he notes, is gradually coming to be seen as also characteristic of the classical epics,[43] which are themselves rooted in the controlled destruction that lies at the heart of Vedic sacrifice.

Finally, let us return to the issue of role models with which we began. Sally Sutherland has written a trenchant essay entitled 'Sītā and Draupadī: Aggressive Behavior and Female Role Models in the Sanskrit Epics.'[44] She offers a comprehensive interpretation of Vālmīki's Sītā that is encapsulated in what she says about Sītā's refusal in the *Uttarākāṇḍa to* rejoin Rāma, being reabsorbed instead by the earth:

> Sītā's repudiation of Rāma comes to represent to the vast majority of the audience, not merely a wife refusing a husband, but an expression of a socially acceptable and highly sublimated act of counter-aggression against a figure of authority.. .. [In contrast with Draupadī's aggression that] is directed outwards—towards her husbands, especially Yudhiṣṭhira . . . —Sītā . . . expresses her anger at her love object inwardly, and this manner of aggression, i.e., through masochistic actions, appears to be more societally normative in ancient and modern India for both men and women.[45]

Such a line of thought obviously has far-reaching implications for understanding Indian behavior in a wide variety of contexts. I do not presume to reject it out of hand. The evidence we have considered in this essay, however, suggests the inadequacy of understanding any role model as monolithic, as promoting a single type of behavior. It is perhaps easier to overlook the multiple dimensions of such models if one considers but a single text, though postmodern analysis has alerted us to the presence of multiplicity even there. Certainly the *Adbhuta Rāmāyaṇa* invites us, both scholars and inhabitants of India, to think about who Sītā is in new ways. The presence of the *Adbhuta* and its kindred folk *Rāmāyaṇa*s suggests that such thinking has been going on in India for a very long time. It attests to the fact that, as Ursala Sharma puts it, 'women in India have always been able to draw upon a stock of cultural imagery which represents women not as weak and passive but as endowed with power and energy'.[46] This line of thinking is also clearly relevant to those who would change the condition of women in contemporary India for the better. And so I close with a quotation from one of India's major agents for such change, Madhu Kishwar, who writes: 'Our cultural traditions have tremendous potential within them to combat reactionary and anti-women ideas, if we can identify their points of strength and use them creatively. The rejection of the harmful is then made much easier than attempts to overthrow traditions totally or to attack them arrogantly from the outside, as most of us Westernized modernists tend to do, since we have been completely alienated from our own culture and the people who hold it dear.'[47]

Sītā need not always fight, nor Rāma always swoon. But clearly the possibilities are much greater than most of us have previously realized.

NOTES

EPIGRAPHS: A.K. Ramanujan, 'Three Hundred *Rāmāyaṇas*: Five Examples and Three Thoughts on Translation,' in Paula Richman, ed., *Many Rāmāyaṇas: The Diversity of a Narrative Tradition in South Asia* (Berkeley: University of California Press, 1991), 46. Sītā addressing Rāvaṇa in Laṅka, Vālmīki, *Rāmāyaṇa* 5.2.20–21. Swamiji quoted in Kirin Narayan, *Storytellers, Saints, and Scoundrels: Folk Narrative in Hindu Religious Teaching* (Philadelphia: University of Pennsylvania Press, 1989), 106.

A first version of this essay was presented in the Intercultural Lecture Series on 'Gender and Religion' at the University of Pennsylvania. I am most grateful for the warm welcome and stimulating response provided by the audience. A somewhat different form of the essay was published in *Manushi: A Journal About Women and Society* 90 (1995): 5–16, and appears here by permission. I am much indebted to Cynthia Ann Humes and Rachel Fell McDermott for their very helpful comments on the *Manushi* essay that have led to the current revised version.

1. Sudhir Kakar, *The Inner World* (Delhi: Oxford University Press, 1981), 218n30. Kakar here cites P. Pratap, 'The Development of Ego Ideal in Indian Children' (PhD thesis, Banaras Hindu University, 1960).
2. Sudhir Kakar, *Intimate Relations: Exploring Indian Sexuality* (Chicago: University of Chicago Press, 1989), 131.
3. For example, Paula Richman, *Questioning Rāmāyaṇas: A South Asian Tradition* (Berkeley: University of California Press, 2001); Monika Thiel-Horstmann, ed., *Rāmāyaṇa and Rāmāyaṇas* (Wiesbaden: Otto Harrassowitz, 1991); Richman, *Many Rāmāyaṇas*; and V. Raghavan, ed., *The Rāmāyaṇa Tradition in Asia* (New Delhi: Sahitya Akademi, 1980).
4. For an excellent study of the qualities that Sītā models in Vālmīki's *Rāmāyaṇa*, see Sally Sutherland, 'Sītā and Draupadī: Aggressive Behavior and Female Role-Models in the Sanskrit Epics', *Journal of the American Oriental Society* 109, no. 1 (1989): 63–79. However, the inadequacy of taking a single text as the basis for understanding a role model is one of the major points I wish to make in this essay.
5. Narendra Nath Bhattacharyya, *History of Indian Erotic Literature* (New Delhi: Munshiram Manoharlal, 1975), ix.
6. Frank Whaling, *The Rise of the Religious Significance of Rāma* (Delhi: Motilal Banarsidass, 1980), 199n2 places the *Adbhuta Rāmāyaṇa* 'slightly

later' than the *Adhyātma Rāmāyaṇa*, which Philip Lutgendorf, *The Life of a Text Performing the Rāmcaritmānas of Tulsidas* (Berkeley: University of California Press, 1991), p. 7, dates to the late fifteenth or early sixteenth century. The argument for the northeastern provenance of the text is, as we shall see, its partial resemblance to *Rāmāyaṇa* versions studied by W.L. Smith in *Rāmāyaṇa Traditions in Eastern India* (Stockholm: Department of Indology, University of Stockholm, 1988). But, as we shall also see, there are similarities to Tamil *Rāmāyaṇas*: see *Two Tamil Folktales: The Story of King Matanakama, and The Story of Peacock Rāvaṇa*, trans. Kamil V. Zvelebil (Delhi: Motilal Banarsidass, 1987), and David Shulman, 'Sītā and Śatakantharāvaṇa in a Tamil Folk Narrative,' *Journal of Indian Folkloristics* 2, nos. 3–4 (1979): 1–26. A revised version of Shulman's article appears as 'Battle as Metaphor in Tamil Folk and Classical Traditions,' in Stuart H. Blackburn and A.K. Ramanujan, eds., *Another Harmony: New Essays on the Folklore of India* (Berkeley: University of California Press, 1986), 105–30.

7. *Adbhuta Rāmāyaṇa*, Sanskrit text with Hindi translation by Camanlal Gautam (Bareilli: Samskrti Samsthan, 1990); *Adbhuta Rāmāyaṇa*, Sanskrit text with Hindi translation by Jvalaprasad Misra (Bombay: Venkatesvara Press, 1990); *Adbhuta Rāmāyaṇa*, Sanskrit text with Hindi translation by Rām Kumār Rai (Varanasi: Prachya Prakashan, 1989); and *Adbhuta Rāmāyaṇa*, Sanskrit text with Hindi translation by Urvasi Jayantilal Surati and Jasvanti Hasmukh Dev (Lucknow: Bhuvan Vani Drast, 1983–1984). The four editions are in very close agreement on the number of verses per chapter as well as on the text proper. I cite the Prachya Prakashan edition below. An inquiry into the audience for these publications would clearly be a fruitful future line of inquiry, a matter to which I return at the end of this essay.
8. Kathleen Erndl, 'The Mutilation of Śūrpanakhā,' in Paula Richman, ed., *Many Rāmāyaṇas: The Diversity of a Narrative Tradition of South Asia* (Berkeley: University of California Press, 1991), 82.
9. Whaling, *Adbhuta Rāmāyaṇa*, 198–99. Whaling, 199n2, 334n1, notes that the one exception to this pattern is found precisely in our text, the *Adbhuta Rāmāyaṇa*.
10. John Braisted Carman, *The Theology of Rāmānuja* (New Haven: Yale University Press, 1974), 243.
11. 'He [Rāvaṇa] plays ball with the sun and the moon' (17.45); 'he regards the ocean as a puddle in a cow's hoofprint, all the worlds as bits of straw' (17.63).
12. *Two Tamil Folktales*, trans. Zvelebil, xl–xli.
13. Shulman, 'Sītā and Śatakantharāvaṇa in a Tamil Folk Narrative', 3.
14. Ibid., 7.
15. Ibid., 16.

16. Velcheru Narayana Rao, 'A *Rāmāyaṇa* of Their Own: Women's Oral Tradition in Telugu,' in Paula Richman, ed., *Many Rāmāyaṇas: The Diversity of a Narrative Tradition of South Asia* (Berkeley: University of California Press, 1991), 114–36. We shall return to this material.
17. See my *Encountering the Goddess: A Translation of the Devī-Māhātmya and a Study of Its Interpretation* (Albany: State University of New York Press, 1991), 14, 24–27, 77, 153, 171, 172, 202–3n35, 203n40, 223–24n22.
18. The label 'triumph' is C. Mackenzie Brown's: *The Triumph of the Goddess: The Canonical Models and Theological Visions of the Devī-Bhāgavata Purāṇa* (Albany: State University of New York Press, 1990). See *Srimad Devi Bhagawatam*, trans. Swami Vijnanananda, 2nd ed. (1921–23; rpt., Delhi: Oriental Books, 1977), 229–40.
19. Biardeau has addressed the topic at hand throughout her work. For convenience I here draw selectively on her superb article, 'The Śamī Tree and the Sacrificial Buffalo,' *Contributions to Indian Sociology*, n.s., 18, no. 1 (1984): 1–23. This is a translation by Richard Nice in collaboration with the author of her 'L'Arbre *śamī* et le buffle sacrificiel,' *Puruṣartha* 5 (1981): 215–44.
20. Biardeau, 'Śamī Tree,' 6, 7.
21. Ibid., 4.
22. Ibid., 19, 16. The best documentation, in text and sculpture, of the interplay between Mahiṣa and Śiva remains Heinrich von Stietencron's, 'Die Gottin Durgā Mahiṣāsuramārdini: Mythos, Darstellung und geschichtliche Rolle bei der Hinduiseirung Indiens,' in *Visible Religion: Annual for Religious Iconography* (Leiden: E.J. Brill, 1983), 118–66.
23. Biardeau, 'Śamī Tree', 15.
24. Ibid., 23.
25. Cornelia Dimmitt, 'Sītā: Fertility Goddess and *Śakti*,' in John S. Hawley and Donna M. Wulff, eds., *The Divine Consort: Rādhā and the Goddesses of India* (Berkeley, Calif.: Berkeley Religious Studies Series, 1982), 210–11.
26. In order to provide some sense of the way the text both condenses and expands the familiar Rāma story, I attach a table of contents of the *Adbhuta Rāmāyaṇa* as an Appendix to this essay.
27. George A. Grierson, 'On the *Adbhuta-Rāmāyaṇa*,' *Bulletin of the School of Oriental Studies* 4, no. 1 (1926): 12, 15. The author does, however, provide a very useful, though unevenly developed, abstract of the *Adbhuta's* contents.
28. Smith, *Rāmāyaṇa Traditions in Eastern India*, 137.
29. Various motifs in this story are found elsewhere—in the *Bhāgavata Purāṇa*, the *Mahābhārata*, and Tulsidas's *Rāmcaritmānas*—but never in the same precise configuration. See Grierson, 'On the *Adbhuta-Rāmāyaṇa*,' 16n, 17n.
30. For a useful discussion of issues in this debate, see Alf Hiltebeitel, 'Religious Studies and Indian Epic Texts,' *Religious Studies Review* 21, no. 1 (January 1995): 26–32.

31. The 'tantalizing evidence' comes from Shana Sippy, co-curator of the 'Sītā in the City' exhibition that accompanied Columbia University's 'Sītā Symposium' (30 April–2 May 1998). She reports (personal communication) that, in an isolated episode in the interviews she and Anne Murphy conducted with immigrant New Yorkers on their understandings of Sītā, 'an elderly woman at a store-front temple in Queens did tell us how Rāvaṇa's wife became pregnant from eating a fruit from the field that she was not supposed to eat and how Rāvaṇa got angry with her 'immaculate conception.'' But she has no broader context for this report.
32. See chapter epigraph above.
33. A.K. Ramanujan, 'Toward a Counter-System: Women's Tales,' in Arjun Appadurai, Frank J. Korom, and Margaret A. Mills, eds., *Gender, Genre, and Power in South Asian Expressive Traditions* (Philadelphia: University of Pennsylvania Press, 1991), 33–55.
34. See Appadurai, Korom, and Mills, *Gender, Genre, and Power in South Asian Expressive Traditions*, and Wendy Doniger, ed., *Purāṇa Perennis: Reciprocity and Transformation in Hindu and Jaina Texts* (Albany: State University of New York Press, 1993).
35. See n. 16 above.
36. See n. 33 above.
37. Rao, '*Rāmāyaṇa* of Their Own,' 115.
38. Smith, *Rāmāyaṇa Traditions in Eastern India*, 21–22.
39. Ibid. As an example of what Smith refers to in his last sentence, see the chapter epigraph from Vālmīki.
40. John P. Ferguson, 'The Great Goddess Today in Burma and Thailand: An Exploration of Her Symbolic Relevance to Monastic and Female Roles,' in James J. Preston, ed., *Mother Worship: Theme and Variations* (Chapel Hill: University of North Carolina Press, 1982), 295.
41. See Sanjukta Gupta and Richard Gombrich, 'Kings, Power and the Goddess,' *South Asia Research* 6, no. 2 (November 1986), esp. 125–26.
42. For extended treatment of the incest motif in Hindu mythology, see Wendy Doniger O'Flaherty, *Asceticism and Eroticism in the Mythology of Śiva* (London: Oxford University Press, 1973), chap. 4.
43. Hiltebeitel, 'Religious Studies and Indian Epic Texts,' 31.
44. See n. 4 above.
45. Sutherland, 'Sītā and Draupadī: Aggressive Behavior and Female Role-Models in the Sanskrit Epics,' 78–79.
46. Ursala Sharma, 'Foreword' to Joanna Liddle and Rāma Joshi, *Daughters of Independence: Gender, Caste and Class in India* (London: Zed Books, 1986), 1. I am indebted to Mary McGee for this and the following reference.
47. Madhu Kishwar and Ruth Vanita, *In Search of Answers: Indian Women's Voices from Manushi* (London: Zed Books, 1984), 47.

APPENDIX

Table of Contents of the *Adbhuta Rāmāyaṇa*
(with number of verses in the Prachya Prakashan edition)

1. Procession of Rāma and Sītā from the highest Brahman (24)
2. King Ambarīṣa's reception of a boon from Nārāyaṇa (50)
3. Nārada and Parvata arrive in the king's court (38)
4. The incarnation of Rāmachandra (81)
5. The cause of Sītā's incarnation (57)
6. Description of Harimitra and the coming of Kauśika, etc., to Vaikuṇṭha (91)
7. Nārada gains the power of singing (66)
8. Description of Sītā's birth (44)
9. The heavenly form of Śrī Rāma is revealed to Paraśurāma to be within Rāmachandra (33)
10. The four-armed heavenly form seen by Hanumān/Mahāvīra (22)
11. Rāma describes Sāṃkhya-Yoga to Hanumān (55)
12. Account of the secret teaching (*upaniṣad*) (24)
13. Rāma tells of *bhakti yoga* (32)
14. Conversation of Rāmachandra and Hanumān (55)
15. Hanumān praises Rāma (25)
16. Rāma kills Rāvaṇa and accedes to the throne (20)
17. Sītā's story: the story of the 1,000-headed Rāvaṇa (68)
18. Description of Rāvaṇa's army (71)
19. Description of the battle with the sons of 1,000-headed Rāvaṇa (42)
20. Battle of those assembled (31)
21. The scattering of Rāma's army by Rāvaṇa (21)
22. Rāma passes out (51)
23. The killing of the 1,000-headed Rāvaṇa by Sītā (72)
24. The gods resuscitate Rāma (44)
25. Rāma praises Sītā with 1,000 names (159)
26. Description of Rāma's triumph (47)
27. Rāma arrives in Ayodhya (32)

PART II

Rethinking Blood, Cadavers, and Death

4

Traditions of Human Sacrifice in Ancient and Tribal India and their Relation to Śāktism

FRANCESCO BRIGHENTI

Comparative study of religious cults provides evidence that human sacrifice functioned as a fertility magic rite in ancient and even in recent times throughout the world: for example, in the American continents, some regions of Africa, the central-eastern Mediterranean basin, and parts of the Indian subcontinent, the Indian archipelago, and Oceania. According to Mircea Eliade, the ritual significance of this extreme and dramatic form of blood sacrifice must be traced back to the archaic theory of the periodical regeneration of the sacred forces of nature. Human sacrifice is a ritual repetition of the act of creation as performed at the beginning of the universe through the dismemberment of the celestial body of a supreme being. Since the vegetable kingdom is often believed to have originated out of the blood and flesh of a mythical primordial being, the regenerative power of seeds, grains, and plants is believed to become powerfully reinforced by the ritual repetition of this cosmogonic act through the dismemberment of a human victim, who is conceived of as an earthly projection of the body of the mythic demiurge. Such a conception underlies all forms of blood sacrifice, whether human or animal.[1]

This essay focuses on the medieval Śākta practice of human sacrifice and the question of its origins. I argue that continuous interchange of socioreligious customs and of mythical, doctrinal, and ritual elements relating to human sacrifice has taken place since protohistoric epochs in the Indian subcontinent. Further, this process of cultural interaction, out of which the whole Tantric religious complex has originated, had as its vectors the 'people of the Veda' on the one hand, and peoples of disparate ethnic origins (Dravidian, Austro-Asiatic, Austronesian and Tibeto-Burman) on the other.

Harking back to Narendra Nath Bhattacharyya's studies on the history of the Śākta religion, I regard the Śākta ritual to be the final outcome of a long process of cultural syncreticism through the development, contact, and combination of diverse ethnocultural streams. Some constant themes will emerge, which should help the reader to consider the reciprocal links between the numerous human sacrifice traditions discussed in this paper. In my conclusion, I hope to contribute to a more coherent explanation of the themes of human sacrifice in the Śākta tradition.

MYTHIC ARCHETYPES IN THE VEDIC TRADITION

In a famous Vedic cosmogonic myth, the universe was manifested through Indra's dismemberment of the body of Vṛtra, the cosmic serpent or dragon.[2] This cosmogonic act simultaneously constituted the prime cause of creation's multiplicity and made Indra and the other gods responsible for breaking the initial unity (nonduality) of the universe.

A. K. Coomaraswamy describes this breaking of One into the Manifold as the 'original sin' (*kilbiṣa*) of Indra and the gods. Man, living in the manifold creation and thus unaware of the actual oneness of the cosmos, is excluded from drinking the divine Soma—the Water of Life—except through the transubstantiation of an analogous substance. To heal this fracture, man must reintegrate the Manifold into the One ritually by performing Sacrifice, renouncing the self to be born again into the One Principle.[3]

Brāhmaṇical doctrines of sacrifice in the post-Vedic period elaborated the Indra-Vṛtra myth. Although lauded in ancient Vedic times, in the post-Vedic period, the slaying was used to discuss Brāhmaṇicide and other related questions, particularly by nascent Vaiṣṇava and Śaiva groups that sought to disparage Indra's 'great deed' so as to reduce the residual authority still enjoyed by him and, conversely, to highlight Viṣṇu or Śiva. Post-Vedic commentators identified some *asuras* (commonly understood as demons) as Brāhmaṇas, including Vṛtra, and portrayed Indra, presumably the *deva* (divine being) being pursued and tormented by a terrific ogress—the fury of Brāhmaṇicide, Brahmahatyā.[4] In both the *Mahābhārata* and the *Rāmāyaṇa,* the personified Brahmahatyā is placated only after an *aśvamedha* (horse sacrifice) purifies Indra.[5] Other Vedic texts offer a modified form of the Indra-Vṛtra cosmogonic myth, replacing the ophidic figure of Vṛtra with the anthropomorphic figure of Puruṣa, the Macrocosmic or Primordial 'Male,' who contained in himself the entire undifferentiated totality. When offered as a sacrifice by the gods, Puruṣa's body, like Vṛtra's, was dismembered into numberless portions resulting in the origination of all that exists.

Coomaraswamy maintains that no essential value would be really changed by substituting the name Vṛtra for Puruṣa in the *Puruṣa Sūkta* hymn (*Ṛg Veda* 10.90).[6] The same argument pertains elsewhere to the manifestation of a new cosmic order by Prajāpati through an exhausting process of self-differentiation from a primeval state of self-concentrated wholeness to multiplicity.[7] Prajāpati's prostrate and powerless condition is subsequently revitalized by the Sacrifice, which is said to be the 'image' (*pratimā*) of his mode of being. The secondary creator, Prajāpati, the Lord of Sacrifice, is the same as the Universal Puruṣa. Vṛtra is the *asura* counterpart of the *deva* Cosmic Man. Unlike the Cosmic Man, Vṛtra refuses self-sacrifice. Indra's 'cruelty' to Vṛtra, the predestined victim of the cosmogonic 'sacrifice,' is a consequence of the latter's resistance.[8] Without resistance, there is no cruelty, explaining why the victim of human sacrifice in India, both in Sanskritized and in tribal contexts, should preferably be willing; his or her consent must be obtained ritually. That is also why the 'pain' (*śuc*) and 'evil' (*pāpam*) suffered by sacrificial victims must be transferred to substitutes that ritually take on themselves the impurity of sacrifice. This doctrine of ritual substitution has been found in Sanskritized forms of blood (human as well as animal) sacrifice, in both Vedic and Śākta-Tantric contexts.

HUMAN SACRIFICE IN VEDIC INDIA

The Vedic form of human sacrifice is known as *puruṣamedha* or *nṛmedha*. Regardless of whether it was actually practiced, at minimum it was abolished or fell into desuetude in a very remote epoch.[9] Jan Gonda maintains that the *puruṣamedha* was aimed at procuring for the royal sacrificer all of the benefits impossible to gain through the *aśvamedha*,[10] for 'the *puruṣamedha* is everything.'[11] Universal supremacy, for instance, was also the goal of the *sarvamedha*, the sacrifice of all (*sarva*) animal and vegetable essences performed by a Vedic king 'who wishes to become this all'. According to *Śatapatha Brāhmaṇa* 13.7.1, the *sarvamedha* consisted of a ten-day *soma* sacrifice aimed at propitiating all gods; it included the building of a firebrick altar (*agnicayana*); the slaying of a horse (*aśvamedha*), of a man (*puruṣamedha*), and of all other animals meet for a sacrifice; as well as the offering of many kinds of herbs and trees. The archetypal model for the royal sacrificer in this rite was Brahman Svayambhū, that is, Prajāpati, whose cosmic emission and subsequent instauration of sacrifice established the supremacy and the lordship over all creatures.[12]

The liturgical literature associated with the *Yajur Veda* suggests that human sacrifice is patterned on the mythic motif of the primeval sacrifice performed by the Puruṣa. The *Taittirīya Brāhmaṇa* (3.4), the *Vājasaneyi Saṃhitā* (30.5–22), and the *Śatapatha Brāhmaṇa* (13.6) enumerate a host of men and women suitable as victims in the *puruṣamedha*, and specify that they should be released after being consecrated and replaced with animals.[13] *Śatapatha Brāhmaṇa* 13.6 explains that the forty-day rite was performed first by Puruṣa Nārāyaṇa for the attainment of universal sovereignty.[14]

The *Śaṅkhāyana Śrauta Sūtra* (16.10–14) and *Vaitāna Śrauta Sūtra* (37.10–38.9) describe the *puruṣamedha* exactly the same way as the horse sacrifice in the *aśvamedha*. The ritual of human sacrifice as prescribed in these later *sūtras* might have constituted either the prototype or a theoretical imitation of the *aśvamedha* ritual.[15] The ultimate purpose of this particular form of *puruṣamedha* is the healing of the sacrificer's bodily ills—not self-realization, the attainment of immortality, universal supremacy, or the like. The victim—a Brāhmaṇa or a Kṣatriya purchased for a thousand cows and a hundred horses—was taken care of and given a free hand for the duration of one full year (just like the *aśvamedha*'s horse), at the end of which he was adorned, decorated, and ritually murdered by suffocation. As with the *aśvamedha*, the principal wife of the sacrificer lay with the corpse, followed by an obscene and abusive ritual dialogue between the Brāhmaṇas and the women attending the ceremony.[16]

In the Vedic period, man was included among the five *paśu* victims (man, horse, bull, ram, and he-goat) suitable to be immolated in the *agnicayana* ceremony, the ritual building of the stratified firebrick altar (called *uttaravedi* or *agniciti*) conceived as the periodical reconstruction of the dismembered body of the willing victim, Prajāpati.[17] According to the *Aitareya Brāhmaṇa*, the gods killed man as a sacrificial victim, after which his *medha*—'marrow'—took shelter in a horse and then, in succession, in a bull, a ram, and a he-goat. This is why the he-goat is considered to be the best-suited animal for sacrifice, epitomizing all five sacrificial animals. The *medha* finally passed into the earth and turned into rice.[18] According to J.C. Heesterman,[19] human and animal victims, as well as vegetable offerings, coexisted side by side in the Vedic epoch by virtue of the close interrelation of man, animals, and vegetation in archaic symbolic thinking. The revaluation of the lowest *paśu* victim (the goat) as the recapitulation of the higher four ones, making it apparently equal to man—considered the highest of sacrificial victims, in that he is the nearest to Prajāpati—may, in the opinion of B.K. Smith,[20] indicate that the hierarchical order of things was at a certain time subverted and rendered meaningless by rival groups of Vedic sacrificers who competed for status and social position by changing the principles on which the sacrifice had been based.

Numerous sources report the ritual establishment of human heads beneath the foundations of buildings or altars.[21] The *Taittirīya Saṃhitā* specifies that the human head to be buried under the brick altar must be purchased, and must belong to either a Kṣatriya or a Vaiśya who was killed in battle or by lightning.[22] The human head provides the foundations of the fire altar's strength or functions as a type of 'guardian'.[23] The sacrificial reintegration of the dismembered Puruṣa's body is achieved in the *agnicayana* through the piling, brick on brick, of the fire altar. The *puruṣamedha* and *aśvamedha* appear to have represented the sacrificial reintegration of the microcosm into the macrocosm. The *puruṣamedha,* in particular, was subsequently perpetuated and continued—more or less openly according to the historical circumstances—by Śākta-Tantrism.

THE RELIGIOUS ROOTS OF THE INDUS CIVILIZATION

In recent years, Asko Parpola has argued that we must examine the pre-Vedic ritual complex for answers to the origin of Vedic ritual. Cults entered the northwestern regions of the Indian subcontinent starting from *c.* 1900 BCE with an early (pre-*Ṛg Vedic*) wave of proto-Aryan immigrants, identified by Parpola with the Dāsas of the *Ṛg Veda,* the archenemies of the Vedic Aryans. The original religion of the so-defined Dāsas greatly differed from the Vedic Aryans' own worship of Indra and the cultic drink of Soma. The Dāsa religion pivoted on the worship of gods called *asuras*, whose sovereign was Varuṇa, and whose partial incorporation into the *Ṛg Vedic* pantheon of *devas* had already occurred in Bactria and Margiana, where the two distinct, successive Aryan peoples fused together around the eighteenth century BCE (see map 1). This cultural amalgamation continued when the *Ṛg Vedic* Aryans met up with the early Indian branch of the Dāsas in the Punjab and the Ganges-Yamuna Doab (*c.* 1700–1400 BCE). These Dāsas were installed as the ruling elite of the Late Harappan Dravidian culture. Through contact with the Dravidian culture, the non-*Ṛg Vedic* Aryan elites had developed the complex fire altar ritual (not mentioned at all in the *Ṛg Veda*). This amalgamation explains the vast differences between the various *Ṛg Vedic* texts as well as the emergence of new mythological themes, including the ideology of Puruṣa/Prajāpati and his (self-)sacrifice, which is connected in Vedic doctrine with human sacrifice and with the fire ritual.[24]

Parpola suggests that the religion of Indian Dāsas—itself the

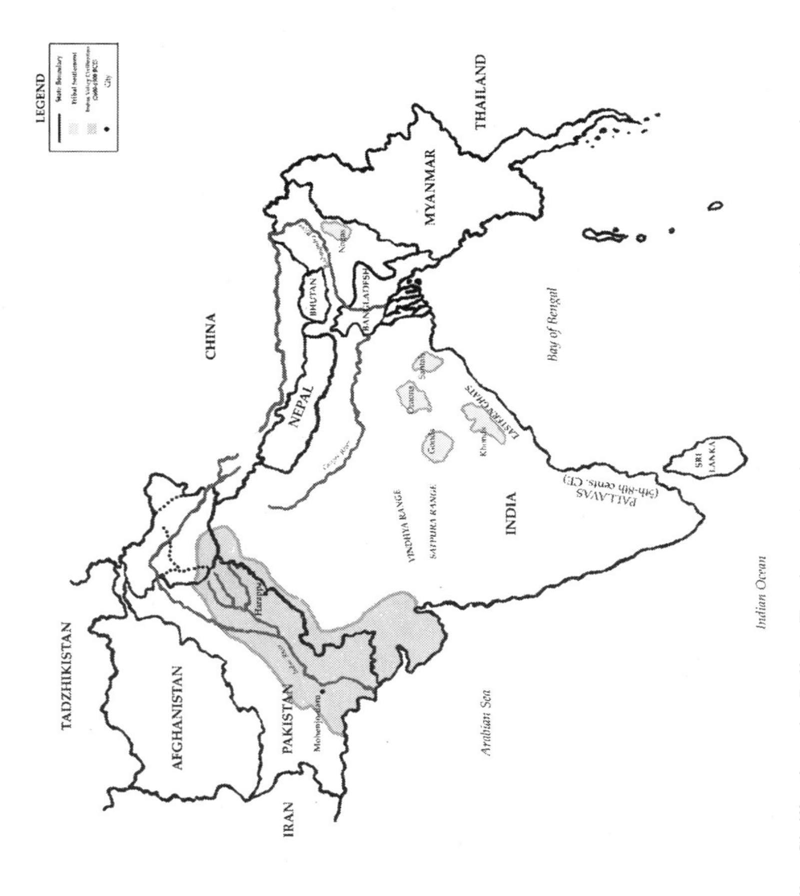

Map 1: The Indus Valley Civilization, the Pallava Empire, and various contemporary tribal groups, as shown within the present political boundaries of South Asia. Artwork by Ben Royas.

result of a syncretistic amalgamation of Harappan-related and proto-Aryan mythic and ritual traditions—evolved into the later *vrātya* rites. Bands (*vrātas*) of unidentified Aryan nomads were described in later Vedic texts as living beyond the pale of Brāhmaṇical culture, in close contact with eastern barbaric peoples (*mlecchas*) worshipping *asuras* and speaking a (Dāsa-related?) old Indo-Aryan language, similar to the old Magadhi language.[25] The *vrātyas* kept certain religious observances (*vratas*) through which they were ritually consecrated (initiated) and bound to a mysterious brotherhood. They were connected with *Atharva Vedic* magic and sorcery as well as some proto-yogic and ecstatic practices, in which Mircea Eliade sees the traces of an archaic shamanistic complex.[26] The *vrātyas* were also consecrated warriors who had vowed to fight to the death—either their own or their opponents'—with nothing to offer as sacrifice but their own lives and skill in battle. They mounted alternating war expeditions and potlatch-like competitions between rival clans. At the outset or return from raids, *vrātya* brotherhoods celebrated the communal rite *vrātyaṣṭoma* to purify themselves.[27]

The main festival associated with the *vrātya*, the well-known *Mahāvrāta*, included among its multifarious ritual performances sacred sexual intercourse of a prostitute and a bard, accompanied by obscene dialogue. This *Mahāvrāta* finds striking parallels in the simulated mating and obscene dialogue in the mating of the chief queen (*mahiṣī*) with the sacrificial victim—either horse or man—in the *aśvamedha*. Moreover, the *Mahāvrāta*, *aśvamedha*, and *puruṣamedha* all prescribe a year-long sacrificial session, characterized by the free roaming of the consecrated victim. In Parpola's opinion, the rite of sexual union celebrated on the occasion of the *Mahāvrāta* is likely to have originally involved the slaying of a human victim.[28]

There is an intriguing affinity between the myth of Prajāpati committing incest with his daughter Uṣas[29] and the Indra-Vṛtra cosmogonic myth. After being shot by Rudra's arrow, Prajāpati ejaculates outside his daughter's womb, and thus originates the whole cosmos: Vṛtra releases the Cosmic Waters after his body is rent by a thunderbolt from Indra; and likewise originates the universe. The mythical figure of Vṛtra is interpreted by some scholars as a negative doublet of Varuṇa,[30] and the latter is, in his turn, regarded by some scholars as the primal divine figure from whom the creator god Prajāpati evolved.[31] Therefore, whether they were conceived as *deva*s or *asura*s, these three figures function in a remarkably similar fashion: a cosmic being offered as a sacrifice at the beginning of time, whose immolation had to be ritually and cyclically reenacted in human sacrifice.

Many of Parpola's hypotheses are of great importance to understanding the religious ideas and beliefs that were at the root of the practice of human sacrifice in ancient India. He tells us, for instance, that human sacrifice may have developed in proto-historic India as a form of royal sacrifice in which a sacred king or his substitute, equated with the supreme vegetation god, was put to death and replaced by a new king, whose consecration marked the beginning of a new time (and vegetative) cycle that coincided with the beginning of a new solar year.[32] In matrilineal (and Dravidian) Kerala, until the seventeenth century CE, the *zamorin* (king) of Calicut was purportedly 'obliged to cut his throat in public at the end of a twelve years' reign'.[33]

Further, Parpola argues that the Harappan seals depicting a buffalo-horned human figure may indicate an archaic buffalo-god, later assimilated as Varuṇa by Vedic Aryans.[34] This buffalo-god was likely the model for the divine king slain cyclically on his sacred marriage with the earth goddess. The epithet *mahiṣī* (buffalo cow) referred to the Vedic king's consort when she lay with the horse sacrificed in the *aśvamedha*, suggesting that the original animal immolated during this rite was a water buffalo, not a horse. Vedic ritual texts show that the king identified himself with the sacrificial victim, as well as with its divine counterpart, Varuṇa. In the Brāhmaṇa texts, Varuṇa is the only god who receives water buffaloes in sacrifice. Having power over both life and death, Varuṇa is, on the other hand, intimately connected with the Vedic god of death, Yama, a partial doublet of his, whose *vāhana* in later Hinduism is the water buffalo.[35]

Third, according to Parpola, the *aśvamedha/puruṣamedha* rite may originally have been conceived of as a cyclical repetition of the dismemberment of the pre-Vedic divine buffalo, equivalent to the Cosmic Man of later Vedic literature. In the period of the Brāhmaṇas, Prajāpati, a 'new' form of the Cosmic Man, partially inherited the functions originally attributed to the cosmic deity Varuṇa and came to be associated with the *aśvamedha/puruṣa-medha* ritual as the Lord of Sacrifice, the personification of both the sacrificer and the victim.[36]

Finally, Vedic ritual texts are comparatively silent about the role of the goddess: what, for instance, is the relationship of the victims of the *aśvamedha* and *puruṣamedha* with the *mahiṣī*? Was the *mahiṣī*'s role similar to that of South Indian Hindu goddesses, whom D. Shulman has efficaciously defined as 'Murderous Brides',[37] thought to be united with the buffalo(-demon) destined to be their victim? Nor does the Brāhmaṇa literature help to explain why human sacrifice in India, both in tribal and Hindu contexts, aims to propitiate female deities. In Vedic literature, there is no proof whatsoever of goddesses being offered human sacrifices. Nevertheless, offering human victims to goddesses appears to be extremely ancient in India and is central to the meaning and logic of *śakti*-worship.[38] Parpola argues that much can be clarified on these points by studying the archaeological remains of the Indus civilization, which likely influenced the Vedic and later Hindu traditions.

Indeed, there seems to be archaeological evidence of human sacrificial rituals in the Indus civilization (see map 1). A Harappan terracotta seal depicts a male figure brandishing a sickle-shaped object while approaching a seated female figure with disheveled hair and her hands raised in supplication. On the obverse, a naked female figure is shown upside down with legs wide apart, and plants issuing from her womb. Two tigers stand at her left side. According to J.H. Marshall, this figure may represent Mother Earth or, at any rate, a female divinity of fertility connected with animal genii, to whom the scene on the obverse side of the seal, interpreted as a scene of human sacrifice, is connected.[39] This seal may constitute one of the earliest pieces of archaeological evidence in the Indian subcontinent of human sacrifice done to propitiate a fertility goddess.

A terracotta seal from Mohenjo-daro may bear witness to the prevalence of human sacrifice to a tree goddess or tree spirit. The so-called 'fig deity' seal[40] (see fig. 4) boasts a nude anthropomorphic figure standing between two branches of an *aśvattha* tree. A half-kneeling figure—distinguished by a horned crown, like the object of his (or her) worship—appears to worship the 'fig deity', interpreted as a tree goddess or tree spirit first by J.H. Marshall and E.J.H. Mackay and subsequently by J.N. Banerjea.[41] Parpola suggests, however, that another detail of this seal is significant: the human head placed on a throne or sacrificial altar beneath the fig tree. This might be the head of a decapitated warrior because of its 'double-bun' hairstyle, and the scene depicted on the seal demands comparison with the self-decapitation of ancient Tamil warriors to the goddess of victory and fertility, Durgā. The interpretation of

Fig. 4: A 'fig diety' seal from Mohenjo-daro, showing a warrior's severed head placed before a goddess. From Asko Parpola, *Deciphering the Indus Script* (Cambridge: Cambridge University Press, 1994), fig. 14.35, p. 260.

this scene as human sacrifice is reinforced by the isolated pictogram placed opposite the human head beneath the fig tree; Parpola notes that the pictogram appears in another seal, which illustrates what appears to be the sacrifice of a buffalo. Parpola parallels the warrior's severed head depicted on this seal to the pot termed *mahāvīra* or 'great hero', conceived of as the head of the mysterious demon Makha, used in the *pravargya* rite associated with the *agnicayana*.[42] The *mahāvīra* was normally placed on a throne just like the warrior's truncated head of the Harappan 'fig deity' seal.[43]

If both seals are admitted to record actual practice of human sacrifice to a goddess, the mode of offering the victim entails bloodshed, requiring the use of a sword or sickle. This method is contrary to the 'classical' Vedic sacrificial doctrine, which proscribed the use of cutting and prescribed suffocation instead. Decapitation or cutting the victim's throat was also the method resorted to by the Śāktas of later epochs, and was the method used by most of the diverse tribal peoples of India to sacrifice victims.

In Śāktism and in most of the tribal religions of India, Harappan sacrificial prototypes have played a more prominent part than later Vedic ones in determining the ritual modalities of sacrifice, both human and animal. A Harappan seal from Chanhudaro shows a bison, *Bos gaurus* (Skt. *gaura mṛga*), a wild bovine assimilable in Indian symbolic thinking to the *mahiṣa-mṛga,* or untamed water buffalo, having sexual intercourse with a recumbent female figure. The female wears a peculiar headdress featuring a plant-sprout (possibly *pīpal*) comparable to those found on the headdresses of other figures such as the 'fig deity.' This scene of bison-woman intercourse presages the simulated mating of the chief royal consort (*mahiṣī*) with the sacrificed horse of the *aśvamedha*.[44] Thus, the royal horse sacrifice most likely evolved from a more archaic Harappan buffalo sacrifice, which itself replaced earlier forms of human sacrifice.

THE ŚĀKTA TRADITION OF SELF-IMMOLATION IN ANCIENT TAMIL NADU

The *Saṅgam* literature of Tamilnadu, commonly dated to the first to second centuries CE,[45] constitutes the only ancient non-Aryan literary sources for the proto-Śākta traditions of South India. Over two thousand years after the creation of the Harappan 'fig deity' seal, depicting, as some believe, a warrior's severed head placed before a goddess, some classical Tamil works from this literary corpus describe the self-immolation of South Indian warriors, hunters, and cattle raiders, who sought to win the favor of certain regional goddesses, assimilable to Durgā or Kālī, by cutting off their own heads and offering the blood gushing from their severed necks.

In the *Tolkāppiyam*, the earliest extant Tamil grammar (*c.* first or second century CE), when warriors were setting out on a cattle raid, a cattle-rescuing expedition, or a military operation, they propitiated the goddess Koṟṟavai for success and victory with sacrifices of buffaloes, humans, and their own heroes' blood.[46] An important contemporaneous Tamil novel in verse, the *c.* second-century CE, Buddhist-oriented *Maṇimekhalai,*[47] vividly describes a temple of the forest goddess Kāḍamarselvi. Located within a terrifying burial and cremation ground, the temple is surrounded by ramparts, has a sacrificial altar before its main entrance, and is faced by tall trees whose branches bow under the burden of the severed heads of votaries who have sacrificed themselves in devotion to the goddess.[48] Such devotees supposedly tied their necks with ropes to the branches of a sacred tree and then severed their heads. In this case, suicide is not performed in fulfillment of a vow to the goddess of victory (Koṟṟavai/Durgā). The supreme sacrifice is dedicated to the proto-Tantric goddess of death (Kāḍamarselvi/ Kālī) residing in a *śmaśāna* (burning ground) within a forest located amidst ghosts and demons.

The later *Śilappadikaram*, a famous novel in verse, most likely dating to the end of the second or the beginning of the third century CE,[49] has an entire chapter that takes place in the temple of the goddess Aiyai, worshipped by hill, forest, and desert tribes whose main occupations were hunting, food-gathering, capturing others' cattle herds, and launching raids for plunder. Here the Eyiṇars adore the goddess in the person of a virgin attired like her. Some Eyiṇars fulfill their vow to offer her their own heads and their blood in a rite called *avippali,* a Tamil term derived from Skt. *havisbali*, 'offering at the sacrificial altar.' The ritual acceptance of the heads and blood by the virgin impersonating the goddess is called *palikkoḍai* (a Tamil term derived from Skt. *balidāna*, 'invoking the deity to partake of the offering').[50]

Self-sacrifice is visibly represented in the Pallava era (*c.* 325–800 CE) (see map 1) in several Tamil sculptural panels showing a warrior offering his own head to the goddess.[51] Oblatory suicide meant to propitiate or render thanks to goddesses of war, death, or forest to fulfill a vow or to ensure success in war or plunder appears to be a peculiar feature of the spirituality of ancient Dravidian groups of warriors, hunters, and plunderers, or of proto-Tantric *vīras* ('heroes').

J.C. Heesterman has described instances of *sarvayajña*, 'sacrifice of all', or symbolic Vedic sacrificial suicide.[52] Probably reminiscent of earlier self-immolation ruled out by Vedic ritual, *sarvayajña* was performed only liturgically, without causing the actual death of the sacrificer, by symbolic drowning, death in fire, or starvation; decapitation is conspicuous by its absence. The symbolic self-immolation rite was framed within the *sattra*, or communal *soma* sacrifice performed by initiates acting as priests, whose expanded one-year session was closely connected with the *Mahāvrāta* feasts.[53] This reminds us again of the *vrātya*s and their cyclic calendrical rites held at the beginning and end of raiding expeditions. The idea and practice of self-immolation were immanent in the *vrātya* ritual, which Heesterman opines to have preceded, indeed originated, the *śrauta*.[54] The *vrātya*s often had nothing to offer in sacrifice but their own lives. The prize they sought was the *dakṣiṇā* offered by a rich sacrificer in exchange for a fallen warrior's head to bury under his *agniciti*. In sum, due to their low position on the social scale, *vrātya*s vowed themselves to death by uniting in sworn bands of poor consecrated warriors who offered themselves as *dakṣiṇā* gifts to enhance their social status.[55]

The self-sacrifice performed by Eyiṇar warriors and cattle raiders of the *Śilappadikāram* is not fundamentally different from the self-sacrifice traditions of the *vrātya*s of the Vedic period. However, in the Tamil epics, the self-sacrifice is for the first time in Indian literature said to be offered as a self-decapitation to a

'Dravidian' goddess, which may have constituted either a South Indian adaptation of the unorthodox *vrātya* ritual hinted at in the Brāhmaṇas or, conversely, the survival of a Harappan-related 'Dravidian' tradition.

Particularly in South India, a modified human sacrifice was offered. One of the most dramatic instances during the Pallava period was the *navakaṇḍam*, the offering of flesh from 'nine parts' of one's own body.[56] The practice of cutting off pieces of one's own flesh and surrendering them as sacrificial gifts (*dakṣiṇā*) appears to have been already known to Vedic audiences, with no connection, explicit or implicit, with the worship of female deities.[57]

Ritual self-wounding in honor of Mahādevī is first mentioned in Sanskrit sources in the *c.* sixth-century CE *Devī Māhātmya,* representing the first appearance of independent Śāktism in Sanskrit literature. We find there an account of a king and a Vaiśya worshipping the Great Goddess with blood from their own limbs.[58] Yet, it was above all early medieval Śāktism—possibly on the basis of the model provided by ancient South Indian warriors—that caused this ritual performance to spread all over India, as may be evinced from a great many Sanskrit literary sources dating from the post-Gupta epoch and later.[59]

The Munda-speaking peoples of the Chhota Nagpur Plateau (see map 1), who were to some extent exposed to Śākta-Tantrism, adopted at an indeterminable time the so-called 'thigh-blood sacrifice' (Mundari *bul-maeom*; Santali *bul-mayam*), which involves the outpouring of one's own blood. The thigh-blood sacrifice is most likely a substitute for actual human sacrifice—a practice that was perhaps never adopted by these tribes—in the propitiation of certain divinities or spirits, known as *saket-bongas*. The term *saket* is a cognate of the Skt. term *śakti*, and *bonga* means divinity.[60] Among the Santals in particular, *saket-bongas* are tutelary deities of *ojhās* (medicine men, exorcists and diviners), who used to offer their own blood in fulfillment of a vow. Although the vowed sacrifice itself is called *saket* and lends its name to the class of *bongas*, many of whom have Hindu names (including important forms of the Mahādevī such as Kālī, Durgā, Gaṅgā, etc.), the *bul-*

mayam is also offered to *bongas* of purely tribal Santal origin by non-Hinduized tribal priests known as *kudam naeke* (the chief priest or *ato naeke*'s assistant). The *kudam naeke* pricks himself with a thorn and mixes drops of his blood with rice. The malevolent *bongas* propitiated with this sacrifice are spirits presiding over village boundaries and outskirts.[61] The *ato naeke* is also charged with propitiating malevolent hill spirits who, at least in the tradition of the Santals of Mayurbhanj district, northeastern Orissa (see map 1), are said to have been offered human sacrifices.[62] Therefore, it is difficult to ascertain now to what degree such bloody tribal rites were influenced by Śākta-Tantrism.

Bhattacharyya maintains that 'very probably' most of the ancient Śākta cults of South India evolved out of a congeries of local goddess cults having originated during the Neolithic period quite independently of the influence exerted by the Brāhmaṇical religion over the Dravidian agricultural-pastoral communities.[63] This would explain the suicidal and self-wounding practices associated with such goddess cults, not mentioned in Vedic literature. The Tamil warrior's self-immolation to his tutelary war goddess was, in fact, already conceived of as a human sacrifice in honor of a Śākta manifestation, while the Vedic *puruṣamedha*, the offering of a human head on the occasion of the celebration of the Vedic *agnicayana*, and the self-sacrifice of the Vedic desperado warrior, were not at all conceived of this way. In the early historical period, the South Dravidian proto-Śākta cultic complex could have had greater and more direct influence on the religious customs of the human-sacrificing North Dravidian tribes than the then obsolete Vedic human sacrifice traditions. At least since the period of the *Śatapatha Brāhmaṇa*, Vedic forms of human sacrifice had fallen into disuse. Śākta forms of human sacrifice had still to assert themselves in North India. Yet Tamil literature dating from the first centuries of our era mention human sacrifice to goddesses. How do we explain this fact except by hypothesizing an indigenous development of a peculiar tradition of human sacrifice in the context of Tamilian (South Dravidian) Śāktism? A general refashioning and, very likely, even a migration of doctrines and practices related to human sacrifice may have occurred in those centuries from North to South India, as suggested by the famous late Vedic legend of Śunaḥśepa, significant for its ethnocultural implications in regard to the diffusion of the practice of human sacrifice in ancient India.

Aitareya Brāhmaṇa 7.13–18 tells of a childless king named Hariścandra who vowed that if he obtained a son, he would offer him in sacrifice to Varuṇa. That son purchased a substitute for himself: Śunaḥśepa, the son of a poor Brāhmaṇa named Ajīgartta. Varuṇa approved the substitute, and when Śunaḥśepa was bound to the *yūpa* (sacrificial stake), the four officiating *hotṛ* priests all refused to bind or slay the victim, leaving the task of sacrificing his own son to Ajīgartta. Śunaḥśepa was saved by uttering mantras taught him by the *ṛṣi* Viśvāmitra, which effectively appeased Varuṇa. Viśvāmitra resolved to adopt Śunaḥśepa to take him away from his unworthy father (who belonged to the family of Aṅgiras, the mythic sage connected with *Atharva Vedic* magic and sorcery and with the fire ritual, in which human sacrifice was once permissible). Viśvāmitra proposed to his hundred sons to declare Śunaḥśepa the eldest; fifty younger sons assented, but fifty elder sons dissented. Viśvāmitra did declare Śunaḥśepa the eldest, with the new name Devarāta (Beloved-of-Gods), and the sage cursed his fifty elder sons so that their now Dasyu (uncivilized, impious, non-Aryan) progeny would become dispersed. Many of the border tribes descended from these cursed sons who refused to accept Viśvāmitra's adoption of the intended sacrificial victim, Śunaḥśepa, and were subsequently banished beyond the borders of Āryāvarta.[64] These included the Āndhras (South-Central Dravidians), the Śavaras (Vindhya Range tribals), the Pulindas (Āndhra tribals), the Puṇḍras (Bengal and Bihar tribals), and the Mūtibas.

G.S. Ghurye claims that this Vedic narrative suggests a remote Vedic origin for the practice of human sacrifice among the Kondhs, the North Dravidian people living in parts of the immense Āndhra country who, more than others, made this ritual practice routine.[65] To Ghurye, the cursed sons symbolize those Aryans who refused to give up human sacrifice, and Vedic Aryans might have been allowed to carry on human sacrifice only in peripheral areas such as Āndhra Deśa.

HUMAN SACRIFICE AMONG THE MUNDA AND NORTH DRAVIDIAN TRIBES

Human sacrifices are said to have been resorted to by some Middle Indian non-Aryan tribes well into the nineteenth century. Three tribal groups—Kondhs, Gonds, and Oraons (see map 1), speaking Dravidian languages—used to sacrifice human victims to appease the Goddess's wrath or to increase fertility. By contrast, Tamil warriors practiced self-immolation rituals to request victory in battle or fulfill vows made before war expeditions.

Some anthropologists hypothesize on cultural grounds that the Kondhs, Gonds, and Oraons might be ethnic descendants of some pre-Dravidian migrant groups, perhaps speaking languages of the Munda family, or of mixed groups of Dravidian and Munda peoples.[66] The Munda-speaking ancestral kinsmen of the Kondhs, Gonds, and Oraons were so influenced by Dravidian cultures that they adopted numerous Dravidian forms of speech. During such 'Dravidization' of language, certain South Dravidian forms of the cultus might also have been adopted, such as the ritual of human sacrifice to propitiate wild and ferocious female divinities. First-century CE Tamil works mention human sacrifices to the Great Goddess, central to Śāktism, and although the tribal-like Tamilian rites of head offering do not seem to have been popular among the Dravidian-speaking populations of Middle India, the latter could have borrowed many Śākta sacrificial doctrines and practices from their South Indian ethnic kinsmen at a time when the influence of the Sanskritic culture of North India had yet to become prominent in the uplands of the Chhota Nagpur Plateau, Vindhya and Satpura Ranges, and Eastern Ghats.

The earliest references to tribal populations of Middle India sacrificing human beings to propitiate goddesses are found in the works of the Sanskrit poet, Bāṇabhaṭṭa (early seventh century CE), who lived at the court of the North Indian monarch Harṣa of Kanauj. Bāṇabhaṭṭa describes in his celebrated *Kādambarī* and *Harṣa-carita* the religious practices of hunters named Śavaras. The common offerings of human flesh and blood caused the Śavaras' bodies to be rough with scars from knives used to make their own blood flow out, and buffaloes were offered to a goddess identified with the Hindu Durgā/Kālī. Similarly, Vākpati (early eighth century CE), in his Prakrit *kāvya* praise poem of Kanauj king Yaśovarman entitled *Gauḍavaho*, describes the cave shrine of Vindhyavāsinī, slayer of the buffalo demon, worshipped with daily human sacrifices by the Śavaras of the Vindhyan region.[67] It is probable that the Śavaras mentioned by early medieval Sanskrit and Prakrit authors as champions of human sacrifice actually formed, along with the Bhīllas, Pulindas, and so on, a block of non-Aryan tribes—partly influenced by Hinduism, yet fiercely opposing the political and military penetration of the Aryans into their lands—distributed right across central and eastern India, who worshipped female manifestations (assimilable to the Hindu Goddess, and installed in shrines described like Hindu temples) as their chief divinities or spirits.[68] Large groups of indigenous tribes from different ethnic stocks—possibly even including among them the Dravidian-speaking Kondhs or other Dravidian tribes—were lumped together categorically by the Aryans as Śavaras. These 'literary' Śavaras are mainly described as warlike cattle seizers and hunters;[69] their socioeconomic status was, thus, similar to that of the bands of Tamil warriors, hunters, and plunderers that in the *Śilappadikaram* practice self-immolation to goddesses craving human blood.

In Bhattacharyya's studies of the history of religions, he posits a dialectical relation of religious forms and social forces; this seems to be substantiated by the common adoption of a human sacrifice pattern by heterogeneous groups of Indian tribes whose economy was based on war-making and cattle raiding. Both Sanskrit and Dravidian medieval texts mention raiders pillaging crops, herds, and houses, who often are alleged to capture victims for human sacrifice.[70]

In anthropologist R. Rahmann's view, the ritual of human sacrifice was adopted by some tribal populations of Middle India under the influence of their Śākta-oriented Hindu rulers in a relatively recent period of Indian history.[71] Other scholars, however, do not attach so great an importance to the influence historically exerted by the Śākta rites. At least in the case of the Kondh groups worshipping the earth goddess Tari Penu as their chief divinity, human sacrifice might have had a more ancient origin. The influence of Hindu Śāktism on the Dravidian tribes of Middle India appears more evident in the cases of the Gonds living in the Bastar ex-state and the Oraons, whose main historical settlements are located on the Chhota Nagpur Plateau.

The occurrence of human sacrifices among the Oraons of Chhota Nagpur is mostly attributable to Hindu influence. The Oraon ritual of human sacrifice was known as *otonga*, or also *urka*.[72] These terms were also employed to indicate one who searched, or else was believed to search, the countryside for poor people (preferably female) to waylay and spirit away for sacrifice.[73] Such dreaded persons were considered the emissaries of local Hinduized landowners, or zamindars, to whose families they often belonged. This sort of 'hunt', even when it was not led to its logical conclusion, was a means for the *otonga* to gain increased respect, social prestige, and the benevolence of the zamindari family.[74]

According to P. Dehon, an authority writing at the beginning of the twentieth century, the recipient of human sacrifice among the Oraons was the goddess Anna Kuārī (a variant from the Sanskrit, Annakumārī, meaning the Virgin-Who-Gives-Food), presiding over the crops, wealth, and epidemics. Anna Kuārī is presently unknown to the Oraons. She was probably a Śākta goddess propitiated with human sacrifices by certain Hinduized Oraon landlords of the Chhota Nagpur Plateau. The victims were selected by the *otonga*s in April or May after sowing. The victim's throat was cut, as in Śākta buffalo sacrifices, and the upper part of the ring finger and the nose were severed.[75] S.C. Roy mentions an aniconic and androgyne guardian of Oraon villages named Mahādāniā, who is said to have been propitiated with human sacrifices in times past. The Mahādāniā cult is known to have been patronized by Hinduized Oraon landlords.[76] The Oraons of Chhota Nagpur, however, today recognize Mahādāniā as a tribal deity of their own, not a Hindu one.[77] The sacrifice of human victims to unseen powers was also believed by the Oraons to dispel contagious illness, and was performed by families inspired by *sokhas*, the tribe's head sorcerers and witch-finders, whose tutelary deity is always Mahādeo (a tribal form of Śiva).[78] The influence of Śaivism-Śāktism on the Oraon tradition of human sacrifice was, on the whole, a patent fact.

The Oraons' Munda neighbors practiced *ondoka*, a Mundari term referring to the rite and the victim, as well as to the person performing the sacrifice under the inspiration of a *deonra* (Śaivite Munda sorcerer and witch-finder). The *ondoka* rite was intended to appease an angry evil spirit causing calamities. The victim—generally a male—was brought by the sacrificer and friends at dead of night to a secluded spot, where he was decapitated and the corpse was hidden after some of its blood had been collected and a finger cut off (as in the case of the Oraon *ottanga*). The blood and finger were then buried in the sacrificer's house under the floor of the *ading* (sacred household tabernacle).[79]

Stories about persons being kidnapped in the countryside to be sacrificed to malevolent spirits (generally hill spirits called *pats* or *buru-bongas*) are recorded among the Santals of Bihar and Orissa. The kidnappers were called *ondgas* (cf. the equivalent nouns *otonga*, current among Oraons, and *ondoka*, current among Mundas). Human sacrifice was also performed at the suggestion of diviners. The selected victim was beheaded, and some of the blood was offered to the *pat* in a small earthen pot.[80]

Whether or not the Gondi-speaking tribes of Bastar ever performed the rite of human sacrifice independent of any Hindu influence is an even more complex question. The only available sources are nineteenth-century British records, which state that human victims were cyclically offered by the *rājās* of Bastar to the tutelary goddess of the kingdom, Danteśvarī.

Danteśvarī, a regional form of Durgā/Kālī, has been the family deity of the Cālukya monarchs of Bastar since their ancestors left the Warangal kingdom (Andhra Pradesh) in the fifteenth century CE to install themselves on the throne of Bastar.[81] The Cālukyas retained the local Gond cults, but superimposed the worship of Danteśvarī on them. The Gond peasants, who customarily offered a share of their agricultural produce to their traditional village mothers, began to offer the shares to Danteśvarī, instead, re-interpreting her to be one of many 'sisters'.[82] Human sacrifices were supposedly offered to Danteśvarī, since her main shrine was established at Dantawada by the *rājās* of Bastar. Human victims, called *junnas* by the Hindus, were supposedly offered for the success of the forthcoming autumnal war expeditions led by the *rājās* and Gond feudatories, betraying the Hindu character of this ritual practice.[83] This view is mainly supported by reports from the 1830s compiled by British officers on the basis of local hearsay. Yet, W.V. Grigson argues, such sacrificial rites have never been proven to have actually occurred in Bastar.[84]

A 'tribal' tradition of human sacrifice may have grown among the Gond tribes of Bastar independent of Śākta influence, however. The Muria Gonds have a legend in which one of their chief deities, Lingo Pen, asks them to offer him human sacrifice; they also have a game in which boys imitate seizing a human sacrificial victim, carrying him off, and then pretending to offer him in sacrifice in a mock decapitation.[85] Moreover, certain Maria Gond peasants of Bastar were said to practice an agricultural rite that consisted of mixing their seed with human blood before sowing to improve their crops. According to 1930s police reports, blood was procured by wounding sleeping victims at night, generally women, and then dipping the bloodstained weapon into a pot full of rice seed steeped in water. Before wounding their victim, these Gonds used to offer near the victim's cot a little rice and turmeric so as to 'ritualize' their action.[86]

The practice of human sacrifice by Gonds and other tribes was not confined to Bastar alone, extending to regions further south. This reinforces the hypothesis, advanced here, of an interaction between North Dravidian (tribal) and South Dravidian (Hindu) human sacrifice traditions. Moreover, all of the Dravidian-speaking or Dravidian-related tribes settled along or in close proximity to the Eastern Ghats may have been influenced by the *meriah* sacrifice once prevalent among the Kondhs, who inhabited the north-central tracts of that mountain range.

THE KONDH TRADITION OF HUMAN SACRIFICE TO THE EARTH GODDESS

Some of the Kondh tribes practiced human sacrifice to the earth goddess, Tari Penu, regarded as their supreme deity. Few if any peoples have sacrificed human victims in the routine fashion of the hill-Kondhs. B.M. Boal even claims the hill-Kondhs to be the likely originators of the Dravidian tribal traditions of human sacrifice in honor of the earth goddess in Middle India, who then passed it to the Gonds and the Oraons.[87] The areas peopled by the Kondhs were in a location which might suggest this. In the west, their domain overlapped that of the Bastar Gonds, and in the north, Hinduized Kondhs who presently speak Oriya, but may have been pure tribal Kondhs until a few centuries back, live in close contact with some Oraon groups.[88] Substantial evidence points to a dialectical interchange of religious doctrines and rites connected with human sacrifice in Middle India, possibly having the *meriah*-sacrificing Kondhs as one of its principal vectors.[89]

The Kondhs of southwestern Orissa comprise different tribes, speaking either Kui or Kuvi, two cognate Dravidian languages. Some Kondh clan groups, although belonging to different Kondh tribes, believed in a supreme earth goddess, paired with a creator sun god, Bura, and did not practice human sacrifice. Most Kondh tribes, however, practiced the *meriah* rite, centering on the offering of a human victim to Tari Penu, usually during the great annual festival held in January, called *tonki*.[90] The victim was also called *tonki* by the Kondhs, whereas the word *meriah*—perhaps a corrupted form of the name of the Kondh deity Mervi Penu, brother of Tari Penu—was introduced by the British.[91] The *meriah* rite seems to have been part of a wider female-oriented religious complex forming the common spiritual background for both the Kondh followers of Tari Penu and the Hindu devotees of the most bloodthirsty forms of the Mahādevī. I shall limit my discussion here to the *meriah*-practicing Kondhs and, more specifically, to their cosmogonic myths connected with human sacrifice.

The *meriah* was meant to ensure immunity from various diseases and to bring fertility, especially to the commercial crop turmeric, which the Kondhs believed could not have a deep red color without the outpouring of human blood on the fields where it was cultivated. The victim was often a child or a young boy (less frequently a girl), who had to be purchased from Hindu outcaste intermediaries named Panos, whose role was ritualized such that a human sacrifice would be rendered invalid if they were uninvolved. The Panos thus carried out trade in children, paying with grain and cattle in the lowlands, or alternatively kidnapped them from Hindu villages or sold their own children as *meriahs*. On the day preceding the appointed day for the sacrifice, the *meriah* was dressed in new clothes, taken in procession with music and dancing through village streets, and finally tied to a wooden pole (see fig. 5), often erected in a sacred grove, a remnant of the old forest kept untouched by an axe for ceremonial purposes and believed to be haunted by vegetation spirits. The victim was thereafter besmeared with oil, clarified butter, and turmeric, and offered flower garlands, and he received people's homage. People spent the whole night preceding the *meriah* sacrifice dancing, singing, and playing music with general intoxication. The sacrificial rite proper started at noon the next day. The young victim, generally intoxicated with rice beer or stupefied with opium, was killed by various methods. In all cases, all the leading men attending the rite rushed with knives to cut off pieces from the corpse. A young man visited every house in the village with the victim's head on his shoulder, and finally placed the head behind the village's *darni* or *jakari* (a cairn made of four stones, regarded as the abode of Tari Penu in each Kondh village). In some areas the priest-shaman of Tari Penu (*jani*) cut a piece of flesh from the *meriah*'s body and subsequently buried it with ceremony near the *darni*. All the heads of village clans and representatives of allied clans who were invited to the ceremony received a morsel of the *meriah*'s flesh or, alternatively, a bone. Such relics were immediately sent to several other villages to be buried in a ceremonial way under their best fields. The *meriah* victim's head and bones were cremated in a funerary ceremony associated, as is still customary in Kondh funerals, with buffalo sacrifice, and were subsequently strewn over village fields. The *meriah*'s flesh and ashes were regarded by the human-sacrificing Kondhs as powerful divine agents of fertilization. In some areas, the skull was kept in a basket in the *jani*'s house as a sort of trophy; the penis, testicles, nose, ears, lips, tongue, and liver were cooked on the sacrificial hearth (as is also common in Śākta buffalo sacrifices) and offered to Tari Penu, after which they were buried in the middle of the village.[92]

Fig. 5: A *koru munda* (buffalo post) used by the Kutia Kondhs at water buffalo sacrifices. Village Pandamasaka, Kandhamal district, Orissa, December 2001. Photograph by Francesco Brighenti.

The *meriah* sacrificial rite was believed to bring prosperity and safety not only to those making the offering, but also to all humankind. The *meriah* protected the world, because it caused the deity to lay aside, at least for some time, her inborn anger and to stop bringing calamities.[93] Such a complex of socioreligious beliefs is likely to have taken shape after tribal ancestors of the Kondhs, along with other waves of non-Aryan migrants, were pushed by Aryan colonists from the Orissan coastal plains up into the hill tracts of the Eastern Ghats. In a fragmented and inhospitable territory, the tribes needed a socioreligious mechanism to maintain their independence and unity.[94]

The theory that the Kondh *meriah* tradition is an adaptation of Śākta sacrificial rites to a tribal environment is insufficient to account for its complexity. The exclusive relationship of these Kondh clans with the lands they occupied, embodied by the earth goddess herself, was greatly stressed in the cyclical performance of the *meriah* sacrifice. The Kondhs' impulse to offer human victims to a paramount goddess appears to have risen from within their society's socioreligious exigencies, and not to have been culturally superimposed on the latter at the initiative of influential Hindu or Hinduized ruling classes, as appears to have been the case with the Oraons.

Some cultural traits common to other human sacrifice traditions of ancient India can be discerned in the *meriah* tradition. First, as with most religious rituals, its main purposes are increasing wealth—in this case wealth from the produce of Kondh hill clearings—and protection from disease and natural calamities. Yet, the inter-clan involvement to cement military alliances is similar to another trait, the interrelationship of war activities and human sacrifice to goddesses, which, if not already well-established among the Harappans, is found as a common motif in ancient Tamil epics, and thereafter becomes a distinctive element of medieval pan-Indian Śāktism. Third, the purchase of the *meriah* victim parallels the purchase of the head of a Kṣatriya or a Vaiśya by the Vedic sacrificer who intended to bury it in the foundations of the fire altar in the opening session of the *agnicayana* ritual. Fourth, the freedom enjoyed by the consecrated *meriah* for years before his/her ritual immolation parallels the roaming of the consecrated victim of both the *aśvamedha* and *puruṣamedha* for one year before being sacrificed. Alf Hiltebeitel notes that such freedom is also the prerogative of the buffalo sacrificed in Dravidian countries in honor of Hindu village goddesses.[95] Finally, in the nineteenth century, the human-sacrificing Kondhs accepted the forced substitution of a buffalo victim as commanded by British authorities, suggesting man and buffalo as interchangeable sacrificial victims. Buffalo sacrifice is still performed by some Kondh tribes on the occasion of certain religious festivals.[96]

An eastern Kondh myth recorded in the nineteenth century by S.C. Macpherson and subsequently, with few variants in characters and setting, by Edgar Thurston, unites the themes of divine self-immolation and fertility. In the first version, Amali-Baeli is a disguised form of the earth goddess who reveals to the Kondhs the secret of human sacrifice. The action takes place in a mythic age during which the earth was one immense morass. One day, when her man was out, this mythic woman cut one of her fingers while peeling vegetables. When some of her blood dripped onto the ground, the mud solidified and became fertile; later on, animals were born. Amali-Baeli then proposed to the Kondhs that they cut her body into pieces to complete the process of creation, but they refused, thinking that she was one of them, and resolved to start sacrificing other human victims instead.[97] The other version describes a primordial mother named Karaboodi (the word *būḍhi* means 'old woman' in Oriya). She has in this case no man, and is said to have come from the earth itself. Karaboodi, too, accidentally cut her little finger, and the blood made the ground become dry and hard. The next day the woman told her son that he should sacrifice her by cutting her flesh away and then burying it. On his doing so, all kinds of plants and animals sprang up. Later she appeared in a dream to her son and told him that if he offered another human victim, lands would be very fertile and cattle would flourish. This request ultimately gave rise to the *meriah* tradition.[98] Karaboodi, like Amali-Baeli of the other myth, likely represents a mythic projection of the earth goddess, the creatrix, great ancestress, and mythical founder of the tradition of human sacrifice.

The specifically female self-immolating primordial being of Kondh mythology contrasts with the male sacrificial being of Puruṣa in the Veda. Verrier Elwin has argued that the tribal mythologies of India record the same archaic myth of self-immolation in two principal forms: 'In one the body of a person (who may be taken to represent the Mahāpuruṣa) is turned into the world; in the other the world is established, or made firm, by the blood of a human sacrifice.'[99] The mythology of Tari Penu, a female self-immolating demiurgic divinity, seems to reflect a different religious tradition, better represented by an Indonesian tribal cult of a self-immolating rice/corn mother than by the male-oriented Puruṣa ideology of the Vedic Aryans.[100]

We may further add that even the Brāhmaṇical theology of the Śākta *pīṭhas* appears indebted to a shamanistic mythic archetype of this sort: the myth of the dismemberment of the goddess Satī, which forms the nucleus of the medieval *pīṭha* ideology, also incorporates the element of the goddess's self-immolation, thus, presenting two essential features—dismemberment and self-sacrifice—which are also noticed in the shamanistic and agrarian mythologies of Southeast Asia concerning the figure of a rice/corn mother.[101] One might even argue, in this respect, that the mythic fall of the pieces of Satī's body is believed by the Śāktas to have made the soil of India sacred, just as drops of the earth goddess's blood are believed by her Kondh votaries to have made their own hill clearings firm and fertile. In both cases, the power of the goddess, be it sanctifying or fertilizing, is still today believed to decrease if there is a lack of blood sacrifices.

THE HEAD-HUNTING COMPLEX OF THE NAGA TRIBES

The Indian hill tribes settled south of the Brahmaputra River (the Tibeto-Burman Nagas, Garos and Kukis and, possibly, also the Austro-Asiatic Khasis; see map 1) used to practice a form of ritual head-hunting that involved exposing the trophies on posts, trees, heaps of stones, or house porches (see fig. 6). After a ritual to augment its magical power, the head was believed to promote and enhance the fertility of villagers, their cattle, and their crops, especially when the head was that of a woman with long hair.[102] Naga tribes procured heads in war,[103] by ambushing individuals walking alone along the road, or by purchase. A Naga might sacrifice a victim by various methods: (a) decapitation during the well-known Feasts of Merit (at which prominent Naga tribesmen normally used to sacrifice the *mithun,* or *Bos frontalis*, a big, barely domesticated bovine traditionally serving as the chief work animal of this people); (b) live burial under the foundations of a new wooden edifice in the belief that doing so would magically make the foundations firmer and more solid; and (c) tethering the victim

Fig. 6: Konyak Naga head-hunting trophies made with human skulls and water buffalo horns. From Aglaja Stirn and Peter Van Ham, *The Seven Sisters of India: Tribal Worlds Between Tibet and Burma* (New York: Prestel, 2000), p. 143. Photograph by H. Sanghvi.

to a post in the middle of a newly cleared field and burning him or her alive along with the surrounding dry felled jungle, in the conviction that this would increase the fertility of the forthcoming crops. Like the Kondhs, the Nagas used to make their victims drunk before sacrificing them.[104]

Similar head-hunting practices are known to have characterized past religions of some Tibeto-Burman and Austro-Asiatic tribes settled in Burma, and they were once widespread all over the Indian Archipelago, the Philippines, Taiwan, and the whole of Oceania.[105] Anthropologist R. Heine-Geldern believed that the head-hunting complex could be ascribed with certainty to prehistoric Austronesian cultures (the Indonesian, Micronesian, Melanesian, and Polynesian),[106] whose socioreligious customs might have influenced the ancient tribes of Burma and Assam via Indo-China. As Bhattacharyya notes, head-hunting rituals as practiced by some of the tribal peoples of Assam might, in turn, have influenced the development of the Śākta tradition of human sacrifice in north-eastern India.[107]

The Naga head-hunting complex may seem to have little in common with other human sacrifice traditions in India mentioned here, but a striking parallel can be drawn with a typically Śākta sacrificial theme. In both, the buffalo/human victim of the sacrifice is opposed to the deified tiger, which has long been connected with the Great Goddess in the Śākta view. The following two elements can be taken in support of this hypothesis: (a) Naga warriors often stuck a pair of *mithun* horns on the skull of their slain enemy to create a more imposing head-hunting trophy, and the two classes of victim were considered interchangeable on the occasion of their Feasts of Merit.[108] Most Naga tribes, before their Christianization, thought man to be endowed with three souls, one of which was that of a *mithun*;[109] (b) among certain Naga tribes (e.g., the Sema, the Konyak, and the Ao), a class of seers or warriors is believed to have the faculty to change into were-tigers or were-leopards. Their souls temporarily leave their sleeping bodies, fall into a cataleptic state at night, and then enter feline bodies, each becoming a sacred alter ego in the form of a freely roaming tiger or leopard.[110] Those Sema and Konyak Naga chieftains and warriors to whom these abilities were attributed were dreaded for their dangerous magical powers.[111]

CONCLUSION

The social prerequisite for the rise and development of traditions of human sacrifice in the Indian subcontinent appears to have been the ascent of a community whose economic maintenance mainly depended on violent activities such as war-making, cattle seizing, crop pillaging, and inter-village raiding. This fact is evident in the studied cases of the ancient South Indian communities of warriors and cattle raiders practicing self-immolation in honor of their tutelary goddesses, of the wild Śavara tribes and, more recently, of the *meriah*-sacrificing Kondhs and the head-hunting Assamese tribes, as well as in some Gond legends and in eighteenth-century British descriptions of their customs. In the case of the nomadic *vrātya* warriors and cattle seizers of the Vedic period, we can only hypothesize the occurrence of human sacrifices in connection with their cyclical aggressive raids and chivalrous inter-clan competitions. As regards the celebration of human sacrifices in connection with war activity proper, we have suggested the continuation of rituals of this kind, performed on the initiative or for the benefit of kings or military leaders, from the Indus civilization to medieval Śāktism, passing through the ancient South Dravidian practices of self-immolation meant to honor deities or to celebrate success in battle. We may furthermore stress the fact that the *puruṣamedha/aśvamedha* sacrificial complex of the Vedic period also had a link with the expansion of the power of the royal sacrificer through military conquest. Even when there is no association with war or raiding, as in the case of the human sacrifices that some scholars infer once took place among the Oraon, Munda, and Santal, the victim was violently ambushed or kidnapped.

A second principal aim of human sacrifice is the stimulation of the fertility of the earth through the outpouring of human blood on it, or the burial of human flesh in it. This practice appears to be structurally and organically related to the first aim I just noted—

that is, the request for divine blessing of war and raiding. Such divine blessing serves as a magical means to increase the general prosperity of a tribe, caste, nation, or royal lineage and to enhance its prestige by the accumulation of wealth. In some Indian sacrificial complexes such as the Kondh (tribal) and the Śākta (Hindu), the earth is fully identified with a goddess, to whom human victims are offered to satisfy her inexhaustible hunger. In this particular outlook, the goddess embodies the world as a living organism that must be cyclically and incessantly fed with blood and flesh to regenerate and perpetuate her life-giving potentialities.

Third, I conclude that humans and bovines (buffaloes, *mithuns*) were ritually interchangeable. The recipient of the sacrifice, or in certain cases, the sacrificer himself, might be a feline, the strongest and most ferocious predator of both humans and bovines in Indian jungles. This opposition is found in some very archaic sacrificial complexes, such as the Kondh and Naga. These, however, cannot be assumed to have evolved out of the Śākta tradition, where the opposition in question is between the human/buffalo victim and the Great Goddess associated with a lion or tiger as her celestial mount, or *vāhana*, to whom the sacrifice is offered. Hiltebeitel's theory about the religious meaning of the scene depicted on the so-called 'proto-Śiva' seal from Mohenjo-daro traces a Harappan matrix to this sacrificial opposition, or at least shows that the latter has been present in Indian religious thinking from Harappan times.[112] The fact that the Vedic king sits on a tiger or lion skin after the ritual slaughter of the horse carried out during the *aśvamedha* is also suggestive.[113] The bovine-feline juxtaposition, which is found in both tribal and Śākta contexts, points to a ritual identification of the sacrificer with the formidable spirit of the feline.

Our materials present us with a fourth inference. Decapitation was the probable method of human sacrifice among the Harappans. This mode of sacrifice was continued by all other human-sacrificing groups about which we have evidence, the non-Aryan tribes as well as the Śāktas of all epochs (starting with the self-immolating ancient Tamils). This is in distinct contrast to the prescriptions recorded in the *puruṣamedha*/*aśvamedha* rituals of the Veda, where suffocation is the typical means of killing. We can conclude that this bifurcation signaled an innovation on the part of the Vedic Aryans, who deviated away from bloodshed.

Finally, this study has demonstrated an age-old, continuous, and multilinear interplay of religious customs, doctrines, beliefs, and practices concerning animal and human sacrifice among both tribal peoples and Hindu adepts of the Śākta religion. One of the great methodological challenges facing the study of Śāktism today is defining, explaining, and interpreting the various stages in this process of tribal-Śākta interaction, which may necessitate moving beyond the ancient limits of Vedic India, as shown by the work of Narendra Nath Bhattacharyya and others.

NOTES

1. Mircea Eliade, *Patterns in Comparative Religion,* trans. Rosemary Sheed (New York: New American Library, 1974), 345–57.
2. According to Ananda K. Coomaraswamy, 'Angel and Titan: An Essay in Vedic Ontology,' *Journal of the American Oriental Society* 55, no. 4 (December 1935): 394, the fullest and perhaps most interesting account of the Indra-Vṛtra myth occurs in *Ṛg Veda* 1.32.
3. Heinrich Zimmer, *Myths and Symbols in Indian Art and Civilization*, ed. Joseph Campbell (1946; rpt., New York: Harper & Brothers, 1962), 189-90, and Ananda K. Coomaraswamy, *Hinduism and Buddhism,* ed. Keshavaram N. Iengar and Rama P. Coomaraswamy, 2nd rev. edn. (New Delhi: Indira Gandhi National Centre for the Arts, 1999), 11.
4. Zimmer, *Myths and Symbols in Indian Art and Civilization*, 189.
5. *Rāmāyaṇa* 7.75ff., quoted in Jan Gonda, *Le religioni dell'India. Veda e antico Induismo* (Milan: Jaca Book, 1981), 302; *Mahābhārata* 12.272.28–31, trans. in Wendy Doniger O'Flaherty, *Hindu Myths: A Sourcebook Translated from the Sanskrit* (New York: Penguin Books, 1975), 86–90.
6. Coomaraswamy, 'Angel and Titan,' 400.
7. Gonda, *Religioni dell'India*, 251ff.
8. Ibid., 97.
9. A. Daniélou, *Hindu Polytheism* (New York: Bollingen Foundation, 1964), 71.
10. Gonda, *Religioni dell'India*, 233.
11. *Śatapatha Brāhmaṇa* 13.6.1.3 and 11, in *The Śatapatha Brāhmaṇa: According to the Text of the Mādhyandina School*, trans. Julius Eggeling, reprint of The *Sacred Books of the East* (Delhi: Motilal Banarsidass, 1963–78), 5: 404, 406.
12. Ibid., 417–21.

13. Ibid., xxxiii, n1, and, for the translation of the list of human victims in the *Vājasaneyi Saṃhitā*, 413–17; *The Veda of the Black Yajus School, Entitled Taittirīya Saṃhitā*, trans. Arthur Barriedale Keith (Cambridge, Mass.: Harvard University Press, 1914), 1: cxxxvii–cxxxviii.
14. *Śatapatha Brāhmaṇa,* trans. Eggeling, 5: 403–13.
15. Gonda, *Religioni dell'India*, 233.
16. *Śatapatha Brāhmaṇa,* trans. Eggeling, 5: xli–xlv; *Veda of the Black Yajus School,* 1: cxxxviii. See also Frits Staal et al., *Agni: The Vedic Ritual of the Fire Altar* (Berkeley, Calif.: Asian Humanities Press, 1983), 2: 118.
17. See, e.g., *Atharvaveda* 11.2.9 quoted in Doris Srinivasan, 'The So-Called Proto-Śiva Seal from Mohenjo Daro: An Iconological Assessment,' *Archives of Asian Art* 29 (1975–76): 56, and *Śatapatha Brāhmaṇa,* trans. Eggeling, 1.2.3.6 (vol. 1, p. 50). *Śatapatha Brāhmaṇa* 6.2.1.2–20 and 37–39 state that the five sacrificial victims were slaughtered for the first time (through decapitation) by Prajāpati himself, who put their heads on his own body (the transcendental nucleus of the fire-altar) and made the bricks to build the fire-altar with their trunks. When the sacrificer buries the heads of the five sacrificial animals in the bottom layer of the *uttaravedi*, and then builds the fire-altar with the bricks consecrated through the immolation of such animals, he is thought to restore the unity of the bodies of the slain victims. *Śatapatha Brāhmaṇa* 3, trans. Eggeling, 162–71.
18. *Aitareya Brāhmaṇa* 2.8 quoted in Gonda, *Religioni dell'India*, 202–3.
19. J.C. Heesterman, *The Ancient Indian Royal Consecration: The Rājasūya Described According to the Yajus Texts and Annoted* (The Hague: Mouton, 1957), 138–39n71.
20. Brian K. Smith, *Reflections on Resemblance, Ritual, and Religion* (Delhi: Motilal Banarsidass, 1988), 177–80.
21. *Śatapatha Brāhmaṇa* 7.5.2.1ff., quoted in *Veda of the Black Yajus School,* 1: cxxxviii, states that for a successful *agnicayana,* the sacred fire should be carried for one year in a pot (*ukhā*), into which the heads of a man, horse, bull, he-goat and ram should then be placed, and the pot ritually buried in the bottom layer of the stratified *agniciti* to impart stability to its foundations.
22. *Taittirīya Saṃhitā* 5.1.8.1 quoted in *Veda of the Black Yajus School,* 1: cxxxix. J.C. Heesterman, 'The Case of the Severed Head,' *Wiener Zeitschrift für die Kunde Süd- und Ostasiens* 11 (1967): 40, hypothesizes that the head of the Vaiśya was customarily obtained in battle by bands of Aryan cattle raiders, Vaiśyas consisting in ancient Vedic times mainly of agriculturists or cattle-breeders, who were often attacked by bands of Vedic nomads. This is also supported by the *Āpastambīya Śrauta Sūtra* (16.6.2), quoted in Gonda, *Religioni dell'India*, 256.
23. *Veda of the Black Yajus School,* 1: cxxxix.
24. Asko Parpola, 'The Pre-Vedic Indian Background of the Śrauta Rituals,' in Staal et al., *Agni,* 2: 44–46; and id., *Deciphering the Indus Script* (Cambridge: Cambridge University Press, 1994), 148–55.

25. Parpola, 'Pre-Vedic Indian Background of the Śrauta Rituals,' 46–48.
26. Mircea Eliade, *Yoga: Immortality and Freedom*, trans. Willard R. Trask (1958; 2nd edn., London: Routledge & Kegan Paul, 1969), 101–5.
27. J.C. Heesterman, 'Vrātya and Sacrifice,' *Indo-Iranian Journal* 6 (1962): 7; and id., 'Self-Sacrifice in Vedic Ritual,' in S. Shaked, D. Shulman and G.G. Stroumsa, eds., *Gilgul: Essays on Transformation, Revolution and Permanence in the History of Religions* (Leiden: E.J. Brill, 1987), 97–100.
28. Parpola, 'Pre-Vedic Indian Background of the Śrauta Rituals,' 51–53. The analogy between the obscene verses being recited during the performance of the *Mahāvrāta* and those being recited during the performance of the *aśvamedha* was already noticed by A. Hillebrandt, *Vedic Mythology* (1927–29; 2nd rev. edn., Delhi: Motilal Banarsidass, 1980), 2: 365n399.
29. See O'Flaherty, *Hindu Myths*, 28–31, and Stella Kramrisch, *The Presence of Śiva* (Princeton: Princeton University Press, 1981), 22–26. In the two *Ṛg Vedic* hymns the two protagonists of the primordial incest are simply mentioned as the (Sky) Father and the (Virgin) Daughter.
30. Coomaraswamy, 'Angel and Titan,' 391n24; Mircea Eliade, *A History of Religious Ideas,* vol. 1: *From the Stone Age to the Eleusinian Mysteries,* trans. Willard R. Trask (Chicago: University of Chicago Press, 1978), 202–3; and id., *Patterns in Comparative Religion,* 428–29.
31. Ananda K. Coomaraswamy, *Yakṣas: Essays in Water Cosmology*, ed. Paul Schoeder (1928–31; new rev. edn., New Delhi: Indira Gandhi National Centre for the Arts, 1993), 122.
32. On this point see also K.F. Johannsen quoted in Coomaraswamy, *Yakṣas*, 114–15, and Heesterman, *Ancient Indian Royal Consecration*, 138n71.
33. E.A. Gait, 'Human Sacrifice (Indian),' in James Hastings, ed., *Encyclopaedia of Religion and Ethics* (New York: Scribner, 1913), 6: 853.
34. Here Parpola follows the argument in Alf Hiltebeitel, 'The Indus Valley 'Proto-Śiva' Reexamined Through Reflections on the Goddess, the Buffalo, and the Symbolism of Vāhanas,' *Anthropos* 73 (1978): 789.
35. Asko Parpola, 'The Harappan 'Priest King's' Robe and the Vedic Tārpya Garment: Their Interrelation and Symbolism (Astral and Procreative),' in Janine Schotsmans and Maurizio Taddei, eds., *South Asian Archaeology 1983* (Naples: Istituto universitario orientale, Dipartimento di studi asiatici), 1: 385–403, esp. 396, 400; and Parpola, *Deciphering the Indus Script*, 188, 219–20.
36. See also Coomaraswamy, *Yakṣas*, 117 and 121.
37. David Shulman, 'The Murderous Bride: Tamil Versions of the Myth of the Devī and the Buffalo-Demon,' *History of Religions* 16 (1976): 120–46.
38. David Kinsley, *Hindu Goddesses: Visions of the Divine Feminine in the Hindu Religious Tradition* (Berkeley: University of California Press, 1986), 146.
39. John H. Marshall, ed., *Mohenjo-Daro and the Indus Civilization* (London: Arthur Probshtan, 1931), 1: 52 (the seal in question is reproduced in ibid.,

pl. 12, fig. 12); and Pupul Jayakar, *The Earthen Drum* (New Delhi: National Museum, 1980), published in a revised edition as *The Earth Mother* (New Delhi: Penguin Books [India], 1989), 67.

40. Reproduced in Marshall, *Mohenjo-Daro and the Indus Civilization*, 1: pl. 12, fig. 18.
41. Marshall, *Mohenjo-Daro and the Indus Civilization*, 1: 63–65; E.J.H. Mackay, *Further Excavations at Mohenjo-daro* (Delhi: Government of India Press, 1938), 1: 337–38; J.N. Banerjea, *The Development of Hindu Iconography*, 2nd edn. (Calcutta, University of Calcutta, 1956), 168.
42. The *pravargya* is the introductory ceremony of the *soma* sacrifice (*agnicayana*), at which fresh milk is poured into a red-hot pot.
43. Parpola, 'The Harappan "Priest King's" Robe,' 400; Parpola, *Deciphering the Indus Script*, 260–61, 270–72. On the other hand, K. Rönnow, quoted in Staal et al., *Agni,* 1: 119, has tried to show that human sacrifices were offered at both the *pravargya* and the *agnicayana*, regarded as relics of a pre-Vedic '*asuric*' religion characterized by human sacrifice.
44. H. Mode, *Das frühe Indien* (Stuttgart: Gustav Kilpper, 1959), 69.
45. R. Nagaswami, *Tantric Cult of South India* (Delhi: Agamkala Prakashan, 1982), 3.
46. Ibid., 6. The *Tolkāppiyam* refers here to some particular ancient Tamil poetic compositions, called *Koṟṟavai milai*, which describe the sacrifices to Koṟṟavai as performed by soldiers.
47. Cāttaṉār, *Manimekhalai (The Dancer with the Magic Bowl) by Merchant-Prince Shattan*, trans. Alain Daniélou with the help of T.V. Gopala Iyer (New York: New Directions Books, 1989), xvi.
48. Cāttaṉār, *Manimekhalai*, canto 6 (pp. 23–26); Nagaswami, *Tantric Cult of South India*, 16–17.
49. Prince Ilangô Adigal, *Shilappadikaram*, trans. Alain Daniélou (New York: New Directions, 1965), ix.
50. Ibid., canto 12 (pp. 76–85); Nagaswami, *Tantric Cult of South India*, 9–11.
51. T.V. Mahalingam, 'The Cult of Śakti in Tamilnad,' in D.C. Sircar, ed., *The Śakti Cult and Tārā* (Calcutta: University of Calcutta, 1967), 27.
52. Heesterman, 'Self-Sacrifice in Vedic Ritual,' 93–95.
53. Gonda, *Religioni dell'India*, 218–21.
54. J.C. Heesterman quoted in Parpola, 'Pre-Vedic Indian Background of the Śrauta Rituals,' 47.
55. Heesterman, 'Self-Sacrifice in Vedic Ritual,' 97–100.
56. Mahalingam, 'Cult of Śakti in Tamilnad', 27.
57. *Taittirīya Saṃhitā* 7.4.9 quoted in Heesterman, 'Self-Sacrifice in Vedic Ritual,' 94n14.
58. *Devī Māhātmya* 13.9, quoted from the translation by Thomas B. Coburn, *Encountering the Goddess: A Translation of the Devī-Māhātmya and a Study of Its Interpretation* (Albany: State University of New York Press, 1991), 83.

59. See, e.g., David N. Lorenzen, *The Kāpālikas and Kālamukhas: Two Lost Śaivite Sects* (Berkeley: University of California Press, 1972), 16–17.
60. R. Rahmann, 'Shamanistic and Related Phenomena in Northern and Middle India,' *Anthropos* 54 (1959): 684–85, 688–89, 753–54.
61. J. Troisi, *Tribal Religion: Religious Beliefs and Practices among the Santals* (New Delhi: Manohar, 1978), 98–99, 102, 210.
62. C. Mukherjea, *The Santals*, 2nd rev. edn. (Calcutta: A. Mukherjee, 1962), 153, 277–80.
63. Narendra Nath Bhattacharyya, *History of the Śākta Religion* (1974; 2nd rev. edn., New Delhi: Munshiram Manoharlal, 1996), 80–81.
64. *Aitareya Brāhmaṇa* 7.13–18. See *Śatapatha Brāhmaṇa,* trans. Eggeling, 5: xxxiv–xxxvii; A.A. Macdonnell and A.B. Keith, *Vedic Index of Names and Subjects* (Varanasi: Motilal Banarsidass, 1958), 1: 8, 23–24, 349, 536; *Veda of the Black Yajus School,* 1: cxl; J. Dowson, *A Classical Dictionary of Hindu Mythology and Religion, Geography, History, and Literature* (1891; reprint, New Delhi: Oriental Books, 1973), 308, 365–66. The early Vedic archetype of this legend is constituted by the three hymns of the *Ṛg Veda* (1.24/25/28) mentioning the figure of a *ṛṣi* named Śunaḥśepa, who is said in *Ṛg Veda* 1.24.12ff. to be imploring Varuṇa to release him from the chains that bound him to three pillars, with this possibly representing a *Ṛg Vedic* allusion to the rite of human sacrifice. See Pio Filippani-Ronconi, *Miti e religioni dell'India*, 2nd edn. (Rome: Newton Compton, 1992), 61; Margaret Stutley and James Stutley, *A Dictionary of Hinduism: Its Mythology, Folklore and Development 1500 B.C.– A.D. 1500* (London: Routledge & Kegan Paul, 1977), 289.
65. G.S. Ghurye, *The Scheduled Tribes* (1943; 3rd edn., Bombay: Popular Prakashan, 1963), 221–22.
66. J.H. Hutton, *Census of India 1931* (Delhi: Government of India Press, 1933), 1: 358; Charles von Fürer-Haimendorf, *The Raj Gonds of Adilabad: A Peasant Culture of the Deccan, Book I: Myth and Ritual* (London: Macmillan, 1948), 2–3; and B.M. Boal, *The Konds: Human Sacrifice and Religious Change* (Warminster, U.K.: Aris & Phillips, 1983), 212.
67. Verrier Elwin, *The Religion of an Indian Tribe* (Bombay: Oxford University Press, 1955), 16-18; A.K. Bhattacharya, 'A Nonaryan Aspect of the Devī,' in Sircar, *Śakti Cult and Tārā*, 58–59; Bhattacharyya, *History of the Śākta Religion*, 99; Alf Hiltebeitel, 'Rāma and Gilgamesh: The Sacrifices of the Water Buffalo and the Bull of Heaven,' *History of Religions* 19 (1980): 205.
68. Elwin, *Religion of an Indian Tribe*, 19, 496–97.
69. Ibid., 19–20.
70. A.L. Basham, *The Wonder That Was India*, 2nd edn. (Calcutta: Rupa, 1981), 200.
71. Rahmann, 'Shamanistic and Related Phenomena in Northern and Middle India,' 720–21, 728–29, 736, 746, 745–47.

72. P. Dehon, 'Religion and Customs of the Uraons,' *Memoirs of the Asiatic Society of Bengal* 1 (1905–7): 141; and K.N. Sahay, 'Oraon,' in Sachchidananda and R.R. Prasad, eds., *Encyclopaedic Profile of Indian Tribes* (New Delhi: Discovery, 1996), 3: 773.
73. S.C. Roy, *The Orāons of Chotā Nāgpur: Their History, Economic Life, and Social Organization* (1915; reprint, Ranchi: Man in India Office, 1984), 91.
74. Oral communication from K. Oraon, Ranchi University, January 2001.
75. Dehon, 'Religion and Customs of the Uraons,' 141–42.
76. S.C. Roy, *Orāon Religion and Customs* (Ranchi: Man in India Office, 1928), 36–38.
77. Oral communication from K. Oraon, Ranchi University, January 2001.
78. Rahmann, 'Shamanistic and Related Phenomena in Northern and Middle India,' 706, 745–46.
79. S.C. Roy, *The Mundas and Their Country* (1912; rpt., Bombay: Asia Publishing House, 1970), 279–80.
80. Mukherjea, *The Santals*, 277–80.
81. G. Busquet and C. Delacampagne, *Les Aborigènes de l'Inde* (Paris: Arthaud, 1981), 116–17; and H.L. Shukla, *History of the People of Bastar* (Delhi: Sharada, 1992, 132–33.
82. H.L. Shukla, *Tribal History: A New Interpretation* (Delhi: B.R., 1988), 96.
83. P. Mukherjee, 'Human Sacrifices Among the Khonds of Orissa—A Note,' *Orissa Historical Research Journal* 8 (1959–60): 166–67; and Shukla, *Tribal History*, 79.
84. W.V. Grigson, *The Maria Gonds of Bastar* (1938; 2nd rev. edn., London: Oxford University Press, 1949), 8, 7–9n1.
85. Verrier Elwin, *The Muria and Their Ghotul* (Bombay: Oxford University Press, 1947), 226, 563.
86. Grigson, *Maria Gonds of Bastar*, 221.
87. Boal, *Konds*, 209–18.
88. B.C. Mazumdar, 'The Kui or Kondh People,' *Man in India* 12 (1932): 246.
89. For a more complete treatment of this subject, see Francesco Brighenti, *Śakti Cult in Orissa* (New Delhi: D.K. Printworld, 2001), chap. 5.4.
90. Samuel Charters Macpherson, 'An Account of the Religion of the Khonds of Orissa,' *Journal of the Royal Asiatic Society of Great Britain* 13 (1852): 216; and Boal, *Konds*, 50–53, 284.
91. D.P. Behera, 'Eradication of Meriah or Human Sacrifice from the Social Life of the Kondhs of Orissa in the Nineteenth Century,' in B.C. Ray, ed., *Tribals of Orissa: The Changing Socio-Economic Profile* (New Delhi: Gian, 1989), 69.
92. This narrative is based upon the accounts of the *meriah* rite given by E.T. Dalton, *Descriptive Ethnology of Bengal* (1872; reprint, Calcutta: Firma K.L. Mukhopadhyaya, 1960), 276ff.; Edgar Thurston, *Castes and Tribes of Southern India* (Madras: Government Press, 1909), 3: 373ff.; Eliade, *Patterns in Comparative Religion,* 344–45; Verrier Elwin, 'Notes on a Kondh Tour,'

Man in India 24 (1944): 54; M.N. Das, 'Suppression of Human Sacrifice Among the Hill Tribes of Orissa,' *Man in India* 36 (1956): 21–48; N.R. Hota, 'Human Sacrifice Among the Khonds of Orissa,' *Orissa Historical Research Journal* 8 (1959–60): 158–63; and Boal, *Konds*, 151.

93. See also Eliade, *Patterns in Comparative Religion*..
94. Boal, *Konds*, 155, 211–12, 217–19.
95. Hiltebeitel, 'Rāma and Gilgamesh,' 189.
96. On Kondh festivals centering on buffalo-sacrifice, see N.A. Watts, *The Half-Clad Tribals of Eastern India* (Bombay: Orient Longmans, 1970), 42, 51.
97. Samuel Charters Macpherson, *Memorials of Service in India: From the correspondence of the late Major Samuel Charters Macpherson, C.B. Political Agent at Gwalior during the mutiny and formerly employed in the Suppression of Human Sacrifice in Orissa,* ed. William Macpherson (London: John Murray, 1865), 96, 121.
98. Thurston, *Castes and Tribes of Southern India* 3: 368–71.
99. Verrier Elwin, *Myths of Middle India* (Madras: Oxford University Press, 1949), 10.
100. G. Hatt, 'The Corn Mother in America and in Indonesia,' *Anthropos* 46 (1951): 882–89.
101. Eliade, *Yoga: Immortality and Freedom,* 346–48.
102. W.C. Smith, *The Ao Naga Tribe of Assam: A Study in Ethnology and Sociology* (London: Macmillan, 1925), 121–24; J.H. Hutton, 'Head Hunting,' *Man in India* 10 (1930): 207–12; and Verrier Elwin, *Nagaland* (Shillong: Research Department, Adviser's Secretariat, 1961), 11.
103. J.H. Hutton, *The Sema Nagas*, 2nd edn. (London, Oxford University Press, 1968), 167ff.
104. Christoph von Fürer-Haimendorf, *The Naked Nagas* (Calcutta, Thacker, Spink, 1933), 128; id., *The Konyak Nagas: An Indian Frontier Tribe* (New York: Holt, Rinehart & Winston, 1969), 95ff.
105. Hutton, 'Head Hunting,' 212–14; Renato Biasutti, et al., *Le razze e i popoli della terra* (1941; 4th rev. edn., Turin: Unione tipografico / Editrice torinese, 1967), 2: 757, 774, and 778–79.
106. R. Heine-Geldern quoted in R. Rahmann, 'The Ritual Spring Hunt of Northeastern and Middle India,' *Anthropos* 47 (1952): 884–85, 888–89.
107. Narendra Nath Bhattacharyya, *The Indian Mother Goddess* (1970; 3rd rev. edn., New Delhi: Manohar, 1999), 67–76.
108. Hutton, *Sema Nagas*, 174, 176, 246; and Smith, *Ao Naga Tribe*, 104–5.
109. J.Jacobs, *Les Nagas* (Geneva: Oligane, 1991), 86.
110. Smith, *Ao Naga Tribe*, 94; J.H. Hutton, 'Lycanthropy,' *Man in India* 11 (1931): 213–14; Fürer-Haimendorf, *Naked Nagas*, 209.
111. Hutton, *Sema Nagas*, 200ff.; Fürer-Haimendorf, *Konyak Nagas*, 56–57.
112. Hiltebeitel, 'Indus Valley "Proto-Śiva . . .",' 776–79, 783–89.
113. Gonda, *Religioni dell'India*, 231.

5

Sitting on the Corpse's Chest

The Tantric Ritual of *Śava sādhana* and its Variations in Modern Bengal

JUNE McDANIEL

Tantra has often been understood as a set of strange and frightening rituals, a corruption of religion. Narendra Nath Bhattacharyya did much to change this approach; his books *History of the Tantric Religion* and *History of the Śākta Religion* contextualized Tantric practices, making a significant contribution. Without such detailed histories, Tantric practices could easily be dismissed as unimportant, incoherent acts, based on magic and superstition, which have appeared periodically throughout Indian history. Bhattacharyya's observation that Tantra is fundamentally anti-caste, popular, regional, and heterodox has now been widely accepted; so, too, his thesis that Tāntrikas reject many external religious formalities and orthodox perspectives, holding to the 'deliberate theoretical orientation that the structures of the microcosm and the macrocosm are identical and that the key to the knowledge of nature is to be found in the body'.[1] That this approach disturbs the Brāhmaṇical elites can be observed even today among those opposed to Tantric practices and Tantric philosophy. When put into historical and ritual contexts, we are able to understand the growth, permutations, and overlapping of meanings in Tantric ritual and interpretation, as well as offer meaningful observations of patterns in its historical development. Analytic approaches are dependent on descriptive surveys, and Narendra Nath Bhattacharyya has laid a solid foundation for future studies of Tantra as a religious issue.

This essay primarily explores the branch of Tantra that privileges the Goddess as supreme, namely, Śākta Tantra. In Śākta Tantra, Śakti, or Power, the Goddess, is inherent in Śiva, as the power of burning is in fire.[2] The adherent may invoke or become the deity through processes of identifying his or her body, the microcosm, with the macrocosm, the universe. The field of Śākta Tantra has burgeoned in recent years, as texts have been edited, translated, and made available in accessible publications. Future directions for such study will require both continued literary translation and analysis, as well as fieldwork among current practitioners. Literary study is in some ways far easier; once acquired, the text is an 'open book,' even if composed in obscure language. On the other hand, Tantric practitioners often prefer to remain underground and are hesitant to speak with outsiders. Yet to understand Tantra as a living religion, we need to hear the voices of its practitioners.

Among the most controversial of Tantric practices, and therefore one of the most difficult topics to gather ethnographic details about, is *śava sādhana*, the ritual practice of sitting on a corpse. The corpse ritual has been incorporated into the Tantric path known as *vāmācāra* (the way of the left or reverse practice) or *kulācāra* (the way of the *kula*, family group or secret religious lineage; thus, esoteric practice). Its opposite, *dakṣiṇācāra*, is the orthodox application of Tantra devoid of the impure and less socially acceptable aspects common in *vāmācāra*. In the Śākta Tantras, it is the *vāmācāra* rites that predominate.[3] The *vāmācāra* goal is to loosen the person from the bonds of *saṃsāra* through a radical breaking of attachment; he or she is no longer emotionally attached, neither hates nor fears, is ashamed of nothing, and has transcended all traditional notions of good and evil, purity and impurity. This destruction of attachment is echoed in the conception of the corpse as the destruction of life. Moreover, the philosophical view of *śava sādhana* meshes well with the yogic/Tantric approach, in which the practitioner is exhorted to identify himself with the corpse (*śava*)—often understood as Śiva himself. Once such an equation is realized, destroying all individual passions in the process, the *avadhūta*, or perfected one, attains immortality.

Śava sādhana boasts multiple interpretations and goals, reflecting the long and varied history of Tantra. From a folk or magical perspective, *śava sādhana* might wield power over death, bringing supernatural power over life. From a yogic perspective, burning ground rituals can help lead to detachment from the physical world and union with a transcendent ground, understood to be either the god Śiva or Brahman. From a devotional perspective, the corpse may be a vessel or icon, into which the Goddess descends for a temporary dwelling. Alternatively, the corpse may be one of her favorite objects, and so attract her interest and favor. Thus, devotionally, *śava sādhana* contributes to the development of a loving relationship with a deity who has a form and personality (*saguṇa*), and who can grant salvation by grace. All of these possible perspectives are present in the ritual and literature of the *śava sādhana* rite today as it has developed over time through the weaving together of so many varied sources. I found these overlapping perspectives among my Bengali informants as well.[4]

The continued prominence of the *śava sādhana* rite is underscored by the fact that descriptions of it can be found throughout contemporary popular Bengali literature. Most of the common elements can be summarized in the following way:

> On either a new moon night, or the eighth or fourteenth day of the moon, the practitioner should bring a corpse to a burning ground or some other lonely spot, such as a deserted house, a riverside, under a *bilva* tree, or atop a hill. The corpse should be of a young and attractive person who died by violence, drowning, or snakebite, usually low-caste. The practitioner should wash the body and place it on a blanket or deer or tiger skin. After worshipping it, the practitioner should then sit on the corpse and contemplate the god or goddess. He or she will experience fearful images and sounds, as well as temptations, but the practitioner must remain emotionally detached—or else he or she may go insane. If the practitioner is successful, he may gain the power to use a mantra (*mantrasiddhi*), or become one with Śiva through the mediation of the corpse, or have a vision of the Goddess. If the latter, the Goddess may seem to possess the corpse, or appear as a beautiful woman, a little girl, or a savioress in the sky.[5]

While there are variations, the theme of a lone practitioner sitting on a corpse in pursuit of some manner of communion with a deity or transcendent reality is essential. Interviews with practitioners in modern West Bengal (see map 2) reveal that Tāntrikas still respect the rite, and some still engage in its performance. This essay illustrates the roots of contemporary Bengali *śava sādhana* practices, which continue to blossom, if in a hidden fashion, and shows that there are distinct differences in interpreting the ritual, although they are primarily differences in emphasis, not of kind.

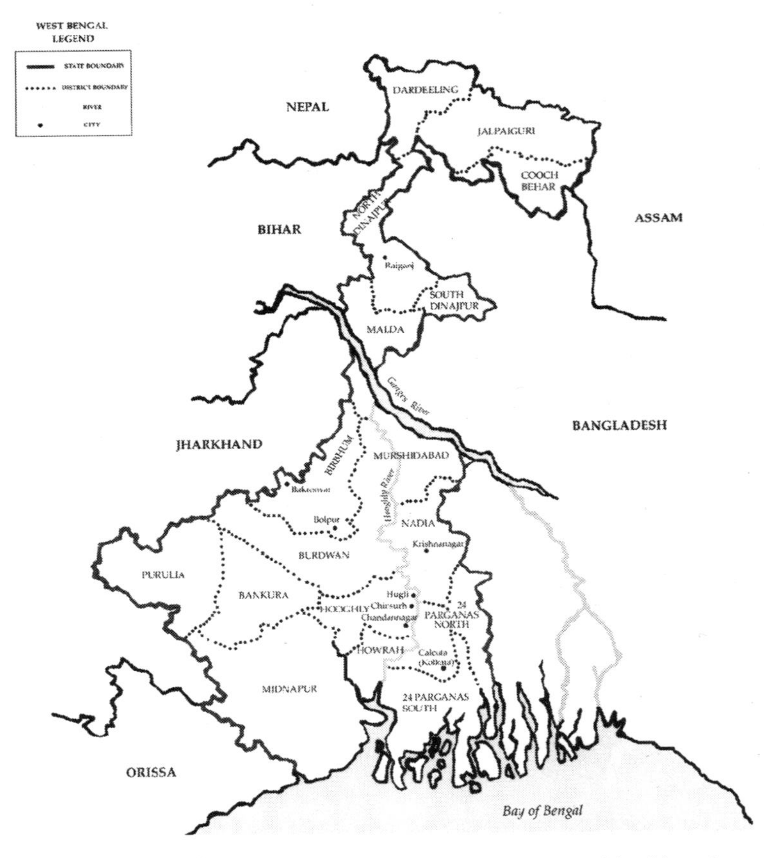

Map 2: The state of West Bengal, highlighting cities discussed in this volume by McDaniel, Sengupta, and McDermott. Artwork by Ben Royas.

THE CIRCLE AND THE CORPSE: DEAD BODIES AS TOOLS OF MAGIC AND RITUAL

In Western literature, *śava sādhana* is commonly associated with black magic and its philosophical and religious dimensions are neglected. For example, in Mircea Eliade's *Encyclopedia of Religion*, André Padoux states, 'Another secret worship is done with a corpse. It is used to achieve particular goals, usually evil.'[6] Many hold that the *śavavāda,* or way of the corpse, is a ritual of black magic, *nīla sādhana*, 'dark practice'. The primary purpose of dark practice is to gain control over another.

Such magical and manipulative dimensions, for instance, which have characterized sects such as the Kāpālikas and Kālamukhas since the first few centuries CE,[7] have been sensationalized in numerous memoirs and exposes by Indian writers, who have associated the Tāntrikas' powers with the criminal and perverse.[8] Early Western observers (especially missionaries and Victorians) were on the whole repulsed by Tantrism and saw it as demonic[9]—much as their descendents today view modern neopaganism and goddess religions as Satanic. In India, mainstream Brāhmaṇical thought attributes impurity, the opposite of dharmic religion, to corpses. Such impurity is threatening, and even modern followers of traditional Hinduism (*sanātana dharma*) associate Tantric ritual with tribal religion, human sacrifice, and degeneracy.[10] Tāntrikas respond to suspicion and accusations by keeping advanced rituals secret, ignoring the accusations, or calling their calumniators 'spiritually primitive, like animals [*paśus*]'. These strategies have contributed to the suppression, in the descriptions of the ritual by both Tāntrikas and their opponents, of the religious dimensions of *śava sādhana*.

It is of course true that magical elements are an integral part of certain *śava sādhana* practices, in the sense that the corpse is used as a ritual instrument—an object more than a subject—for the gaining of powers (*siddhis*), boons, or desires. The individual soul of the dead person is often of little or no interest to magical ritualists; in fact, at its most basic level, the magical perspective views the corpse as a kind of battery that can store and release energy (*śakti*).

One can see some of these magical elements at work in the *śava sādhana* prescriptions given in the medieval Śaiva Āgama text, the *Nīla Tantra*, which is constructed as a dialogue between Śiva and Devī:

102–4. (The practitioner) should offer *kuśa* grass at the feet of the corpse, and then pull together the corpse's hair and bind it into a topknot or tuft. He should then do the highest worship (*pūjā*) before the corpse, which takes on the form of the god (*devarūpī*). He should then rise and stand in front of the corpse, reading these mantras (in Sanskrit). Then he should draw a three-pointed design (*yantra*) at the feet of the corpse.

105–7. After doing this, the corpse will not be able to rise and will be motionless. Having drawn (the image), he extends the arms and legs, and *kuśa* grass is placed on the hands and feet. His lips are joined together, and his mind and senses are stilled, and in his heart the practitioner meditates on the Devī and begins chanting (*japa*). If the corpse moves, that is, if it keeps moving, the practitioner will become afraid.

108. If he becomes afraid, the practitioner should speak in Sanskrit: 'O Deveṣi! This evening I shall offer to you whatever you ask for. What is your name, tell me?'

109. Having spoken this in Sanskrit, the practitioner again fearlessly continues to chant mantras. Then, if he speaks his own name sweetly, he will (be able to) speak Sanskrit.

110–11. Then the practitioner, who is bound by (his) vow, prays hard for the desired boon. If he does not attain it, then he must be disciplined and single-minded, and he must start chanting again. If he does gain his boon, then the practitioner should abandon chanting.

112. If he gains the desired fruit of the ritual practice, then he should release the topknot of the corpse's hair which he has bound, and carefully wash the corpse according to custom. He must then ritually establish the corpse, clasp its feet, and then release it.

113. Having released the corpse's feet, he should throw all *pūjā*

supplies into running water. Then the corpse itself should be placed in the water or into a pit, and the practitioner should bathe.[11]

Here, although deities are invoked and the corpse is believed to be identified with Śiva, the main point of the ritual is the attainment of boons.

The primary goal of the *śava sādhana* is similarly to attain a supernatural servant—a ghost—who will serve the practitioner unquestioningly and for no remuneration, as Jonathan Parry points out in his study of the Śaivite *aghorīs* (terrible ones) of Varanasi:[12]

According to the descriptions I was given, the corpse is held fast during the *śava-sādhana* by a silken thread, which binds its wrist or ankle to a stake in the ground. A protective circle then surrounds it, within which the evil spirits of the cremation ground cannot penetrate, and outside of which are placed meat and liquor for them to consume. These spirits will try to engage the adept in a dialogue, which he must at all costs resist. Provided that he is sufficiently resolute, they will eventually tire and accept the offerings he has left for them. This is a sign that his austerities will be rewarded. The corpse's mouth will relax, allowing the *aghorī* to feed it a tiny quantity of *khir* (rice pudding). He will subsequently decapitate it in order to acquire the skull, or cut a bone from the spine, and finally immerse its remains in the river. This is followed by a period of severe ascetic restraint, which completes his mastery over the deceased's spirit. The *ojha*, who is a specialist in the control over the malevolent dead, is also said to perform *śava-sādhana* for similar ends. But while the *aghorī* sits on the corpse's chest, the *ojha* sits on the stomach.[13]

According to this description, remarkably similar to that found in the *Nīla Tantra*, the corpse is bound or tied down in order to conjure greater power. Likewise, no religious transformations take place in the *aghorī*; he merely wishes to gain a skull and control over a spirit through whom he may communicate with other spirits.[14] *Śava sādhana* here involves a magical process in which evil spirits try to penetrate the protective circle, and the practitioner becomes successful by ignoring them. Eventually, through his austerities, he also conquers the soul of the deceased.[15]

In an article published in *North Indian Notes and Queries* in 1895, Nanda Lal Ghosha describes a *śava sādhana* rite under the title, 'How to Make a Demon Subservient to Your Will.' He describes this method as used in Bengal; its goal is to attain a supernatural servant. The major decision maker, here in the form of a cat, is not identified (though it seems likely that it would be a type of deity called down by the ritual):

When a man dies on the fifteenth day of the Hindu month, being a Saturday, go with your teacher in the magical arts to the cremation ground and seat your teacher on a tree at least a mile from the place. Go to the cremation ground alone with the body and lay it on the ground with the feet to the south. Tie the hands and feet of the corpse to four iron pegs, securely driven into the ground. Sit on the breast of the corpse with a bottle of wine beside you and repeat mantras on a rosary made of bones. After repeating the mantras one hundred and eight times, drink some wine, and pour some into the mouth of the corpse. Then the corpse will begin to make faces at you and try to get up and fight you. But fear not; it cannot harm you as long as you retain your courage. You should at times call to your teacher and take his directions as to the mode of performing the rite. He will tell you to go on repeating the mantras and using the wine as before. As you go on repeating the mantras at intervals of one hundred and eight repetitions, animals of hideous form will appear, but heed them not. At last a cat will come, and will ask you what you want. You must say that you need the services of the ghost of the corpse on which you are seated. This the cat will grant. Then make a fire, sacrifice with meat and wine and return home, marking your forehead with the ashes of the sacrifice. As you go home do not look back nor reply to any questions put to you. The ghost will then serve you for the rest of your life.[16]

Related corpse rituals center on the possibility of the dead body serving as a vehicle for possession. Although now rarely practiced, the Bengali *Gambhira* rites involved a corpse dance, during which the body was 'awakened'. Life was instilled, but without visible signs. The corpse was purified by mantras and placed in a pool or tied to high branches of a tree. A Hāḍī or low-caste scavenger would then decorate it with *mālā* wreaths and vermilion and tie a cord around its waist. The presence of the corpse would inspire the god Śiva to possess his devotees, and they would become *bhar*—strong—with Śiva's presence and endurance. The possessed were understood to be capable of withstanding various austerities. Needles and nails would be driven into the body, through the tongue, and into the sides, and blazing cloths hung from the spikes after being dipped in ghee and set on fire. There was also possession by ghosts (*bhaginīs* and *pretas*) or by the goddess Maśān Cāmuṇḍā Kālī, and the participants would sing songs to avert evil.[17] Apparently, the goal of the ritual was unity with the god or goddess by possession, and possession of the corpse acted as the trigger or catalyst for the possession of the devotee.

Some corpse practices appear to have involved ritual sexuality. The Kaula text *Vīra Cūḍāmaṇi* has the practitioner sit naked with his female partner upon the corpse, first chanting mantras and then having ritual sex (while still sitting on the corpse). A similar ritual is *śava śṛṅgāra*, which is said to have been performed in Orissa by Śaivite Kāpālikas. These skull-bearing monks have sex with the unburned corpse of a young girl in order to obtain her *śakti* (spiritual power), but the corpse must be virginal or the ritual will not succeed.[18] As in the *śava sādhana* ritual, the corpse is used as a source of power.

Other forms of the corpse ritual incorporate violence. For example, one ritual requires a perfectly intact corpse, which is bathed and marked with sandalwood paste at midnight. The practitioner should next hold its head, and cut it off with one single stroke (of a sword). This pleases the yoginīs, who are understood as forms of Śakti, and they grant the practitioner the eight supernatural powers.[19]

In sum, the goal of all of these rituals is the gaining of magical power or a supernatural servant—whether deity, ghost, or cat—who will serve the practitioner and grant his wishes. Such approaches to *śava sādhana* are hence heavily magical and do not appear to have a traditionally religious end in sight, such as devotion to a god or entrance into Brahman. By contrast, they emphasize power, a value still prized today in Tantric contexts. Indeed, many contemporary Bengali Tāntrika interviewees claimed to have gained *śakti* through *śava sādhana*, as we shall shortly see.

ŚIVA AND THE NET OF MANTRAS

Many descriptions of the *śava sādhana* rite that we find in Hindu Tantras, ritual texts, and even dramas, present the powers and boons attained through its auspices as dependent upon the grace, or favor, of a deity.[20] Often this deity is Śiva.

For example, Śaivite Kāpālikas and Kālamukhas in the first few centuries CE were ascetic worshippers of Śiva Bhairava, and they made use of skulls and bones, as well as smearing themselves with ash from the burning ground. The Kāpālika carried a skull (*kapāla*), which was used as an eating bowl, and wore a loincloth and animal skins. The word *kapālin* (skull-bearer) occurs in a third-century CE *sūtra* (the *Yajñavālkya Smṛti* III.243), and Kāpālikas are mentioned by name in texts from the fifth to sixth centuries CE on.[21] They were known for their austerities and Tantric practices. In Rāmacandra's medieval *Kaumudīmitrānanda*, a Kāpālika offers oblations of human intestines into a fire and revives a corpse (who then strikes the Kāpālika).[22]

We also see a corpse ritual performed to Mahākāla, a form of Śiva, called the *Mahākālahṛdaya* rite. Bāṇa dramatically describes it in his seventh-century CE work the *Kādambarī*. This rite was performed in the burning ground at night, in order to gain a boon. It was sponsored by King Prabhākaravārdhana of Kanauj and performed by the ascetic Bhairavācārya with three assistants, after the ascetic had given the king a great enchanted sword.

The king and the ascetic came to the burning ground after fasting, the king bringing his sword. The assistants wore daggers and had magical knots in their turbans. They burned resin and incense in magical lamps, and in the center of a great circle of ashes, Bhairavācārya sat on the chest of a corpse wearing red garlands, clothes, and ornaments, as well as red sandalwood. Bhairavācārya wore black, and he offered black sesame seeds to the corpse as he lit its mouth with fire. Demons arose to fight them, but they prevailed, and at midnight the earth burst open into a fissure. From this chasm, a Nāga demon with dark skin and red eyes rushed upon the group. The king killed him with his magical sword. Then the king saw the goddess Lakṣmī in a vision, who blessed him to become the founder of a mighty line of kings because of the devotion he had shown to Śiva.[23] Interestingly, we have here a Śaivite ritual with a boon given by a goddess.

Some ritual prescriptions are more overtly religious, with *śava sādhana* being presented as a form of ritual worship, or *pūjā*, in which a deity, usually a form of Śiva or Devī, is worshipped within the corpse. In such cases the identification of the aspirant with the deity is the major goal.

The *Nīla Tantra* once again provides verses that exemplify the importance of Śiva's homologization with the corpse and, through means of Tantric meditation practices, the Tāntrika himself:

58–59. By means of (the ritual of) *śodhanyāsa*, he makes his own body identical to (that of) Śiva. He then performs *nyāsa* on the corpse (placing mantras in various places), using the Tārā *śodha* or the Tārā mantra, and begins *pūjā*. Concentrating on the mantras and visualizations of ritual worship, he does one-pointed meditation on mantra and *japa*. If the mantra has one consonant, then he performs mantra *japa* 10,000 times. . . .

63–64. While seated in *śavāsana* (upon the corpse) he will not glance in any direction, and if any friends arrive at that place, he will pay no attention to them. Seated in *śavāsana*, having begun *japa*, he may see many things in his imagination: water, fire, dangerous snakes or elephants, *rākṣasas*, animals, birds, insects, demons (*piśācas*), and other illusions. All of these may be understood to be dream-images, and while performing *śava sādhana*, he (the practitioner) should abandon all fear.

65. Hey, Devī! When *śava sādhana* is finished, and the practitioner has gained wealth and power for himself, he should offer gifts to his guru, his guru's son, or his guru's wife.

66. During *śava sādhana*, if the practitioner enters fully into the form of the mantra (*samyakrūpe*) then nothing remains unattainable (for him). Great *mantrasiddhi* cannot be described, and if he attains perfection (*siddhi*) in a mantra, the practitioner becomes equal to Śiva (Śivātulya).[24]

Here we see that the Tantric practitioner makes his own body ritually identical to that of Śiva, and the corpse also takes on the form of the god through *nyāsa* (the practice of placing mantras in the body that render various deities incarnate). The Śaivite Tāntrika seeks total concentration and conquest of fear, and worships the gods all around him and in the corpse. As David Kinsley states, 'Surrounded by death in the place of death, those aspects of reality that end in the fires of the cremation ground become distasteful . . .

attachment to the world and the ego is cut, and union with Śiva, the conqueror of death, is sought.'[25]

Ideally, in the Śaivite form of *śava sādhana*, the Tāntrika becomes unified with Lord Śiva. This differs from the Śākta goal of the ritual.

THE TEN-ARMED MOTHER AND THE CORPSE

In contrast with Śaivite forms of *śava sādhana*, the Śākta approach to the corpse ritual tends to differ in emphasis; it is understood to be a sign of devotion, an evidence of one's love of the Goddess. In this more *bhakti*-oriented, Śākta attitude, *śava sādhana* is a form of *pūjā*, in which the Goddess is worshipped within the corpse that functions as her *mūrti*. Through devotion, the corpse can be brought to life under the benevolent gaze of the deity. A popular Sanskrit play on words posits that 'Śiva without Śakti is a corpse [*śava*].' Iconographically, Śiva is portrayed as a corpse, with the Goddess in the form of the beautiful and terrifying Kālī, who may stand over or even sit upon his unmoving form (see fig. 7). The practitioner meditates upon Śakti, visualizing her form in his heart lotus: she wears the dead bodies of two boys as earrings, with a belt made of dead men's hands, and sits upon the *pretas* (spirits) of Brahmā, Viṣṇu, Rudra, Īśvara, and Sadāśiva. These gods are dead, because they cannot act without her power.[26] She is naked and surrounded by jackals. In her form as Ucchiṣṭacaṇḍālinī, she is wearing a red sari and ornaments, carrying a skull and a sword, and is sitting on a corpse. She is worshipped with impure objects when the practitioner is in an impure state.[27] Ideally, the corpse ritual brings about a vision of the Goddess. As Sir John Woodroffe notes:

> In successful Śavāsana the Devī, it is said, appears to the Sādhaka. In Śava-sādhana the Sādhaka sits astride on the back of a corpse (heading [toward] the north), on which he draws a Yantra and then does Japa of Mantra with Ṣodhānyāsa and Pūjā on its head. A corpse is selected as being a pure form of organized matter, since the Devatā that is invoked into it is the Mahā-vidyā whose Svarūpa is Nirguṇa-brahman, and by such invocation becomes Saguṇa. The corpse is free from sin or desire. The only Vāyu in it is the Dhanaṁjaya, 'which leaves not even a corpse.' The Devatā materializes by means of the corpse. There is possession of it (Āveśa)—that is, entry of the Devatā into the dead body. At the

conclusion of a successful rite, it is said, that the head of the corpse turns round, and, facing the Sādhaka, speaks, bidding him name his boon, which may be spiritual or worldly advancement as he wishes.[28]

Fig. 7: Kālī, goddess of the corpse ritual. This powerful image is said to have been worshipped by the Thugs for many centuries. South Calcutta, 1994. Photograph by Jim Denosky.

The devotee sits upon the corpse to call down the Goddess, who saves him when he is threatened by demons or ghosts. As the *Tantra Tattva* phrases it: If her son is in trouble, Ma runs down from her golden throne on Mt. Kailāśa, 'without even staying to arrange Her dress', and extends her ten fear-dispelling arms in ten directions, crying, 'fear not'.[29]

The Mother's compassion towards her children is a well-known theme in Bengali song and story; the poet Dāśarathi Rāy (1807–1857) describes the compassion of the Goddess as Jagadāmbā:

Mother does not care for the children who mix with others
And go about laughing and playing.
She does not go to them, she rests instead
[But] She takes the child who weeps on her lap.[30]

Here the Tāntrika is the child of the deity, overwhelmed by fear and love, who seeks to dwell in the lap of the Goddess. This is the *bhakti* surrender of the devotee, who passes the ocean of birth and death to dwell in eternity with his Goddess. The ritual of *śava sādhana* is a powerful way to call down the Goddess, for her *śakti* is understood to dwell most strongly in corpses, burning grounds, jackals, and natural sites.[31] In this ritual, the corpse itself becomes the body of the deity, and the practitioner also becomes ritually sanctified.

In addition, the Goddess is often worshipped in other bodies, where the power of the mantra (*mantraśakti*) reveals her true form. She may be worshipped as Kumārī in the bodies of young virgins, as Umā in jackals, as Mother of *siddhis* within the *brāhmini* or kite.[32] She may enter the corpse itself and speak through its mouth, or she may appear in a vision. The Goddess descends in the midst of fear:

When all earthly means fail . . . when in that terrible and pitiless great cremation ground, where horrors do a frantic dance, there is, despite the presence of the all-good Mother, nothing in all the infinite world which for our safety we can call our own; in that deep darkness of a new-moon night, haunted with destructive Bhairavas, Vetālas, Siddhas, Bhūtas, Vaṭukas and Dākinīs . . . when the firm and heroic heart of even the great Vīra shakes with fear; when even the intricate bonds of the Sādhaka's posture on the back of the corpse which is awakened by Mantra, is loosened; when with a faning [*sic*] heart the Vīra feels as he sits the earth quake furiously under him; when without means of rescue he is about to fall and be crushed; when he is overtaken by the swoon of death—if even at such times the Sādhaka but . . . extends his uplifted hands, saying, 'Save me, I pray thee, O Gurudeva!' then the Mother of the world, who is Herself the Guru, at once forgets all his faults, dispels all his difficulties with Her glance, and stretching forth ten hands instead of two, says: 'Come, my child, there is no more fear', and blesses the Sādhaka by raising him to Her assuring bosom.[33]

One of the earliest stories of the Śākta form of the *śava sādhana* ritual is the story of Sarvānanda of Mehar. This story was told to me by several informants in Calcutta and seems to be an important origin story for Bengali Tāntrikas. Sarvānanda is believed to have lived in the late fourteenth or early fifteenth century and to have attained *siddhi* by means of this ritual on a new-moon night (*amāvasya*).

The story of Sarvānanda begins with his grandfather, Vasudeva Bhaṭṭācārya, of Tipperah (in what is now West Bengal). He was a devoted Śākta, who went to Kāmākhyā in Assam to practice *śakti sādhana*. Vasudeva heard a voice say that he would attain liberation in his next life, when he would be reborn as his own grandson. He gave to his servant Pūrṇānanda a piece of copper engraved with his mantra (or according to some sources, a *yantra*), for worshipping the Goddess.

Later, Vasudeva's grandson, Sarvānanda, was attended by Pūrṇānanda, now an old man. The boy was uneducated, and both neighbors and family jeered at his lack of intelligence. While wandering about depressed he was initiated by a passing *sannyāsi*, who told him to perform *sādhana* with Pūrṇānanda. Pūrṇānanda told him about the most powerful form of *sādhana*, the *śava sādhana* ritual.

Sarvānanda and Pūrṇānanda got all the ritual implements together and only needed a recently dead corpse to serve as the seat of the Tantric practitioner. Pūrṇānanda volunteered for this so that he might be blessed for his sacrifice, and Sarvānanda agreed. Pūrṇānanda strangled himself, warning Sarvānanda that he should be neither tempted nor afraid, and only ask for the vision (*darśana*) of the Mother.

Sarvānanda sat on the corpse of Pūrṇānanda; he saw horrible ghosts, terrible storms, beautiful nymphs (*apsaras*es), and finally the vision of the Mother. He remained detached throughout. The Goddess blessed him and revived Pūrṇānanda, and Sarvānanda became a *siddha puruṣa*, a liberated person. The dark, new-moon night was miraculously transformed into a shining full-moon night. He also gained the power of *vāk siddhi*, so that all of his statements became true. He was the first Tāntrika to see the Goddess in all of her ten major forms in one night (the Daśamahāvidyās).[34]

Thus the corpse ritual evoked the Goddess, who blessed Sarvānanda with wisdom. She also gave him the gift of bringing his devoted servant back to life. His practice was unusual, and came by inspiration, but over time, the ritual became acceptable to and even required for Śākta Tāntrikas, with a threat of hell for its nonperformance. The *Kālī Tantra* describes a Śākta version of the ritual, in which the goal is not union with a deity, but rather the pleasing of the Goddess:

8. At the root of a *bilva* tree, having carefully placed a corpse on his own lap, [the Tāntrika] should perform the *narasiṁha mudrā*. Observing the corpse, he should chant the *mātṛkā mantra* and the *puṭita mantra*.

9. Having chanted these one thousand times, he will become master of all powers [*siddhis*].

10. Carrying the corpse to the root of a banyan tree and worshipping the Goddess there, he will chant mantras while laying down and become the master of all powers.

11. Holding the belt of hands [*karakāñcī*], decorated with a necklace made of skulls, decorated with markings of ash from the burning ground, if he chants mantras even once at the burning ground, he will become the master of all powers. . . .

12. He who worships (the goddess) Pārvatī without the corpse ritual will live a terrible life in Naraka (a hell-world) until the great destruction at the end of the world.[35]

So crucial is *śava sādhana* that the text warns that if the Goddess is worshipped without the corpse ritual, she will throw the Tāntrika into the hell-world of Naraka.

Another famous practitioner of *śava sādhana* was the Śākta poet Rāmprasād Sen (*c.* 1718–75). Sen performed this ritual on a funeral pyre (*cita sādhana*) using a *mālā* or rosary made of human bone. He also performed it under a *bilva* tree and on a seat made of the skulls of five animals, including humans (*pañcamuṇḍa āsana*).[36] He, too, was blessed by a vision of the Goddess.

According to Śākta folklore, it is the devotion of the practitioner that brings the Goddess down to him. He is so loving that he is willing to risk the dangers of the burning ground, including its ghosts and demons and jackals, to incite the Goddess to manifest herself. She may enter his heart or she may enter the corpse when it becomes a suitable dwelling place (*mūrti*) for her. Its head is said to turn around and begin speaking affectionately (or sometimes terrifyingly) to the devotee. When the devotee asks for a boon, the Goddess cannot refuse.

To bring Śakti into the corpse is also to bring life and power (*śakti*) into it, as Śakti is said to enliven Śiva. Some Tāntrikas compare the devotee's own body to a corpse, saying that the Goddess must enter into the heart to enliven it. Others say that the practitioner himself becomes both the Goddess and the corpse, realizing in him or herself both the divine spirit and the physical body.

If one keeps in mind, therefore, these more devotionally oriented forms of burning ground rituals, as prescribed by Śāktas, as well as the monistic interpretations of the aspirant's union with Śiva, as recounted in the last section of this essay, it becomes clear how reductionist it is to categorize Tantric rituals like the *śava sādhana* as purely manipulative, magical, or motivated by selfish intentions. Defamers who level such charges are not seeing beneath the surface. Nevertheless, it is a challenge to separate out the three strands of meaning and approach to the *śava sādhana* practice—the magical, yogic, and devotional. Rites, like people, are complex. In privileging only one element, interpreters misconstrue and omit many important insights into Tantric practice in modern Bengal, which is more diverse than it appears and in need of further exploration. The ritual resonates with several layers of meaning.

SOME MODERN TĀNTRIKAS: RITUALS AND PROBLEMS

In modern West Bengal, there is great prejudice against Tāntrikas, and therefore they are difficult to locate and interview. In 1983–84 and 1993–94, I interviewed nearly twenty Tāntrikas. Informants were much harder to find in the 1990s; most had disappeared and nobody could tell me where they had gone. Those I could locate said that they were being harassed by government officials in West Bengal. Some officials blamed Śaiva and Śākta Tāntrikas for Bengal's difficult financial state after the collapse of the USSR and accused them of being malingerers and false *sādhus*. Several renunciant Tāntrikas told me that they had been threatened and attacked by goondas—professional tough guys who assault people for a price—as well as by children, who were organized by communist clubs in the public schools to harass and throw rocks at them. This assertion was corroborated by an elementary school principal interviewed, who described the clubs and their recruitment techniques in some detail. The householder Tāntrikas, who were teachers, doctors, and engineers, explained that their jobs would be in danger if they admitted publicly to being Tāntrikas. Some reported that they had received anonymous phone calls threatening to expose their Tantric leanings to superiors. Because there is high unemployment in the state, this is a significant threat, leading to the hiding of one's Tantric identity.

In concert with the stereotyping of Tantric rituals that we have seen in the previous sections of this chapter, Tāntrikas are commonly feared because they are believed to be black magicians, madmen, and hypnotists. Bengali parents will sometimes threaten their misbehaving children by saying that the Tāntrika will come and get them if they are bad. In folk stories, Tāntrikas are frequently villains, portrayed as capturing innocent young girls to be sacrificed to the goddess Kālī.[37] This latter charge is problematic, as I was told by several Tāntrikas that the Goddess never accepts female sacrifices, which indicates that the writers of these stories do not portray Śākta Tantra accurately. This popular image, and attendant misunderstanding, many say, goes back to medieval times. Bhavabhuti's play *Mālatīmādhava* features outrageous Kāpālikas, 'skull-bearing' ascetics bent on killing innocents to serve as their offerings in *śava sādhana*, and folk stories of King Vikramāditya portray him as rescuing fair maidens from murderous Tāntrikas.[38] On the other hand, there are some textual sources which support the use of female corpses. Indeed, the *Nīla Tantra* mentions the efficacy of sacrificing a pregnant woman.[39]

The issue of sacrificing live humans for use in the *śava sādhana* is important, because it dramatically affects the popular understanding of Tāntrikas today. Besides being eccentric, are Tāntrikas actually murderers, deliberately killing their victims in order to offer an appropriate sacrifice to the Goddess or a good corpse for the *śava sādhana* ritual? Some writers have suggested that Tāntrikas may become murderers. 'The corpse should be undiseased, of one who has died of an accident,' Narendra Nath Bhattacharyya notes. 'But how is it possible that a Candala will, conveniently for the aspirant, have an accidental death on a fixed day of the calendar and at the right moment?'[40]

This is a reasonable question. 'The common practice is, therefore, to tempt a youthful Candala to get him drunk and finally kill him,' Bhattacharyya continues. 'Then the body is to be anointed and used for the purpose of *sādhana*.'[41] While Bhattacharyya's comment here accurately reflects the opinions of many people about Tāntrikas, this conclusion may be empirically unwarranted, or at minimum, the practice is best not characterized as 'common'.

I asked several Tāntrikas who had performed or planned to perform the corpse ritual about whether Tāntrikas kill people to serve as corpses in *śava sādhana*. They agreed that it was wrong and immoral to kill anybody for such a ritual, and they stressed that Kālī would disapprove of it. None admitted knowing anybody who had ever done this.

These informants—who were mainly Śākta—said instead that the corpse would be provided by the Goddess. The spontaneous appearance of a suitable corpse was a major way that a Tāntrika knew it was the appropriate time to perform *śava sādhana*. One Tāntrika interviewed in 1994 outside Calcutta spoke of the special bond between Tāntrikas and Ḍoms, the low-caste workers who dispose of bodies. He said that he maintained a relationship with a

Ḍom working in a Calcutta hospital, who would inform him of various deaths and advise him whether there were any bodies that appeared particularly suitable for *śava sādhana*.

Sometimes accusations of murder occur in rural areas, where the atrocity is variously attributed to Tāntrikas, tribals, or people hostile to Westerners. During fieldwork in the Bolpur area in 1984, I was warned by local informants to avoid certain villages. They said that villagers were using human corpses to worship the Goddess, and that several tourists had disappeared in that area over the past years. Some informants stated that it was Santals rather than Tāntrikas who had been cutting the bodies to pieces and spreading them around their land to make it more fertile. My informants noted that these villagers were using passing Westerners as sacrifices because the victims did not have relatives who could avenge them, and they gambled that itinerant Westerners would not be missed by the authorities.

In general, however, murdering someone to obtain a corpse does not fit the criteria for Śākta Tantra. If the purpose of *śava sādhana* is primarily to please the Goddess, performing it in a way that would irritate her is pointless and a waste of time. If the Goddess is pleased, she will grant boons to the performer, but if not, nothing comes of the ritual. According to my informants, she does not want others to provide the corpse; that is her job, and she gets particularly angry if a woman is killed. In this case, then, a devotional perspective provides the underlying framework for attitudes toward the dead body.

The corpse ritual may be effective for other purposes. For example, I recorded one incident, told to me by a Kālī priest in a 1994 interview, in which the *śava sādhana* was used to bring a corpse back from the dead:

An interesting incident happened many years ago. When my father was just a child, he was very ill, and he was declared to be dead by the doctor. My grandfather took him into the forest. There were hundreds of jackals and vultures surrounding him, but no animal came near or tried to attack him. My grandfather went into a meditative trance and was full of devotion for the Devī. After three or four days, my father began to move, and he regained his life and his strength. The Goddess saves people in her many forms—Durgā, Kālī, Tārā—but it is my belief that my father was saved by the intervention of Kālī.[42]

Here we have a Śākta practitioner meditating upon the corpse of his son and calling down the Goddess, not for his own good, but for the life of his child. The possibility of reanimating the corpse is central to the ritual process of *śava sādhana*, but here the effect is not to limit the corpse's reanimation to the duration of the ritual, or to place its soul under the authority of the practitioner, as with the *aghorī*, but instead to ask the Goddess's blessing in the restoration of its life.

This same Kālī priest had an altar of skulls painted red, as the souls, he said, would help him in meditation. When he sat beneath his five trees, or over the *pañcamuṇḍa āsana* (the seat of five skulls) that had been his grandfather's meditation place, the souls would help him. He explained:

The Goddess is normally invisible before us, but through meditative practice, we can see her. One ritual that I perform here is the feeding of skulls [*muṇḍake khāoāno*]. Generally, they like puffed rice, though some like fried lentils, curries or wine. After an animal sacrifice, I feed them with meat. [Note: feeding in this case means offering a plate of food before each skull.] The feeding is accompanied by a ritual fire [*homa*] and *yajña* [Vedic style sacrifice]. After the feeding, I bathe them in ghee, yogurt, milk and honey, and then I arrange them for worship. Sometimes I do this when I need more mental balance or physical strength.

Skulls are useful, because the dead person's soul often stays with the skull. The soul can predict the future, and help the *sādhu*. People used to do the corpse ritual [*śava sādhana*] and sit on the dead body of a virgin girl. She would then become Kālī, and the body would come back to life and talk. My grandfather performed the corpse ritual, but people today are afraid of it—if you make one mistake, you die or go insane. This *sādhu* in orange that you see roaming around here in the burning ground did the corpse ritual wrongly, and he was made insane by it. But he will return to sanity one of these days.

I feed the skulls on the altar, and they help me. I learned the skull-feeding ritual from my grandfather. When the skulls are fed, they are pacified and they become protectors. Then they are strong enough to fight off the evil souls [*ātmas*] who wish to distract or harm the *sādhu*. When negative spirits [*bhaginīs* and *pretas*] try to disturb the *sādhu*'s meditation, then the good souls fight the bad souls and keep the *sādhu* on the right path. *Sādhus* often have helpers. Sometimes the corpse ritual is performed with a woman, who is called the *uttarā sādhikā*.[43] She is very skilled and helps the male through meditation if he is distracted by bad spirits. When the *sādhu* draws a circle around himself to protect him from these spirits, she is within the circle. Sometimes the *sādhu* may invite his guru in subtle form to watch over him and help him.

Today, it is widely believed that there are no ghosts, but really there are souls who do not die. They are always around us. Sometimes they may enter into our physical bodies and cause problems or even tragedies. It is only by meditative practice, and by dedication to the Goddess, that we gain control over them. Then they can work for our benefit. We become immune to fear, hate, and intense desire with their help. I show them loyalty, and they guard me.

The skulls in this temple mostly come from people who died in epidemics, especially cholera epidemics. Large numbers of people used to die, and there was no effective system of cremation at that time. Corpses would lie on the roadside or in the forests.

Under the altar of this temple there are 108 skulls buried. Some altars have 1,008 skulls. Skulls awaken the Goddess, and make her present here. Male gods have stones [*śilas*] or *liṅgas*, but goddesses have skulls. Some skulls are used for *pañcamuṇḍa āsana*. People use the skulls of a low-caste man [usually a Caṇḍāla], a jackal, a tiger, a snake and a virgin girl. They must be young, and die suddenly by violence. Nobody wants the skulls of people who died of disease or old age.[44]

The ghost of this man's grandfather also helped him. He taught the priest both while he was alive and also after his death, in ghostly form. He would come to visit and teach while his grandson sat on the seat of five skulls. Because of the priest's love and respect for his grandfather, their relationship continued even after the old man's death. However, my informant had not yet performed the corpse ritual, partly because he did not believe he was yet ready. He felt that the Goddess would let him know when and if he should perform it.

A *sādhikā* interviewed in Bakreswar, a renunciant yoginī and head of an ashram,[45] explained that the five-skulls ritual is based on a theory of exchange:

The *pañcamuṇḍa āsana* is a meditation site where five skulls are buried in the earth, beneath the practitioner, and it is an old Tantric rite for gaining power. It is based on exchange. A *sādhaka* is contacted by unsatisfied spirits [*atripta ātma*], who wish to gain liberation [*mokṣa*]. The *sādhu* [usually understood to be a *siddha puruṣa* or a *muni*] knows the mantras that the spirits can use to escape from their unpleasant state. The spirits come to the *sādhu* and donate their power in exchange for *mantraśakti*, thus trading salvation for power. They are understood to have traveled through many different worlds, gathering strength as they went. The spirits point out their skulls to the *sādhu*, directing him to their location, and telling him which to use. Sometimes they bring the skulls flying through the air to him. The *sādhu* then builds the *pañcamuṇḍa āsana*, and in meditation the exchange occurs. While sometimes the skulls are of five different species, more frequently they are all of human origin. The *āsana* may only be used once, for after the trade is completed, the spirits are no longer associated with the skulls. Used skulls cannot give the requisite power.[46]

She also noted that in the vicinity of the Bakreswar *śakti pīṭha* where we spoke, there was a *lākhmuṇḍa āsana*, a buried pile of 100,000 skulls. Most skulls were not visible, placed deep in the tree roots or built into a thick base of soil surrounding the tree at this site (see fig. 8). There were some skulls scattered around, as well as thigh bones, and one skull painted red that sat about five feet up from the base of the tree and was suspended from a rough iron trident. The *lākhmuṇḍa āsana* had been built in the nineteenth century by a *sādhu* named Aghor Bābā. The *sādhikā* explained to me the history of the skulls and the sacred site in some detail.

She said that Aghor Bābā had been born in Orissa, and studied Tantric practice for a long time in Tibet. He later returned to India and did meditation at Tārāpīṭha, a Śākta site, while the *sādhu* Bāmākṣepā (1837–1911) lived there. During that time, Aghor Bābā performed meditation in which he identified with Śiva Mahākāla and performed *aghorī sādhana* (eating human flesh and living in the burning ground). Eventually, Bāmākṣepā received a dream command from Tārā Mā (the major goddess of Tārāpīṭha) to expel Aghor Bābā from the town, because Aghor Bābā did not belong there.

Aghor Bābā was removed by force, and he was very unhappy and angry at Tārā Mā. He went to Howrah near Calcutta and sat there for meditation. He received a dream command to go to Gorakhpur. There he met a yogi named Gorakhnāth, and Aghor Bābā told him about Tārā Mā's orders. Gorakhnāth called Tārā Mā to Gorakhpur to find out why Aghor Bābā had been removed. Tārā Mā came in the form of a tribal woman, and was very angry, for it is a long trip from Tārāpīṭha to Gorakhpur, even for a goddess. She said that she had wanted Aghor Bābā removed because he had gone as far as he could spiritually in Tārāpīṭha, and he needed to go elsewhere to attain *siddhi*. She told Gorakhnāth to tell Aghor Bābā to go to Bakreswar in Birbhum and meditate there, doing Tantric *sādhana*.

However, when Aghor Bābā went to the burning ground at Bakreswar, he found it already occupied. A Kāpālika and his three *bhairavīs* were already living there, and they did not wish to move. However, Aghor was commanded by Tārā Mā to be there, and he

Fig. 8: A *lākhmuṇḍa āsana*, or 100,000-headed seat, said to have captured the power of many spirits of the dead and hence to be a potent place for Tantric meditation. Bakreswar, West Bengal, 1994. Photograph by Jim Denosky.

insisted on staying. He fought with the Kāpālika, killing him and his consorts. He did not allow these four souls to gain liberation, but instead kept them in the burning ground to gain knowledge from them. Their skulls were the first four skulls of the *lākhmuṇḍa āsana*.

He then collected other skulls from the burning ground. Sometimes bodies were only half-burnt and tigers and other predators ate the flesh. Aghor Bābā took the bones. By means of Tantric practice, he would draw the souls to the bones and use their power for his *sādhana*. However, he eventually reached a dead end and could progress no further. Finally, a *sādhikā* named Maheśvarī Devī, who was a *bhairavī* from East Bengal, came to Bakreswar. With her help, he attained *siddhi*, and he spent his remaining years in Bakreswar.[47]

In this case, we do have a story of a murder by a Tāntrika, but the purpose of the killing does not fall into the pattern commonly attributed to *śava sādhana*. It was also performed by an *aghorī*, rather than by a devotional Śākta Tāntrika. However, it is interesting to note that the *aghorī* was believed to be able to prevent the Kāpālika and his consorts from gaining liberation with the help of Tārā Mā, who accepts the use of these spirits in meditation—an indication that even a devotional aspect to the corpse ritual narratives does not always remove a search for power. This pile of skulls is still a site of practice, and my informant would often meditate there in the evening.

The search for supernatural power is, indeed, found among many types of Tāntrikas. In West Bengal, there are practitioners known as Piśāca Tāntrikas, those who have gained power over *piśācas* or demonic creatures. Piśāca Tāntrikas are exorcists who ply a good business in protective amulets and supernatural revenge. One such Tāntrika interviewed in Calcutta in 1984 had a back room full of dusty, gray-brown human skulls and bones, and I was told by informants there that these objects had the most power (*śakti*) of anything in his supply. He had on the wall a picture of a skeleton sitting in meditation upon a corpse, with a red *maṇḍala* of the *kuṇḍalinī* at the navel area. In this image, the corpse was symbolic of the physical body left behind during meditation. This Piśāca

Tāntrika was considered to be a powerful magician and consented to speak with me only if he sat on my lap and I fed him rice with my hand. He was a large man, and very heavy. (The informant who had driven me there on his motorcycle told me on our way back that this was a very good turn of events: I had fed him on my lap and was therefore his mother, and no Tāntrika would ever hurt his mother, even if he got angry.) The Piśāca Tāntrika spoke of how the majority of his clients were family members who were antagonistic toward one another and called on him for revenge in fights and problems of inheritance. I asked about the skulls and bones, but he would not say how the bones got into his shrine; he replied that they were given by the Goddess. As they were understood to be empowered and used for spells, I assumed that he got them by some ritual means.

Many Tāntrikas find the powers granted to them through their Tantric practices to bring great personal satisfaction as well as an income. For instance, Tantric *sādhaka*s with whom I spoke at the Śākta site of Tārāpīṭha Temple in 1984 in West Bengal reclined on piles of skulls and bones to address their devotees. Tārāpīṭha is somewhat notorious in Bengal for its nontraditional rituals, and its burning ground is said to be a great locale for *śava sādhana* practice. There are many rumors of drug use, murders, and orgies. However, the Tāntrika there with whom I spoke the longest was a rather cheery soul. He explained that he had spent his life as a conductor on the Indian railroad and was simply bored to death. He had long looked forward to retirement so that he could do something interesting with his life. He was lying across a pile of skulls, happily stating that now his life was fine, because there was always something new happening, some ritual or gift from the Goddess or interesting visitor, and now his life was worthwhile.[48]

One Śākta practitioner, a householder, used to spend time down at the burning ground with Tāntrikas, smoking cigarettes and learning rituals. He learned about *śava sādhana*, but did not practice it himself. He spoke of the Goddess:

I worship Kālī because she is the soul of nature, she is *Prakṛti*. In the West, they call it animism, and I believe in it, because nature is full of soul and dynamic power. Śiva is a static male: if he acts, it must be through Śakti. The feminine force in Hinduism is controlled by the male force, as God creates out of nature. As the practitioner, you take the role of Śiva, you take over the feminine force to accomplish things.

Kālī doesn't mind being used in this way, if you do enough *pūjā* to her. If she hears you, she gives you power, and you can use it to your own ends. She may support the black part of magic, if it is justified by karma, but basically she is a good goddess. I give nature a form in Kālī. I worship her to gain power to deal with problems in life. I pray to her, and I go to the temple and talk to her. Sometimes it is easier to talk to her in the temple, because it is a focus of Kālī's power. I worship on Kālī Pūjā at Kālīghāṭ, and I concentrate on her photograph at home. I bring her energy into my body, and I use the power of my body as a receptacle for her power. I use my mind to draw her in. . . .

Every Bengali is a 'Kālī freak' [English in original]. Bengalis may also worship Durgā and Śiva, but Kālī is both dangerous and benevolent. Her power of illusion [*māyā*] is very strong. In her worship, blood, power, and black magic create a dark, strange *māyā* among the people. In Bengal, more people worship Kālī than Kṛṣṇa. Kālī is Bengali, she is one of us, but Kṛṣṇa is a foreigner from northern India, born in Uttar Pradesh or Gujarat. . . .

I used to speak with many Tāntrikas. Tāntrikas take spirits into their bodies and use them for magic, and they play with the spirits. . . . Sometimes I call spirits into my body to communicate. It is a strange feeling, having a spirit in your body: it is a 'cheap thrill' [English in the original]. If the spirit is good, it is a positive experience. But some spirits won't identify themselves, and make you confused and make you think about things that you don't want to think about. There are many kinds of spirits. I have only known a few kinds.[49]

He further noted that burning grounds, where they burn the bodies with wood, have more supernatural power than electric crematoriums, which are becoming popular. The spirits of the dead can even infuse the statues of nearby Śiva and Kālī temples with power, which Tāntrikas can then use. Thus the *śava sādhana* ritual is a major technique of empowerment.

According to another informant, a singer of songs to Kālī or a Kālī *kīrtanīya*, one may approach the Goddess in two ways: by emotion (*bhāva*), and by ritual (*sādhana*). He performed a *śava sādhana* practice many years ago with a friend who was a Śākta Tāntrika, and he sensed the presence of the Goddess at that time. He still sees the friend occasionally, and they periodically do meditation at the burning ground. He described his relationship to the Goddess; he had lost faith in her but found it again among the bodies burning at the crematorium:

> I used to believe that Kālī was the only goddess, and did special *pūjā* to her, and would never worship any other deity. Now I think that I was narrow-minded at that time. My approach changed because of personal problems, and these caused me to lose faith in the Goddess. I stopped worshipping her and removed her picture, and worshipped other gods and goddesses, for Kālī did not prevent my tragedy. But one day a stranger asked me if I sang songs to Kālī, and arranged for me to sing all night at a crematorium for Kālī Pūjā. The people there were greatly affected by the songs, asking me to sing to bless people and help the dying. I realized the powerful effect of these songs on people's lives, and I was again drawn toward the Goddess.[50]

He remarked that singing at the burning ground was the best way to worship the Goddess, for she is vividly present in death.

A renunciant *sādhikā* and head of an ashram in Jadavpur told me of her guru's dedication to the Goddess, and his emphasis on morality for Tantric practitioners, especially those performing such dangerous rituals as *śava sādhana*. As she stated of her guru, Satyānanda:

> He said that those who follow the Śākta path may sit in the cremation ground at midnight and repeat mantras in order to overcome fear, but they must always focus upon the benevolent aspect of the Divine Mother, her gentle and peaceful form. Her weapons are only wielded against evil, and her other hands only shower blessings and give assurances to bring forth the power [of] good and right action. He described Śakti as the principle of Motherhood to his disciples and described his visions.

My informant continued:

> He had many beautiful visions of Mother Bhavatāriṇī. He described her color as like blue lightning. He said, 'She is like a dazzling electric light within a glass container. It cannot be compared in any way with the physical bodies in this mortal world. Yet She has a definite form.' The form in which he saw her in meditation represents the whole universe. I remember that he said to us, 'When I was looking at the sky, it seemed that it was the Mother's form that was spread over the entire universe. Her hair was spread all over the sky. Her shining face was like blue lightning, with blue eyes blooming in the sky. The moon's crescent resembles a crown on Her head, the stars appear as jewelry on Her hands, the whole of nature adorns Her body. The clouds full of lightning make up Her sari.'
>
> He also noted that while the Divine Mother protects and guides her devotees, one must still take spirits into account, 'for dead family members may interfere with initiation, preventing a disciple from hearing the mantra, and influencing people on earth.' The Divine Mother is always protecting her devotees, especially from bad spirits while they are asleep, like a mother who keeps covering her

child in cold weather. Both detachment from the world and its desires and devotion to the Goddess are important. Thus, a place like the burning ground can be useful for Śākta devotees, for the rituals performed there overcome attachment to the body, and draw down the Goddess.[51]

In sum, as all of these accounts of my experiences with Śākta Tāntrikas in West Bengal indicate, not only are Tāntrikas *not* immoral murderers, they are also convinced that the presence of Kālī is fundamental to their ritual practices. To be sure, this is no *bhakti*, pure and simple, for the Tantric rites in which they participate also include room for spirits, ghosts, and the quest for power. But the desired *siddhis* are mediated through, or given by, the Goddess, and the result is a sense of gratitude, contentment, wonder, and even new realization.

CONCLUSION

As we have seen, the corpse ritual combines many layers of Indian tradition. The folk and magical desire for supernatural power, or *siddhi,* is seen in the conquest of the corpse and the physical collecting of skulls and bones, as was evident with the Piśāca Tāntrika using the power of death for his clients and the Aghorī Tāntrika building his seat of 100,000 skulls. In both of these cases, the skulls and bones were public and open to view. This type of corpse ritual in West Bengal is generally intended to produce fertility, healing, or harm. We may also note that the high gods require a full corpse for the ritual, while the spirits with partial powers only need parts of bodies (such as skulls). The nature of the corpse used for the ritual may reflect the nature of the deities who are invoked.

When discussing even what would seem to be a very specific rite, ethnographic research reveals that there are in fact profound differences of interpretation that reflect a religious view. Those who are devoted primarily to Śiva, with attendant yogic and nondual understandings of the divine, use the *śava sādhana* to improve their meditation, and become one with Śiva.

The Śākta perspective on the ritual, however, while containing magical and yogic elements, is primarily devotional. In Śākta *śava sādhana*, ritually invoked possession of the corpse by the Goddess is a form of deity establishment or *prāṇa pratiṣṭhā*. The Goddess is called down into the corpse that is to be her *mūrti*, which is then empowered and made alive. The goal is for the corpse to be born again, of the Goddess's power, alive with a Goddess who loves the burning ground. The corpse is, in a sense, an apt place for a Goddess to descend and communicate; it can speak and transform the lives of those ritually acting upon it in the name of the Goddess—as expressed by the Kālī priest whose father's corpse had been revived through devotion. The corpse ritual here gives devotional love, *bhakti*, for the Goddess and protection to the devotee.

While the majority of the Tāntrikas I interviewed in Bengal expressed their love for the Devī, many also emphasized the *siddhis* they received through rituals performed under her auspices. This indicates the complexity of the intertwining strands of *śava sādhana* in contemporary practice. Power, liberation, and love are all motivations for a practice almost universally condemned in the popular literature, yet revered by Tāntrikas seeking a greater understanding of the supernatural worlds.

NOTES

1. *History of the Tantric Religion: A Historical, Ritualistic, and Philosophical Study* (New Delhi: Manohar, 1982), 1.
2. Ibid., 66.
3. Ibid., 341.
4. My field sites were primarily Calcutta and Bakreswar. I interviewed nearly twenty Tāntrikas during the years 1983–84 and 1993–94.
5. Descriptions along these lines are found widely in Bengali popular literature, especially in the biographies of Śākta saints, such as Bāmākṣepā, and the paperback worship texts found at Śākta shrines, such as the *Ḍākinī Tantra*.
6. André Padoux, 'Hindu Tantrism' in *The Encyclopedia of Religion*, ed. Mircea Eliade (New York: Macmillan, 1987), 14: 279.
7. See David N. Lorenzen, *The Kāpālikas and Kālamukhas: Two Lost Śaivite Sects* (Berkeley: University of California Press, 1972).
8. In Somadeva's eleventh century *Kathāsaritsāgara*, a Kāpālika worships a corpse within a ritual circle, or *maṇḍala*, to gain power over a woman with whom he has fallen in love. Also in this text, a Kāpālika brings a woman back to life while she is already on a blazing funeral pyre and takes her to his cave by using his magical powers. Her husband follows and throws the

Kāpālika's magical *khaṭvāṅga* staff into the Ganges River. Somadeva comments, 'Thus heretics, who make a mockery of the *Śivāgamas* for the pleasure of evil accomplishments, fall (into ruin), as they had already fallen (into sin).' Cited in Lorenzen, *Kāpālikas and Kālamukhas*, 64. For another example, see Bhavabhuti's use of the Kāpālika motif in his *Mālatimādhava* play.

9. See Cynthia Ann Humes, 'Wrestling with Kālī: South Asian and British Constructions of the Dark Goddess,' in *Encountering Kālī: At the Margins, At the Center, In the West*, eds. Rachel Fell McDermott and Jeffrey J. Kripal (Berkeley: University of California Press, 2003), 145–68.
10. I was advised by many scholars and pandits in West Bengal not to do research on Tāntrikas, who were said to be corrupt magicians and dangerous people. However, none of the people I found who called themselves Tāntrikas appeared to fit this stereotype.
11. Selected verses from the *Nīlutantram*, ed. Jyotirlāl Dās (Calcutta: Nababhārat Publishers, 1388 [1981]), chap. 16, 'Śavasādhanapaddhati,' lines 23–113. This is a Sanskrit text with Bengali translation. All English translations are my own.
12. Jonathan Parry, 'Sacrificial Death and the Necrophagous Ascetic,' in *Death and the Regeneration of Life*, eds. Maurice Bloch and Jonathan Parry (New York: Cambridge University Press, 1982), 78.
13. Ibid., 104–5.
14. *Aghorī* practice in the cremation ground is said to grant many *siddhis*, or powers, including curing the sick, raising the dead, flying in the air, and entering other bodies, as well as control of spirits.
15. Bengal, too, has its share of Śaivite *aghorīs*. The Bakreswar Temple is a gathering place for many of them, and informants warned me not to visit an *aghorī* living nearby, because he tended to throw excrement and parts of corpses at visitors. Buddhadeb Chaudhuri describes a Bakreswar *sādhu* known as Aghorī bābā or Jaṭā bābā, who lived in a hut near the burning ground and Śiva temple. It was said that he would construct a sitting platform made of corpses and cook his meals with the fat of dead bodies. The local villagers respected him and believed that he protected them through his divine powers. When an epidemic broke out, it was believed that he had stopped it by absorbing its evil, from which he died. See Buddhadeb Chaudhuri, *The Bakreshwar Temple: A Study of Continuity and Change* (Delhi: Inter-India, 1981), 22–23.
16. Nanda Lal Ghosha, 'How to Make a Demon Subservient to Your Will,' *North Indian Notes and Queries* 5, no. 4 (July 1895): 57.
17. Benoy Kumar Sarkar, *The Folk Element in Hindu Culture: A Contribution to Socio-Religious Studies in Hindu Folk-institutions* (1917; rpt., New Delhi: Cosmo, 1972), 89–90. Even in 1917, Sarkar mentions that these rites were uncommon. *Maśān* is a local idiom for *śmaśān*.
18. This ritual was cited by Apurba Chandra Barthakuria in his book *The*

Kapalikas: A Critical Study of the Religion, Philosophy and Literature of a Tantric Sect (Calcutta: Sanskrit Pustak Bhandar, 1984), 30.

19. Vidya Dehejia, *Yogini, Cult and Temples: A Tantric Tradition* (New Delhi: National Museum, 1986), 59.
20. The phrase 'net of mantras' derives from *Nīla Tantra* 72: 'Having brought the corpse to the place of *śava sādhana*, he should first wash it off. Then he should perform *nyāsa* over the whole [body], thus creating a web or net of *nyāsa* [*nyāsajal*].'
21. Lorenzen, *Kāpālikas and Kālamukhas*, 13–14.
22. Cited in ibid., 62.
23. R.N. Saletore, *Indian Witchcraft* (New Delhi: Abhinav, 1981), 73–75.
24. *Nīlatantram*, ed. Dās (see n. 11 above). It is interesting that when everything is going well in the ritual, Śiva is said to be in control. When, however, there is the threat of trouble, it is the Goddess who is invoked for aid.
25. David R. Kinsley, 'The Death That Conquers Death: Dying to the World in Medieval Hinduism,' in *Religious Encounters with Death: Insights from the History and Anthropology of Religions*, ed. Frank Reynolds and Earle H. Waugh (University Park: Pennsylvania State University Press, 1977), 100.
26. From the *Devī Gītā*, cited in Jadunath Sinha, *The Cult of Divine Power: Saktisadhana* (Calcutta: Sinha, 1977), 87. Similar descriptions are found in the sixteenth-century *Tantrasāra* of Kṛṣṇānanda Āgambāgīś and in the medieval *Kālī Tantra*.
27. Chintaharan Chakravarti, *Tantras: Studies on Their Religion and Literature* (Calcutta: Punthi Pustak, 1963), 88.
28. Sir John Woodroffe, *The Serpent Power: Being the Ṣaṭ-Cakra-Nirūpaṇa and Pādukā-Pañcaka* (1913; 14th edn., Madras: Ganesh, 1989), 204n.1.
29. Sriyukta Siva Candra Vidyarnava Bhattacarya Mahodaya, *Tantra-Tattva*, ed. Sir John Woodroffe as *Principles of Tantra* (1914; 5th edn., Madras: Ganesh, 1978), 2: 318–19.
30. Ibid., 1: 140. Slightly rephrased.
31. Ibid., 2: 298.
32. Ibid., 296.
33. Ibid., 256–57.
34. This is a conglomerate story from both informants and literature. For a good middle ground version, see Swami Tattwananda, *The Saints of India* (Calcutta: Nirmalendu Bikash Sen, n.d.), 87–91.
35. *Kālī Tantra*, ed. Paṇḍit Nityānanda Smṛtitīrtha (Calcutta: Nababharata, 1388 [1981]), 6.8–11, 36, 40. Sanskrit text, with Bengali translation.
36. Bhattacharya, *Tantra-Tattva*, 360.
37. For instance, see P.V. Jagadisa Ayyar, *The Legends of Vikramaditya* (Calcutta: D. Bose, 1924). Ironically, King Vikramāditya is also a devotee of Kālī who performs Tantric feats, but he is a Tantric hero rather than a villain.

38. Shaikh Chilli, *Folk-tales of Hindustan* (Bahadurganj: Bhuwaneswari Asrama, 1920), 126.
39. *Nīla Tantra* 6.71–73: 'As to the goal of *śava sādhana*, if the corpse obtained is a boy of more than two years old, or aged five years, or a young man, or if it is a woman pregnant for seven or eight months, or if the corpse obtained is a Caṇḍāla or some other very low caste person, then this corpse will quickly bring success (lit., be fruitful).'
40. Bhattacharyya, *History of the Tantric Religion*, 137.
41. Ibid., 137.
42. Kālī priest, interview, Calcutta, 1994.
43. The *uttarā sādhikā* helps, and often guides, the male practitioner in the performance of Tantric ritual. In the case mentioned here, she was a renunciant *sannyāsinī*.
44. Kālī priest, interview, Bolpur, 1994.
45. This *sādhikā* had not performed the *śava sādhanā* ritual, through she knew many Tāntrikas who had done so.
46. *Sādhikā,* interview, Bakreswar, 1993. While some Tāntrikas believe that ghosts stay with their skulls and will serve whoever performs proper meditation on them, others believe that ghosts may only obey one person, in exchange for mantras that will liberate them. Once they gain these mantras, they are freed from attachment to the body and place, and travel the spiritual path to rebirth or to afterlife worlds. If anybody else wants supernatural help at that site, he or she must contact a different ghost. While some of the *pīṭhas* gain power and notoriety from the presence of such ghosts, most have power from a more traditional source, such as a body part of the goddess Satī.
47. *Sādhikā,* interview, Bakreswar, 1993.
48. *Sādhaka,* interview, Tārāpīṭha Temple, 1984.
49. Xerox shop owner, interview, Calcutta, 1994.
50. Kālī kīrtanīya, interview, Calcutta, 1993.
51. Ashram head, interview, Jadavpur, 1993.

6

Corpses, Severed Heads, and Sex

Reflections on the Daśamahāvidyās

DAVID R. KINSLEY

The Mahāvidyās are a group of goddesses, usually ten (*daśa*) in number, who bestow *vidyā* (wisdom), and who are prominent primarily in Tantric literature and in a few late Śākta Purāṇas and Upapurāṇas (minor, later, or subsidiary Purāṇas). The order in which the Mahāvidyās are given varies somewhat, as do the goddesses included in the group. In contemporary sources and calendar art (see fig. 9), in the following order, we find: (1) Kālī, (2) Tārā, (3) Tripurasundarī (Ṣoḍaśī), (4) Bhuvaneśvarī, (5) Chinnamastā, (6) Bhairavī, (7) Dhūmāvatī, (8) Bagalāmukhī, (9) Mātaṅgī, and (10) Kamalā. The ten are described in remarkably similar detail.

1. Kālī is black, which is in fact what her name means. She has a fierce countenance, stands on the supine body of the god Śiva, and has four arms. Her upper left hand wields a bloodied cleaver, and her lower left hand holds a severed head. Her upper right hand makes the sign of 'fear not', and her lower right hand makes the gesture of bestowing boons. She is naked, apart from a garland of severed heads and a girdle of bloodied arms; her hair is unbound and disheveled; and she is often standing in a cremation ground surrounded by jackals or on a battlefield. Her lips are sometimes said to gleam with fresh blood, and she has large fangs. Sometimes she is shown in 'reverse' sexual intercourse (which in the Indian context means that the woman is on top) with the great 'auspicious' god, Śiva. Although the texts indicate that she is seated on Śiva, iconographically it is more common to see her standing on her

Fig. 9: Calendar art illustration of the ten Mahāvidyās.

lover. Kālī is almost always mentioned as the first of the Mahāvidyās and occupies a preeminent place in the group. In some texts and in some settings, it is clear that the other Mahāvidyās are understood to arise from her and to be her different forms.

2. Tārā is usually given as the second Mahāvidyā, and in appearance she is similar to Kālī: she is dark; her left foot is placed on a corpse or on Śiva; she wears a tiger skin; her hair is tied in a long braid; she is potbellied (which may suggest that she is pregnant); and she has four arms. In her left hands she holds a knife and a severed head; and her right hands make the signs of giving boons and granting fearlessness. She often stands in the midst of a cremation fire.

3. Ṣoḍaśī (also known as Tripurasundarī, Lalitā, and Rājarājeśvarī) is a beautiful young girl of sixteen with a red complexion. She is sometimes shown astride Śiva in sexual intercourse. Their pedestal

or couch is supported by the gods Brahmā, Viṣṇu, and Rudra, with the fourth member being either Indra or Yama. Sometimes she is said to sit on a lotus that emerges from the navel of Śiva, who is reclining below her. Her four arms hold a noose, goad, bow, and arrows.

4. Bhuvaneśvarī, who is said to nourish the three worlds, holds a piece of fruit in one of her four hands, makes the sign of assurance with another, and holds a goad and a noose in the other two. Her breasts are large and ooze milk. She has a bright, light complexion and smiles pleasantly.

5. Chinnamastā—she with the severed head—has cut off her own head with a sword (fig. 10). Her left hand supports her head on a platter, and her right hand holds the sword with which she cut it off. Three jets of blood gush from her neck: one stream enters the mouth of her severed head; the other two enter the mouths of two female companions. Chinnamastā stands on the copulating bodies of Rati and her husband Kāma, the deities of passion and sexual lust. They, in turn, are lying on a lotus or occasionally a cremation pyre. Sometimes Chinnamastā is shown astride Śiva copulating with him as he lies beneath her. Her hair is loose, and she is naked.

6. Bhairavī has a fierce appearance; her primary role in the cosmic process is destruction. Her complexion is said to be as bright as thousands of rising suns. She wears a garland of skulls and clothes made from the skins of demons she has killed; her feet and breasts are covered with blood. Her four hands hold a rosary and a book and make the signs of fearlessness and granting wishes. The *Kālikā Purāṇa* (74.90–94) says that her eyes roll from intoxication and that she stands on a corpse.

7. Dhūmāvatī is tall, with a pale complexion and a stern, unsmiling face. She is dressed as a widow, in white clothes with no adornments. Her clothes are dirty and her hair disheveled. She is toothless, her breasts long and pendulous, and her nose large and crooked. She is hungry and thirsty, has a quarrelsome nature, and rides a crow or is seated on a chariot. She holds a winnowing basket and sometimes a trident.

8. Bagalāmukhī means 'she who has the head of a crane'. Typically, however, she is depicted with a human head, and the crane is present as her vehicle, or *vāhana*. She usually sits on a throne of jewels, which is sometimes in the midst of a body of water. She is dressed in a yellow sari. In one hand she holds a club, with which she is about to beat a dark-complexioned enemy. With another hand she is pulling his tongue. Sometimes she sits on a corpse (see fig. 11).

9. Mātaṅgī is usually portrayed as a beautiful young woman with a dark or black complexion. The moon adorns her long hair, and she sits on a jeweled throne. She wears a beautiful robe and a garland of flowers. Her four hands hold a goad, noose, sword, and club. Her eyes are described as intoxicated from passion.

10. Kamalā is a beautiful young woman with a golden complexion. Two elephants flank her and pour pitchers of water or nectar on her while she sits on a lotus and holds lotuses in her hands. She is clearly a form of the goddess Lakṣmī, one of whose common epithets is Kamalā, lotus.

It is not clear either historically or structurally how and why this group of goddesses has been brought together to form the Mahāvidyās. It is an odd combination of goddesses. Some of the individual goddesses are very well known, such as Kālī and Kamalā. Others are obscure and hardly known at all outside the group, such as Bagalāmukhī and Dhūmāvatī. Each goddess has her own particular history and distinct meaning. Despite the diversity, there are several striking characteristics of the group as a whole that invite comment and interpretation. I should like to comment on three such characteristics. First, death imagery, especially corpses and cremation grounds, is prominent in Mahāvidyā iconography. Second, severed heads and skulls are central in several of the goddesses' depictions and descriptions. And third, sexual intercourse or overtly sexual themes are frequently mentioned in connection with several members of the group. Narendra Nath Bhattacharyya, in a conversation with me in Calcutta in October 1992—appropriately, during Kālī Pūjā—said that when Kālī stands on Śiva, as in the Dakṣinā-Kālī images, the message is sexual: it

Fig. 10: Chinnamastā, from a street display of the ten Mahāvidyās at Kālī Pūjā, Calcutta, November 1988. Photograph by Rachel Fell McDermott.

Fig. 11: Calendar art depiction of Bagalā.

symbolizes her dominance during intercourse. Such sexual union between the two is often actually shown and is sometimes part of the *dhyāna* (meditation) mantras of other forms of Kālī. Death imagery and sexual imagery are often dramatically conjoined. What might be the significance of these striking features of Mahāvidyā iconography and cult?

CORPSES AND CREMATION GROUNDS

Corpses are remarkably often associated with the Mahāvidyās, and cremation grounds seem to be highly favored as places in which to worship members of the group. Kālī, Tārā, Bagalāmukhī, Tripurasundarī, Mātaṅgī, and Bhairavī all stand or sit upon corpses. Kālī, Tārā, Chinnamastā, and Dhūmāvatī are often described or pictured as dwelling in cremation grounds. On several occasions, the *Mantramahodadhiḥ*, a text that focuses on the Mahāvidyās, stipulates that *sādhana* (spiritual endeavor) should be done while sitting on a corpse or on a place where a corpse has recently been buried. For example, in an almost matter-of-fact way, the text says, 'Bringing a corpse on a Tuesday or Saturday . . . bury it one foot deep in the ground beneath the door of the house. Then, sitting on that spot . . . perform 108 Japas [repetitions] every day . . . . Through such a Japa for eight days the [*sādhaka*, 'adept'] becomes the lord of various Siddhis ['perfections', magical powers].'[1] The same text, again, instructs the *sādhaka* as follows: 'Sitting on a Śavāsana [a corpse seat] . . . the Sādhaka should begin the Japa at sunrise and continue it without break till the next sunrise. Through such a [process] the Sādhaka becomes fearless and master of various Siddhis.'[2] In discussing the empowerment or perfection of mantras, which is accomplished primarily by repetition, the *Mantramahodadhiḥ* says: 'A Sādhaka who, sitting on a corpse, performs one lakh (100,000) [repetitions] of this mantra, his mantra becomes potent and all his cherished desires are soon fulfilled.'[3] In discussing the relative power of different 'seats', the *Mantramahodadhiḥ* describes the *komalāsana*, which uses an aborted fetus or the corpse of a five-year-old child, and the *viṣṭarāsana*, which is made of woven grass and 'consecrated with a corpse'.[4] The *Tantrasāra*, a text devoted primarily to the Mahāvidyās, has detailed descriptions of both *śava sādhana* (spiritual endeavor with a corpse)[5] and *cita sādhana* (spiritual endeavor on a cremation pyre).[6] These rituals are not described as applicable to a particular goddess among the Mahāvidyās, so probably both techniques are appropriate in the worship of any, or at least several, of the Mahāvidyās.

It is important to reflect on these associations if we wish to come to an understanding of certain individual Mahāvidyās and of the group as a whole. As a group, they seem to be associated with a type of spirituality that relies heavily on death imagery. This is perhaps most explicit in the case of Kālī, the first and most important of the group. But corpses and cremation grounds are central in descriptions of several of the other goddesses as well, and worship of nearly all of them is said to be most effective if undertaken in a cremation ground.

It is tempting to suppose that this death imagery belongs to the ascetic, world-denying vein of Hinduism, in which renunciation of worldly desire is central. In such a context, death imagery and death rituals make sense: they reinforce the renunciant's decision to pursue spiritual liberation by giving up the lures of the world. Meditation upon death puts worldly pleasures in a perspective where their attraction can be minimized or subverted altogether.[7] And surely corpses and cremation grounds do play this role in Mahāvidyā *sādhana*.

The cremation ground also plays the role of a 'forbidden thing', a kind of sixth *tattva*, which the heroic *sādhaka* must confront in order to glimpse the underlying nature of reality, which is that all things, no matter how polluted or terrible, are pervaded by *śakti* (energy or power).[8] To meditate upon, to meditate in, or to live in a cremation ground functions as a spiritual test. In what has been termed the '*sāmadhi* [heightened or intensified consciousness] of horror',[9] the adept discovers a distaste for the world that encourages him or her to see beyond or through its lures to underlying spiritual truths. The goddess herself is sometimes described as putting the male gods through similar tests. In the *Mahābhāgavata Purāṇa*, she assumes a terrible form to test Brahmā, Viṣṇu, and Śiva. To avoid looking at her, Brahmā turns his head away, and Viṣṇu closes his eyes and plunges into the cosmic ocean. Only Śiva is able to continue to gaze on her, and for this heroic ability she blesses him to become a great yogi.[10] In a similar scenario, the goddess appears to the three male gods as a rotting corpse. Śiva thinks her stench is fragrant incense, and he takes her corpse on his breast. The goddess blesses him by placing his *liṅga* in her *yoni*.[11] The Tantric *sādhaka* is tested, as it were, in the cremation ground. The challenge is for the spiritual aspirant to be able to perceive the presence of the goddess even in the most terrible, gruesome, and polluting objects and places.

There is some evidence that cremation grounds are sometimes used for initiation into certain Tantric cults.[12] Insofar as initiation rites often involve the symbolic death and rebirth of the initiate,[13] a cremation ground seems an appropriate venue. It is a place of transformation, where people die to one mode of being and are born to another. It is the locale of the greatest human transformation, that from life to death. If the candidate's initiation into a Tantric cult is meant to signify dramatic transformation, the cremation ground is a most suitable place for it.

However, something beyond this seems to be involved in the use of corpses and cremation grounds for Mahāvidyā worship, because my fieldwork reveals that people undertaking these rituals are often householders who have not renounced the world, are not engaged in ascetic practices, do not seem primarily concerned with affirming the underlying divinity of the forbidden or the polluted, and are not undergoing initiation into a Tantric cult. It is also clear from their testimony as well as from Tantric texts that the desires that motivate this type of spirituality are often worldly: power over one's enemies, kingly authority, eloquence in speech, and so on. The aim of this *sādhana*, that is, seems to be not so much to triumph over the lures of the world or even to see through its illusory façade to its underlying reality as *śakti*, but rather to gain success and well-being in the world. Corpses and cremation grounds seem to function as more than dramatic reminders of the transience of worldly existence and the futility of physical and mental desires, and thus as appropriate accoutrements or contexts for the spiritual quest. They also seem to function as objects and places of power by means of which or in which extraordinary achievements may be obtained. Power seems to accrue to the individual who associates with corpses and frequents cremation grounds. Why might this be so?

Texts describing the Mahāvidyās and their worship assume the existence of a world of spirits that is parallel to the physical world and impinges upon it. This assumption persists in and to a great extent dominates contemporary Hinduism in both its popular and its refined, literary forms. The inhabitants of this world include gods, goddesses, *rākṣasas*, *asuras*, *vetālas*, yoginīs, *ḍākinīs*, *gandharvas*, *kiṃnaras*, *siddhas*, *mūḍhā bhaginīs*, *pretas*, *piśācas*, *nāgas*, and other classes of beings that are not visible under usual conditions but that appear from time to time in the physical world. All of these beings are more powerful than humans or have some ability or cunning that surpasses normal human abilities. Their manifestations within the visible world of human beings can be beneficial or harmful, unexpected or willed. Examples of harmful and unexpected eruptions are illnesses, bad luck, and accidents. These are often attributed to the actions of *bhaginīs* and *pretas* (spirits of the dead, ghosts), but also to other inimical spirits or deities. Such eruptions may result from either bad karma on the part of the victim (who caused the disease by wicked deeds or thoughts) or unsatisfied passions or desires on the part of the spirit being, who tries to satisfy them by possessing the human victim. Much of Hindu belief and practice concerns warding off or dealing with such inimical intrusions into human affairs.

On the other hand, another large part of Hindu ritual and practice deliberately seeks contact with this invisible world for a variety of purposes, and it is in this context that much Tantric ritual probably should be understood. In many cases, Tantric rituals are aimed at crossing the barrier between the visible and invisible worlds, either by allowing the *sādhaka* to enter the spirit world, or by enticing or forcing spirit beings to appear in the visible world. The goal of the *sādhaka* is often made explicit: to gain a blessing, usually in the form of some kind of power or ability, from a being in the spirit world—usually a deity. Contacting the spirit world deliberately (as opposed to being contacted by it unexpectedly) is also assumed to be both difficult and dangerous, and often terrifying. This practice of seeking otherworldly contact is where the importance of corpses and cremation grounds becomes understandable in Tantric worship.

Where might one hope to contact the unseen, spiritual world? Where might the barrier between the visible and invisible worlds be most permeable? One place is certainly the cremation ground, which is where Hindus believe that all human beings eventually and inevitably make contact with the spirit world as they pass from life to death. Indeed, to a great extent, this is precisely what death is: the transition from one mode of being to another, from that of a physical to a nonphysical being. The cremation ground is the 'terminal' where such transitions routinely take place. In this sense, it represents a more or less permanent 'opening' to the spirit world and the beings that inhabit it. It is a place of spirit traffic, of coming and going from one world to another.[14] It is a liminal place,[15] betwixt and between worlds, where radical transformations take place, and contact between worlds is relatively common.

Corpses—particularly of the recent dead—are vehicles with which one can traverse worlds. A recently dead person, particularly if the proper death rituals have not yet been done, still hovers in the physical world while already having been transformed into a spirit being. He or she is a liminal being with a foot in each world, as it were. He or she is on the way to the 'other world'; to ride that person's corpse, or otherwise associate with or dominate it, is to make that transition as well. References to reviving or gaining control over a corpse, or the spirit that inhabits it, are not infrequent. The *Uḍḍīśa Tantra* gives mantras for reviving a corpse.[16] The *Kathāsaritsāgara* also mentions revitalizing corpses, gaining control over them in order to use them at will, and acquiring the ability to fly by eating human flesh.[17] Elsewhere we read, 'Dead and putrefying corpses submerged near cremation grounds are still brought to life by the force of the sādhaka's mantras, and made to render aid to sādhana and siddhi.'[18] These references make it clear that a corpse is a numinous object particularly useful for making contact with the spirit world and acquiring powers and abilities associated with spirit beings.

This impression is reinforced in the description of *śava sādhana* in the *Tantrasāra*. In the context of worshipping the corpse that the *sādhaka* intends to become the seat of a goddess, he addresses the body, saying: 'You are the lord of all heroic persons, lord of kulas, blissful, you are the form of Ānandabhairava [a form of Śiva], and you are the seat of the goddess. I am heroic myself, and I bow to you. Please arise for the purpose of making my worship of Caṇḍikā fruitful.'[19] At another point, the *sādhaka* sits on the corpse in the manner of riding a horse. Later, the *sādhaka* binds the feet of the corpse with a silken cord, remounts the corpse, and presses its hands firmly down while reciting a particular deity's mantra. It seems clear that the *sādhaka* is acting out mastery or control over the corpse and by association, the corpse's spirit.[20]

Yet this description does not clearly delineate whom the *sādhaka* is trying to contact or propitiate in *śava sādhana*. Is it the spirit of the corpse itself, or is it another spirit or goddess? Exactly whom the *sādhaka* might be worshipping and whom he might be trying to control is not indicated in this description of *śava sādhana*. At some points, it seems clear that he is propitiating the corpse itself, and at other points, the corpse as the seat or location of a deity. Finally, the matter of whose voice might issue forth from the corpse and address the *sādhaka* in this ritual remains unclear. It might be the deity whose mantra he is reciting, or the spirit of the corpse, or even a *preta* or *bhūta* (ghost) now associated with the corpse.

The *Tantrasāra* mentions yet another possibility: a goddess named Karṇa Piśācī, who lives in the heart of a corpse. She favors the successful *sādhaka* by coming invisibly to him and whispering in his ear the correct answer to any question. The text says: 'Ascending her, getting her power, he [the *sādhaka*] can go anywhere and see the past, present, and future.'[21]

Karṇa Piśācī has clear shamanistic overtones. A central theme in shamanism is the acquisition of a spirit who gives the shaman special or mystical knowledge from the spirit world. Both in *śava sādhana* and in the propitiation of Karṇa Piśācī, it seems that the *sādhaka* is interested in gaining access to such a spirit.[22] It is in cooperation with, or through the power of, this spirit that the adept comes to possess certain magical powers for overcoming, controlling, or defeating his or her enemies. Cremation grounds are believed to be the places where such 'spirit allies', or 'helpers' may be found, and corpses are often the actual sources of such spirits.

Thus, though householders who worship the Mahāvidyās might not identify themselves as Tāntrikas per se, they are nevertheless heir to a Tantric tradition that valorizes the belief that power accrues to the individual who associates with corpses and frequents cremation grounds.

SKULLS AND SEVERED HEADS

Another remarkable feature of Mahāvidyā iconography is the prevalence of skulls and chopped-off heads. Kālī, Tārā, Chinnamastā, Mātaṅgī, and Bhairavī all wear garlands of skulls or severed heads and are often said to hold a freshly cut head or a skull in their hands. Skulls also adorn Tārā's forehead and sometimes Kālī's hair. Some texts devoted to worship of the Mahāvidyās prescribe skulls as seats upon which effective *sādhana* may be performed. The *Mantramahodadhiḥ*, for example, stipulates that the *sādhaka* should bring a human skull to a remote place in the woods, purify it, bury it, and perform worship while seated on that spot.[23] The most dramatic example of a chopped-off head in the context of the Mahāvidyās, of course, is that of Chinnamastā, a Mahāvidyā herself, who has severed her own head. What might be the significance of all these dislodged and displaced skulls and heads for Mahāvidyā iconography and practice?

Perhaps the most obvious interpretation of these skulls and heads concerns head offerings. Animal (and sometimes human) sacrifice was fairly common in the Hindu tradition, and the typical way of killing the victim was by decapitation. During the Vedic period, animal sacrifices were commonly offered to many deities; later, most blood sacrifices were directed to goddesses. Contemporary Hinduism continues the centuries-old tradition of blood sacrifice, which is still almost invariably associated with certain goddesses. At some goddess temples, daily sacrifices are made, usually of goats and chickens. In almost all cases, the animal's head is cut off and offered to the image of the goddess, often on a platter. The *Tantrasāra* devotes a section to *bali*, 'blood sacrifice', and makes it clear that the proper method of killing the victim (which according to the text may be a human being) is by decapitation.[24] The chopped-off heads that several of the Mahāvidyās wear or sit upon can be thought of as sacrificial offerings. That these human heads are always male in Mahāvidyā iconography is still reflected in contemporary practice, which uses male animals almost exclusively.

A tradition of voluntary head offering to goddesses may also shed some light on the prominence of skulls and heads in the Mahāvidyā iconography and cult. The eleventh-century CE Tamil text *Kaliṅgattuparaṇi* contains a gruesome description of a Kālī temple in South India: 'Like the roaring sound of ocean waves, the shouts of heroes offering their heads in return for the bestowal of boons were echoing all over the area.'[25] In another passage from this text, 'the process of offering a head is portrayed. The sacrificer cut his head at the bottom of the neck and placed it on the hands of Kālī. The head thus presented sang the greatness of Kālī while the remaining trunk stood saluting the Goddess.'[26] In Pallava sculpture particularly, but elsewhere as well, the theme is quite common, although whether the sculptures depict actual devotional suicide by self-decapitation is not certain.[27]

Examples of a devotee offering his or her head in a fit of devotional frenzy are found in many Hindu texts. In the Tamil epic *Śilappadikaram*, the goddess Aiyai, who is worshipped by hunters, routinely receives blood sacrifices, and she also accepts the blood that flows from the severed heads of her devotees.[28] There is also a north Indian story associated with the Jvālamukhī temple in Himachal Pradesh that features a head offering. According to the story, a devotee of the goddess Jvālamukhī named Dhyānu wished to visit her temple but was prohibited from doing so by the Muslim emperor Akbar, who claimed that the Hindu goddess had no power. The emperor declared Dhyānu could proceed only if he agreed to leave his horse behind and Akbar would kill it. If Dhyānu's goddess were able to revive the horse, Akbar pledged, he would spare Dhyānu's life. Dhyānu accepted the challenge. Akbar duly killed Dhyānu's horse and locked its carcass in a room. At Jvālāmukhī's temple, Dhyānu performed devotional ritual to the goddess, but she did not appear or answer his pleas to prove her power to the emperor. In desperation, Dhyānu decided to offer his own head to the goddess. Taking a sword, he was about to cut off his head, when she suddenly appeared and granted him his boon of restoring his horse to life. In some versions of the tale, Dhyānu actually cuts off his head, which the goddess subsequently restores. Actual decapitation is the version usually shown in pictures, with Dhyānu kneeling in front of the goddess, offering her his head on a platter. A large tableau in a recessed niche of the Jvālāmukhī temple depicts the story. Dhyānu kneels before the goddess holding his severed head in his two hands. The practice of cutting off one's tongue, I was told, is practiced to this day at the temple. In these cases, as with Dhyānu, the goddess is believed to restore the devotee's tongue in recognition of his or her devotion.

In some sense, skulls and severed heads are objects of power containing special qualities, particularly for ritual purposes. Their use in iconography to represent letters[29] or sounds, the 'seeds' from which all creation proceeds, is no doubt connected to the mouth or head as the source of language or sound. The head as the chief of the body's parts also houses the person's essential being. Without the head, a person is without identity. This belief is made clear in myths concerning transposed heads, in which the identity of the person follows the head, not the rest of the body.[30]

Another possible interpretation of skulls and severed heads accords well with the importance of corpses and cremation grounds in Mahāvidyā worship and iconography. The severed head or skull, especially when worn as an ornament of one of the Mahāvidyā goddesses, might be thought to symbolize transformation. By means of spiritual exercises in the cremation ground and with corpses, the *sādhaka* seeks transformation through a direct encounter with the spirit world to acquire powers associated with spirit beings: superior power or even omnipotence; expanded knowledge, or omniscience; transcendence of time and space, including precognition or clairvoyance; and the ability to change form at will, to become small or light, or to fly.[31] In short, the adept seeks to transcend the limitations of the physical, earthbound human condition in some manner by direct association with the spirit world.

That these spirit powers often denote transcendence of corporeal limitations and the expansion of consciousness—the ability of the consciousness to drift free of the body and roam at will—suggests a divorce of body and mind, the liberation of the mind from the body. Those severed heads and skulls might be symbolic of *sādhakas* who, by a particular goddess's blessing or their own efforts, have accomplished these feats. They might be thought of as symbolic of transformed consciousness in two ways. First, they have achieved the status of spirit beings by having died; the theme of symbolic death in many religions functions in just this way, namely, to denote a drastic change in status.[32] Second, the severed heads exemplify consciousness that has transcended the limitations of physical, worldly existence: the mind (symbolized by the head) has left the body and is no longer attached to or limited by it.

A common motif in world religions is the quest by a spiritual master to acquire techniques for transcending the human condition. The shaman and the mystic are both examples of this motif. Both undertake spiritual journeys to achieve an unmediated and transformative experience of the spirit world, and in so doing, they must often undergo a symbolic death and dismemberment. The shaman is often said to be torn asunder by spiritual beings, who then reconstitute his or her body with indestructible pieces, signifying a new, transcendent condition. Just such a dismemberment was described by Pāgal Haranāth (b. 1865), a Bengali Vaiṣṇava. While traveling in Kashmir, he fell into a deep trance. Caitanya, the famous Bengali Vaiṣṇava reformer, appeared to him, divided his body into sixty-four parts, and then proceeded to clean and purify them. When his body was reassembled, Haranāth had acquired magical, shamanic powers, that is, expanded consciousness.[33]

Mystics often pass through a 'dark night of the soul', in which they feel as if they have died, before experiencing the bliss of union with the divine. In the cremation ground, in association with corpses, Tantric *sādhakas* undergo a symbolic death before entering the spirit world, where they are reconstituted as spiritual beings equipped with powers that go beyond the limitations of earthy existence. The severed heads that the goddesses wear might signify both the symbolic death and the transcendent consciousness of successful *sādhakas*. That all of these chopped-off heads seem to wear a look of peace and satisfaction seems to confirm this interpretation.

SEXUALITY AND AWAKENED CONSCIOUSNESS

Mahāvidyā mythology, iconography, worship, and ritual are often dominated by implicit and explicit sexual symbolism. Sexual intercourse is explicitly portrayed in the *dhyāna* mantras and portraits of Kālī, Chinnamastā, and Tārā,[34] and most of the Mahāvidyās are described as sexually attractive and powerful. The mythology concerning the origin of particular individual Mahāvidyā goddesses (for example, Chinnamastā and Mātaṅgī) stresses sexual tension. The *yantras* and *maṇḍalas* or mystic diagrams that represent the Mahāvidyās contain implicit sexual symbolism, and the central metaphor of awakening the *kuṇḍalinī śakti,* or serpentine power, residing in the spine may be interpreted as the arousal of sexual energy. It is also the case that most of the Mahāvidyās may be worshipped through the *pañcatattva* ritual, in which sexual intercourse is the culminating act. The centrality of sexual imagery in Mahāvidyā worship and iconography deserves further comment and analysis at this point.

To a great extent, sexual imagery in Mahāvidyā materials must be related to the Tantric philosophy and ritual that are its primary religious context. This imagery can be understood on several different, but related, levels. On the most abstract level, sexual imagery reflects the Tantric vision of reality as the dynamic interaction and tension between the two great principles, Śiva and Śakti. As the fundamental underlying principles of reality, the basic components of the essential texture of the cosmos, Śiva and Śakti have been understood in a wide variety of ways. Several sophisticated philosophical systems center on the meaning and interpretation of these two principles, Kashmir Śaivism perhaps being the most developed and systematic. Śiva and Śakti are present in the mutual attraction and complementarity of the sexes. At the level of human existence and human relationships, they are inherent and embodied in individual males and females. In the context of Tantra, sexual attraction, sexual behavior, and sexual intercourse suggest the underlying texture of reality, which is the manifestation of the dynamic, energetic, creative, and harmonious interaction of Śiva and Śakti.

At a more concrete, but still fairly coded level, sexual imagery suffuses the *yantras* and *maṇḍalas* associated with all of the Mahāvidyā goddesses (as it does Tantric *maṇḍala* structure and symbolism generally). The dominant forms of the *yantra*—the triangle and the lotus—both have sexual connotations. The triangle, particularly when it is pointing downward, is symbolic of the vulva. A triangle pointing upward is sometimes held to represent the phallus. When the two are superimposed on each other, as in most of the *yantras* representing the individual Mahāvidyās, they denote sexual union. Another feature of *yantra* design is the presence of a small dot called a *bindu* in the very center of the diagram. This dot is often said to represent either the two principles of Śiva and Śakti in union, or the male seed, particularly when it is enclosed in a triangle pointing downward toward the center of the *yantra*. The lotus also has implicit sexual connotations. It is often a symbol of generation, that from which all creation proceeds or that in which all creation is contained. As it opens and blossoms, the cosmos emerges. In this sense, the lotus represents the womb from which the world is born and may be associated with the womb or sexual organ of Śakti, from whom creation emerges, and in whom it is contained.

The *yantras* representing the Mahāvidyās are also charged with a group of powers—male and female deities—who are located at various points in the design. The *sādhaka* places these powers in the *yantra* while either drawing or imagining it during *sādhana*. In many of the Mahāvidyā *yantras*, the petals of the inner lotus are charged with the presence of different forms of Rati and Kāma, deities associated in particular with sexual vitality and desire. In their general structure, then, the Mahāvidyā *yantras* may be understood as schematic renderings of sexual imagery and containers of sexual power. As representations of both the goddess in question and the cosmos generally, which she is held to embody, the *yantra* again expresses the idea that reality, in its basic nature, is sexually charged.

In Mahāvidyā iconography, sexual imagery is often quite explicit. Kālī and Tārā are sometimes shown copulating with Śiva; a copulating couple, usually identifiable as Kāma and Rati, figures in Chinnamastā and Tārā iconography. Sexual motifs and activity also figure prominently in certain Tantric rituals associated with the Mahāvidyās. In the *pañcamakāra* or *pañcatattva* ritual, the culminating act—the fifth *makāra*—is *maithuna*, in which the *sādhaka* and his *śakti* perform ritual sexual intercourse. This act as described in the *Tantrasāra* is highly ritualized.[35] *Maithuna* involves the careful purification of many elements and a lengthy worship by the *sādhaka* of his female companion (the text is written from the male point of view). Some interpreters have suggested that the primary aim of the ritual is for the male *sādhaka* to demonstrate that he has mastered his sexual desires. They claim that he does not ejaculate during intercourse, but redirects his semen 'upward' or inward, thereby controlling or channeling his sexual energy to achieve spiritual ends.[36] In the *Tantrasāra*, however, it is clear that the man does ejaculate into the woman. As he does so, he says a particular prayer comparing his ejaculation to an offering: 'The fire of *ātman* has been made blazing by the offering of clarified butter; by means of my mind ladle I am ever engaged in offering the modality of my senses through the *suṣumnā* channels.'[37] This utterance implies that the *sādhaka* does not withhold his semen, but rather, that he interprets his ejaculation as part of a process that awakens *kuṇḍalinī śakti*. It is not sublimated or curbed sexual activity that awakens the *kuṇḍalinī* but sexual activity properly understood—or perhaps properly appreciated.[38]

Sexual imagery in Mahāvidyā iconography and worship plays a symbolic role. It may be understood metaphorically as suggesting the dynamic polar rhythm of reality, the interaction of Śiva and Śakti that creates and suffuses the cosmos. The *Kulārṇava Tantra* says that the world does not bear the likeness of the *cakra*, the lotus, or the thunderbolt, but rather, the likeness of the *liṅgam* and *yoni*, thus reflecting the form of Śiva and Śakti. Wherever there is the union of the two, 'the devotee experiences deep trance [*samādhi*]'.[39] Sexual imagery also may symbolize awakening consciousness. The rising of the *kuṇḍalinī śakti* and the bliss of her union with Śiva in the highest energy node located at the top of the head (*sahasrāra cakra*) may be symbolized by sexual union. Sexual activity seems an appropriate metaphor for the rousing of the *kuṇḍalinī*, as both are highly energetic processes accompanied by heightened awareness.

On the other hand, it also seems likely that in some cases sexual imagery reflects real practice, as in the *pañcatattva* ritual, in which actual sexual intercourse might be used as a means of awakening the *kuṇḍalinī śakti*. Substitutes may be used in the ritual, however, which implies that sexual intercourse is not essential to the awakening of the *kuṇḍalinī*. Tantric texts sometimes warn that only those of a certain accomplished character and heroic nature should engage in this ritual. To suggest that sexual activity is a necessary part of Mahāvidyā worship would thus be an exaggeration. On the other hand, sexual practices clearly have a role, and for some *sādhakas* in some situations, the Tantric tradition asserts that sexual intercourse may be an option that can lead to an intense spiritual experience.

THE CONJUNCTION OF DEATH AND SEXUAL IMAGERY

It is striking that the imagery of both death and sex should be so central in our Mahāvidyā materials, and that both are so often dramatically juxtaposed in the characterization of these goddesses as well as certain rituals in their worship.

Some Mahāvidyā texts prescribe shocking descriptions of rituals as appropriate to Mahāvidyā worship. In its section on Tārā, for example, the *Mantramahodadhiḥ* says that the *sādhaka* who seeks lordship should sit naked on the heart of a corpse in a cremation ground and offer the goddess one thousand flowers, each covered with his semen, while reciting her mantra.[40] The same section of the text describes a ritual in which the *sādhaka* should imagine the goddess seated on the chest of a corpse engaged in sex with her consort on a fifteen-petaled lotus while the *sādhaka* is also having sexual intercourse. Also in the section on Tārā, the *Mantra-mahodadhiḥ* mentions a ritual in which the *sādhaka* sets a human skull at the place where he is to recite the goddess's mantra. Then, while repeating the mantra, he is to gaze upon, touch, and sexually enjoy a woman.[41] The *Uḍḍīśa Tantra* gives directions for improving the erotic appeal of a woman, which are followed immediately by rules governing *śava sādhana*.[42]

What might this juxtaposition of sex and death imagery mean? I suggest two interpretations. First, Tantric *sādhana*, which is so intimately associated with Mahāvidyā worship, places a premium upon direct, unmediated experience. As mentioned above, Tantric *sādhana* is secret and private. It is undertaken by an individual in a lonely place. Priests are not necessary, and while the *sādhaka*'s guru may be present, or the *sādhaka* may take part in a collective ritual on rare occasions, it is primarily a lone adept who undertakes the rituals described in Mahāvidyā and related Tantric texts. Further, the texts are also explicit concerning at least one of the aims of *sādhana*: to become one with the deity being worshipped, or to be blessed with a vision of the deity—a transformative experience. We may typify the Tantric *sādhaka* as someone who seeks concrete religious experience, for whom rituals are a means to experiencing an intensity of feeling and emotion. Both dying and sex are overwhelming human experiences that can leave a person uprooted from and unprotected by social conventions and ritual insulation. Both, of course, are highly ritualized in almost every culture, precisely because the strong emotions they engender are so apt to cause social disruption. But no amount of ritual can guarantee the taming or orderly channeling of either of these basic human experiences. It is the 'explosive' nature of death and sex imagery that makes them so central in Tantric *sādhana*, which puts such a premium on achieving transformative religious experiences. As symbols, they are particularly powerful in evoking feelings or events that can deeply affect and alter a person—they can trigger the kind of experience the *sādhaka* seeks.

Second, the juxtaposition of death and sex imagery appropriately expresses the nature of reality as constant, and yet simultaneous, creation and destruction. The waxing and waning of all beings and all things, from individual organisms to the infinite cosmos itself, is appropriately suggested in the simultaneous presentation of sexual and death imagery. If such juxtaposed imagery shocks us, it is because we are in the habit of masking the destructive dimension of reality so insistently that its inevitable appearance is upsetting. That sex and death imagery 'do not belong together', that we find the juxtaposition in 'bad taste', is simply an admission that our view of reality is warped and unrealistic. Those Mahāvidyā goddesses who juxtapose sexual and death imagery are icons of revelation to the *sādhaka*, who seeks an expanded consciousness, an awareness of the truth of things that does not pander to wishful thinking concerning one's own mortality and frailty. They are images that help the *sādhaka* tear the veil of illusion.

NOTES

This essay was submitted to the editors in 1994. After David Kinsley's death on 25 April 2000, we corrected and fine-tuned several points in the chapter as minimally as possible by drawing on several of his works, especially David's book *Tantric Visions of the Divine Feminine: The Ten Mahāvidyās* (Berkeley: University of California Press, 1997). We are thankful to Carolyn Kinsley for her permission to publish her late husband's essay.

1. *Mahīdhara's Mantramahodadhiḥ*, ed. and trans. Ram Kumar Rai (Varanasi: Prachya Prakashan, 1992), 1: 214.
2. Ibid., 214.
3. Ibid., 146; see also 145.
4. Ibid., 198.
5. Kṛṣṇānanda Āgamavāgiśa, *Bṛhat Tantrasāra*, ed. Rasikmohan Caṭṭopādhyāy and translated from Sanskrit to Bengali by Candrakumār Tarkālaṅkār (Calcutta: Nababhārat, 1982), 438–44.
6. Ibid., 434–38.
7. See David R. Kinsley, 'The Death That Conquers Death': Dying to the World in Medieval Hinduism,' in Frank E. Reynolds and Earle H. Waugh, eds., *Religious Encounters with Death: Insights from the History and Anthropology of Religions* (University Park: Pennsylvania State University Press, 1977), 97–108.
8. The *pañcatattva* ritual, which is prescribed in left-handed Tantra, includes the partaking of five 'forbidden' things: wine, fish, meat, *mudrā* (some kind of parched grain, possibly a hallucinogenic drug), and sexual intercourse. The logic of the ritual may involve the radical affirmation in a

ritual context that nothing is forbidden, that underlying and pervading all things is *śakti*.

9. The term is used in reference to rituals in the cremation ground by Tantric Buddhists in Nepal by P.H. Pott, *Yoga and Yantra: Their Interrelation and Their Significance for Indian Archaeology* (The Hague: Martinus Nijhoff, 1966), 77.
10. *Mahābhāgavata Purāṇa*, 3.15–70; cited in Wendy Doniger O'Flaherty, *Sexual Metaphors and Animal Symbols in Indian Mythology* (Delhi: Motilal Banarsidass, 1981), 98.
11. *Bṛhaddharma Purāṇa*, 2.31.16–36; cited in O'Flaherty, *Sexual Metaphors and Animal Symbols,* 99.
12. Mark S.G. Dyczkowski, *The Canon of the Śaivāgama and the Kubjikā Tantras of the Western Kaula Tradition* (Albany: State University of New York Press, 1988), 6–7.
13. See Mircea Eliade, *Rites and Symbols of Initiation: The Mysteries of Birth and Rebirth* (New York: Harper & Row, 1958).
14. For a vivid description of the cremation ground as the locale of a host of spirits, see Mary Shepherd Slusser, *Nepal Mandala: A Cultural Study of the Kathmandu Valley* (Princeton, N.J.: University Press, 1982), 1: 333. For a discussion of making contact with spirits in the cremation ground, see Robert Svoboda, *Aghora: At the Left Hand of God* (Albuquerque, N.M.: Brotherhood of Life, 1986), 187–210.
15. See Victor Turner, *The Ritual Process: Structure and Anti-structure* (Harmondsworth, U.K.: Penguin Books, 1969), for a definition and discussion of the 'liminal' as central to many sets of rituals.
16. *Uddīsa Tantra*, chap. 9; cited in S.C. Banerjea, *A Brief History of Tantric Literature* (New Delhi: Naya Prakash, 1988), 325.
17. Banerjea, *Brief History of Tantric Literature*, 496–97.
18. Cited in June McDaniel, *The Madness of the Saints: Ecstatic Religion in Bengal* (Chicago: University of Chicago Press, 1989), 112.
19. *Tantrasāra* 438–44; see also *Kaulāvalī*, chap. 15, and *Nīla-tantra*, chap. 16, summarized in Banerjea, *Brief History of Tantric Literature*, 251–52.
20. At many points in this ritual, it appears that the *sādhaka* is seeking to revive or control the spirit of the corpse, which will then be used as a 'power instrument,' as it were, to bring about desired goals. See Narendra Nath Bhattacharyya, *History of the Tantric Religion: A Historical, Ritualistic, and Philosophical Study* (New Delhi: Manohar, 1982), 137–41.
21. *Tantrasara*, 468.
22. See *Kaulāvalī*, chap. 19, concerning gaining power from a corpse by reviving it. The particular power (*siddhi*) mentioned in this case is the ability to see through solid objects and substances.
23. *Mantramahodadhiḥ*, 214.
24. *Tantrasāra*, 682–83.

25. Cited in R. Nagaswami, *Tantric Cult of South India* (Delhi: Agam Kala Prakashan, 1982), 2.
26. Ibid.
27. J.P. Vogel, 'The Head-Offering to the Goddess in Pallava Sculpture,' *Bulletin of the School of Oriental Studies* 6, no. 2 (1931): 539-43; see also U.N. Ghosal, *Studies in Indian History and Culture* (Bombay: Orient Longman, 1965), 333–40.
28. Prince Ilangô Adigal, *Shilappadikaram*, trans. Alain Daniélou (New York: New Directions, 1965), 539–43.
29. See Sir John Woodroffe, ed., *The Garland of Letters (Varṇamalā)* (Madras: Ganesh, 1922).
30. For examples, see M.B. Emeaneau, trans., 'Jambhaladatta's Version of the Vetālapañcaviṃśati,' *American Oriental Society* 4 (1934): 59–63 (this story of transposed heads is originally from *Kathāsaritsāgara* 6. 80), and Wendy Doniger O' Flaherty, *The Origins of Evil in Hindu Mythology* (Berkeley: University of California Press, 1976), 351, for the theme of transposed heads in the myth of Reṇukā's beheading.
31. The *aṣṭasiddhis*, which are eight superior powers or 'perfections' achieved by means of yoga, include some of these abilities and are ancient in the Hindu tradition. A well-known example of the ability to change form at will, including changing into animal form, is that of Mahiṣāsura, the buffalo demon whom Durgā slays in the *Devī Māhātmya*.
32. Kinsley, 'Death that Conquers Death,' 97–108.
33. McDaniel, *Madness of the Saints*, 58. Bodily dismemberment, significantly including decapitation, is mentioned as part of an Aghora *sādhanā* called *khaṇḍa maṇḍa yoga*. In this ritual, the *sādhaka* cuts off his own limbs and head and throws them into a fire, from which the parts emerge twelve hours later to rejoin the body; see Robert E. Svoboda, *Aghora II: Kundulini* (Albuquerque, N.M.: Brotherhood of Life, 1993), 114.
34. In Ajit Mookerjee and Madhu Khanna, *The Tantric Way: Art, Science*, Ritual (London: Thames & Hudson, 1977), pl. 3, which is identified as Kālī, is actually Tārā.
35. *Tantrasāra*, 692–702.
36. For example, Mookerjee and Khanna, *Tantric Way*, 166–67, 185.
37. *Tantrasāra*, 702.
38. A contemporary *aghorī* says sexual excitement is greatly increased in the context of the *pañcatattva* ritual and that, 'if you know what you are doing, all this excitement will help you awaken your Kuṇḍalinī'. Cited in Svoboda, *Aghora II*, 96.
39. *Kulārṇava Tantra* 108–9; cited in McDaniel, *Madness of the Saints*, 111.
40. *Mantramohodadhiḥ*, 145.
41. The *Mantramahodadhiḥ*, like most Tantric texts, assumes the *sādhaka* to be male.
42. *Uddīśa Tantra*, chaps. 7–9; cited in Banerjea, *Brief History of Tantric Literature*, 325.

PART III

The Contributions of Art History

7

The Northernmost Representation of an Indian Goddess of Power

BRATINDRA NATH MUKHERJEE

One of the most remarkable archaeological sites in former Soviet Central Asia is about seventy kilometers east of Samarkand, on the outskirts of the present-day town of Pendzhikent,[1] on the Zeravshan River in western Tadzhikistan (see map 3).[2] Systematic excavations at the site since 1946 have laid bare a large city of forty-seven acres, consisting of a citadel (belonging to the local rulers), the town proper, a suburban settlement, and a cemetery.[3] Archaeologists believe that Pendzhikent came into existence as an urban settlement within what was then Sogdiana in the fifth or early sixth century CE[4] and that it was deserted, as a result of the Arab conquests, 'between the twenties and the seventies of the 8th century'.[5] The excavations therefore yield important evidence about Sogdian history in particular, as well as about pre-Muslim Central Asian urban life and culture in general.[6]

Apart from building structures, excavators have unearthed more than 1,500 coins, remarkable wooden sculptures and carvings, sculptures and ornaments in clay and stucco, and a rich profusion of wall paintings used to decorate homes and temples. These give interpreters clues as to contemporary clothing styles, textile patterns, jewelry, weapons and horses' harnesses, metal vessels, architectural structures, furniture, kings' thrones, and religious cults.[7] The subject of this chapter is a part of a wall painting found in one of the two temples discovered in the main town of Pendzhikent. Painted onto 'the central portion of the south wall of the main hall' of temple no. 2 (see fig. 12)[8] is a female figure in a

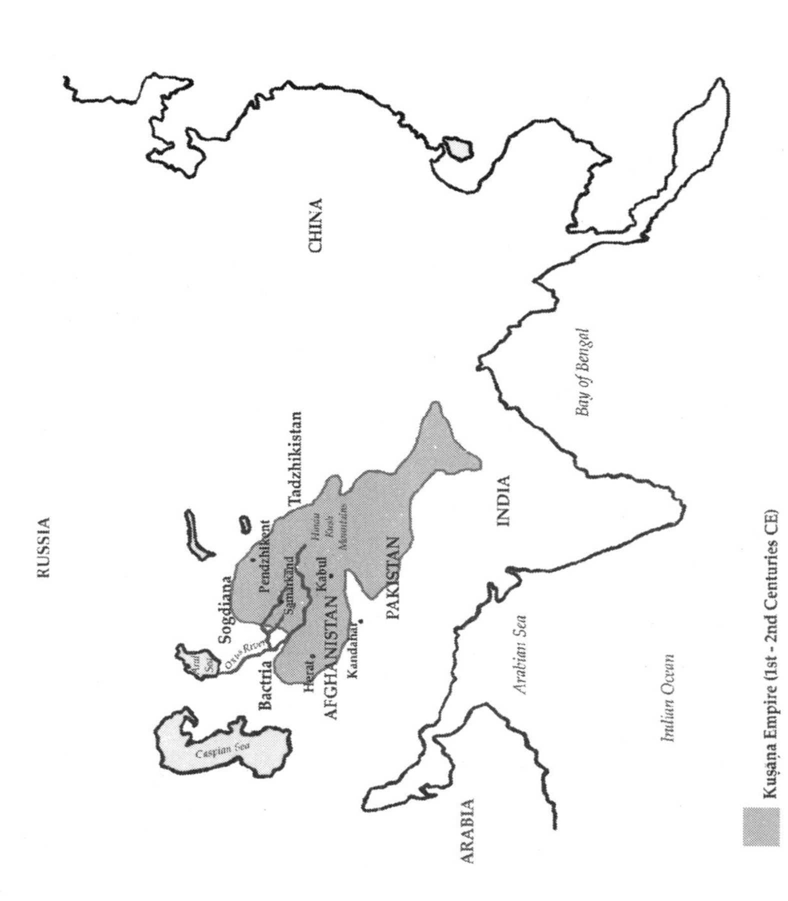

Map 3: Central Asia in the first and second centuries CE. Artwork by Ben Royas

half-sitting and half-standing posture. She wears a bejeweled waist belt and various types of ornaments. She was originally depicted as a four-armed female. Her two left hands are still visible, but the right hands are now effaced. Her face is partially obliterated. Traces of a halo were detected behind her head at the time the representation was unearthed. This feature and the extra hands allude to her supernatural character.

One of the left hands of the figure presses down a standing animal, recognizable as a bull (or cow) or buffalo. Its mouth is partly open, and its tongue is slightly jutting out. Its body is somewhat covered by the garment of the female figure, which is woven with square patterns and other embellishments. The front

Fig. 12: Female figure painted on the wall of temple no. 2, Pendzhikent. From Alexander Belenitsky, *Central Asia*, trans. James Hogarth (Cleveland: World, 1968), fig. 126.

legs of the animal are placed on the body of a demon-like figure lying on the ground, which has the body of an animal with clawed feet and a grotesque half-human, half-animal face. The bull (or buffalo), or rather the demon, is being pierced by what looks like either a spear or a trident held in the second hand of the female figure. On a segment of the garment covering the lower side of the female one can notice the white traces of the figure of a lion walking to its right. All the figures are set on an oval platform or pedestal and against a stela, a part of the outline of which is seen to the left of the female figure.

The female figure has been recognized by Russian scholars as a four-armed goddess.[9] However, to date she has not yet been properly identified.

A clue to the identification of the female deity is supplied by the Śiva *liṅga* in the foreground of the picture. The *liṅga*, depicted in black color and set on the above noted pedestal, is adorned with a garland placed along the higher side of the shaft (see fig. 12).

We thus find in this tableau the presence of the phallic representation of the Brāhmaṇical god Śiva in front of a female deity in a killing posture, as well as the spear (*śakti*) or trident (*triśūla*) in her hand, both of which are recognized in Indian iconographic texts as weapons of Śiva's consort.[10] This combination immediately suggests that the sculpture depicts the female figure of Durgā, shown in her form as Mahiṣāsuramardinī, or Caṇḍī, the slayer of the buffalo demon Mahiṣa.

Mahiṣāsuramardinī is one of the most well-known forms of the great Brāhmaṇical Mother Goddess. Even now she is worshipped with pomp and pleasure in autumn in different parts of India, particularly in its eastern region.[11] The autumnal worship of the Goddess in the company of four other deities (Gaṇeśa, Kārttikeya, Sarasvatī, and Lakṣmī), looked upon as her family members, marks in popular belief the annual visit to her paternal home. But the real and age-old idea behind the worship of this Śakti, the active power of energy of Śiva, seems to be twofold: the purging of evil, as embodied by the demon, by a superior good and divine force, as represented by the Goddess; and the ensuring of the regeneration of the earth and fertility, as indicated by a portion of the green trunk and leaves of a banana tree that is placed by the side of the icons of Durgā and her family members during the period of worship.[12]

The inclusion of family members in iconographic depictions of the ten-armed Caṇḍī is mentioned in the *Kabikaṅkan Caṇḍī* of Mukundarām Cakrabartī (sixteenth century CE).[13] Prior to the late medieval age, however, one does not find such familial representations, as the Goddess is generally worshipped alone. In the early and early medieval periods, she is shown (with a very few exceptions) standing by the side of or riding on a lion and killing—in the earliest sculptures—a buffalo, then slightly later a buffalo-headed male, and then even later, a male coming out of a decapitated buffalo.[14] The number of her hands varies from two to twenty-two, and even thirty-two.[15] However, in her earliest forms, she has only two or four hands.[16] The story of the battle between the Goddess and the buffalo demon is described in detail in the *Devī Māhātmya* section of the *Mārkaṇḍeya Purāṇa* (chaps. 81–93), while textual details of the iconography appear later in the *Viṣṇudharmottara*, *Matsya*, and *Agni Purāṇas*.[17]

Central to the demon-slaying aspect of the Goddess are (a) her association with the lion; and (b) her killing of the demon, symbolizing evil. The earliest Mahiṣāsuramardinī image is not datable prior to the middle of the first century BCE, but it occurs during a period of fruitful contact between India and West Asia, when the tribes who later formed the Kuṣāṇa empire in the first century CE were settling in the Oxus Valley and mixing with preexistent Greeks and Scytho-Parthians.[18]

The impact of these contacts can be discerned in the development of the cult concerned. For her lion mount, the Goddess was immediately indebted to several ancient goddesses datable to before the rise of the Kuṣāṇas: the Babylonian mother goddess Nanā, evidence for whom is found in classical sources, temple epigraphy, sculpture, clay votive tablets, and seals and coins;[19] the Sumerian Ninlil (Ninhursag); the Phrygian and Lydian Cybele; the Akkadian-Assyrian Ishtar; the Greek Rhea and Athena; and the Persian Anāhita. All of these had the same animal as their mount or at least as an associate.[20] According to a Hellenic tradition, Athena, the Greek war goddess and protectress of good from evil, participated in the war between the gods and the giants.[21] In a scene from this episode, sculpted on an altar at Pergamon (in Turkey), datable to the second century BCE, she is shown as inflicting a wound on a giant with a spear, while her lion mount is attacking the latter or another giant.[22] The Persian mother goddess, Anāhita, for whom we have evidence at least from the fourth century BCE,[23] has been traced to a ritual called the Taurobolium, that is, the sacrifice of a bull that embodies evil force, and the destruction of which ensures regeneration and fertility.[24] The ritual became connected also with the popular god Mithra, who had some association with Anāhita and Cybele.[25] These several examples serve to illustrate the popularity of Nanā and other lion-riding goddesses identified with her in parts of Western Asia in the centuries immediately before the turn of the Common Era—either regions included in what became the Kuṣāṇa empire or places with which they traded.

The Kuṣāṇas built up an empire that stretched from Central Asia to at least southern Bihar, and fostered a 'composite empire comprising regions inhabited by people of different origins, creeds, and artistic traditions, a kind of centralized "Commonwealth" with some of its component parts connected more or less loosely with each other, their relationship with the central government being often that of tributary allegiance rather than complete submission. . . . The syncretism prevailing throughout the Empire—Buddhism, Hellenism, Hinduism, Zoroastrianism and other creeds—is well reflected in the coins minted during [their] rule.'[26] Indeed, the Kuṣāṇa emperors incorporated Nanā into their royal coinage: we see her on the obverse of coins depicting Huvishka (mid-second century CE) and Kanishka III (third century), where she is depicted sitting on a lion;[27] and a backless sculpture from the Kuṣāṇa school at Mathura shows a female figure standing on a lion, with a trident and a drum—both signs of Śiva—in her hands.[28] It is this 'goddess on lion', originating by the time of the imperial Kuṣāṇas, that thus eventually becomes Durgā Siṁhavāhinī. For the employment of a lion as a mount of a female deity, the belief in her participation in a gigantomachy, and the killing by her of an animal symbolizing the evil force, noticeable (fully or partly) in the cults of earlier mother goddesses, also formed the main conceptual and iconographic elements in the cult of Mahiṣāsuramardinī.

No doubt, some innovations were discernible in the cult of Mahiṣāsuramardinī, which evolved through a centering on Durgā (Umā), the Indian Mother Goddess. For instance, the evil demon and demonic animal were understandably identified with each other (at least in the initial stage of the development of the Indian cult), and the bull was replaced by the buffalo, as the former animal had already been considered sacred to Śiva, Durgā's consort. She was also shown in the early representations of her Mahiṣāsuramardinī form as pressing or crushing the buffalo demon, an action that justified the name Mahiṣāsuramạrdinī (literally, presser, crusher, or destroyer of the buffalo demon). From about the late Kuṣāṇa age, the artists concerned began—at first sporadically—to show her using a trident to kill the animal.[29] These innovations, however, cannot minimize the value of the hypothesis that the broad concept and iconic traits of the Indian cult were indebted to the mother goddesses noted above. The explicit unification of Nanā with the consort of Śiva took place in the Indian subcontinent around the first century BCE and after,[30] during the Scytho-Parthian and then Kuṣāṇa ages. The Mathura area might have been one of the territories where it became popular in the initial stage. of its development.[31] By the time we reach the fourth- to fifth-century Gupta period, the coins of Candragupta I, Candragupta II, and Kumaragupta reveal this Indianization to be even more pronounced, with the Goddess seated on a lion in different *āsanas* and holding a lotus.[32]

Turning from this general picture to the specific region of Pendzhikent, we know from numismatic and other archeological data that Nanā was popular in Transoxiana from an early period.[33] In fact, four-armed Nanā rides on a lion in a panel of woodcarvings dated from the seventh–eighth century CE found at Pendzhikent (see fig. 13).[34] Furthermore, in several scenes on a wall painting from room 41 of Sector VI at Pendzhikent, she appears within the clouds, watching the action of a hero riding a horse as he vanquishes his enemies. She sends him a half-flower half-woman, who holds out to him a necklace of honor.[35] Perhaps Nanā was viewed as the patron goddess of the area.[36] Anāhita, another contributory goddess, was also known in that region from an age much earlier than the beginning of the town of Pendzhikent.[37]

In the painting under review in this essay, a garland adorns the Śiva *liṅga*, as if it were offered to the latter by a devotee. The figure of the goddess and others are placed on a pedestal and against the background of a stela. Such a disposition of the figures gives the impression that the artist wanted to draw a cult icon. But while drawing it he made an innovation or a modification. He depicted the deity as killing a demon, whose form corresponded to the local concept of a demon (or a dragon). Again, the artist showed the goddess as pressing an animal (buffalo) and thereby combined two iconic types of the goddess into one. The deity appears in a painting on a wall of a temple. All these indicate the knowledge of, reverence for, lively interest in, and perhaps local adaptation of the cult of Mahiṣāsuramardinī among the people of Pendzhikent.[38]

Fig. 13: A wood carving of a four-armed Nanā riding on a lion. Pendzhikent, seventh–eighth century CE. From Gregoir Frumkin, *Archaeology in Soviet Central Asia* (Leiden: E.J. Brill, 1970), pl. 25.

This inference need not cause surprise. The familiarity of the people, or at least of a section of them, at Pendzhikent with Śiva and his consort is suggested by a wall painting at this locality depicting a human figure with three faces: two representing the benevolent and malevolent aspects of the god, and the third, that of a female, reminding one of Umā, his consort.[39] Other 'Hindu-type' finds include a stucco sculpture of a goddess sitting on a throne, surrounded by flames, and a three-armed and three-headed deity, reminding one of the Hindu Trimūrti.[40] In another painting located in the same area, Śiva is depicted dancing with a halo behind his head and wearing a short garment (apparently made of tiger or deer skin). A part of his signature trident can be discerned behind his right thigh. He is being worshipped by two devotees, and some other people outside the main section of the picture are shown as covered in the upper parts of their bodies with loose wrappers impressed with the marks of the Śaivite trident.[41] Some terracotta figures of naked ascetics wearing only rosaries and bangles, unearthed at Khatyn-Rabad and the site of Old Termez, may be associated with the Śaiva Pāśupata sect.[42] Alexander Belenitsky, leader of the Soviet archaeological expedition at Pendzhikent from 1954 until the late 1960s, believed that the wall paintings found in the city even corresponded to scenes from the later Indian *Pañcatantra*.[43]

All these data suggest the presence of the cults of Śiva and Mahiṣāsuramardinī in the territory to the north of the Oxus by the early half of the first millennium CE. These could have reached there through a Central Asian route from the northwestern section of the Indian subcontinent and via eastern Xinjian (China) and a section of western Central Asia. However, a more probable route could have been through Arachosia, the region in southeastern Afghanistan including the locality of Kandahar (or Parapomisadai, to the southeast of the Hindu Kush and extending to the Kabul-Begram area), and Bactria (situated to the northwest of the Hindu Kush, south of the Oxus and east of Herat). As shown elsewhere, there is enough evidence to vouch for the popularity of Śaivism in Bactria in the early centuries of the Common Era.[44] A few images of Mahiṣāsuramardinī and a sculpture in stone representing Umā and Maheśvara, all datable to the first millennium CE, have been unearthed in certain areas of eastern Afghanistan to the southeast of the Hindu Kush mountains.[45]

Thus by the seventh or eighth centuries CE, the cult of the great Indian Goddess of power made an impact in an area now included in the western part of Central Asia. Her mural representation in a temple and in a territory far outside the Indian subcontinent, the main region of its development, alludes to a wide dissemination of the Durgā Mahiṣāsuramardinī cult. This religious history has been preserved not by textual data, but by religious art. The Pendzhikent painting is the northernmost representation of the cult of Mahiṣāsuramardinī.

NOTES

1. Also spelled Pyandzhikent and Pjandzikent.
2. Alexander Belenitsky, *Central Asia*, trans. James Hogarth (Cleveland: World, 1968), 154–60, 185–89; Gregoir Frumkin, *Archaeology in Soviet Central Asia* (Leiden: E.J. Brill, 1970), 72; and Galina Anatol'evna Pugachenkova and L.I. Rempel, *Ocherki iskusstva Srednei Azii: Drevnosti srednevekove* (Moscow: Iskusstvo, 1982), 129. Note that the sources on this archaeological site were written by Russian scholars and do not postdate the early 1980s, when Soviet researchers ceased—for military and political reasons—to have access to the region.
3. The archaeological team was a joint collaboration between the Institute of Archaeology of the Soviet Academy of Science, the Institute of the History of the Tadzhik Academy of Science, and the Hermitage Museum in former Leningrad. See Belenitsky, *Central Asia*, 155, and Frumkin, *Archaeology in Soviet Central Asia*, 72.
4. Belenitsky, *Central Asia*, 155.
5. Ibid.
6. For an excellent history of Sogdiana and its sites, see *The Encyclopedia of World Art* (New York: McGraw-Hill, 1959–87), vol. 8 (1967), cols. 121–33.
7. See Belenitsky, *Central Asia*, 160, 186.
8. Ibid., figs. 127 (black and white) and 133 (color); and *Encyclopedia of World Art*, vol. 1 (1959), col. 823; and vol. 8 (1967), col. 129. The female figure to be discussed is one of three haloed deities painted in the central portion of the south wall of the main hall of temple no. 2.
9. See Belenitsky, *Central Asia*, 245.
10. For an example, see the *Agni Purāṇa* 50.1–6. Refer also to Marie-Therèse

de Mallmann, *Les Enseignements iconographiques de L'Agni-Purana* (Paris: Presses universitaires de France, 1963), 143–47.

11. Kṛttibās, author of the Bengali *Rāmāyaṇa*, is usually credited with establishing autumn as the authoritative time to worship Durgā, as Rāma does so before his battle with Rāvaṇa, in an untimely (*akāl*) season. Note, however, that long before Kṛttibās, the *Devī Māhātmya* had exhorted the Goddess's devotees to worship her in autumn. See B.N. Mukherjee, *Śaktir Rūp Bhārate o Madhya Eśiyāy* (Calcutta: Ānanda, 1990), 14.
12. Jitendra Nath Banerjea, *The Development of Hindu Iconography* (1941; 4th ed., New Delhi: Munshiram Manoharlal, 1985), 489–92; *Deś* (a Bengali weekly), Autumn 1983, 11–12; B.N. Mukherjee, 'Foreign Elements in Iconography of Mahishāsuramardinī—The War Goddess of India,' in *Zeitschrift der Deutschen Morgenländischen Gesellschaft* (Stuttgart: Franz Steiner, 1985), suppl. 6, 402–14; B.N. Mukherjee, 'Pictures from Woodcut Blocks: An Iconological Analysis,' in *Woodcut Prints of Nineteenth-Century Calcutta* (Calcutta: Seagull, 1983), ed. Ashit Paul, 108; and Mukherjee, *Śaktir Rūp*, 14–15.
13. See the section called, '*Gaurīr Khed*', lines 14–16, in Mukundarām Cakrabartī, *Kabikaṅkaṇ Caṇḍī* (Calcutta: Basumatī-Sāhitya-Mandir, 1963), 24.
14. B.N. Mukherjee, *Nanā on Lion: A Study in Kushāṇa Numismatic Art* (Calcutta: Asiatic Society, 1969), pl. 11, no. 41; pl. 13, nos. 45–46; Nalini Kanta Bhattasali, *Iconography of Buddhist and Brāhmaṇical Sculptures in the Dacca Museum* (Dacca: Rai S.N. Bhadra Bahadur, 1929), pl. opp. p. 198; Gritli von Mitterwallner, 'The Kuṣāṇa Type of the Goddess Mahiṣāsuramardinī as compared to the Gupta and Mediaeval Types,' in *German Scholars on India: Contributions to Indian Studies*, ed. Cultural Dept. of the Embassy of the Federal Republic of Germany, New Delhi (Varanasi: Chowkhamba Sanskrit Series Office, 1973–76), 2: fig. 6.
15. Banerjea, *Development of Hindu Iconography*, 497–500, and Mukherjee, 'Foreign Elements,' 406 and n. 16.
16. Mukherjee, *Nanā on Lion*, pl. 11, no. 41; Herbert Hartel, 'Some Results of the Excavations at Sonkh: A Preliminary Report,' in *German Scholars on India: Contributions to Indian Studies*, ed. Cultural Dept. of the Embassy of the Federal Republic of Germany (Varanasi: Chowkhamba Sanskrit Series Office, 1973–76), 2: fig. 36; and Mitterwallner, 'Kuṣāṇa Type', figs. 1–3.
17. *Viṣṇudharmottara Purāṇa*, quoted in T. Gopinath Rao, *Elements of Hindu Iconography* (Madras: Law Printing House, 1914), 1, pt. 2: 346; *Agni Purāṇa* 50.1–6; and *Matsya Purāṇa* 260.55–70. The goddess is referred to as Caṇḍīkā in the first and as Kātyāyaṇī in the last text.
18. See *Deś*, Autumn 1983, 16–17; and Mukherjee, 'Foreign Elements,' 408–13; *Nanā on Lion*, 3–30, and *Śaktir Rūp*, 16–20. The dates of the Kuṣāṇa empire

are hard to fix with certainty. The Kuṣāṇas were a nomadic group from northwestern China who migrated into Bactria (modern northwestern Afghanistan and Tadzhikistan) in the second century BCE. They established a dynasty in the mid first century CE that lasted until the fourth or fifth centuries, when they succumbed to the Iranian Sasanians.

19. Mukherjee, *Nanā on Lion*, 3–4 and 12–18, pl. 5, nos. 15–20; and B.N. Mukherjee, *Mathura and Its Society—the Śaka-Pahlava Phase* (Calcutta: Firma K.L. Mukhopadhyay, 1981), 206–7.
20. Mukherjee, *Nanā on Lion*, 12–18. See also James Hastings, ed., *The Encyclopedia of Religion and Ethics* (New York: Scribner, 1913). For Ninlil, see 2: 296, 7: 430, and 10: 161; for Cybele, see 4: 377–78 and 8: 848–49; for Ishtar, see 7: 428–34; for Rhea, see 1: 147, 4: 377, 7: 116, and 8: 847–48; for Athena, see 1: 72, 6: 381, and 12: 695; and for Anāhita, see 1: 415 and 797.
21. Hastings, *Encyclopedia of Religion and Ethics,* 12: 695; Karl Schefold, *Myth and Legend in Early Greek Art* (New York: Harry N. Abrams, 1966), 64; and Jean Charbonneaux, Roland Martin, and François Villard, *Hellenistic Art (330–50 B.C.)*, trans. Peter Green (New York: Braziller, 1973), 265–66 and fig. 288.
22. See n. 20 above.
23. See Mukherjee, *Nanā on Lion*, 3.
24. Hastings, *Encyclopedia of Religion and Ethics,* 8: 752, 850; 10: 645.
25. Ibid., 8: 754.
26. Frumkin, *Archaeology in Soviet Central Asia*, 52.
27. For a detailed discussion of Kuṣāṇa coins and the evidence therein for goddess veneration, see Mukherjee, *Nanā on Lion*, 9–30.
28. See ibid., 19–20, and fig. 43. For more examples, see Mukherjee, 'Foreign Elements,' 410–11.
29. Mukherjee, *Nanā on Lion*, 19–20, and *Śaktir Rūp*, 15 and figs. 4–5; and Hartel, 'Some Results of the Excavations at Sonkh,' 92.
30. Mukherjee, *Nanā on Lion*, 12–15, and *Śaktir Rūp*, 18–19.
31. Mukherjee, *Mathura and Its Society*, 208–09, and *Nanā on Lion*, 19–20; and *Deś*, Autumn 1983, 20.
32. Mukherjee, *Nanā on Lion*, 33–34.
33. Mukherjee, *Nanā on Lion*, pl. 4, no. 8A; and Pugochenkova and Rempel', *Ocherki iskusstva Srednei Azii*, 129.
34. Frunkin, *Archaeology in Soviet Central Asia*, pl. 25. On p. 78, Frumkin identifies this Pendzhikent woodcarving as 'a goddess (?) seated on the back of a lion'.
35. Pugochenkova and Rempel, *Ocherki iskusstva Srednei Azii*, 129.
36. Ibid.
37. Mukherjee, *Nanā on Lion*, 89–90; pl. 14, no. 47; Belenitsky, *Central Asia*, 215.
38. The face of the demon has some superficial resemblance to that of a *makara*, the mythical monster associated with the river goddess Gaṅgā as her vehicle

mount. We are not certain whether the artist at Pendzhikent had any idea of this fabulous animal and wanted to introduce it into the iconography of Mahiṣāsuramardinī.

39. Guitty Azarpay, *Sogdian Paintings: The Pictorial Epic in Oriental Art* (Berkeley: University of California Press, 1981), 29, fig. 5, and 143.
40. Frumkin, *Archaeology in Soviet Central Asia*, 78.
41. Ibid., 75 and fig. 17; Mukherjee, *Śaktir Rūp*, 35n33.
42. *Informatsionnyi Biulleten*, International Association for the Study of the Cultures of Central Asia, Moscow, no. 11 (1986): 22, 25; Mukherjee, *Śaktir Rūp*, 31.
43. Belenitsky, *Central Asia*, 189.
44. Mukherjee, *Śaktir Rūp*, 31. See also Irina Timofeevna Kruglikova, *Dil'berdzhin: Materialy sovetsko-afganskoi arkeologicheskoi ekspeditsii* (Moscow: Nauka, 1986), 1: 65–66, and fig. 60.
45. Jaya Goswami, *Cultural History of Ancient India: A Socio-Economic and Religio-Cultural Survey of Kapiśa and Gandhāra* (Delhi: Agam Kala Prakashan, 1979), 49–53; Nilima Sen Gupta, *Cultural History of Kapiśa and Gandhara* (Delhi: Sundeep, 1984), 130, 189; P.L. Gupta and D.C. Sircar, 'Umā-Maheśvara Image Inscription from Skandar (Afghanistan),' *Journal of Ancient Indian History* 6, pts. 1–2 (1972–73): 1–4; Mukherjee, *Śaktir Rūp*, 31–32; and G.S. Gai, 'Umā-Maheśvara Image Inscription from Skandar,' in *Studies in Indian Epigraphy* (Mysore: Epigraphical Society of India, 1975–77), 1: 1–6.

8

An Unnoticed Form of Devī from Bengal and the Challenges of Art Historical Analysis

GAUTAM SENGUPTA

In one of his important essays, Narendra Nath Bhattacharyya discussed the process through which innumerable local goddesses in Bengal were identified with the supreme Goddess of the Śāktas. 'The Śākta Devī in her developed form absorbed within herself innumerable goddesses representing different streams,' Bhattacharyya observed. 'Gaurī, Śatākṣī, Śākambharī, Śrī, etc. were undoubtedly developed forms of rudimentary Earth and Corn Mothers.'[1] Citing the *Devī Bhāgavata Purāṇa*, Bhattacharyya continued:

> In every creation of the universe, it is said, the *mūlaprakṛti* assumes the different gradation[s] of *aṁśarūpiṇī*, *kalārūpiṇī*, and *kalāṁśarūpiṇī* or manifests herself in parts, smaller parts and further subdivisions. In the first grade she is represented by Durgā, Lakṣmī, Sarasvatī, Sāvitrī, and Rādhā; in the second by Gaṅgā, Tulasī, Manasā, Ṣaṣṭhī, Maṅgalacaṇḍikā, and Kālī; and in the third by the *grāmadevatās* or village mothers and by women folk in general. This indicates that with the development of the conception of an all-embracing Female Principle when need was felt for regarding the local goddesses as the manifestations of the Śākta Devī, they were primarily given recognition to represent the fragments of *mūlaprakṛti*, the primordial female force of creation, while the more important and popular goddesses were given relatively higher positions. The presiding deities of the *pīṭhas* (holy resorts of the Goddess) were also originally local goddesses, and the story of Satī's death, the falling of her limbs in different *pīṭhas*, etc., were obviously invented to bring all these goddesses in relation to the Śākta Devī.[2]

Bhattacharyya's perceptive comments help us understand a

significant process in the context of traditional Bengal. In this brief paper, I propose to look at the process with reference to a particular iconic type. Such an attempt is always fraught with several problems —methodological and conceptual. How does one identify unnamed goddess sculptures, which might help us to understand the development over time of goddess worship in Bengal, when iconographic texts and sculptural types often bear such little correspondence to one another? I shall highlight the issue by introducing a sample problem: a small (11 cm × 7.5 cm) portable image of a Devī presently housed at the State Archaeological Museum, Calcutta (see fig. 14).[3] The precise find-spot of the image is unknown, since it forms part of a cache of confiscated antiquities seized by the District Police of North Dinajpur at Raigunj (see map 2) in July 1992.

Some hints to the image's provenance are immediately clear. The general style of the image is indicative of its origin in northern Bengal in the early medieval period. Another important consideration is the rock-type employed in carving the piece; the rock is actinolite-sericite schist, which is found in the neighboring Himalayan region.

The Devī is seated in *lalitāsana*, with her left leg folded underneath her on a double-petaled lotus and her right leg pendant. She holds a child on her lap by the left hand, and the corresponding right hand shows the *varadā mudrā*, or boon-conferring gesture. Each of the upper two hands holds a branch of a tree with three leaves. On the base of the image are carved two seated figures, probably representing the donor couple, with folded hands (*añjali mudrā*). The Devī is decorated with a number of ornaments, including a crown, a necklace, and anklets. Her garment is shown by neat rows of parallel lines. The pedestal is of an irregular *triratha* type, with a central projection and two lateral depressions; the back slab is almost devoid of any decoration. What appears to be rather unusual, however, is the perfunctory workmanship of the child and the donor figures, which stands in sharp contrast to the graceful appearance of the Goddess. Stylistically, the figure may be dated to *c.* ninth to tenth centuries CE, as it shares most of the features seen in contemporaneous figures: semicircular back-slab, absence

Fig. 14: Devī, State Archaeological Museum, Calcutta. Photograph courtesy Gautam Sengupta.

of ornamentation, and simplicity of physical form. From a broad, generic identification of the figure as a Devī, one can proceed toward a more specific and precise identity. Central to this exercise are two cognizable features: (a) the child on her lap and (b) the bunch of leaves in her two upper hands.

Starting from these two characteristic features, I shall proceed, in a detective-like fashion, to try to identify this Raiganj figure, to give voice to this silent goddess. Ideally, one would like to know her name, her provenance, her ritual significance, and some information about the circumstances of her creation. My method is typical of that used by all art historians: I sift through as many data as possible—textual, historical, and sculptural—noting points of connection to, and difference from, the original image, and I try to decide what can be judiciously inferred.

I begin with the first of the two prominent attributes of the Raiganj figure, the child, and look for named goddesses who also hold children. In actuality, the association of a child with a goddess is not an unusual iconographic feature. This is vividly reflected in the iconography of the *mātṛkās*, or mothers, whose number was standardized to seven (*saptamātṛkās*) in the Gupta period. It should be pointed out, however, that the textual tradition—embodied in such works as the *Mahābhārata*, the Purāṇas, and the *Bṛhatsaṁhitā*[4] —mentions specific linkage between the *mātṛkās* and children in only a generic fashion. According to the seventh-century *Kādambarī* of Bāṇabhaṭṭa, and in later Purāṇas such as the *Brahmavaivarta* and *Devī Bhāgavata*, *mātṛkās* are worshipped as children's guardian deities.[5] Besides the *mātṛkās* mentioned in these various texts, there are other goddesses associated with children, although—conforming to the practices prevalent in the iconographic studies—these are not designated as *mātṛkās*. Such iconic types appear in Bengal and eastern India, and it is these that I shall have occasion to discuss later in this essay.

I begin with textual evidence—the iconographic data available in the *Devī Purāṇa*—that gives us our first candidate for consideration: Diti. The *Devī Purāṇa* is one of the most important Śākta Upapurāṇas. According to R.C. Hazra, it is 'an East Indian work written in Bengal'.[6] Hazra further suggests that 'the date of the present *Devī Purāṇa* which was known far and wide in the eleventh century, can never be placed later than 850 A.D.'.[7] In its 128 chapters, the *Devī Purāṇa* describes the

exploits and worship of the Devī (the Great Goddess) who incarnated herself on the Vindhyas as a maiden mounted on a lion and became known as Vindhyavāsinī. In this Purāṇa, Devī is not only called the Sleep of Spiritual Trance (Yoganidrā) and the Primordial and Preeminent Energy (Ādyā Parā Śakti, 7.20) and at the same time said to be the same as Umā, the wife and Śakti (Energy) of Śiva, but is also identified with the Śaktis of other gods as well as with the *mātṛkās* and other female deities such as Dākṣāyanī, Kālī, Caṇḍī, etc. who are called Devī's various forms. It gives us important information about the different incarnations of Devī and her original nature and relationship with Śiva and other gods; about Yoga and the method of its practice; about Śākta iconography and the Śākta vows and worship.[8]

The fiftieth chapter of the work is particularly rich in iconographic details. Here sixty forms of Devī are divided into three groups:

twenty *sāttvika* forms constituting the first grade, viz., Maṅgalā, Vijayā, Bhadrā, Śivā, Śānti, Dhṛti, Kṣamā, Ṛddhi, Vṛddhi, Unnati, Siddhi, Tuṣṭi, Puṣṭi, Śrī, Umā, Dīpti, Kānti, Yaśā, Lakṣmī, and Īśvarī; 2) twenty *rājasa* forms constituting the second grade, viz., Brāhmī, Jayāvatī, Śakti, Ajitā, Aparjitā, Jayantī, Mānasī, Māyā, Didi, Śvetā, Vimohini, Śaranya, Kauśikī, Gaurī, Vimalā, Rati, Lālasā, Arundhatī, Kriyā, and Durgā; and 3) twenty *tāmasa* forms of the third grade, viz., Kālī, Raudrī, Kapāli, Ghaṇṭākarṇā, Mayūrikā, Bahurūpā, Surūpā, Trinetrā, Ripuhā, Ambikā, Māheśarī, Kumārī, Vaiṣṇavī, Sura-pūjitā, Vaivasvatī, Ghorā, Karālī, Vikaṭā, Aditi, and Carcikā.[9]

Hazra's is among the most elaborate lists describing the iconic forms of Devī. For each particular form, it specifies the time schedule for worship, the iconographic details, and proper methods of worship. There can be very little doubt that there is a great deal of overlap and repetition in the list, but it indicates in no uncertain terms the identification of diverse forms with the all-pervasive presence of Devī. Many of the deities described in this list do not correspond to the known corpus of Devī images from Bengal or eastern India. But a Devī image that is relevant to this essay is found in the iconographic features of Diti. In chapter 50, Diti is invoked as Daityanutāṁ (She Who Is Praised by the Demons) and is described thus:

daṇḍāsanasthitāṁ bhadrāṁ sarvābharaṇabhūṣitām |
phalanīlotpalakarām utsaṅgaśiśubhūṣitām ||[10]

[We adore] that auspicious lady who is in a fully prostrate position, is bedecked with all ornaments, and is carrying a fruit, a blue lotus, and a baby in her lap.

She is said to be worshipped in a particular year called Manmatha with fragrant flowers and so on. Elsewhere in the same chapter, Diti is described as Devamātā (Mother of the Gods) and Bahuprajā (She with Many Subjects).

bhadrāsanasamārūḍhā gītibhir bālakairvṛtā |
phalapuṣpāpahastā ca śiśupālanakrodhanā ||[11]

She is seated in *bhadrāsana*, with both legs dangling, surrounded by a group of boys involved in singing. She holds flowers and fruits in her hand and is busy rearing a child.

Significantly, in both descriptions, Diti's association with children is emphasized. No less important is the other iconographic feature, the occurrence of flowers and fruit in her hand. Thus the *Devī Purāṇa* verses establish the basic typology of such forms; they are unequivocally identified as the mothers (*mātṛs*). It is significant that among all the goddesses in the *Devī Purāṇa* list, Diti alone is associated with a child. However, we typically find no Diti sculptures, which makes me hesitate to lend her name to the Raigunj goddess.

Turning thus from the *Devī Purāṇa* evidence, we may now explore a range of contemporaneous images to establish relevant points of comparison. Images broadly comparable to the Raigunj Devī are not unknown in early medieval eastern India, although the iconographic features do not always correspond in every single detail. More important, some of the images are inscribed, and the dedicatory labels reveal the names by which such forms were known to the donors. One such goddess has been variously named Puṇḍeśvarī, Muṇḍeśvarī, and Gausavā.

For example, Rakhal Das Banerji noticed an intriguing image in the collection of the Indian Museum, Calcutta, which he described in the following words: 'It represents a goddess seated on a cushion with one leg down resting on a lotus. She has four hands, in which she holds an elephant goad and a round object in the left, while in the right she has a curious wand, ending in the head of a *makara*, the remaining one holding a child on her lap. A pair of lions is also seen in the pedestal. The image was discovered at Ghosrāwān in the Patna District and an inscription on the pedestal records its dedication by one Candraka son of Viṣṇu in the village of Tentadī. The main figure is called Muṇḍeśarī or Puṇḍeśarī.'[12] D.C. Sircar, however, observed that 'the correct reading of the name of the deity is Puṇḍeśvarī and not Muṇḍeśvarī'.[13] Priyatosh Banerjee noticed another image from Rajauna in Bihar, 'a four-armed image of the goddess called Puṇḍeśvarī with a child on her lap'.[14] Since the image is now untraceable, one cannot make out its iconographic details. However, the dedicatory inscription, which still survives, is fairly elaborate. It refers to the 'pious gift' (*deyadharma*) of Sanaka, who dedicated the image of Puṇḍeśvarī in Mahātrikada of Krimilā, which was both an administrative division and its headquarters, on the twenty-fourth Āṣādha of the thirteenth regnal year of Nayapāladeva (second quarter of the eleventh century CE). Similar images were noticed by D.C. Sircar at Valgudar, not far from Rajauna, and some other sites of South Bihar. Unfortunately, Sircar's descriptions of the images are cryptic and devoid of iconographic detail. Sircar does, however, mention children on the laps of such Devīs:

> It may be mentioned here that such images of the Devī with child were noticed by me in many places in South Bihar. She must have enjoyed great popularity amongst the people of the region in the early medieval period. . . . The deity seems to have been the primitive mother-goddess worshipped under different local names in various parts of East India, though she may have been associated with the Buddhist deity Hārītī as well as the *Brāhmaṇical* goddess Pārvatī with Skanda on her lap. . . . It seems that the same primitive mother-goddess with a child on her lap, sometimes represented with a lion pedestal and sometimes with a snake canopy, was worshipped under different names in different parts of East India, the snake-canopied form being later endowed with the name Manasā in Bengal. The Jain Ambikā seems to be an adaptation of the same deity.[15]

As Sircar has so clearly demonstrated, the marker of a child, as in the case of Puṇḍeśvarī and Muṇḍeśvarī, does not necessarily tell us anything and, in fact, leaves open the possibility of such an image belonging to a wildly disparate array of sectarian contexts: local, Buddhist, Brāhmaṇical, Jain, or primitive.

In some instances, dedicatory inscriptions do not specify the name of the Devī, probably because she was sufficiently popular not to need labeling. D.C. Sircar referred to 'another image of the same goddess, but not exactly with the same attributes, [that] was recently unearthed at Jaynagar'.[16] A pedestal inscription engraved in the Gauḍīya character of about the twelfth century records the pious gift of a lay worshipper, described as a *paramopāsikā* (supreme worshipper) of the Mahāyāna Buddhist order. Another image of Devī on display in the Asutosh Museum of Indian Art, University of Calcutta, is seated on a double-petaled lotus with her leg supported beneath by a second lotus. The Devī holds a child with her lower right hand, while her lower left hand makes the hand gestures of *varadā* and *śriphala* (a small *bilva* fruit in the palm of her hand). The upper left hand holds what looks like a shaft, and the upper right hand is broken. On the pedestal are carved a lion, a pot (*ghaṭa*), a heap of offerings (*naivedya*), and a garland-bearing donor. The image is dated in the sixth regnal year of the Pāla king Rāmapāla (*c.* 1078–79).[17]

More important is another image from Jaynagar, currently preserved in the Victoria and Albert Museum, London, which has an inscription revealing her name to be Pūrṇeśvarī.[18] The name Pūrṇeśvarī occurs in the *Kālikā Purāṇa* as one of the many names of the great goddess Yoganidrā. Yoganidrā was called Pūrṇeśvarī at Pūrṇagiri, located beyond Kāmarūpa, in eastern India (Prācya).[19] Despite some amount of uncertainty about the geographical information in the *Kālikā Purāṇa*, the text has an obvious bias in favor of eastern India and its sacred geography. This would imply that Pūrṇeśvarī was an important appellation of Devī in eastern India.

The Jaynagar image shows a four-handed Devī very close in terms of general appearance to the one noticed by Rakhal Das Banerji. The child on the lap of the Devī and a small pitcher-like object on the lower left hand are identical in both images. However, the attributes in the two upper hands differ. In both her upper hands, the Jaynagar Devī holds what seem to be wands: the one in the upper left hand is topped by a seated elephant, whereas the one in the upper right is surmounted by a lotus. Another significant difference between the Ghosrāwān and Jaynagar figures is their pedestals; a pair of lions sits on the former, and a water pot on the latter. But the most important iconographic element in the Jaynagar image is the presence of Gaṇeśa by the side of the Devī, a feature not represented in other images. The inscription on the pedestal records the installation of the image of Pūrṇeśvarī at the city of Campā by Ūtakva. The benedictory phrase expresses the desire that the merits of the work should go to the communities of *siddhas* and the congregation of *śramanas*, as well as to all the relatives of Ūtakva, who are bound by the fetters of worldly existence. The date of the image is the thirty-fifth year of Pālapāla, around the close of the twelfth or the beginning of the thirteenth century.[20]

It remains an open question as to whether the Devī was incorporated into the Buddhist pantheon or whether the donor was a lay worshipper with allegiance to other popular cults. The evidence of the inscription is not sufficiently categorical in this regard. Whatever the case, as I have argued above, Devī with a child was a popular iconic type of unspecified cultic affiliation in early medieval eastern India, and she was known under different names, such as Puṇḍeśvarī and Pūrṇeśvarī. Available evidence tends to indicate that eastern and southeastern Bihar were the main areas in which such iconic types were concentrated.

Another iconic type with which the Raigunj figure has much in common is that of the goddess under a serpent hood. On the basis of *dhyānas* in the *Brahmavaivarta Purāṇa* and other Sanskrit texts of the late medieval period, this deity has been identified as Manasā. In one of her *dhyānas*, cited by Nalini Kanta Bhattasali, she is described as having a child (*śiśusutā*) on her lap.[21] Prithvi K. Agarwala has drawn our attention to an exceedingly important *dhyāna* cited in the ninth-century *Pratiṣṭhālakṣaṇa-sārasamuccaya* of Vairocana. Agarwala observed: 'Stating first indeed the iconographic form of the leading snake goddess Manasā, who is described only in her two-armed form, the texts goes on to enumerate her associates, namely, Jaratkāru (the male sage), Manasā-parivāra, i.e. her two (?) boyish attendants or "sons", and the goddess Svaṅgā.'[22] Svaṅgā's iconography, as envisaged in her *dhyāna*,[23] has definite bearing on the image discussed in this essay.

Svaṅgā is distinguished by three important iconographic features, namely: (1) a serpent canopy made of seven hoods (*saptabhogā*), (2) *parṇavallī*, a betal leaf creeper in the upper two hands, and (3) a child on her lap. Dr. Gouriswar Bhattacharya has informed me about an image in a private collection that conforms to these features and has an inscription on its pedestal, which describes the image as Svaṅgā, 'fair-limbed'.[24]

Closely related to this type is another image, now on display at the State Archaeological Museum, Calcutta (see fig. 15). Collected from Kushmandi in the West Dinajpur district of West Bengal, the image represents a four-handed Devī seated on a double-petaled lotus in *lalitāsana* with her pendant right leg placed on a lotus. She holds a child on her lap with her lower left hand and with her lower right hand displays the *varadā mudrā* and *śriphala*. Each of the two upper hands hold a *dhānyamañjarī*, or bunch of rice paddy. Two female attendants with fly whisks are seated on either side of the Devī; a devotee with folded hands and a bird are carved on the pedestal. Despite mutilation, the bird can be identified as an owl.[25] The central figure has been variously identified as the Buddhist Vasudhārā-Hārītī; the Jaina Śāsanadevī, who sits on a peacock mount, 'a syncretistic icon . . . much influenced by the Jaina or the Buddhist conception'; or the Brāhmaṇical Dhānya-Lakṣmī.[26] Like all other attempts at ascertaining the precise identity of this figure, the recent exercise by Enamul Haque identifying the goddess as Dhānya-Lakṣmī stands on uncertain ground, since there is no definite textual description for such an iconic category; hence such a suggestion should be viewed as tentative.[27] Nevertheless, whoever she is, this deity and the Svaṅgā mentioned above are close multiforms of our Raigunj figure because of their shared child and vegetal motifs.

We may close the discussion of comparable iconic types with a reference to Ṣaṣṭhī, the 'sixth part' of *prakṛti*, and the wife of Skanda. It appears that there are two distinct trends in the iconography of Ṣaṣṭhī and the rituals connected with her worship. The first is represented by the Ṣaṣṭhī images from Mathura of the Kuṣāṇa period, first to third centuries CE. In a recent essay, N.P. Joshi has tried to identify thirteen images of the Kuṣāṇa period as

Fig. 15: A four-armed Devī from Kushmandi in West Dinajpur district, West Bengal. Photograph courtesy Gautam Sengupta.

representing Ṣaṣṭhī, on the basis of textual data available 'from some works on *Āyur Veda* datable to early centuries of the Christian era'.[28] Joshi notes: 'Revatī, known as Ṣaṣṭhī as well, has been talked of in details in the *Cikitsā Adhyāya* and *Revatī-kalpa* of the *Kāśyapa-Saṁhitā* by Vṛddha Jīvaka. . . . Herein it has been observed that Revatī pleased Skanda by her penance. He gave her the status of his sister and further placed her on the sixth position. . . . Thus Revatī came to be known as Ṣaṣṭhī and became as powerful as Skanda himself.'[29]

Joshi further observes that Kuṣāṇa works on Indian medicine refer to Ṣaṣṭhī as (1) closely associated with Skanda; (2) responsible for the growth and protection of children; (3) endowed with six faces and various garments and ornaments; (4) beautiful, boon-imparting, and competent to assume forms at will; and (5) stationed for worship between her two brothers Kumāra and Viśakha.[30]

Joshi proposes to group these thirteen figures into two types. The first type 'shows the deity standing between two males, often [indicating] *abhayamudrā* [by a raised hand signaling "fear not", and] carrying a spear in their other hand'. In the second type, 'the central figure of the goddess remains unchanged, but the two brothers flanking her are absent'. In all these images, the two-handed goddess Ṣaṣṭhī, standing with her right hand raised in a protection-imparting attitude, 'has a beautiful face, nice hairdo, usual ornaments, *sāḍi* and upper garment. She has her left hand akimbo, which sometimes holds a water vessel as well. Behind her head and shoulders, often mounting a canopy like motif covering her head, there appear five emanating female figures seen up to the waist only.'[31]

In contrast with the Ṣaṣṭhī of the Kuṣāṇa period, the Bengali Ṣaṣṭhī, while maintaining her connection with children, is not typically sculpted in high art form. Textual references support her motherly characteristics, whereas the stone images of the goddess tend to be aniconic, and the connection with children is maintained solely by ritual.

To elaborate, in the *Brahmavaivarta Purāṇa,* well known as a Bengali text, Ṣaṣṭhī appears, 'but absolutely in a new garb'.[32] In chapter 1, seven verses are devoted to Ṣaṣṭhī.[33] She is equated with the consort of Kārttikeya (Devasenā and Kārttikeyasyakāminī). She is chief among the mothers (*mātṛkāsu pūjyatamā*), an ascetic (*tapasvinī*), and a devotee of Viṣṇu (*Viṣṇubhaktā*). She is called Ṣaṣṭhī because she represents one-sixth of *prakṛti* (*ṣaṣṭhaṁśārūpa prakṛtestena Ṣaṣṭhī prakīrtitā*). She is the giver of sons and grandsons (*putrapautrāpradātrī*), and she nurses the world (*dhātrī ca jagatāṁ sadā*). She is a bewitching young woman who accompanies her husband. She appears as an old woman and a yoginī. She is to be worshipped on the twelfth month, on the sixth and twenty-first days after the birth of a child. Finally, she is described as appearing in the dreams of children (*śiśūnāṁ sapnagocarā*).

Similar statements are made in the eleventh-century *Devī Bhāgavata Purāṇa*, chapter 43, which presents a fairly detailed account of how the worship of the goddess Ṣaṣṭhī was introduced on earth by King Priyabrata.[34] Ṣaṣṭhī brought to life the dead son of the king, who in gratitude initiated Ṣaṣṭhī Pūjā. Here in this chapter, Ṣaṣṭhī is called Bālakādhiṣṭhātrī (Superintendent of Children), Bālānāṁ Dhātrī (Support of Children), Skandabhārya (Wife of Skanda), and Siddhiyoginī (Ascetic Perfected in Spiritual Powers). There is virtually nothing on Ṣaṣṭhī's iconography. The goddess appears before Priyabrata as a beautiful, perpetually young (*susthira yauvanā*) woman. She has the complexion of a white *campaka* flower and a smiling face (*iṣad hāsya prasannāsyā*), and she is bedecked in precious stones and jewelry (*ratnā-bhūṣaṇabhūṣitā*). She is full of compassion (*kṛpāmayī*), accomplished in yoga, and confers boons on devotees (*bhaktānu-grahakātarā*). In addition,

śālagrāme ghaṭe vātha vaṭamūle thavā mune |
bhittayāṁ puttalikāṁ kṛtvā pūjayitvā vicakṣaṇā ||[35]

She can be worshipped in a *śālagrama* stone, a sacred pitcher, on a road, at the roots of a banyan tree, or in toys placed on the floor.

What is significant in this verse is the indication that the worship of Ṣaṣṭhī does not involve the use of any standardized icon, for she can even be invoked symbolically in toys. It may be pointed out in this connection that in rural Bengal, we do come across abstract forms of toys representing Ṣaṣṭhī. A well-known variety comes from Panchmura village in Bankura district of West Bengal. It shows a female form resembling a tree with children attached to it. Asutosh Bhattacharya, who studied the cult of Ṣaṣṭhī in Bengal in great detail, comes to the conclusion that the goddess Ṣaṣṭhī was not represented in any image and that her worship took place mostly in vacant places known as Ṣaṣṭhītalās or within houses in earthen pitchers, or *ghaṭas* (goddesses are often invoked in the shape of jars or pitchers filled with water that are kept in the house).[36]

Recently, Enamul Haque has attempted to ascribe iconic forms to Ṣaṣṭhī.[37] He has argued that five types of Devī images from Bengal should be more properly identified as Ṣaṣṭhī. In the first type, Devī is two-armed, with her right hand gesturing a *varadā mudrā* and her left holding a child. To her right and left, respectively, stand Gaṇeśa and Kārttikeya; a pot, a lion, and some devotees are carved on the pedestal in front of her; and a Śiva *liṅga* is positioned over her head. The second type of Devī is four-armed—in one example, she holds what looks like a branch of a tree—with a pot and a lion visible on the pedestal. Type three shows a four-armed goddess without the lion or the pot at her feet; she holds an *aṅkuśa* or *gadā* (goad or mace), a sword and a shield; and a child is seated on her lap. The fourth type is similar to the third, except that her upper two hands grasp a three-stringed instrument (*tridaṇḍī*) and a lotus. The fifth type is very elaborate. It shows the four-armed Devī, again without any lion or pot, seated in *vajrāsana* (on an adamantine throne). She holds a child on her lap with the two lower hands, while with the upper two hands, she displays a fish and a bowl. These images come from different sites in West Bengal and Bangladesh; Haque found them at Muroil in Bogra district, Mirpur in Rajshahi district, Deulpota in South 24 Parganas district, and Paikpara in Dacca district. They are datable between the tenth and twelfth centuries CE. Haque's argument is based on the testimony of the *Brahmavaivarta Purāṇa*, which discussed at length the worship of Ṣaṣṭhī. Haque further argues that the antiquity of Ṣaṣṭhī worship goes back to a date earlier than the eleventh century CE, because Al-Beruni (*c*. 973–1048/49 CE), the author of the *Tarikhu'l Hind*, or *An Account of India*, mentioned the *Brahmavaivarta Purāṇa*, along with other texts.

Indeed, this is a far-fetched argument. In the first place, Al-Beruni did not write anything either about the worship of Ṣaṣṭhī or about the goddess's iconographic features. Second, the date of the *Brahmavaivarta Purāṇa* is uncertain.[38] Some of the available portions of the *Brahmavaivarta Purāṇa* come very close to the late-medieval Maṅgalakāvyas in their ethos. Third, even the extant versions of the *Brahmavaivarta Purāṇa* do not provide any worthwhile information on the iconography of Ṣaṣṭhī; whatever little information is available does not have any clear correspondence with the images proposed to be identified as Ṣaṣṭhī by Haque. Despite Haque's attempt to label certain types of images as Ṣaṣṭhī, the empirical basis of Asutosh Bhattacharya's observations remains valid.

In sum, during the Kuṣāṇa period, Ṣaṣṭhī's importance was largely due to her association with Skanda-Kārttikeya. In Bengal, although her association with Kārttikeya is not entirely forgotten, she is a mother goddess in her own right, often identified with Maṅgalacaṇḍī, another powerful maternal figure, and sculpted images of Ṣaṣṭhī are unknown. Ṣaṣṭhī's essentially aniconic mode of worship occurs outside temple precincts and without the intervention of Brāhmaṇa priests. Indeed, in Bengali village practice, Ṣaṣṭhī is commonly worshipped in birth rituals for the protection of infants. 'The goddess, generally represented by a stone, is invoked for safeguarding the mother and the child against the influence of malevolent spirits. The cowrie shell, regarded as a symbol of the Mother Goddess, on account of its apparent similarity with the female generative organ, is used as an amulet which children carry in order to protect themselves against evil spirits.'[39]

Thus, the identification of the Raigunj image type, showing the Devī with a child, with or without a lion vehicle and pot, and holding different attributes in two or four hands, remains unresolved, and cannot be adequately explained by standard iconography and its variants, although Svaṅgādevī perhaps comes closest, iconographically, to the goddess in question. One rather clear conclusion that emerges out of the inscriptional and contextual evidence, however, is that the acceptance of Devī cut across sectarian lines and was prominent in Bihar, Bengal, and Assam from the late medieval period on.

Whatever the Raigunj Devī's local affiliation, and however divergent her attributes or other iconographic features, her association with a child remains the most decisive element in her iconography. As mentioned above, the second most important iconographic element noticed in the Raigunj image is a bunch of three leaves on each of her upper hands. This is a rather unusual iconographic formula, although there exists an unbroken tradition associating goddesses with vegetation. In the *Devī Māhātmya* section of the *Mārkaṇḍeya Purāṇa*,[40] the Devī is made to convey this message. In two famous *ślokas* or verses, Devī assures the Devas that she will feed mankind through the lifesaving vegetation growing out of her body, and will thus be known as Śākambharī, 'she who supports with vegetables'. Devī as the source of vegetation has also been represented by means of different iconographic formulae. For example, both at Harappa and in a group of Devī figures in south India and the Deccan, vegetation comes out of the female organ.[41] In a Bhita seal assigned to the Gupta period, a lotus supported on its stalk originates from the torso of the Devī.[42]

In eastern India, the vegetal connection is suggested by Devī's identification with the nine plants during her autumnal worship at Durgā Pūjā. A banana plant, along with eight other varieties of fruit, roots, and bunches of leaves, are tied together and covered by a sari, which is then installed near the icon of the Goddess. R.P. Chandra observes: 'An important aspect of Durga worship, called *navapatrikā* or the worship of the nine plants (lit. 'leaves'), also clearly shows that the goddess was conceived as the personification of the vegetation spirit.'[43] Citing the authority of the *Puraścaryārṇava*—a later Tantric text from the eighteenth century—Chandra further argues that Devī, in her nine different forms, namely, Brahmāṇī, Kālikā, Durgā, Kārtikī, Śivā, Raktadantikā, Śokarahitā, Cāmuṇḍā, and Lakṣmī, presides over the following plants: *kadalī* (banana), *kacī* (mango), *haridrā* (turmeric), *jayantī* (nutmeg), *bilva* (maremelos), *dāḍimba* (pomegranate), *aśoka* (saraca asoka), *māna* (arum), and *dhānya* (rice paddy).[44] J.N. Bandyopādhyāy argues that in several later Tantric texts (*Kulacūḍāmaṇī*, *Śāktataraṅginī*, and *Tantrasāra*) the reference to plants (*kulavṛkṣa*) in the context of Śākta ritual signifies the vegetal aspect of the Goddess.[45]

The point of citing all these examples is to emphasize the relevance of the vegetation motif in the iconography of the Devī. From proto-historic civilization to medieval times, this association continues to be reflected in Devī iconography. Returning to our Raigunj image, the basic characteristics of the leaves in the upper hands are as follows: they are simple, lanceolate in shape, with an obtuse apex, a base not clearly visible, and an entire margin. The midrib is broad, distinct, and continues from base to apex; the venation is sub-opposite. It appears from the sculpture that the leaf is thick and leathery.

One may compare the leaves carved in this image with two well-known leaves, the *āmra* (mango) and *aśoka*, associated with Hindu rites and rituals. Neither one appears to be the exact model. *Āmra* leaves are generally offered in a bunch of five. Furthermore, they are longer than they are wide, and hence different in shape from the leaves shown in the Raigunj image. *Aśoka* leaves are associated with the worship of Ṣaṣṭhī. N.P. Joshi refers to the representation of *aśoka* leaves on a Kuṣāṇa-period sculpture.[46] But the basic features of *aśoka* leaves are different. These are elongated, spear-shaped, with an acute apex, and a crenulated or wavy margin. The best leaves with which to compare those in the Raigunj image's upper hand are those of the *putrañjīva* (*Putranjiva roxburghii,* the 'lucky bean tree' or 'amulet tree'); they are alternate, smooth, short petioled, oblong in shape, and with an obtuse apex, an oblique base, an entire or slightly wavy margin, and a distinct midrib. This tree is seen throughout tropical India, and in the lower reaches of the Himalayas, eastward in Myanmar and southward in Sri Laṅka.

William Roxbourgh, who first wrote of this tree in English in the early nineteenth century, observed that: '*Pootrunjeeva*' is the Sanscrit name. *Pootra* signifies a son and *jeeva* life. Dr. Berry of Madras informs me, the nuts are known, and sold in the bazars at that place by the very same appellation; and observes that they are strung by parents, and put round the necks of their children, to preserve them in health.[47]

Clearly, there is a deep-rooted popular belief in the healing qualities of the tree, especially with respect to children. This is reflected in the names by which the deified Putrañjīva is known in regional languages: Jīvaputraka in Marathi; Jiyāputā in Bengali;

and Jiyāsuta in Hindi.[48] All the names convey the same meaning: desire for the longevity of the (male) child. It is a common belief in rural Bengal that the Putrañjīva tree holds spiritual protective power, and is capable of destroying all evil spirits that might harm children. It is appropriate, therefore, that its leaves are seen in the hands of the Raigunj Devī with the child on her lap.

What can we conclude, therefore, after this extended discussion of the two characteristic features of the Devī in question? Together, the iconographic elements depicted in our problematic Raigunj image effectively convey its intended symbolism. A child on the lap of the Devī continued to recur unfailingly in all such images as a standard iconographic formula, revealing it to be emblematic of the archetypal image of the pan-Indian Mother Goddess. However, such forms, unless provided with a designation in the dedicatory records, remain nameless. Any attempt at imposing a cultic affiliation and a name amounts to the rejection of iconographic diversities, as observed in a large number of Devī images. In the Raigunj image the maternal aspect is illustrated in very convincing terms through the child on Devī's lap and the Putrañjīva leaves in her upper hands.

The foregoing discussion makes us increasingly aware of the limitations of textual sources in situating the bewildering varieties of Devī forms in early medieval eastern India, since it remains a frustrating fact that most of the iconographic forms as described in texts do not conform to images as they are actually found in temples, museums, or archaeological sites. Given this impasse, one would like to think that popular and oral traditions would provide clues to the identification of local goddesses, many of whom were, after all, created and sustained by the nontextual, popular milieu. Such a methodological move is, of course, fraught with obstacles. First, many icons awaiting identification are now divorced from their original worship contexts and displayed in museums or in private collections, where their devotees may lose touch with them. Second, even if one were to find, say, a Svaṅgādevī-like stone or clay deity worshipped in a contemporary setting, one might be loath, in the absence of inscriptional evidence, to trust local efforts at identification, particularly if one suspected that the deity had moved up to become linked with a goddess of larger or more well-recognized provenance. In other words, charting the early stages of the process postulated by Narendra Nath Bhattacharyya—the tendency of local goddesses to become enveloped by the supreme Goddess—is hampered by the results of the very process itself, as a result of which local deities' names are forgotten or layered over. Nevertheless, image-centered ethnographies—consulting folk stories, oral traditions, and religious beliefs surrounding particular styles of images and their spiritual powers—ought to be added to the methodological arsenal of art historians hoping to interpret medieval iconographic forms from predominantly rural areas. Such interpretive challenges aside, these local memories may be our best resource to arrive at some means of breaking the deadlock occasioned by mutually nonreinforcing texts and sculptural artifacts.

One can learn a lot in the attempt, however, even if all of our best efforts fail to produce a definitive conclusion. One must retain a sense of humility in the process of scholarship, recognizing what we can know and refraining from the temptation to assert certainty when there is none.

As Bhattacharyya cogently reminds us, although the impulse of Śāktism flowed in many streams, representing manifold 'religious beliefs and practices belonging to peoples of different cultural grades . . . and diverse historical conditions, . . . [f]rom the tenth century onward, the Śākta-Tāntric cults gained a qualitatively changed character and became woven into the texture of all the religious practices current in India.'[49] Perhaps the very pervasiveness of the Śākta element is so successful that the isolation of any one element, be it name, provenance, ritual significance, or information about the circumstances of an image's creation, is nearly impossible.

NOTES

1. Narendra Nath Bhattacharyya, 'Mother Worship in Bengal,' in Asok Datta, ed., *Studies in Archaeology: Papers Presented in Memory of P.C. Dasgupta* (New Delhi: Books & Books, 1991), 355.
2. Ibid.
3. I am thankful to Sri Banibrata Basu, IPS, then superintendent of police,

North Dinajpur District, who handed over the sculpture under discussion to the State Archaeological Museum, West Bengal; to Dr. S. Sengupta; and to Sri S. Chakraborty for infrastructural and academic support.

4. For references in the *Mahābhārata*, see *Vana-parva* 215.16, 18, 21–22; 217; 219.20–48; and *Śalya-parva* 45. *Mātṛkās* are also referenced in the following Purāṇas: *Agni* 50.21–22, 30–37, 144.30–37; *Bhāgavata* 2.10.37–39, 10.63.6–29; *Devī Bhāgavata* 5.28–29; *Devī Māhātmya* 8.38, 44, 49, 62; *Matsya* 179.9–32, 261.33–38; *Vāmana* 30; and *Viṣṇudharmottara* 1.227, 17.33–37. For a description of the contents of these and other Purāṇic sources, see David R. Kinsley's chapter on 'The Mātṛkās' in his *Hindu Goddesses: Visions of the Divine Feminine in the Hindu Religious Tradition* (Berkeley: University of California Press, 1986), 151–60; and Katherine Anne Harper, 'Appendix: Post-Seventh Century References on the Mātṛkās,' in *The Iconography of the Saptamātṛkās: Seven Hindu Goddesses of Spiritual Transformation* (Lewiston, U.K.: Edwin Mellen Press, 1989). For a discussion of *Bṛhatsaṁhitā* 57.56 and 60.9, see Thomas B. Coburn, *Devī-Māhātmya: Crystallization of the Goddess Tradition* (Delhi: Motilal Banarsidass, 1985), 325.
5. See Kinsley, 'Mātṛkās,' 155–56. For a discussion of the *Brahmavaivarta Purāṇa*, see below in this essay.
6. R.C. Hazra, *Studies in the Upapuranas*, vol. 2: *Śākta and Non-Sectarian Upapuranas* (Calcutta: Sanskrit College, 1963), 35–36.
7. Hazra, *Studies in the Upapuranas*, 94. Ludo Rocher, however, suggests an earlier date: the latter half of the sixth century CE. See his *The Purāṇas*, vol. 2, fasc. 3 of *A History of Indian Literature*, ed. Jan Gonda (Wiesbaden: Otto Harrassowitz, 1986), 167.
8. Hazra, *Studies in the Upapuranas*, 36.
9. Ibid., 51–52.
10. *Devī Purāṇam* (in Bengali), ed. Pañcānan Tarkaratna (Calcutta: Nababhārat, [1384] 1977), chap. 50, pt. 2, vv. 29–30.
11. Ibid., pt. 3, v. 32. *Apahasta* means 'striking or throwing away or off', so the second part of the verse may mean, 'throwing a fruit and a flower'. *Krodhanā* means 'inclined to wrath, passionate, angry; a passionate woman; the name of a mother [*mātṛ*] in Skanda's retinue'.
12. Rakhal Das Banerji, *The Eastern Indian School of Mediaeval Sculpture* (Delhi: Manager of Publications, 1933), 31, pl. 12.C.
13. D.C. Sircar, editorial comment on P. Banerjee's 'Some Inscription from Bihar,' in *Journal of Ancient Indian History* 7, pts. 1–2 (1973–74): 108n.27.
14. P. Banerjee, 'Some Inscriptions from Bihar,' in *Journal of Ancient Indian History* 7, pts. 1–2 (1973–74): 108–9.
15. D.C. Sircar, 'Three Inscriptions from Valgudar,' *Epigraphia Indica* 28, pt. 3 (July 1949): 138–39. Sircar's research at Valgudar 'introduces us to a different name of Devī. The image, datable to *c.* eighth to ninth century, is described as the goddess Gausavā (or Gausevā?). The image, a pious gift by

Nṛkaṭṭa, was installed at the above-mentioned city of Krimilā' (ibid., 145).

16. D.C. Sircar, 'Jaynagar Image Inscription of Year 35,' *Journal of the Bihar Research Society* 41, pt. 2 (June 1955): 146.
17. Information courtesy of Dr. N. Goswami, curator, Asutosh Museum of Indian Art, University of Calcutta.
18. Susan L. Huntington, *The 'Pala-Sena' Schools of Sculpture* (Leiden: E.J. Brill, 1984), fig. 80.
19. *Kālikā Purāṇam*, ed. Pañcānan Tarkaratna (Calcutta: Nababhārat, [1384] 1977), chap. 18, vv. 49–50.
20. D.C. Sircar, 'Jaynagar Image Inscription,' 151–53.
21. Nalini Kanta Bhattasali, *Iconography of Buddhist and Brāhmaṇical Sculptures in the Dacca Museum* (Dacca: Rai S.N. Bhadra Bahadur, 1929), 227.
22. Prithvi K. Agarwala, 'Notes on Two Problematic Images from Bengal,' in *Studies in Art and Archaeology of Bihar and Bengal: Nalinikanta Satavarsiki; Dr. N.K. Bhattasali Centenary Volume, 1888–1988*, ed. Debala Mitra and Gouriswar Bhattacharya (Delhi: Sri Satguru, 1989), 93.
23. See ibid., 95n21, for the Sanskrit description of Svaṅgādevī.
24. I am not aware if this singularly important image has yet been published.
25. Gautam Sengupta, *Treasures of the State Archaeological Museum, West Bengal*, vol. 2: *Sculptures* (Calcutta: Directorate of Archaeology, Government of West Bengal, 1991), pl. 12.
26. The opinion of D.K. Chakravarty is here cited by Enamul Haque in his *Bengal Sculptures: Hindu Iconography up to c. 1250 A.D.* (Dhaka: Bangladesh National Museum, 1992), 283.
27. See ibid.
28. N.P. Joshi, 'Sasthi in Literature and Art,' in Devendra Handa, ed., *Ajaya-Sri: Recent Studies in Indology: Prof. Ajay Mitra Shastri Felicitation Volume* (Delhi: Sundeep Prakashan, 1989), 2: 392.
29. Ibid., 392.
30. Ibid.
31. Ibid., 393.
32. Ibid., 392.
33. *Brahmavaivarta Purāṇam*, ed. Pañcānan Tarkaratna (Calcutta: Nababhārat, [1386] 1979), *Prakṛti Khaṇḍa* 1.73–79.
34. 43.3-19. See *Srimad Devi Bhagawatam*, trans. Swami Vijnanananda, 2nd edn. (1921-23; rpt., New Delhi: Oriental Books, 1977), 987–88.
35. Note, however, that Swami Vijnanananda translates *bhittayām puttalikām* as 'figures drawn on the floor' (*Srimad Devi Bhagawatam*, 987); N.P. Joshi, as 'painted on the walls' ('Sashti in Literature and Art,' 391).
36. Asutosh Bhattacharya, 'The Cult of Sasthi in Bengal,' *Man in India* 28, no. 3 (1948): 152–62.
37. Haque, *Bengal Sculptures*, 261–67 and pls. 211–13. Earlier, R.C. Majumdar had made a similar suggestion with regard to a *devī* image from Mirpur or

Rajshahi, Bangladesh. See Mazumder, ed., *The History of Bengal* (Dacca: University of Dacca, 1943), 1: 461, and pl. 14 (p. 38).

38. Rocher, *The Purāṇas*, 163, opines that although the kernel of the *Brahmavaivarta Purāṇa* may derive from as early as the tenth century, the text as we have it now dates only to the fifteenth or sixteenth century and was probably produced in Bengal.
39. Narendra Nath Bhattacharyya, *The Indian Mother Goddess* (1970; 2nd edn., Columbia, Mo.: South Asia Books, 1977), 46–47.
40. *Devī Māhātmya* 11.44–45; see Thomas B. Coburn, *Encountering the Goddess: A Translation of the Devī-Māhātmya and a Study of Its Interpretation* (Albany: State University of New York Press, 1991), 78.
41. For a discussion of these seals, see Jitendra Nāth Bandyopādhyāy, *Pañcopāsanā* (in Bengali) (Calcutta: Firma K.L. Mukhopādhyāy, 1960), 217–19. See also Narendra Nath Bhattacharyya, *Indian Mother Goddess*, 19–20.
42. Bandyopādhyāy, *Pañcopāsanā*, 220.
43. R.P. Chandra, *The Indo-Aryan Races: A Study of the Origins of Indo-Aryan People and Institutions* (1916; rpt., New Delhi: Indological Book Corp., 1976), 131, cited in Bandyopādhyāy, *Pañcopāsanā*, 282.
44. Cited in Chandra, *Indo-Aryan Races,* 282–83.
45. Ibid., 283.
46. Joshi, 'Sasthi in Literature and Art,' 394.
47. William Roxburgh, *Flora Indica; or, Descriptions of Indian Plants* (Serampore: W. Thacker, 1832), 3: 767.
48. H. Sentapau, *Common Trees* (New Delhi: National Book Trust, 1966), 118–19.
49. Narendra Nath Bhattacharyya, *Indian Mother Goddess*, 230.

PART IV

Experiencing Śākta Power

9

A Festival for Jagaddhātrī and the Power of Localized Religion in West Bengal

RACHEL FELL McDERMOTT

One of the first places Narendra Nath Bhattacharyya took me to after my arrival in West Bengal in 1988 was Chandannagar, a former French colony in the district of Hooghly, about an hour's train ride north of Calcutta (see map 2).[1] In the late afternoon, we hired a bicycle-rickshaw from nearby Chinsurah, Naren-da's hometown, and after a long, bumpy ride, we reached our destination. Chandannagar seemed magical to me. I saw, in the soft, dusk light, bamboo poles being erected at street intersections, cul-de-sacs, and empty municipal lots; atop the poles were men in precarious positions stringing them together to form outlines of huge, two-to-three-storey buildings and temples. Jagaddhātrī Pūjā was imminent, Naren-da told me, and the city's builders, engineers, and electricians were busy creating the elaborately decorated temporary structures, or *pāṇḍāls*, that would house the Goddess during her three-day sojourn in the city. A few days later he brought me back, and this time goddesses greeted my astonished gaze at every corner.

Over the thirteen years that I was privileged to be Naren-da's student and friend, he told me many stories and took me to see many places—all of them connected with or situated in his home district of Hooghly. He was known as a sort of regional savant, an expert on the historical, archaeological, and religious history of the area, in which he spent his entire life. It is fitting, therefore, to include an essay on Jagaddhātrī Pūjā in this volume of tributes to his memory, for Jagaddhātrī is a goddess associated especially with the Hooghly and nearby Nadia districts of West Bengal. Even today,

Jagaddhātrī Pūjā is synonymous with Chandannagar and a few towns close by.

Jagaddhātrī is widely believed to be a form of the goddess Durgā. In the nineteenth century, Jagaddhātrī Pūjā was prescribed in times of distress, when the typical three-day Durgā Pūjā could not be held; Jagaddhātrī Pūjā occurs exactly one month after Durgā Pūjā and is similar in many ways, except that prescriptions for the seventh, eighth, and ninth days of Durgā's nine-day festival are amalgamated into one day, the ninth. Because of the close relationship between these two forms of the Goddess, I have chosen to present this overview of Jagaddhātrī Pūjā as a comparison with Durgā Pūjā. This will afford us the opportunity to see in what ways regionalization and localization can change a pan-Bengali deity.[2]

THE CURIOUS QUESTION OF ORIGINS

The festival as we know it today is not very old, and probably does not predate the mid-eighteenth century. There are numerous variants on its origin story, but almost all of them involve the presence of the famous maharaja, Kṛṣṇacandra Rāy of Nadia (*c.* 1728–82), the towns of Krishnanagar[3] (see map 2) and/or Chandannagar,[4] and the uneasy political climate under the *nawābs*.

The core of the most popular story is as follows: Kṛṣṇacandra Rāy had been imprisoned by one of the *nawābs*. It was nearing Durgā Pūjā season, and he prayed to be released in time to get home to Krishnanagar, his capital in Nadia district, in order to be able to perform his worship of the Goddess. He was indeed released, but too late; even by rushing home by boat as fast as possible, he was unable to arrive before the ninth day of the festival. Discouraged and exhausted, he dreamed that a goddess on a lion with weapons in her hands appeared to him and reassured him, saying, 'Worship me next month, on the ninth day of the bright fortnight of Kārtik, and you will not be deprived of my blessings.' He thereupon described the goddess he had seen to his artisans so that they could make an image of her and worshipped her as instructed.[5]

A rival story associates the rise of Jagaddhātrī Pūjā not with Kṛṣṇacandra Rāy or Krishnanagar, but with the *dewān* of the French trading town of Chandannagar, a man named Indranārāyaṇ Caudhurī, who introduced the festival in the rice-selling business section of town, Laksmiganj at Caulpatti. It was due to the Pūjā's growing fame that Indranārāyaṇ's friend Kṛṣṇacandra came to Chandannagar, where he consulted a locally renowned Tantric Brāhmaṇa to learn how he, too, could perform this new Pūjā and import it to Krishnanagar.[6] A third story reverses the order of influence, stating that it was Indranārāyaṇ who initiated his worship of Jagaddhātrī on the model provided by his friend Kṛṣṇacandra in Nadia.[7]

No origin story dates the annual public worship of the Goddess further back than the mid eighteenth century. But could her worship possibly be older than these legends suggest? What clues do we get from Sanskrit and Bengali textual sources?

The name Jagaddhātrī, or 'She Who Supports the World', does not appear to occur as an epithet of the Goddess until the Purāṇas, where it occurs infrequently and is not accompanied by any specific iconographic description or mention of a separate cult.[8] Several Tantric texts also mention her name tangentially; for example, she occurs in *Kāmākhyā Tantra* 10.8, *Kubjikā Tantra* 3.65, and *Kālikā Purāṇa* 37.24–27,[9] but in none of these is there any iconographic description, and the specific festival in the month of Kārtik is not detailed.

Indeed, the first reference to an annual public worship occurs in Śūlapāṇi's fifteenth-century *Kālaviveka*, where one is instructed to worship Jagaddhātrī, depicted seated on the back of a lion, three times on the ninth day of the bright half of Kārtik.[10] Similar instructions are provided in fifteenth-century works by Bṛhaspati Rāy and Śrīnātha Ācārya Cuḍāmaṇi, the *Smṛtiratnahāra* and the *Kṛtyatattvārṇava*, respectively.[11] One can also find Jagaddhātrī's *dhyāna mantra* in Kṛṣṇānanda Āgambāgīś's sixteenth-century *Tantrasāra*, where she is described as follows:

Seated on a lion's back, adorned with various ornaments,
With four hands, the Great Goddess, a snake for a sacred thread,
In her two left hands a conch and a bow,
In her two right hands a discus and five arrows,
Wearing a red garment, her young body outshining the sun,

Served by Nārada and other sages, the beauteous wife of Bhava,
The three folds of her navel shine like a clump of lotuses.
She is seated on a blooming lotus on top of a lion on a gem-encrusted island.[12]

Given the steady, albeit lightly trickling, stream of references to the Pūjā since the fifteenth century, it is surprising that neither the Bengali poet Bhāratcandra Rāy (1712–60), a patronee of Kṛṣṇacandra Rāy, who in his *Annadāmaṅgal* lists the yearly religious holidays current in his day, nor Raghunandan, the famed seventeenth-century Bengali author of the law book *Aṣṭa-vimśatitattva*, mentions Jagaddhātrī in his work.[13] Perhaps the most one can infer, from the origin stories and the scant textual evidence, is that Kṛṣṇacandra Rāy, an avid Śākta patron, incorporated Jagaddhātrī into his larger program of popularizing Śākta traditions. He had already been credited with the spreading of Kālī Pūjā, and he was also a devotee of the goddess Durgā. It makes sense therefore to assume—even if one does not accept the specifics of the prison story—that this Nadia zamindar used his prestige and wealth to revive the worship of a goddess whose ritual prescriptions, though evidenced in earlier texts, had fallen into disuse by the mid eighteenth century.[14] Such a supposition has merit whether the initial popularizer was Kṛṣṇacandra or his friend Indranārāyaṇ Caudhurī, in Chandannagar: no matter who was first, the festival was a renewal of an older rite and occurred in the context of aggressive Śākta patronage in regions of West Bengal fairly close to Calcutta that were experiencing power struggles under the *nawābs*.

In terms of its comparison with the heavily textually attested Durgā Pūjā, it is obvious that Jaggadhātrī Pūjā was a late addition to the menu of Śākta festivals. Durgā Pūjā's origins are wildly contested, with competing origins stories from the sixteenth and seventeenth centuries and zamindar progenitors deriving from areas as disparate as the hinterlands of West Bengal and the interior of what is now Bangladesh. Durgā Pūjā may be a distinctly Bengali phenomenon, but it cannot be said to be regional in the same sense as its daughter offshoot.

LIKE DURGĀ, LIKE JAGADDHĀTRĪ: DID THE BRITISH SEE JAGADDHĀTRĪ?

A survey of English-language newspapers from the late eighteenth century up to 1947 shows that the British were alternately fascinated by, critical of, and passively reconciled to the events connected with the annual Durgā Pūjā holiday. Scarcely a year went by in which the festival was not mentioned, described, or pontificated about in all the Calcutta newspapers, no matter how friendly or inimical to Indian interests. The same is true, but in a radically reduced fashion, of the Jagaddhātrī Pūjā, which runs a distant third in British news coverage behind the Durgā and Kālī Pūjās.

This occasional reporting is helpful in establishing the existence and popularity of the festival among Hindus, even from an early date. In his four-volume *History, Literature, and Mythology of the Hindoos* (1817–20), for instance, William Ward describes the iconography of 'Juguddhatree' and the large sums spent on illuminations, songs, dances, the entertainment of Brāhmaṇas, and priests employed to read the *Caṇḍī*.[15] There is evidence from the 1820s through the 1840s, when the British were generally open to Hindu festivities and would accept Pūjā invitations from the city's wealthy babus, that Jagaddhātrī was also part of the holiday circuit: English bands and 'nautches', or dance performances, were announced as coming entertainments, and British reporters also noted the Goddess's images, their numbers, and tasteful decorations.[16] Even as late as 1889, when most Britons had ceased to be interested in descriptions of Pūjā events, it was announced in the *Statesman and Friend of India* that 'the Juggodhatri Poojah' had been celebrated 'with great pomp' in the house of 'Baboo Girish Chunder Banerjee in Bhowanipore', when 1,100 Brāhmaṇas, Śūdras, and mendicants were fed.[17] By the early twentieth century, when the Pūjā holiday season was enthusiastically anticipated by Britons, Jagaddhātrī Pūjā was, along with Durgā Pūjā, viewed as a wonderful excuse to escape from Calcutta.[18] Note that English newspapers were very Calcutta-centric in their coverage; the area north and west, from Chandannagar up to Krishnanagar, was not described as the heart of Jagaddhātrī's popularity.

THE GROWTH OF THE PUBLIC PŪJĀ

The developmental changes in Jagaddhātrī Pūjā mirrored, and in some cases even anticipated, those undergone by Durgā Pūjā.

The earliest festivities were patronized by wealthy merchants and businessmen, who paid for the image, the priests, the entertainments (street plays, puppet shows, circuses, and various types of female singers and dancers), and the distribution of food. The oldest celebration in Chandannagar, for instance, was started by Indranārāyaṇ Caudhurī (who died in 1756 in Laksmiganj, Caulpatti), and his descendants continue to do the worship in his name. The oldest Pūjā in nearby Bhadreswar is at Tetutala, Gaurhati, and dates from 1793.[19] In Krishnanagar, the earliest Pūjā is that of Kṛṣṇacandra Rāy, which is still performed by priests in the large Pūjā hall that he built adjacent to his mansion.[20] Another very old Pūjā, founded in Krishnanagar in 1773, is in the Casapara area of town; this Jagaddhātrī is known affectionately as Buḍimā, or the Old Mother.[21] Even in districts not known for their Jagaddhātrī devotion, one occasionally hears of old family worship; at Kagram in Murshidabad, the oldest Pūjā belongs to the Mukherji family, whose ancestor is said to have started it upon seeing Kṛṣṇacandra's festival in Krishnanagar.[22] There is also abundant evidence that respected old families in Calcutta sponsored Jagaddhātrī Pūjā in the nineteenth century—although it must be remembered that all of them added this on to an autumnal worship schedule previously dominated by Durgā.[23]

The changeover from privately sponsored Pūjās to those paid for by groups of friends or kinsmen (called *bāroiyāri*, or those organized by twelve friends) originated not with Durgā Pūjā, as one might expect, but with Jagaddhātrī Pūjā, at Guptipara in the Hooghly district, in 1790. This spreading out of the costs and responsibility for all Śākta festivities reflected the increasingly impoverished state of rural zamindars, who, squeezed by British revenue demands and taxation introduced through the Permanent Settlement, could no longer afford annual displays of wealth. During the nineteenth century, whether in private home or community worship, the immersion ceremonies, when the images would be carried to the riverbanks, were a lavish affair. Chandannagar, in particular, was known for its nighttime *śobhāyātrās*, or processions, in which ninety to one hundred bearers would carry the biggest images, surrounded by parallel lines of bystanders holding kerosene torches.

In the 1920s, a second major change occurred in respect to the autumnal festivals, and this time the pioneers were those focusing on Durgā Pūjā. Partly in response to Gandhi's call to open temples and religious ceremonies to Untouchables, and partly as a mechanism for garnering the greatest possible number of Hindu votes to counteract Muslim and Untouchable calls for separate electorates, politicians in Calcutta in the 1920s coined the phrase '*sarbajanīn* Pūjās', or those that were universal, open to all. Further democratized as a result, Pūjās were now sponsored by entire neighborhoods, civic associations, or caste groupings, and the festivals literally took to the streets, with goddesses temporarily residing in *pāṇḍāls* placed in public roads, alleyways, and vacant spaces between buildings.

Jagaddhātrī Pūjā, as also Kālī Pūjā, followed closely behind. By 1956, residents of Chandannagar and its sister town Bhadreswar began to feel the need for some sort of organizing body to oversee the burgeoning number of community Pūjās, and they therefore established a central committee, whose purpose was to supply, for a membership fee, everything a Pūjā committee would need for its celebration: kerosene, electricity, priests, and arrangements for the final procession after the third day.[24] The number of central committee-approved Pūjās has risen steadily every year since 1956: in 1968 there were 44; in 1977, 89; and in 2002, 132.[25] Only 51 of these 132, collectively taking 210 trucks from four zones of the city, are permitted to join the *śobhāyātrā* to the river (see fig. 16); acceding to its historical pride of place, the image from Laksmiganj brings up the rear. Krishnanagar has its own procession traditions; first, each of its 126 Pūjā committees takes the *ghaṭ*, or pot of water that officially houses the spirit of the Goddess, to the Jalangi River for immersion, and then, later in the evening, the committees return to the river with their images. All processions must pass by the Nadia Rāj estate, where the raja and his wife used to view the images and award prizes; owing to her venerable status in the town's history, the goddess Buḍimā comes last.[26]

Pūjā growth has been reflected not only in Krishnanagar and Chandannagar, bursting every year with more and more goddesses, but also in the enthusiasm for the festival that has spread to surrounding villages and towns along the Hooghly River, up into Nadia district.[27] As we shall shortly see, many of them attempt to outdo their more famous predecessors by introducing some peculiarity that makes their worship of Jagaddhātrī remarkable. In this, they and the hubs of Jagaddhātrī fervor, Chandannagar and Krishnanagar, follow the lead set by the enthusiastic patrons of Durgā.

JAGADDHĀTRĪ IN THE CONCORDE

In its gorgeous displays of pageantry, creativity, opulence, and social commentary, the three-day Jagaddhātrī festival at Chandannagar rivals what one would find for Durgā Pūjā in Calcutta. Towering *pāṇḍāls*, built to imitate almost anything one can conceive of, and

Fig. 16: Getting ready for the *śobhāyātrā*, or procession. Chandannagar. 6 November 2000. Photograph by Rachel Fell McDermott.

associated lighting shows, depicting moving figures in brightly pulsating colors, dazzle the sight, especially when seen against the night sky. Some *pāṇḍāls* are constructed in imitation of temples, the most appropriate settings for images of the Goddess, or even of Buddhist and Christian religious buildings.[28] But Pūjā committee organizers also branch out in novel ways, building *pāṇḍāls* in the shapes of the type of French residence one might have seen in Chandannagar in the eighteenth century, the Eiffel Tower, or an African fort, for example,[29] not to speak of computers, the Titanic, and the man-eating shark from *Jaws*.[30] Lighting shows delight with similarly contemporary scenes: moving depictions of a giraffe eating leaves, peacocks dancing, Humpty Dumpty, Mickey Mouse, Superman, Spider-Man, World Cup soccer, cricket players batting and bowling, the development of the mail system from horses to vans, and even the TV show *Who Wants to Be a Millionaire*.

Perhaps the most intriguing uses of *pāṇḍāls* and lighting exhibitions concern the reflection, and sometimes critique, of social or political events. The Goddess is invoked in a recreation of the dacoit Veeraapan's den, in a Concorde airliner crashing to the ground, in an Indian army base in the Himalayas, and in a simulated flood-torn village.[31] Electricians fashion whirling lighting shows of Gandhi spinning, Amartya Sen receiving the Nobel Prize, a little girl being married to a dog to stave off the bad omens in her horoscope, and nuclear bombs exploding at Pokhran.[32] Some committee organizers use the Pūjā to lobby for pet causes; panels decorating the inside or outside of the *pāṇḍāls* demonstrate the nefarious effects of tobacco, the benefits of donating blood, or the terrible plight of flood victims.

Ever since the mid 1970s, when *pāṇḍāls* for all Durgā Pūjās in West Bengal began to be built in imitation of specific buildings or material items, towns sponsoring Jagaddhātrī Pūjā have enthusiastically followed suit. And, like Durgā and Kālī Pūjā as well, the catholicity of the festivity is proudly advertised and borne out: in Chandannagar, some of the Pūjā committees are headed by Muslims or are entirely run by Harijans or women.[33]

There is indication, however, that just as Durgā Pūjā has been put to political use when Bengali national interests were at stake,

Jagaddhātrī Pūjā has also been employed for raising consciousness or deliberately provoking communal tension. In the 1880s and 1890s, decades of increasing Hindu-Muslim violence, when Muharram and Pūjā processions frequently coincided, the police had to be vigilant against communal violence—and often failed. In Bankimcandra Chatterjee's famous book *Ānandamaṭh* (1882), Jagaddhātrī is a symbol of ancient India, with her triumphant stability and benevolence; she is what had been lost to the successive Mughal and British hegemonies, and the renunciant heros of the story seek to redeem her former glory through their politically subversive activities. During the first partition of Bengal in 1905, Pūjā *pāṇḍāls* were used to garner contributions for the nationalist cause.[34] In 1984, when Jagaddhātrī Pūjā coincided with the assassination of Mrs. Gandhi, several committee organizers, in all parts of the state where the Pūjā was celebrated, affixed photographs of her on their *pāṇḍāl* walls or positioned Mrs. Gandhi next to the Goddess herself.[35]

Because the Communist Party of India (Marxist), which has been in power uninterruptedly in the state since 1977, is extremely sensitive to communalism and actively polices Pūjā *pāṇḍāls* for offensive designs, the Goddess and her Pūjās are less politically charged than they once were, or perhaps could be. In 2001, for instance, artisans were prohibited from fashioning Durgā's adversary, the buffalo demon Mahiṣa, in the shape of Osama bin Laden, and lighting experts were asked not to depict the crashing of planes into the World Trade Center. If the Bharatiya Janata Party were to gain an upper hand in the state, one might begin to see increased recourse to goddess imagery as a means of championing particularly Hindu causes.

WE ARE BETTER THAN YOU

Imitation, rivalry, competition for victory: these are the galvanizing feelings and hopes that motivate most *sarbajanīn* Jagaddhātrī Pūjā committees. The big contest is with Durgā Pūjā—not only to adopt its newest features but also to outdo it. Chandannagar hardly celebrates Durgā Pūjā at all, claiming, rightly, that its Jagaddhātrī

Pūjā, which lasts the same number of days and has just as gorgeous *pāṇḍāls* and even taller images, can outshine Durgā Pūjā anywhere. In the early 1940s, the average Jagaddhātrī was ten to twelve feet high; in 2003, together with her crown, she ranged up to thirty-five feet. Within the city itself, Pūjā organizers compete with one another for a bevy of prizes.

The major rival of Krishnanagar's Jagaddhātrī devotees is not another Pūjā, but the city of Chandannagar. Krishnanagar residents emphasize their special *ghaṭ bisarjan*, festoon their *pāṇḍāls* with depictions of Kṛṣṇacandra Rāy's dream and Jagaddhātrī's appearance to him (see fig. 17), and are now aided by a Bombay merchant firm that has undertaken to help spread the fame of the Jagaddhātrī tradition. Through the awarding of prizes for the best image, *ghaṭ bisarjan*, *pāṇḍāl* design, and lighting exhibition, through advertisements on cable networks, and through the creation of a special web site, they are hoping to reach a larger audience and to outstrip Chandannagar in fame.[36]

Fig. 17: Panel drawing of Rājā Kṛṣṇacandra Rāy's dream of Jagaddhātrī. Decoration of the *pāṇḍāl* at Natunpara, Chandannagar, 6 November 2000. Photoghraph by Rachel Fell McDermott.

Other towns also look to Chandannagar as the standard for judgment. Risra, just a stop or two away on the local commuter rail line, asserts its independence by having a three-day Pūjā as well, but one that starts on the ninth day and extends three days later, when the Chandannagar images have all been immersed. The Bengali newspaper *Bartamān* reported in 2000 that even though Risra's Jagaddātrī Pūjā does not get Chandannagar's 'high profile', it is nonetheless 'superduper'. There are approximately fifty-five community Pūjās, of which fifteen are 'big budget' festivities. That year, one lucky Jagaddhātrī at Risra was welcomed into a huge replica of Buckingham Palace.[37] Guptipara, of historical importance because of its sponsorship of the first *bāroiyāri* Jagaddhātrī Pūjā in 1790, has fallen badly behind in the race for kudos. However, it, too, claims a distinction: Guptipara's goddesses have fireworks displays for their divine amusement.[38]

Another means of Pūjā glorification is the advertised appearance of a celebrity to view or even to inaugurate one's worship; typical invitees are the mayor, councilmen, judges, movie stars, or athletes. In 1995, the Dumdum Naboday Club in Calcutta had a special treat when Mother Teresa opened their Jagaddhātrī Pūjā.[39] Television and news coverage is also a big help to name recognition, as is, increasingly, the Internet. In their reveling in rivalry, Jagaddhātrī devotees equal their Durgā- and Kālī-centered competitors.

A DIMPLE IN HER CHIN

In many ways Jagaddhātrī looks like Durgā. She is beautiful, holds weapons in her hands, sits on a lion, and subdues a demon. However, a closer look reveals important differences. Durgā's ten arms are replaced by Jagaddhātrī's four; the latter holds a discus and arrow in her right hands and a conch and bow in her left. Durgā is usually standing with one leg on the back of her lion; Jagaddhātrī sits on hers in a half-lotus, with one leg hanging down, in the fashion of a South Indian goddess. Durgā is actively spearing Mahiṣa; Jagaddhātrī leaves the goring of the elephant demon to the ferocity of her lion, who squashes the elephant's head with one of his paws.

Absent are Durgā's four children, Gaṇeśa, Kārttikeya, Lakṣmī, and Sarasvatī; Jagaddhātrī, if flanked at all, is accompanied by Jayā and Bijayā, two companions. The Goddess herself is typically yellowish in color and arrayed in white[40]—often the white *solā* decorations that are characteristic of her adornment (see fig. 18).

It is a peculiarity of Durgā, and even to a greater extent Jagaddhātrī—but not Kālī—that their manifestation at the Pūjā season is practically the only time in the year when their devotees get to see and worship them; this is because there are very few permanent temples to either goddess in the state. Although there are a lot of Jagaddātrīs depicted on the walls of brick temples after the time of Caitanya, there is only one temple dedicated to her, in the village of Somra, Balagar subdivision, in the Hooghly district. It was built in 1755 by Dewān Rāmcandra Rāy, and the deity is made of eight stones, common for the expensive tastes of zamindar patrons of the time.[41] This lack of architectural attestation to her popularity prior to the mid eighteenth century serves to confirm what one gleans from her festal history: Jagaddhātrī did not become popular much before the time of Kṛṣṇacandra Rāy,[42] and if one wants to worship her, one must participate in her yearly Pūjā.

Like Durgā, Jagaddhātrī, too, can be classed according to facial types. The oldest Durgā and Jagaddhātrī faces are fairly stylized, with wide faces, elongated eyes stretching to the ears, and relatively tiny mouths. Newer facial varieties, introduced in Calcutta in the 1930s and 1940s, humanize the Goddess's visage; her face is rounded, her features are normalized relative to one another, in imitation of a young woman, and her mouth is sculpted into a charming smile. In present-day Chandannagar, Jagaddhātrī's eyes are decorated with mascara, and her dimpled chin is adorned with a beauty mark. The overwhelming number of Jagaddhātrīs I have seen, either in person in Chandannagar or Calcutta or in newspaper photographs, are of the saccharine, girlish type. Even the famed *sarbajanīn* Pūjā celebration in Baghbazar, Calcutta, dating from the late nineteenth century, which is frequently photographed, never departs from its beauteous goddess.[43]

There are a few Pūjā committees that still commission the old-style images. In the Chandannagar area, there are only two, at

Fig. 18: Close-up of Jagaddhātrī. Rashbihari Avenue, Calcutta, 7 November 2000. Photograph by Rachel Fell McDermott.

Laksmiganj and at Tetutala, Bhadreswar; both of these are old celebrations. Other fiercer, less anthropomorphized goddesses appear in Krishnanagar in the depiction of Buḍimā; at the Mukherji house in Kagram, Murshidabad; in Sorbhujbazar Sutragar, Santipur; and in Calcutta at Baburam Sil Lane and Kumartuli Friends Circle.[44] It is no coincidence that all of these were founded in the eighteenth or early nineteenth century, and that many of them still perform goat sacrifices. Indeed, according to Mr. Sāu, head of the central committee in Chandannagar and Bhadreswar in 2000, the only two Pūjās out of 131 in his jurisdiction that offer sacrifice are the two oldest; at Laksmiganj they sacrifice four or five goats, whereas 902 were given to the Goddess that year at Tetutola.[45]

As with Durgā Pūjā, the impetus toward a sweeter, vegetarian goddess has complex roots: many families or committees prefer to worship Jagaddhātrī in the Vaiṣṇavī, or vegetarian style; the mid-nineteenth-century critique by the British and reform-minded Hindus of the barbaric nature of blood sacrifice caused many orthodox Hindus to emphasize the more pacific aspects of goddess worship; and especially since Independence, the increased democratization and spread of Jagaddhātrī's worship has necessitated a more benign, kindlier persona for popular consumption.[46]

DOUBLES, MULTIFORMS, AND LOCALIZATION

As this survey has demonstrated, the history of Jagaddhātrī's Pūjā, its growth and reflection of current events and trends, the rivalries it engenders among its devotees, and the variations in the Goddess's iconographic depiction, are closely linked with her more important older sister, Durgā. Even though one might claim that in the late eighteenth to late nineteenth century, she may have had a more significant presence than she does now—recall that the first innovation in Pūjā performance, the *bāroiyāri*, occurred in the context of her worship rather than of Durgā's, and when Candramohan Datta, a devotee of Ramakrishna, received a vision of the Goddess, it was Ramakrishna's saintly wife, Sharada Devi, in the form of Jagaddhātrī whom he saw[47]—in most other respects one would have to admit that Jagaddhātrī is less interesting, derivative, and even bland, in comparison with Durgā. She has no myths, is rooted neither in the Purāṇas nor in the Tantras, and is not an example of a local goddess rising to prominence as a result of the sponsorship of a Sanskritizing or Brāhmaṇicizing group of patrons.

Looked at from the opposite perspective, however—Jagaddhātrī as a multiform of the universal goddess Durgā who has become localized—the Goddess of Hooghly and Nadia can tell us some interesting things about the Devī in general. Placed next to a plethora of other Durgā lookalikes, goddesses astride lions or tigers (Śerāṅvālī / Vaiṣṇo Devī of the northwest, Bāgheśvarī of the Gaya region, Kāmākhyā of Assam, Siṁhavāhinī of Bengal and Orissa, Vindhyavāsinī of the Vindhya mountains, the Jain goddess Ambikā, and various forms of tribal and mountain goddesses), Jagaddhātrī gains a context. Although, unlike Jagaddhātrī, many of these other Durgā doubles may have become elevated through a process of Brāhmaṇical absorption of what were once local deities, they share with her a regional jurisdiction and a popularity that lends distinction to their places of residence. What Jagaddhātrī offers her devotees in the towns north of Calcutta on the Hooghly River, many of which were once French, Danish, Dutch, or Portuguese trading posts, is a chance for a second sight of Durgā, a second consideration of her salvific power. As Frederick Burwick puts it in his book *Mimesis and Its Romantic Reflections*, 'the twice-told tale' is 'far from tedious'.[48] Through second tellings, one can catch discrepancies in the story and observe the various narrators' perspectives. For descendants of Raja Kṛṣṇacandra Rāy and other residents of Krishnanagar, Jagaddhātrī's gracious fulfillment of her devotee's wish to worship Durgā at home, away from the clutches of the rapacious *nawāb*, is an acknowledgment of his saintliness (some accounts refer to Kṛṣṇacandra as a *sādhaka*, or holy man), of her willingness to satisfy provincial needs, and of her farsightedness in providing provisions for worship in a time of crisis. Jagaddhātrī's appearance is evidence of the care of the Goddess, who is willing to manifest herself in multitudinous ways for the benefit of specific persons. By contrast, Chandannagar citizens' worship of Jagaddhātrī not only links them to the history of the most famous *rājā* and Śākta patron of the eighteenth century but also serves to embody a uniqueness that continues to set them apart, as their French colonial status did until 1950, from surrounding cities, especially Calcutta. West Bengalis in general are proud of this regional festival, and do not attempt to universalize it. The current web site for the West Bengal Tourism Office has a link to 'Festivals in West Bengal'; Jagaddhātrī Pūjā is described as a festival of Hooghly, and one is encouraged to take advantage of special tourism packages to avail oneself of its wonders.[49]

It is ironic but not surprising that when Jagaddhātrī travels to Hindu communities in the diaspora, she loses her regional flavor. True, she is worshipped almost exclusively by organizations founded by Bengalis—such as the Ramakrishna-Vedanta Societies and the Dakshineswar Ramkrishna Sangha Adyapeath—but the sponsorship of her festival is undertaken as a means of accentuating religious fervor and Bengali identity in general, rather than as a celebration of any specific geographic context. One devotee of the New Jersey-based Dakshineswar Ramkrishna Sangha Adyapeath remarked to me rather mournfully at their celebration of Jagaddhātrī Pūjā in November 2003 that not one of the other 120 members present that day had grown up in Chandannagar, and so none could share in her nostalgia for the Pūjā of her hometown. That Jagaddhātrī has gained a more universal Bengali audience away from home is further demonstrated by her inclusion in the yearly round of festivals performed at the Bangladesh Hindu Mandir in Queens, New York, a tightly knit group of Bangladeshi Hindu refugees who cling fervently to symbols of their Hindu Bengali identity and who agitate, from afar, for justice for minorities in Bangladesh.

Imitation, of course, leads to rivalry. One can see this, in the human realm, in the relationships of children to parents or of junior partners to their senior mentors. It occurs also in the animal world, in the art world, and in the world populated by goddesses. Durgā's doubles seem to 'win' in the regional areas in which they hold sway. But they do this only by borrowing, copying, and indigenizing the great symbol of a martial and maternal, beautiful and fierce, divine female energy sometimes known as Durgā. Jagaddhātrī is the Supporter of the World. Even though, in West Bengal, that 'world' consists principally of two districts west of the Hooghly River, it is her care for them, and her devotees' strong pride in that care, that humanizes Durgā, and hence also the omnipresent Goddess.

NOTES

1. Place-names, including names of districts, subdivisions, cities, towns, villages, and roads, are given here without diacritics. Where there are recognizable anglicized forms of names, I have used those; the names of small towns and villages are as close to the Bengali originals as possible. Since most people living in the time period covered in this essay (the late eighteenth century up to the present) knew Calcutta as Calcutta, and not as Kolkata (which came into effect only in 2001), I spell it Calcutta.
2. I use for comparison material covered in my forthcoming book on Durgā and Kālī Pūjās, *Of Fortunes and Festivals: Money, Power, and the Goddess of Bengal* (New York: Columbia University Press).
3. Krishnanagar is 118 kilometers north of Calcutta, just south of the Jalangi River, and has a current population of 1.3 lakhs. The headquarters of Nadia district, the city became a municipality in 1864, although it was famed as a center of religion, culture, and art at least from the time of its most famous raja in the eighteenth century, Kṛṣṇacandra Rāy. Apart from the raja's crumbling palace and a historic Roman Catholic church, the city is also famed for its clay dolls made in the suburb of Ghurni.
4. Chandannagar comprises about twenty square miles, and as of 2003 had a population of 1.4 lakhs. Although the current spelling and pronunciation of the name implies a derivation from *candan*, or sandalwood trees, the British misspelling, Chandernagore, probably hints at its earlier association with a crescent-shaped (*candra*) bend in the Hooghly River where the town is situated. The French commander Joseph Dupleix was the first to buy land in the area in 1673–74, but it was not until 1688 that the French got permission from Aurangzeb to build a warehouse and to trade, tax-free, in Bengal, Bihar, and Orissa; Chandannagar was settled from 1691. After the British first took Chandannagar in 1757, the town changed hands several times due to Anglo-French rivalry, but from 1815 until 1950 it remained a French colony. See Premtoṣ De, 'Candanagarer Jagaddhātrī Pujo,' *Sāptahik Bartamān* 12, no. 25 (13 November 1999): 8–10.
5. Narrators of this story do not agree on who the *nawāb* was (candidates are 'Alīvardī Khān [1740–56], Sirāj-ud-daula [1756–57], Mīr Ja'far [1757–60, 1763–65], and Mīr Qāsim [1760–63]), and hence on why the rājā was in

prison when this event occurred (was it for arrears of revenue payment, or because of his role in the battle of Plassey?) and why he was released (did the *nawāb* let him out, did the British free him, or was his deliverance due to the prayers of his daughter?). For representative examples of this story, see *Amrita Bazar Patrika,* 23 November 1963, 4; ibid., 20 November 1966, 1 of the Sunday magazine; ibid., 27 October 1971, 4; De, 'Candanagarer Jagaddhātrī Pujo'; Sudhīrkumār Mitra, *Huglī Jelār Debideul* (Kalikata: Aparna Book Distributors, 1991), 30–32; and a web site devoted to Krishnanagar history, www.geocities.com/shatakratu/town/jaga/jaga2/html (accessed 31 July 2005).

6. *Amrita Bazar Patrika,* 17 November 1969, 4; ibid., 27 October 1971, 4; Apūrba Caṭṭopādhyāy, 'Ālor Banyāy Bhāsbe Jagaddhātrīr Candannagar,' *Sāptahik Bartamān* 12, no. 25 (13 November 1999): 11–12; and Ajit Kumar Mukhopadhyay and Kalyan Chakrabortty, *Discover Chandernagore* (Chandannagar, Hooghly: Kumar, 1999), accessed online 1 November 2003. Some commentators note that the Brāhmaṇa in question, Candracuḍ Cūḍāmaṇi, lived during the time of Kṛṣṇacandra's grandson, Giriścandra Rāy; they conclude therefore that Jagaddhātrī was initiated and standardized later, in the early nineteenth century. See De, 'Candanagarer Jagaddhātrī Pujo' and Mitra, *Huglī Jelār Debideul*, 30–32.
7. Mitra, *Huglī Jelār Debideul*, 30–32.
8. In the *Devī Māhātmya*, the Goddess is called Jagaddhātrī twice (1.53, 13.10), Jagatam Dhātrī once (4.27) and Dhātrī once (5.8). See Thomas B. Coburn, *The Devī-Māhātmya: Crystallization of the Goddess Tradition* (New Delhi: Motilal Banarsidass, 1985), 205–6. In *Devī Bhāgavata Purāṇa* 6.6, Jagaddhātrī is one of several epithets used for the deluding goddess to whom the gods go in supplication for help against the demon Vṛtra. See *Srimad Devi Bhagawatam*, trans. Swami Vijñānananda, 2nd edn. (1921–23; rpt., New Delhi: Oriental Books, 1977), 495–99.
9. See *Kāmākhyā Tantram*, Sanskrit text edited with a Bengali translation by Jyotirlāl Dās (Calcutta: Nababhārat, 1978), 78; *Kubjikā Tantram*, Sanskrit text edited with a Bengali translation by Jyotirlāl Dās (Calcutta: Nababhārat, 1978), 33; and *Kālikā Purāṇam*, Sanskrit text edited with an English translation by Biswanarayan Shastri (Delhi: Nag, 1991), 2: 466–67.
10. For the original Sanskrit, see Hamsanārāyaṇ Bhaṭṭācārya, *Hinduder Debadebī: Udbhav o Kramabikāś* (Calcutta: Firma KLM, 1986), 3: 308, and Pratapaditya Pal, *Hindu Religion and Iconology According to the Tantrasāra* (Los Angeles: Vichitra Press, 1981), 42.
11. See Narendra Nath Bhattacharyya, *History of the Śākta Religion*, 2nd edn. (New Delhi: Munshiram Manoharlal, 1996), 168, and Mukhopadhyay and Chakrabortty, *Discover Chandernagore*.
12. See *Bṛhat Tantrasāra*, ed. Rasikmohan Caṭṭopādhyāy and translated into Bengali by Candrakumār Tarkālaṅkar (Calcutta: Nababhārat, 1982), section

called 'Atha Durgā Mantrāḥ,' 488. In most modern images, the Goddess holds one arrow, not five.

13. Bhaṭṭācārya, *Hinduder Debadebī: Udbhav o Kramabikāś*, 308–11.
14. For corroborating opinions, see Mahendranāth Datta, *Kalikātār Purātan Kāhinī o Prarthā*, 2nd edn. (1973; Kalikata: Mahendra, 1975), 130–31, and *Yugāntar*, Tuesday, 1 November 1995, 7.
15. William Ward, *The History, Literature, and Mythology of the Hindoos* (1817–1820; rpt., Delhi: Low Price, 1990), 3:130.
16. See, e.g., *Calcutta Gazette,* 17 November 1825, in *The Days of John Company: Selections from the Calcutta Gazette 1824–1832*, ed. Anil Chandra Das Gupta (Calcutta: Government Printing, 1959), 107; *Bengal Hurkaru,* 30 October 1838, 422; ibid., 5 November 1849, 507.
17. *Statesman and Friend of India,* 3 November 1889, 3.
18. See *Statesman,* 26 October 1930, 1, for a special 'Jagadhatri Poojah' holiday return fare to Sinhachalam on the Bengal-Nagpur Railway.
19. For overviews of the oldest Pūjās in Chandannagar and Bhadreswar, see Caṭṭopādhyāy, 'Ālor Banyāy Bhāsbe Jagaddhātrīr Candannagar,' 11–12; *Dainik Basumatī,* 26 October 1968, 3; Mitra, *Huglī Jelār Debideul*, 30–32; and *Statesman,* 24 November 1982, 3.
20. For a 2002 photograph of this image and its priests in the hall, see www.geocities.com/shataktaru/town/jaga/jaga2/html (accessed 31 July 2005).
21. See *Ājkāl,* 6 November, 2000, 3.
22. *Pratidin,* 30 October 1998, 6. On this village and its celebration of Jagaddātrī Pūjā, see Sudhīr Cakrabartī, 'Jagaddhātrīpujoy Kāgrāme,' *Deś* 57, no. 1 (4 November 1989): 52–55.
23. Famed families include the descendants of Rāṇī Rāsmaṇi in Janbazar, the Nilmaṇi Mitras of Beadon Street, the Deb descendants of the littérateurs Chātubābu and Lātubābu, the Khelātcandra Ghoṣ house on Pathuriaghata Street, various branches of the Dā̃ (Dawn) family, the Dattas of Baubazar's Baburam Sil Lane, and the Pāl family of Sobhabazar.
24. It is not clear to me when Candannagar began its characteristic three-day Pūjā, instead of a one-day Pūjā. However, by 1956, all Pūjās in the city appear to have been three days long.
25. See, respectively, *Dainik Basumatī,* 26 October 1968, 3; *Amrita Bazar Patrika,* 18 November 1977, 5; and www.giridoot.com/puja2.htm (accessed 31 July 2005).
26. On the *ghaṭ bisarjan*, see *Pratidin,* 27 October 2000, 12.
27. Of the additional places in which I have found reference to Jagaddhātrī Pūjā, three are in Nadia (Navadvip, Ranaghat, and Santipur), eleven are in Hooghly (Bandel, Bhadrakali, Bhadreshwar, Chinsurah, Guptipara, Haripal, Hugli, Serampore, Singur, Tarakeshwar, and Uttarpara); one is in Murshidabad (Kagram); and one is in Burdwan (Guskara).

28. In 2000, a seventy-five-foot Buddha was placed on top of a Buddhist temple in Baracanditala; nearby, in Circus Math, Jagaddhātrī sat in a Parisian Catholic church.
29. For photos of the first two, see *Ājkāl,* 3 November 2000, 5, and *Bartamān*, 16 November 1999, 6. The fort I saw in Candannagar at the Moran Road Ambika Electric Club in 2000.
30. For a photograph of the shark, which was at Krishnanagar in 2002, see www.geocities.com/shataktaru/town/jaga/jaga2/html (accessed 31 July 2005).
31. Veerapan's den is described in *Bartamān*, 9 November 2000, 3; for the Indian army dugout, see *Ājkāl,* 1 November 1995, 6. The other two I saw and photographed in Chandannagar in 2000.
32. Lighting shows of this variety are often very topical; Amartya Sen appeared and nuclear bombs exploded in Pūjās tableaus in the fall of 1998, and I saw the little girl's wedding several times in 2000, after a father had actually been arrested for his cruel treatment of his daughter.
33. Caṭṭopādhyāy, 'Ālor Banyāy Bhāsbe Jagaddhātrīr Candannagar,' 11–16, wrote in 1999 that the chairman of the Katapukur Pūjā was a Muslim. In 2000, a Harijan community in Laldighirdhar, Chandannagar, had been doing its own Pūjā for over twenty years (*Statesman,* 4 November 2000, 4), and another, in Mahadanga, also Chandannagar, was performed exclusively by women (ibid., 24 November 1982, 3).
34. For a letter expressing fear of communal violence during Jagaddhātrī Pūjā and Muharram processions, see the *Statesman and Friend of India,* 7 November 1893, 3. Bankim's description of Jagaddhātrī may be found in *The Abbey of Bliss*, trans. Nares Candra Sengupta (Calcutta: Cherry Press, 1902), 40. On the partition, see the *Bengalee,* 5 November 1905, 3.
35. A photograph of one such *pāṇḍāl* can be seen in *Amrita Bazar Patrika,* 3 November, 1984, 36.
36. *Bartamān,* 5 November 2000, 3.
37. *Bartamān,* 9 November 2000, 3.
38. *Pratidin,* 30 October 1998, 6.
39. *Pratidin,* 31 October 1995, 5.
40. See, however, the prescription for red clothing given above in the *Tantrasāra*.
41. Of the 121 freestanding temples to single goddesses (not male gods with their female consorts) described by David McCutchion in his exhaustive survey of Bengali temples, thirty-three are dedicated to Kālī (the oldest dated is from 1712), fifteen to Śītalā (oldest dated from 1811), fourteen to Caṇḍī (oldest dated from 1649), eleven to Durgā (oldest dated from 1705), and ten to Simhavāhinī (oldest dated from 1490). See *Brick Temples of Bengal: From the Archives of David McCutchion*, ed. George Michell (Princeton: Princeton University Press, 1983).
42. The Asutosh Museum at University of Calcutta has an eighth-century image

from Barisal and an eighteenth-century image from Jessore, both in present-day Bangladesh. These scant museum holdings may indicate that Jagaddhātrī was popular earlier and further east than other sources can corroborate at present.

43. For instance, all the Jagaddhātrīs pictured in the Giridoot Chandannagar web site displays (www.giridoot.com/puja3.htm [accessed July 26, 2005]) are of the sweet variety.
44. For photographs, see *Amrita Bazar Patrika,* 28 October 1990, 3; *Pratidin,* 30 October 1998, 6; ibid., 17 November 1999, 6; and the Krishnanagar web site, www.geocities.com/shataktaru/town/jaga/jaga2/html.
45. Mr. Sāu, interview, 6 November 2000. The *Pratidin* article on the Kagram family Pūjā reports that the Mukherjis still offer buffaloes, in addition to goats (30 October 1998, 6).
46. Another indication of British influence may be seen in the descriptions of old images, or images as worshipped in the nineteenth century. In his famed satire *Hutom Pyāṇcār Nakśā,* 2nd edn. (Calcutta: Bose, 1862), 85, Kāliprasanna Sinha describes a typical Jagaddhatri image as nearly twenty hands tall, with a European face, clothed in Jewish and Armenian fashions, and seated on a horse-faced lion decorated with an English crest. In modern times, one can see further evidence of British taste: in the home of the Dawn family of Din Rakshit Lane, North Calcutta, Jagaddhātrī's lion vehicle holds a ball in one paw, just as one might see in a royal coat of arms. Apart from her female attendants, the Dawns' goddess is accompanied by armored equestrians of obviously European descent (*Telegraph,* 13 November 2002 [accessed online, 4 November 2003]).
47. *Bartamān,* 4 November 2000, 12.
48. Frederick Burwick, *Mimesis and Its Romantic Reflections* (University Park: Pennsylvania State University Press, 2001), 162.
49. See www.wbtourism.com (accessed 31 July 2005).

10

Shashibhushan Dasgupta's Lotus

Realizing the Sublime in Contemporary Tantric Studies

JEFFREY J. KRIPAL

From this psychological point of view it may be said that human love, when dissociated completely from selfish carnal desires, not by process of violent suppression, but by a slow and gradual process of strict physical and psychological discipline, has the capacity, in its boundless extent and deep intensity, of producing a transcendental state of mind, which is of the same kind as the state of mind produced through the highest state of divine love, or communion with God. . . . Intense human love, or even sex-emotion, has the capacity of producing a supreme state of arrest. In a unique flow of emotion, uninterrupted by subjective or objective notions there dawns an infinite oneness of mind. . . . though a Freudian explanation of the whole thing may not be absolutely inadmissible in such religious practices, one fundamental point, which we should never lose sight of even from the empirical point of view, is that though the lotus above the surface of the water may have its origin in the mud deep below, mud and lotus cannot surely be placed in the same scale in our general scheme of valuation.

Shashibhushan Dasgupta, *Obscure Religious Cults*

mūrcchito harate vyādhīn mṛto jīvayati svayam /
baddhaḥ khecaratāṃ dhatte raso vāyuśca pārvati.

Swooned, *rasa*, like the breath, drives away diseases; killed, it revives itself; bound, it affords the power of flight.

Haṭhayogapradīpikā, trans. David Gordon White

Through his many books and articles Narendra Nath Bhattacharyya, or 'NNB', as many of us affectionately called him, demonstrated that the Śākta traditions must be understood within the complex matrices of their own socioeconomic environments. It is not enough to talk about gods and goddesses, rituals and myths, saints and temples without at the same time locating those deities, those acts and stories and institutions, within their own social and historical contexts. Bhattacharyya's work is in that respect both a rich resource for present-day scholars and an important model for the future of Śākta studies.

In this essay, I seek to build on these general contextualizing principles and draw on psychoanalytic theory to propose that the larger field of Tantric studies also needs to be more psychologically nuanced. Without denying the very real and important differences between the two systems, I would like to suggest that psychoanalysis can poetically be described as a kind of Western Tantra, as a century-long meditation on the powers of sexuality, the body, life, death, and religion. Psychoanalysis, after all, much like the Tantra, gazes into zones of human experience that were previously forbidden, off-limits, obscene, unthinkable. And, it too, again like the Tantric systems, accesses altered states of consciousness—dreams, hypnosis, hysteria, trance states, fantasy, free association, and so on—to advance its claims about the nature of human being. Moreover, again not unlike the Tantra, psychoanalysis is something of a scandal to the larger culture, an embarrassment to many, a horror to more than a few. And why not? As Freud famously pointed out long ago, psychoanalysis is an offense to humanity's self-assured arrogance (the 'third blow', as it were, after the Copernican and Darwinian revolutions), for it removes the ego from its pedestal and reveals it to be what it has been all along—a social construction, necessary perhaps, but hardly stable, and always threatened by the instinctual forces of the id, an often overbearing superego, and the terrifying whirlpool of the unconscious . . . by no means a permanent condition.[1] Psychoanalysis even possesses a similar esoteric ritual structure, with analysts and analysands trained in closed private sessions, accessing a kind of personal gnosis or *jñāna* reserved for the few who can understand and emotionally accept it. It is not for nothing that Sudhir Kakar once wrote that, '[o]f the many Indian mystical-spiritual cults, tantra is perhaps the most congenial to a psychoanalyst'.[2] I am certain that we can easily make too much of such analogies, but we may also too quickly ignore them and so miss an opportunity to think again about both psychoanalysis and Tantric ritual and symbolism.

Here, I want to address the relationship between sexuality and spirituality in the terms of the psycho-theological category of *sublimation*, literally, a 'making sublime' of the sexualized body, a careful cultivation of the lotus of higher consciousness out of the rich waters of the unconscious and the fertile loam of the sexualized body. More specifically, I want to reflect anew on Freud's original understandings of sublimation in the light of some Nāth Siddha, Sahajiyā, Śākta, and Vajrayāna symbolic systems in order to ask how these iconographies and imaginal physiologies might help us rethink or reconceive the category of sublimation itself, a category that is certainly one of the most undefined, mysterious, and yet important in Freud's thinking. It is not simply, then, 'How can psychoanalysis help us think about Tantric symbolism?' but also, 'How can Tantric symbolism help us think about psychoanalysis?' I thus make no claims to remaining faithful to Freud's thought; indeed, much of what I shall advance here I am certain he would passionately reject. Put differently, my interests are neither therapeutic nor strictly psychoanalytic. Rather, they are comparative and archaeological, that is, I seek to reflect on the psychoanalytic category of 'sublimation' by exploring analogous cultural models and practices in South Asia and Tibet and, by so doing, uncover something of the power and ultimate *aporia* of the category itself, be it psychoanalytically or religiously defined. Such an enterprise is more than justified historically, since, as Volney P. Gay reminds us, 'the concept of sublimation is taken whole cloth from mystical traditions in which a magical process occurs such that one substance is transformed into another'.[3]

In focusing on these questions, I am not seeking to neglect the social and the cultural. What is needed is a simultaneous focus on both, an awareness that psyche and society 'make each other up' in a never-ending dialectic of mutual creation. There is no culture apart from the human psyche, but neither is there a psyche without human culture. This is an insight particularly useful for the interpretation of erotic forms of human religious experience, my own particular area of interest. In this model, the religious value of erotic mysticism does not depend on whether or not the mystical experience in question is 'sexual'. How could it, when each culture attributes different symbolic and ontological meanings to what is 'sexual'? Rather, the hermeneutical challenge consists in trying to understand other, sometimes genuinely mystical, ontological conceptions of human sexuality, which are in turn embedded in an elaborate web of cultural practices and assumptions, and allowing all of these to define and guide, at least initially, one's interpretation. Erotic forms of mysticism, in other words, cannot be discussed comparatively, as if they were all minor variations on the exact same thing. Behind such a discourse lies the unspoken assumption that every time and culture have more or less agreed on the nature of religious and sexual experience and the manner in which they do or do not intersect. It also ignores the very real possibility that different cultural systems set their actors up for radically different experiences of the world, in effect 'creating' different life-worlds with different language games, symbolic systems, and sexualities. Put simply, what is 'impossible' within one cultural register might be entirely probable in another, and vice versa.

MYSTICISM AND PSYCHOANALYSIS: THE RECURRING NONSENSE

Psychoanalysis, understood here as that complex stream of psychological, literary, and feminist theory that has developed from Freud's system over the past one hundred years, is an especially powerful lens through which to glimpse something of these other 'impossible' spiritual and sexual worlds. Why this is so, I would suggest, lies ultimately in the 'mystical' origins of psychoanalysis itself.

Almost half a century ago now, David Bakan advanced the provocative thesis that psychoanalysis—with its oral initiatory ritual structure, its emphasis on esotericism, its understanding of sexual symbolism, its antinomian engagement with the 'lower' or 'infernal' powers of instinct, its strange fascination with numerology, and its rabbinic-like exegetical style—functions as a kind of secularized Kabbalah, and that the former in fact may find its deepest intellectual roots in the latter.[4] Bakan, it turns out, was not the first to advance a thesis about Freud's possible, perhaps even unconscious, indebtedness to Jewish mysticism. Abraham Roback, as early as 1918 and again in 1929 in his *Jewish Influence in Modern Thought*, argued that Freud's method is 'strongly reminiscent' of Kabbalah, and that '[p]sychoanalysis, on the whole, contains a mystical tendency'.[5] Although Freud himself objected strongly to Roback's thesis, calling it 'nonsense,'[6] one wonders if there is not indeed something to it. Certainly contemporary scholarship on the literary and religious dimensions of Freud's system have only added to this 'nonsensical' intuition. One thinks, for example, of Suzanne Kirschner's study of the religious structure and romantic 'naturalized supernaturalism' of psychoanalytic thought, seen again as a type of secularized mysticism,[7] or of Diana Hume George's comparative study of Blake and Freud, in which she attempts a poetic revision of Freud through Blake in the conviction, not only that Blake's work anticipated Freud's, 'but that his mapping of psychic processes actually subsumes Freud's in several identifiable respects'.[8] In the process, she calls on Blake's radical mysticism and psychological poetry to accomplish what I have attempted in my own work on Ramakrishna's Śākta mysticism,[9] that is, an inversion of Freud's notion of sublimation in order to make room in it for other ontological and imaginative possibilities: 'Blake reverses the causal relationship. We are sexual beings and live our lives, think our thoughts, in a sexual context. But intellectual energy was not originally sexual; sexual energy was originally intellective. "The Treasures of Heaven are not Negations of Passion but Realities of Intellect from which All the Passions Emanate Uncurbed in their Eternal Glory." . . . He [thus] inverts the progression and derivation.'[10] In this broad psychoanalytic-literary tradition, then, to think with Freud is not necessarily to think as Freud: one can be inspired and move on into one's own theorizing.

Also particularly relevant here is Michel de Certeau's *The Mystic*

Fable. Bringing together two decades of historiographical research on sixteenth- and seventeenth-century French mystical writers—or what de Certeau calls twenty years of waiting 'near the door' of the radiance with his personal guardian, the seventeenth-century French mystic Jean-Joseph Surin, whom, we are told, he came to know down even to 'the fleas in his fur collar'[11]—and seventeen years' experience at the École freudienne de Paris, the book seeks to locate and then practice a series of characteristic procedures common to both French mysticism and French psychoanalysis (for example, 'desire', the 'splitting' of the subject, the narcissistic mirror, and the vocabulary of sexuality and difference). For de Certeau, this 'dual practice' is not a project involving the mechanical application of psychoanalytic principles to historical materials, as if the former somehow rendered the latter completely intelligible; rather, it involves 'an awareness of theoretical procedures (Freudian and Lacanian) capable of bringing into play what the language of the mystics had already articulated and capable of displacing and amplifying its effects'[12] (we are reminded of George's Freudian Blake and Blakean Freud). Psychoanalytic thought, in other words, not only relives and recalls mystical thought; it also radicalizes the mystical texts and makes their psychic procedures our own. Almost. De Certeau warns us that such a 'mutual seizure' might tempt us to erase the fundamental distinctions that separate these life-worlds, but it also, at the same time, 'occasions, by a movement of frontiers, what we call a reading, that is, innumerable ways of deciphering, in the texts, what has already written us'.[13] A tension remains, then, and with it a distance and the possibility of historical self-understanding.

But perhaps no one has done more to uncover the mystical dimensions of psychoanalysis than William B. Parsons, whose recent historical reconstruction and psychological analysis of the Freud-Rolland correspondence demonstrates quite clearly that Freud's psychoanalysis, *pace* the usual assumptions, possesses, hidden within both its structure and history, profound and respectful engagements with mystical forms of subjectivity.[14] Parson's work is particularly important to my own thought, because it also shows that Freud's earliest theorizing on mysticism was indirectly connected to Bengali Śāktism through the person of Romain Rolland, who related to Freud largely through his own mystical or 'oceanic' experiences, which he saw both mirrored and confirmed in the lives of Ramakrishna and Vivekananda. The psychoanalytic study of mysticism, in other words, began as a conversation discursively defined by a French intellectual (Rolland), Freud, and two Bengali mystics (Ramakrishna and Vivekananda). Perhaps it is no accident, then, that that same twentieth-century study, at least with respect to Hinduism, has returned again and again to a single Śākta saint: the enigmatic figure of Ramakrishna.[15]

Bakan had tried to move beyond what we might call the structural thesis (namely, that medieval Kabbalah and psychoanalysis display certain analogous structural features or theoretical underpinnings) in order to suggest a material, historical connection between Freud and medieval Kabbalah. This he did by speculating whether some sort of historical diffusion might have taken place through Freud's wide reading in Jewish literature. What is so seductive about Parson's work, which is a kind of end-of-the-century return to the Bakanian thesis, is that he is able to show precisely this, namely, a genuine historical diffusion between a mystical system and Freud. Whether or not, then, there are historical connections between psychoanalysis and medieval Kabbalah, there are most certainly such connections between Śāktism and Freud's theorizing about mysticism. I have treated these elsewhere in some detail,[16] and Parsons has dedicated much of an entire monograph to them. Here, building on this dialogic history, I would simply like to add that there are genuine and important analogies between Freud's psychoanalysis and Tantric thought, and, moreover, that each can be understood anew in the mirror of the other.

This speculative structural project is possible, since, as de Certeau demonstrated with respect to French mysticism and psychoanalysis,[17] a 'strange similarity' exists between the psychoanalytic and Tantric systems, particularly, as I shall argue here, between psychoanalytic speculations on and Tantric practices of sublimation. Certainly, however, the analogies run even deeper and wider. Śākta mystical practice, like psychoanalysis, is an exercise in excess, a ritualized confrontation with both universal and culturally constituted anxieties about death, sexuality, pollution, and the dissolution of the socialized self. In the famous *pañca-makāra* ritual or the Five Ms, for example, the male Tāntrika secretly ingests substances or perform acts that are otherwise forbidden and considered highly polluting by his public Brāhmaṇical culture. He thus consumes meat, drinks wine, and engages in sexual intercourse with his Tantric consort precisely to transgress, ritually and emotionally, the orthodox categories of impurity, pollution, and taboo. It is as if his own culture deconstructs itself within this remarkable practice.[18]

THE SUBLIME IN SOUTH ASIAN AND TIBETAN TANTRA

Seen within this same cross-cultural spirit of comparison, the Tantric traditions of South Asia and the Himalayan region are particularly fascinating examples for us to think about and imagine with, as it has long been obvious to these subcultures that one of the easiest, quickest, and most profound ways to alter consciousness is to manipulate the body sexually. Sexual arousal and orgasm generate forms of consciousness that, potentially at least, are more subtle and 'higher', the traditions argue, than our normal banal fare. Whether we are with the Nāth Siddhas and their elaborate hydraulics of the subtle body, and their alchemical equations between mercury and semen, the Sahajiyās and their ritualized reenactment of Kṛṣṇa's love-play with Rādhā as the clearest expression of God's ecstatically blissful bipolar nature, the Śākta *cakra* system in which the human body-consciousness is imagined as one immense thousand-petaled lotus growing directly out of—where else?—the anal and genital regions, or Vajrayāna Buddhism in which the highest state of religious accomplishment, the union of emptiness and compassion, is symbolized and secretly realized by the act of sexual intercourse, the message is provocatively clear: human sexuality, handled correctly and understood properly, can manifest the sacred.

In his pioneering, middle-of-the-century study of Śākta, Sahajiyā, Nāth Siddha, Vajrayāna, and Baul textual traditions, the Bengali historian of literature Shashibhushan Dasgupta saw this same comparative truth in 1946:

The secret yogic practices . . . belong neither strictly to the Buddhist fold nor exclusively to the Hindu fold; they are essentially yogic practices, which by their association with different theological systems, either Buddhist or Hindu, have given rise to different religious cults. The most important of the secret practices is the yogic control of the sex-pleasure so as to transform it into transcendental bliss. . . . This yogic practice with its accessories, being associated with the philosophy of Śiva and Śakti, stands at the centre of the network of the Hindu Tantric systems, and when associated with the speculations on Prajñā and Upāya of later Buddhism, has given rise to the Tāntric Buddhist cults including the Buddhist Sahajiyā system; and again, when associated with the speculations on Kṛṣṇa and Rādhā conceived as Rasa and Rati in Bengal Vaiṣṇavism, the same yogic practice and discipline has been responsible for the growth and development of the Vaiṣṇava Sahajiyā movement of Bengal.[19]

But to say that sexuality is sacred and that the highest forms of consciousness are rooted in the body is not the whole truth, for it is not sexuality per se that is sacralized here, but its 'yogic control' or ritual transformation. Hence the famous Indic symbol of the lotus that grows in the mud but blossoms forth just above the water, opening to the light of the transcendent sun. Dasgupta at least is clear, as quoted in the opening epigraph, that we can affirm the muddy rootedness of this flower in the sexualized body without facilely equating the sexual roots and the mystical bloom or pretending that the lotus flower is 'nothing but' the muddy water. Inspired by such authors as Dasgupta, I have argued the same point elsewhere:

Putting aside for a moment the fact that Indian poetic and religious traditions often see sexual meanings in the shape and nature of the lotus (it is, after all, the reproductive organ of the flower), we might also reasonably ask how anyone could hope to understand something as biological as a lotus without first beginning with the larger ecosystem, that is, with [what Aurobindo called] 'the secrets of the mud in which it grows.' Put bluntly, there just is no such thing as a mudless lotus. We need not and should not end with the mud, but we certainly need to at least begin there. . . . It is pointless to deny the muddiness of the mud, but it is equally silly to deny the beautiful blooming nature of the blossom. Both are aspects of the flower. Only by accepting both, in dialogue and debate, will we be able to see a fuller picture (if never the full picture) of that iconic image and begin to understand its many truths.[20]

In this model, it is correct to say that some carefully specified[21] mystical states of consciousness both are—and are not—sexual; that is, that, although they are rooted in, and draw in, what are originally libidinal forces, they have somehow transfigured these energies into 'higher' structures of being that can no longer be facilely equated with the original libidinal forces. This dialectical, essentially developmental understanding of the relationship between sexuality and spirituality is what I have called 'the erotic'.[22] Previously, I emphasized the dialecticism of the erotic as a *co-incidentia* of sexual and mystical processes. In the next section, I would like to focus on sublimation—what we might call its hierarchical or developmental structure—that is, the erotic transformation *from* the sexual *to* the mystical, where the latter is conceived as a 'higher' or more 'sublime' form of the former.

SUBLIMATION IN PSYCHOANALYTIC THEORY: THE PSYCHOSEXUAL STAGES AND THE EROTOGENIC ZONES

The West is itself, of course, imbued with a linking of sexuality and spirituality analogous to those that we find in the Hindu and Buddhist traditions,—and I have written about these patterns in Christian, Islamic, and Jewish mystical traditions at some length elsewhere[23]—but within Western religious traditions this linking has, in general, been theologized quite differently (and, I would argue, not as successfully).[24] Such erotic theologizing has also, unfortunately, had a very difficult time in public morality and has often become the object of censorship and control. Consider, for example, Leo Steinberg's remarkable *The Sexuality of Christ in Renaissance Art and Modern Oblivion*.[25] This is the text with which Volney Gay launches his study of sublimation in Freud's thought. After beginning his book with the funny but eye-catching sentence, 'In the 1950s it was hard to find pictures of naked people' and a remarkably honest observation about the psychosexual dynamics of one common practice of Catholic piety ('In a Catholic girl's bedroom was the crucifix. On it a naked Christ stretched out on a cross, positioned so that Christ could see the girl and she could see Him'),[26] Gay goes on to summarize Steinberg's study of one striking motif of Renaissance art, what Steinberg calls the ostentatio genitalium, that is, the open display of the infant Christ's genitals. This pattern of displaying or pointing out the infant Christ's genitals, almost always by the Virgin's finger pointing to or touching the child's penis, was common in Renaissance art for a full two hundred years, until it died out in a different cultural milieu that found the motif a cause of pious offense rather than a theological opportunity to reflect on Christ's full humanity and the sacralization of sexuality that the doctrine of the Incarnation can imply. In Gay's terms, '[t]he reconciliation of God with human beings, and the divinity of Christ's sexuality, [made] possible religious art that is also sexual'.[27] Or such, anyway, was the theology of the Renaissance preachers studied by John O'Malley in Steinberg's book. These preachers, we are told, encouraged their listeners to reflect on Christ's sexuality as a potent site of God's humanization. Their theology, then, not only allowed Christ's sexuality: it encouraged and celebrated it as a necessary and admirable component of salvation history.

What happened, of course, was that cultural models of human nature, proper sexuality, and religious piety changed radically over the years, rendering the once divinized and adored sexuality quasi-pornographic. Public morality had changed, and now an important period of Christian art had to be denied, if not literally effaced. The erect phallus swollen with new life beneath the resurrected Christ's garment that Steinberg found in some Renaissance drawings now had to be covered up again—more folds, more cloth, anything. The erect phallus was not there, it *could not* be there, or, if it was, it could only be flaccid. Christ may have had a real body, but he did not have a true sexuality. That was simply unthinkable now.[28]

And this is where Freud's theory of sublimation comes in. What the reigning public morality cannot accept, the psyche of the artist, writer, or religious seer has to somehow disguise or, better, transform in his art, text, or vision. With its sexual roots now 'appropriately' hidden, the message can get through the public censor, often in a form so distant from the original libidinal source that there is almost nothing of the latter left. Thus, Christ may be denied an erect and useable phallus, but when one of his female saints unites with him in a mystical marriage, she sees a gorgeous male angel with a flame-tipped arrow, which he thrusts again and again into the middle of her body as she moans in intense pain and ecstatic pleasure. This visionary sublimation worked, since a marble version of this vision, sculpted by none other than Bernini, now hangs suspended over the altar of a chapel in Rome. The erotic got through the censor.

Bernini's scenario took place in sixteenth- and seventeenth-century Spain and Italy. But the Spanish and the Italians did not invent sublimation. Indeed, the idea of sublimation and the sublime, as Gay reminds us, are thousands of years old, dating back to Greek culture, where the term *hupsos,* 'the sublime', was used to describe that which uplifts human beings, whether it be a poem, a work of literature, the grandeurs of nature, or a god.[29] The term was later carried over into alchemical literature, where the concept was used to describe the mysterious transformation of base metals into gold, this precious metal often functioning as a symbol for the achievement of immortality. Modern chemistry transformed the transformation yet again and used the term to describe the chemical process by which a solid is translated directly into a gas, as when, for example, ice evaporates into the air without first becoming a liquid. Interestingly, when the vapor condenses again back into a solid form, it is said to be 'purified' or 'refined', two terms with clear analogues in mystical traditions. From a solid (the sexual body) to a gas (the spirit) while skipping the liquid phase (sexual emission), the metaphor works beautifully on at least three levels: the chemical, the magico-mystical, and the sexual.

Freud took the common usage of the term in the German (*Sublimierung*) and English words, both of which derive from the Latin *sublimare*, to describe how originally libidinal energies are diverted from their original sexual aims and converted into cultural accomplishments, such as art or literature.[30] *How* exactly this occurs, however, was something of a mystery, and, as we shall see, remained a mystery, even in Freud's otherwise lucent and heavily rationalized corpus.

The problems were many. First of all, there are the related concepts of repression and sublimation. Repression can be said to begin with a kind of 'dam effect' in which 'the libido behaves like a stream whose main bed has become blocked.' Dammed up in this way, the libido 'proceeds to fill up collateral channels which may hitherto have been empty'.[31] These 'collateral channels' then manifest themselves as symptoms, which for Freud are disguised expressions of the libidinal forces, that is, they are ultimately sexual in nature. In another, more contemporary and quite beautiful expression of the same theory, Peter Shabad describes the pathological symptoms of the suffering as 'the most intimate of creations' and 'memorials to one's lonely suffering'.[32] As intimate memorials, however, they are often less than effective, since at the same time that they call attention back to or memorialize the original suffering, they also disguise or hide the true source of that suffering, that is, a sexual trauma. It is as if a German memorial to the Holocaust tried to give expression to the suffering of its own Jewish citizens without ever clearly mentioning the death camps or the collective guilt of the German people. Thus, in Freud's own words now, 'between the pressure of the instinct and his antagonism to sexuality, illness offers him a way of escape. It does not solve his conflict, but seeks to evade it by transforming his libidinal impulses into symptoms.'[33]

Freud considered sublimation to be the opposite of repression: whereas repression attempts to deny libidinal forces and drive them 'below' into the unconscious where they can fester and eventually manifest themselves as neurotic symptoms, sublimation expresses libidinal forces in healthy and culturally creative ways. Put more succinctly, whereas repression produces symptoms and suffering, sublimation produces art and creativity. Paradoxically, however, this does not render sublimation a conscious process. Quite the contrary. Sublimation is an unconscious, automatic, ultimately mysterious process that lies well beyond the control of the ego. Moreover, the shadow of repression and, with it, neurosis is never far behind. Indeed, in his summary of 'The Three Essays,' Freud includes sublimation, along with perversion and repression, as one of the three results of 'an abnormal constitutional disposition'.

> Sublimation enables excessively strong excitations arising from particular sources of sexuality to find an outlet and use in other fields, so that a not inconsiderable increase in psychical efficiency results from a disposition which in itself is perilous. Here we have the origins of artistic creativity; and, according to the completeness or incompleteness of the sublimation, a characterological analysis

of a highly gifted individual, and in particular of one with an artistic disposition, may reveal a mixture, in every proportion, of efficiency, perversion and neurosis.[34]

There is also the problem of how these psychic forces derive a qualitative product (say, a work of art or a religious vision) from a quantity of physical energy (the instinctual drives). There is, in other words, a genuine 'gap' or 'quantum leap' between sexuality and the sublimate, much as we find in the original use of the term in chemistry between the solid and the gas. Gay puts the problem this way:

[Freud] says little about how these invisible elements (quantities) give rise to the visible structures (qualities) of everyday life. Like the alchemists who wished to transform one substance into another, Freud can name this gap. With admirable honesty, he confesses that he cannot bridge it. Hence, sublimation becomes a mysterious process. . . . The origins of the term sublimation point to this fact. For it designates processes by which a substance is transformed from a solid to a gas without passing through the liquid state. In other words, these are exceptional processes which violate the usual sequences of transformation. . . . Freud's many comments on sublimation and his many attempts to employ it reveal their roots in this magical image.[35]

Interestingly, Gay invokes the Indic 'equation of semen with magical fluids and the idea of reigning in male potency' as an important analogue of sublimation, noting, correctly, that whereas Christ's erection is a rarity in Christian art that is soon censored, the ithyphallic Śiva is omnipresent in Hindu myth and iconography and the awareness that spiritual attainment and the retention of semen are related permeates Indian religious culture.[36] Folk wisdom, in both India and the West, Gay notes, 'has always linked creativity to sexual arousal and orgasm'.[37] And yet, 'none of these often beautiful evocations of the idealized power of sexuality is psychoanalytically valid. They are all prepsychoanalytic and usually adamant justifications of magical beliefs.'[38]

It is not entirely clear to me what Gay means by 'magical', although I gather he intends by that expression a vague reliance on external forces that are never rationally defined but that can be manipulated by ritual activity. For him, Freud's theory of sublimation moves beyond such magical frameworks by providing a coherent and reasonable stage theory of psychosexual development and, with it, cogent explanations for both repression (the pushing of sexual instincts 'down' into the unconscious) and sublimation (the expression of sexual instincts 'up' into cultural achievement). These stages are set out for the first time in Freud's famous *Three Essays on the Theory of Sexuality*, where he mapped a series of erotogenic zones in the human body and their attending structural organizations of the libidinal drives, his well-known oral, anal, phallic, latency, and genital psychosexual stages.[39] In this model, the libidinal impulses are not single but *complex*, that is, the sexual organization is put together from multiple somatic functions (like eating, defecation, and ejaculation) and located alternately in different erotogenic zones of the human body over a long period of time. Psychosexual development begins in the pre-genital erotogenic zones of the mouth and the anus and is only much later attached to the genitals (in an initial and incomplete sense in the Oedipal phase but only successfully and permanently during puberty), and then only after considerable developmental risk. If environmental or intrapsychic forces intervene and disturb the normal course of this development, 'fixation' on a particular erotogenic zone or psychosexual stage of development may result and, with it, possible later forms of neurosis. 'Every step on this long path of development can become a point of fixation, every juncture in this involved combination can be an occasion for a dissociation of the sexual instinct.'[40]

For Freud, then, there are 'connecting pathways' in the body along which libidinal forces move and organize themselves over time and through which sexual excitation is connected to various somatic functions and body zones. It is these pathways, moreover, that account for fixations, sexual disturbances, *and* cultural creativity (within which I would certainly include religious creativity). Here is Freud again in *Three Essays*: 'we are led to the suspicion that all the connecting pathways that lead from other functions to sexuality must also be traversable in the reverse direction'.[41] Thus, just as disturbances in the oral function can lead to sexual dysfunction, so too sexual dysfunction can lead to eating disorders. And there is even more, for 'the same pathways . . . along which sexual disturbances trench upon the other somatic functions might also perform another important function in normal health. They must serve as paths for the attraction of sexual instinctual forces to aims that are other than sexual, that is to say, for the sublimation of sexuality.'[42] We are back, in other words, to that 'perilous condition' of the sublimated cultural creative who walks the thin line between neurosis and creativity or, in more traditional religious language, madness and sanctity.

Finally, before we leave Freud, it is important to point out, *pace* his non-reading critics, that the Viennese master remained quite humble throughout his life before the mysteries and accomplishments of sublimation. Hence he could write: 'No other influences on the course of sexual development can compare with releases of sexuality, waves of repression and sublimation—the latter two being processes of which the inner causes are quite unknown to us.'[43] Along similar lines, he believed that sublimation, being an intricate product of numerous variables, including environmental context and individual psychosexuality, is a rare accomplishment 'achieved by a minority and then only intermittently'.[44] Freud is also clear that psychoanalysis can only understand sublimation as a transformation of instinctual drives, that is, the changing of the instincts from one form to another according to predictable natural laws. Transfiguration, on the hand, which Gay defines as 'a spiritual transformation accomplished by the intervention of divine forces',[45] is another matter, and one well beyond the psychoanalytic gaze. But provocatively and crucially, *sublimation is ultimately about transfiguration, not transformation.* Freud again: 'Instincts and their transformations are at the limit of what is discernible by psycho-analysis. From that point it gives place to biological research. . . . Since artistic talent and capacity are intimately connected with sublimation we must admit that the nature of the artistic function is also inaccessible to us along psychoanalytic lines.'[46] These lines, which he penned at the end of his essay on Leonardo da Vinci, that 'rarest and most perfect' of sublimated types, signal for Gay an important confession: 'When Freud uses the term in his later case histories,' he tells us, 'he does so in a descriptive sense which echoes concepts of transfiguration, magic, and spirituality.'[47] The mystery would remain.

THE ALCHEMY OF SUBLIMATION AND THE NECTAR OF THE LOTUS: THE MEDIEVAL SIDDHA TRADITIONS

One could, I think, make the argument that sublimation is the central issue within the Indic Tantric schools, that wave of genius that swept across India beginning in about the sixth century CE and, in the process, preserved the original and most ancient meanings of *ānanda* as mystico-erotic delight[48] within an elaborate body of theory and practice.[49] Appropriately, then, this same sublimatory process glistens at the core of David Gordon White's recent definition of Tantra: 'Tantra is the Asian body of beliefs and practices which, working from the principle that the universe we experience is nothing other than the concrete manifestation of the divine energy of the godhead that creates and maintains that universe, seeks to ritually appropriate and channel that energy, within the human microcosm, in creative and emancipatory ways.'[50] And indeed, a similar 'hydraulics' of sublimation was at the center of his earlier study of the medieval Nāth Siddha schools. Despite the fact that White eschews a psychological hermeneutics in his opening remarks[51] (even as he teasingly suggests such an approach to his own motivations in an opening endnote),[52] for the psychologically oriented comparativist interested in Indic models of psychosexual sublimation, there is no better text than White's magisterial *The Alchemical Body*.

Sublimation, we might recall, is a term derived immediately from the modern science of chemistry and, originally, from medieval European alchemy, where it functioned as both a quasi-scientific technique for attempting to transform cheap ores into precious gold and as a code term for the spiritual transubstantiations that the alchemist was believed to undergo during the same hoped-for chemical processes. Actually, both the terms 'alchemy' and 'chemistry' are probably ultimately derived from the Chinese *kim* or *chin*, which White glosses as 'aurifaction'. White speculates that such techniques were likely carried to the West around the third century of the Common Era. According to White, the Chinese was then transliterated by Pseudo-Zosimos as *chymeia* or *chemeia*, which was later arabicized into *al-chymeia* and introduced through

Islam into Europe as the Latin *alchymia* or 'alchemy'.[53] Here, too, I might add, we have the inspirational source for a good deal of modern Jungian psychology, much of which, in the person of Jung himself, was, to stick to the same chemical metaphor, catalyzed by medieval alchemical texts. We are back, in other words, to a simultaneous mystical-psychological register, further enriched by a (pre-)scientific and cross-cultural history.

Still within this same chemical-psychological-mystical register, what the medieval Indian *siddhas* were after was the sublimation of semen, which they identified with the mineral mercury, into *amṛta* or nectar, a precious liquid that was believed to drip from the blooming thousand-petaled lotus in the head activated through the precise yogic controls of the hydraulics of the inner body that the *siddhas* made the focus of their speculations and practices. This internal yogic process found its external chemical analogue in their alchemical apparatuses designed to extract mercury from cinnabar or mercuric sulfide (*darada*). In fact, at least three different kinds of chemical sublimations were known: upward sublimation (*ūrddhvapātana*), downward sublimation (*adhopātana*), and transverse sublimation (*tiryakpātana*), each performed with a double-drum apparatus (*yantra*) in which mercury was made to sublimate out of heated ores and recondense through the use of cold water. Such mineral transformations, moreover, found their human analogues in the process of what White calls the 'yogic reversal' of *ūrddhvaretas*, literally 'upward semen'. Just as through the fire of yoga semen was thought to sublimate upward into the head and drip down from there as *amṛta* or nectar that the yogin, even 'in the embrace of a beautiful woman', can autoerotically drink,[54] so too when the mercuric sulfide ore was heated properly by an actual fire in the double drum apparatus, the precious mercury would sublimate and condense on the top, on the bottom, or on the side of the apparatus, depending upon the technique used.[55] If, then, sublimation, within a triple-language that was at once erotico-mystical, hathayogic, and alchemical,[56] is the quantum-like transformation of a solid directly into a gas that somehow skips the usual liquid phase, what the *siddhas* desired was to transform the sexual solid of the human body into the gas of spirit-consciousness by a stopping, avoidance, or transcendence of the liquid phase of sexual emission.

Sometimes. In fact, what White demonstrates is that the earliest and most ancient strata of Tantric practice was more concerned with the very solid production of sexual fluids, and not their repression and attempted sublimation into spirit. What he calls 'the earlier Kula practices of primitive tantrism' involved clan-structured funerary practices in cremation grounds and the production and ingestion of sexual fluids with wild goddesses whom the male Tāntrikas identified with their human consorts or yoginīs: 'These "bliss-starved" goddesses, attracted by offerings of mingled sexual fluids, would converge into the consciousness of the practitioner, to transform him, through their limitless libido, into a god on earth.'[57] This early Kaulism was reconfigured in the tenth and eleventh century CE by the brilliant theoretician Abhinavagupta, who effectively aestheticized and 'cleaned up' these early practices in order to create a 'higher' Tantrism. Ritual sexuality, according to White, thus underwent a paradigm shift: 'Sexual fluids themselves were no longer the way to godhead; rather, it was in the bliss of sexual orgasm that one realized god-consciousness for oneself.'[58] Put differently, the sexual fluids ceased to be the 'by-products of a transubstantiating experience of bliss' and became instead internalized 'power-substances' in their own right.[59] Specifically, the sexual fluids became increasingly internalized in the form of a female serpentine force (*kuṇḍalinī*) and an elaborate lotus system through which the Tāntrika could realize a kind of internal ejaculation or interiorized sexual intercourse within the intimate spaces of his body.[60]

This is not to say that Abhinavagupta and his Trika Kaula system ignored the actual production and ritual use of sexual fluids. Indeed, in certain esoteric contexts, Abhinavagupta prescribes the consumption of sexual fluids, which are to be passed from mouth to mouth before they are collected in a vessel and offered to the gods:

In this, the Trika Kaula theoreticians, even as they effected their reformation of Hindu tantra, remained in touch with the concrete ground of the tantric enterprise, which was and remains human sexual fluids and their symbolic correlates. The cosmic force that activates and actualizes every facet of tantric practice—that originates from the womb of the Goddess and passes through every link in the chain of transmission, from guru to disciple and thence to his or her disciple, via the inner channels of yogic transformation and through the channels that energize the mystic diagrams that serve as supports for worship and meditation—is ultimately nothing other than a stream (*ogha*) or flow (*srotas*) of sexual fluid.[61]

And this makes perfect sense within the ontological vision of these traditions, which assert again and again that the world is not an illusion, that it is real, that it is divine, and that it is sexual to its metaphysical depths: 'If then the preservation of the universe depends upon—indeed, is nothing other than—the endless cosmic orgasm of the divine, and if the bliss of orgasm is that human experience which is closest to the very being of godhead, then the stuff of orgasm—male semen and the female sexual emission and uterine blood—will, of necessity, play a vital role in the tantric quest for divine autonomy, immortality, and power.'[62] Here, in other words, we have an elaborate metaphysics and practice of sublimation—the transfiguration of the sexual into the divine, or better, the *realization* that the sexual was *and is always already* the divine, in short, that the sexual is sublime.[63]

KĀMA INTO *PREMA*: THE SAHAJIYĀ TRADITION

Within the later Vaiṣṇava Sahajiyā tradition, which developed out of the extraordinary life and devotional experiences of the Bengali religious leader Caitanya (1486–1533 CE), what I have called the mystery of sublimation is framed in terms of the traditional categories of *kāma* (sexual or libidinal love) and *prema* (transcendent love) and how the latter is to be derived from the former. The theology and ritual dynamics of this essentially alchemical process come out particularly clearly in Edward C. Dimock Jr.'s classic study of Sahajiyā theology and practice, *The Place of the Hidden Moon*, particularly in chapter 5, 'Man and Superman: Physical and Metaphysical Bases for the Sahajiyā Sadhana,' to which we now turn.

Here, in his discussion of the nature of man, Dimock is quick to pick up on the rhetoric of sublimation, which, unlike in our previous treatment of White above, he more or less equates with sexual repression in the dualistic traditions of Manichaean Christianity and orthodox Vaiṣṇavism. In both of these traditions, he writes, 'the solution of the problem of the flesh is a very simple one: deny it. By denying the flesh one sublimates its energy, causing it to flow along more true, or "spiritual" channels.'[64] This, of course, is essentially one traditional psychoanalytic reading. But this sublimation-as-repression was not what the Sahajiyās were about. Rather, they practiced what we might call a sublimation-as-transformation. Or in Dimock's words, 'their methods of control, their technique of chastity, was not one of denial; it was one of transformation'.[65] With Dimock's 'transformation' we are back to a mystery, to a transfiguration or transubstantiation[66] that goes beyond the usual mechanical or mechanistic understandings of classical psychoanalysis to something more, something miraculous or magical in spirit and effect.

All of this, moreover, was made possible by a specific ontology, one that affirmed and celebrated the basic unity of flesh and spirit. Whereas for the orthodox Vaiṣṇavas, *prema* and *kāma* were qualitatively different realities (the former being a gift of Kṛṣṇa's grace, the latter a mere instinct, hence their ascetic rejection of sexuality), for the Tantric Sahajiyās, *prema* could only develop through a transformation of *kāma*, since the two experiences shared the same ontological base.[67] Significantly, Dimock invokes alchemy to express this Sahajiyā understanding: 'The Sahajiyās, somewhat more alchemically inclined, feel that kāma and prema are not qualitatively different, but that kāma becomes prema by a slight rearrangement of motive and object'. Say the Sahajiyās: 'Prema is derived from kāma, but the motives of the two are different'.[68] The Sahajiyās, in other words, took what is essentially a psychoanalytic position on the primacy of the instinctual powers and their relationship to religious experience but understood the ontology of that relationship in a decidedly religious way. Dimock again:

> [I]f one happens to hold a doctrine which says that there is no qualitative difference between the human and the divine, spiritual union of the two is possible, and fleshly union between the two is also not only poetically but actually possible. The search and longing for this union are now the *means* to the ultimate experience,

an actual union of flesh and spirit, of human and divine. The distinctions between spiritual and carnal love and between poetic and doctrinal expression are wiped away. Accordingly, the Sahajiyās adopted the poetic paraphernalia of the orthodox Vaiṣṇavas and read the basic image the other way.[69]

How, though, was this transformation actually effected? Through *āropa*, the imaginal imposition of a divine or mythological persona onto the human one. The *līlā,* or 'play', of Kṛṣṇa's love in Vrindavana, in other words, can be reexperienced by taking on one of the personalities of Kṛṣṇa's female lovers or attendants in Vrindavana. Through such an imaginal absorption in the texts and events of revelation, the nature of the godhead itself (*svarūpa*) is revealed to the devotee through his own devotional nature (*rūpa*). This is the 'slight rearrangement of motive and object' of which Dimock wrote earlier, the magical twist that transforms an otherwise simply sexual situation into a potentially divine event. For most Sahajiyās, this *āropa* seems to have involved an appropriation of one of the female identities of Kṛṣṇa's company, that is, one 'became a woman'. For other more heterodox practitioners, however, this could also mean 'becoming Kṛṣṇa' in relationship to a female consort or lover.[70]

Either way, if handled correctly, this *āropa* was said to release a stream of nectar from the 'place of the hidden moon', that is, the cranial cavity of the practitioner: 'The eternal Vṛndāvana, the projection of the self, the sahaja, the secret place, "the place of the hidden moon", is the place of the eternal pleasure of Rādhā and Kṛṣṇa. The conceit is that a stream of rasa flows perpetually from the eternal Vṛndāvana to the earth, manifested as the stream of rasa flowing to and between men and women.'[71] Dimock's discussion of this mystical process is suffused with sublimating metaphors and models: 'To the Sahajiyās, the body is full of rasa, of the bliss of union, or, speaking purely physiologically, of semen.'[72] Thus, the semen-*rasa* is raised from the lowest lotuses in the genital and anal regions, the 'secret place' (*guhyadeśa*),[73] to the highest in the head, where man 'knows completely the divine *ānanda* within himself'.[74] In this, we might say that the Sahajiyā took the spiritual experience of *ānanda* back to its original and most ancient erotic meanings. But, significantly, this occurs often only after he has learned to become a woman in relationship to Kṛṣṇa, that is, only after he has taken on, through *āropa*, what is, psychologically speaking, a homoerotic orientation to the divine. This, I would argue, is precisely what renders the *prema* 'pure': denied any and every legitimate external object by society, the homoerotic desire turns in upon itself and flows toward its only socially acceptable object, the divine male. Such *prema* is no longer 'sexual', that is, moving toward another human being. It has become nondual, 'erotic'; it has imploded in upon itself in an experience of ecstasy, fervent devotion, and divine love. In this, it is indeed 'pure', in other words, without an external object.

A SNAKE AMONG THE LOTUSES: THE ŚĀKTA TRADITION

Gay refers to Hindu folk models of sublimation as magical and pre-psychoanalytic. Although I would agree with him that these are indeed pre-psychoanalytic to the extent that they do not attempt to move their adherents out of a religious frame into a postcritical, explicitly psychological one,[75] I think Gay seriously underestimates the explanatory power and psychological achievements of one kind of South Asian model of libidinal transformation and transfiguration, otherwise known as the *cakra* system. We, of course, have already seen this 'secondary somatic system'[76] at work in the Nāth Siddha and Sahajiyā traditions. Its basic structure and variants are well known, and we know at least something about its history.[77] Perhaps what is less obvious, however, is the system's complex gender dynamics and the way it dramatically affirms the ontological relationship between sexual and mystical energies. One does not need to think long with the symbolism to realize its most basic message, namely, that the sexual and the mystical exist along a shared organic developmental spectrum, and that, moreover and more radically, it is the sexual and the anal—or what the *Kaulajñānanirṇaya* calls the *gūḍha*, literally 'the hidden' (the anus), and the *guhya*, literally 'the secret' (the genitals)[78]—from which the mystical flower always arises.

In terms of its gender structure, what is interesting and especially Indic is the fact that the penetrating serpent of the system is coded female and displays clear androgynous characteristics. This snake among the lotuses, in other words, although it clearly carries phallic connotations (particularly in its penetration of the feminine lotuses), cannot be read as a dominantly phallic symbol, as we find, for example, in the American snake-handling cults that Weston La Barre has studied.[79] Rather, what we find in the Indian context is an essentially androgynous symbol that functions as both a penetrating phallus and a potentially dangerous but mystically potent feminine-sexual energy.[80] The conclusions reached by Joseph S. Alter in his eloquent study of snakes in the culture of north Indian wrestlers seem equally applicable here: 'I think it can be shown that in India in general and certainly in the world of the wrestler, snakes represent sexuality in many forms.'[81] To back up this claim, Alter discusses the common motif of the snake wrapped around the phallic-shaped *liṅgam* or etched onto the *yoni* on which the *liṅgam* is seated and the similar and no doubt related motif of the *kuṇḍalinī* coiled around the base of the spine. Indeed, 'in the imagery of Kundalini Yoga the seed of shakti is activated at the base of one's spine and shot upward through the serpent to the top of one's head. This metaphor of ejaculation (which, not incidentally, is completely self-contained) provides a symbolic graph of self-realization and metaphysical release in Hindu spiritualism.'[82] The wrestlers Alter worked with expressed what Alter calls 'an abject fear of eroticism in any form' and regarded snakes as 'the symbolic equivalent of lustful women'.[83] Their fear was expressed by the rule that women were not allowed into the *akhara* precinct (the wrestling pit), and the aphorism, '[H]aving sex with a woman is like being sucked dry by a snake'.[84] And this, I should add, also takes us right back to the imagery of *kuṇḍalinī yoga*, where in a text like the *Saṭcakranirūpaṇa,* the sleeping serpentine energy is said to have its mouth directly over the *liṅgam* at the base of the spine, no doubt to drink the precious semen-energy and prevent it from making its way up the *suṣumṇā* channel: 'Over it [the *svayambhū liṅgam*] shines the sleeping Kuṇḍalinī, fine as the fibre of the lotus-stalk. She is the world-bewilderer, gently covering the mouth of Brahma-dvāra [the hollow at the top of the *svayambhū liṅgam*] by Her own.'[85]

To complicate things further, it is also worth pointing out that in other Śākta Tantric texts, like the medieval and classic Tantric digest, the *Tantrasāra*, ejaculation is explicitly enjoined as a kind of sacrificial offering. In the following summary, David Kinsley invokes the category of sublimation to describe what the Tantric ritual of *maithuna* is *not*: 'It is not sublimated or curbed sexual activity that awakens the *kundalini*,' here, 'but sexual activity properly understood or perhaps properly appreciated.'[86]

THE COMPASSION OF JEFFREY HOPKINS: EROS AND THE VAJRAYĀNA TRADITION

Shashibhushan Dasgupta begins his *Obscure Religious Cults* with a study of what he calls the Buddhist Sahajiyā cult as it appears in the earliest Bengali religious text that we have, the *Caryāpadas*, a collection of fifty Buddhist Tantric songs dating somewhere between the tenth and twelfth centuries with clear connections to Tantric Buddhism as it developed in northeastern India under the Pāla kings and, later, in Nepal and Tibet. More recently, Per Kvaerne has given us an elaborate study of the songs as they were translated and interpreted within a Tibetan commentarial tradition,[87] and Miranda Shaw, following Dasgupta's lead, has referred to these same early Tibetan systems as 'Śākta Buddhism'.[88] What interests me here is not so much the *Caryāpadas* themselves or even these early forms of Tibetan Buddhism but the broad Vajrayāna tradition of which they became a part and, more to the point, the manner in which contemporary understandings of Vajrayāna erotics deepen and enrich the earlier discussions of Dasgupta and our present exploration of South Asian models of sublimation.

For a variety of historical and cultural reasons, Vajrayāna Buddhism has received significant scholarly and popular attention in the West over the past fifty years. One of the results of this consistent and studied attention is a much greater awareness of Vajrayāna erotics and its relationship to the tradition's central category of *śunyatā*, or emptiness, and *karuṇa*, or compassion. The Tibetologist John Powers, for example, makes the following point: 'While most exoteric Buddhist texts advise practitioners to reduce desire in order to attain liberation, Tantric texts actually propose to incorporate the energy of desire into the path. The problem lies not in desire per se, but rather in a misdirection of the energy of desire toward objects that lead to suffering and bondage.'[89] The Tantric path, in other words, is one of sublimation.

The Tibetan systems are incredibly complex and generally require many years of practice at different elaborately described stages of doctrinal and meditative development. At the risk of simplifying things, it is worth pointing out that at the very highest stages of practice, yogins are encouraged to use a 'seal' or female partner in conjunction with a sublimating technique: 'It said that in orgasm coarser levels of mind drop away, but most people do not see the potential meditative benefits of the experience. In the practices using seals, the experience of orgasm is conjoined with techniques that draw the winds into the central channel. The result is an indescribable experience of bliss and direct perception of emptiness. The partner is referred to as a "seal" because the practice seals the realization that all phenomena are a union of bliss and emptiness.'[90] Indeed, some aspects of the tradition actually insist that such consorts are absolutely necessary to attaining Buddhahood in one lifetime. According to a Gelukpa tradition cited by Powers, there are only two ways to reach Buddhahood: through a sexual practice involving a female consort, or through the meditative use of one's actual death in an attempt to withdraw the subtle winds of the body.[91] As is so often the case, sexuality and death are understood to be phenomenologically similar experiences, and both are suffused with mystical potentials.

This same advanced practice of using orgasm as a meditative technique is discussed by Jeffrey Hopkins, one of America's premiere Tibetologists and a regular translator for the Dalai Lama. His recent *Sex, Orgasm, and the Mind of Clear Light*[92] is an explicit homosexual manual for the art of gay love in the tradition of the Indian *Kāmaśāstras* modeled after the Tibetan sex manual of Gedün Chöpel, his *Tibetan Arts of Love*, which Hopkins had translated in an earlier work.[93] After revising Chöpel's heterosexual manual for his own gay community, Hopkins turns, in the second part of the book, to a series of incisive 'Ruminations', many of which bear directly on the issues that have concerned me in the present essay.[94] Here, in four such ruminations, Hopkins addresses the sex-friendly nature of Tibetan Buddhism, the structural psychology of Tibetan Tantric Buddhism, the psychological nature of homophobia, and the contemporary practice of Tantric sex. Hopkins's refusal to separate the sexual and the mystical, his insistence on the ontological dimensions of Tantric eroticism, his rejection of a metaphorical or 'spiritual' approach to Tantric sexual symbolism, his subtle adoption of Western psychological and psychoanalytic insights,[95] his solid stance against homophobia, and his awareness that sexual orientation must play into any understanding or practice of Tantra, all resonate beautifully with my own positions as articulated in *Kālī's Child* and subsequent writings, and I am thus particularly fond of this text and its portrayal of Vajrayāna Buddhism.

Hopkins begins his ruminations with the power of iconography: 'On the walls of Tibetan temples there are paintings of males with erect phallus and paintings of male-female couples in sexual union.' 'Sex is clearly not separate from religion,' Hopkins concludes.[96] Or put differently, 'the state of the all-good [consciousness] is harmonious with orgasm'.[97] He then proceeds to state his central thesis about the continuum of mind in Tantric psychology and the consequent compatibility of orgasm and reason: 'Both cognitive states and emotional states have the same basic nature, clear light, and thus are not separated off from each other in separate universes; both have luminosity as their core and exist within a continuum. . . . From this perspective, orgasmic pleasure is a type of mind, and the state of orgasm is even utilized to gain realization of the clear light nature of basic mind which is often compared to the sky.'[98]

This 'mind of clear light'—which Hopkins confesses to know as 'so awesome when one newly becomes aware of it'[99]—can be revealed erotically, since, phenomenologically speaking, 'orgasm involves the ceasing of the grosser levels of consciousness and manifestation of the more subtle levels'.[100] Even more radically, 'the consciousness that manifests in profound orgasm is deeper than reason, and is its basis'.[101] In sum, it must be understood that 'the state of orgasmic bliss is in the same continuum of mind as reason, is even more subtle than conceptual thought, and can be utilized in special states to realize the truth'.[102] Indeed, the Indo-Tibetan system of the Tantra Vehicle or Vajra Vehicle (the Vajrayāna) advanced by the Gelukpa sect highlighted by Hopkins goes so far as to argue that during orgasm, this mind of clear light manifests *to all*, if usually unconsciously.[103]

But why? And, more important for us in the present context, *how*? The why involves the deconstructive and overwhelming characteristics of orgasm: 'The pleasure of orgasm is so intense that the mind becomes totally withdrawn and fascinated such that both the usual conceptual mind and the appearances that accompany it melt away, leaving basic reality.'[104] The consciousness manifested in orgasm then is not a dimming of mind or a depletion of reality—although it might often seem that way to the untrained or fearful—but 'that into which all appearances dissolve and thus the foundation of appearance'.[105] The result is both liberating and emotionally healing. In the words of the first Panchen Lama, Lo-san-cho-gyi-gyel-tsen: 'A great bliss is generated in dependence on a casual motivation that is the desire of gazing, smiling, holding hands or embracing, or union of the two organs. The wisdom of undifferentiable bliss and emptiness, which is this great bliss generated undifferentiably with a mind cognizing emptiness at the same time, consumes completely the afflictive emotions—desire, ignorance, and so forth.'[106]

Sexual pleasure or 'bliss' (a clear Tibetan analogue to the Sanskrit *ānanda*), then, is not a 'depletion' of energy or pressure, as if we were working in some hydraulic system, but a clear manifestation of consciousness and reality. The trick, of course, is how this is done, and this brings us back to a kind of sublimation. Gedün Chöpel's advice is simple: 'Do everything.' More specifically, he advises his readers to learn how to dwell in the midst of intense pleasure and allow it to pervade the entire body. Note again the clear sexual uses of the terms 'bliss', 'the jewel', and 'churning':

If one does not know the techniques of holding and spreading the bliss that has arrived at the tip of the jewel [i.e., the head of the phallus], immediately upon seeing it for a moment it fades and disappears, like picking up a snowflake in the hand. Therefore when, upon churning about, bliss is generated, cease movement, and again and again spread [the sense of bliss throughout the body]. Then, by again doing it with the former methods, bliss will be sustained for a long time.[107]

The point of all of this, of course, is not 'simply sex', but what I have called in *Kālī's Child* 'the erotic', that is, the ultimate nonduality of the energies of human sexuality and the ontological revelations of mystical experience. Hopkins puts the matter this way: 'The aim of sexual yoga is not mere repetition of an attractive state but revelation of the basic reality of bliss and emptiness underlying appearances . . . developed practitioners seek to utilize the blissful and powerful mind of orgasm to realize the truth and the all-good ground of consciousness.'[108]

Such a dialectical ontological vision allows Hopkins to read Tibetan technical terms as simultaneously religious and sexual (again, very much as I have done with Bengali terms in *Kālī's Child*). Take, for example, his discussion of the Tibetan Buddhist notion of 'compassion'. Hopkins points out that the Sanskrit term for compassion, *karuṇā*, is taken in the Tibetan context to mean 'stopping bliss' (Tib. *bde œgog*) and can thus function in *both* a sexual sense ('orgasmic bliss without emission')[109] *and* an ethical way ('in the sense that finding another's state of suffering to be unbearable stops . . . one's own happiness').[110] It is not a matter, then, of one or the other meaning, *but of both*: 'the meaning is that the two exist side by side'.[111] Or more philosophically put: 'Association of compassion and sexual bliss is consonant with the basic Tantric psychology that a mind of orgasm can yield a vision of reality and thus that the supramundane is at the core of the mundane.'[112] It is also consonant with the conviction of Highest Yoga Tantra that a connection exists 'between the capacity of compassion and the capacity to use sexual bliss for spiritual progress',[113] an insight that, as Hopkins points out, has profound implications for the psychological dynamics of sexual violence in both its misogynistic and homophobic forms.

Hopkins ends his ruminations with a wise refusal to turn the sexual acts of Chöpel's or his own sex manual into mere metaphors or 'spiritual' signs for some completely transcendent ideal (for such a move again 'splits' the unbroken continuum of the orgasmic mind and generates the dualistic defilements of homophobia, misogyny, etc.) and issues a call for his readers to see the erotic as a manifestation of the real:

> The religious focus on the mind of clear light does not turn the material on sexual acts into metaphors for union with the divine. Rather, ordinary sex is viewed as a basis for possible development into extraordinary insight. The sky-experience of the mind of clear light stands behind these scintillating descriptions of erotic acts, beckoning the participant to taste reality.[114]

SOME FINAL UNFINISHED WEAVINGS: TOWARD A WESTERN TANTRA

What, then, should we finally make of this recurring koan of the mystical and the erotic, this ever-present coincidentia of spirit and sex in the history of religions? Or, put differently, this time within the rhetorical frame of the present essay, as a community of scholars committed to the tasks of historically contextualizing, sympathetically understanding, critically interpreting, and comparatively synthesizing Tantric symbolism and ritual, where are we now, a little more than fifty years after Dasgupta's pioneering study of those 'obscure religious cults' of Bengal? With so much more textual material and theoretical sophistication at our literal fingertips, I would like to think that we can contemplate the Tantric lotus a little more clearly now. I would also like to imagine that we can someday emerge from our increasingly focused and specialized studies or doctrinal positions, step back a bit, and look at the bigger picture in order to notice that there are other flowers out there that seem to grow, well, a bit differently. Is it time to synthesize this mass of material and methods into a more adequate, if never perfect, vision of South Asian Tantra? And more radically still, do we know enough 'stuff' now? Is there a critical mass of information and perspectives to enable us to put it all on the table with other cultural forms of religious eroticism, so that we might begin to develop a comparative erotics of mysticism that can address both our descriptive or phenomenological needs about this or that cultural tradition and our normative or explanatory questions about 'religion', 'mysticism', and 'sexuality'? Are we ready, in other words, to understand the Part of Tantra through the Whole of the history of mysticism, even as we continue to explore the Whole of the history of mysticism through such Parts as Siddha Yoga, Sahajiyā Vaiṣṇavism, Śākta Tantra, and Vajrayāna Buddhism? Not simply, in other words, 'What does this Nāth Siddha or medieval bridal mystic think or write about this or that?' but 'What do we think about what the Nāth Siddha, the bridal mystic, the Daoist alchemist, and the Sufi have written, how do their individual texts throw light on the others, and what can we say with this new, explicitly comparative perspective?' If the history of religions has anything to offer Tantric Studies—and I think it does—it is this explicitly comparative method. And this is something genuinely new. This is our Western *darśana*, our philosophical 'perspective', our hermeneutical yoga that promises to teach us something more and else about the relationship between the mystical and the erotic, if not in present actuality, then at least in future dream and hope.

Until that comparative dream is attempted, we can make at least a few, fairly reasonable observations and ask some better questions. Here, then, are a few threads of thought that, taken together and related to each other, might be woven into an unfinished Western Tantra.

The Warp and Woof of Sexual Expression–Repression

One of my most important conclusions to the above considerations is connected to the fact that sublimation in Freud's thought is connected to the lifting or removal of sexual repression: 'Premature repression makes the sublimation of the repressed instinct impossible; when the repression is lifted, the path to sublimation becomes free once more.'[115] Here, I think, we begin to approach an answer for why Tantric systems almost always employ a combination of sexual control and sexual expression. It is seldom one or the other. It is usually both. Hence Shashibhushan Dasgupta's psychological rendering of Tantric practice: 'not by process of violent suppression, but by a slow and gradual process of strict physical and psychological discipline'. In more technical terms: sublimation, not repression.

This same dialectic of sexual expression and repression might also help us problematize or rethink the psychoanalytic model. Consider, for example, the dominating sublimation metaphor of both psychoanalysis and the Tantric traditions, that is, the hydraulic metaphor: dam up the libidinal waters (or winds) here, and they will move 'up' and appear as something else there. Sexual repression leads to sublimation: that is the basic logic. But what, then, to do with the Tantric practices of sexual expression that clearly call for ejaculation and orgasm?[116] As we have seen, ejaculation and orgasm are needed in any number of Siddha and Śākta contexts, especially the earliest ones, to generate the sexual fluids that are to be offered to the deities. And, as we have seen in the Vajrayāna, orgasm is believed to possess a whole range of subtle levels of mind not available to the completely abstaining. Clearly there are repressive dimensions to even these practices, as when, for example, the Vajrayāna orgasm is timed with an emptying of the side channels and a filling up of the *suṣumṇā* or central channel (the hydraulics metaphor returns), or when Tantric intercourse is hedged in and controlled with all sorts of yogic techniques, mantras, and ritual acts. Still, the fact remains that such controls are in the service of a kind of sublimated sexual expression and not dammed up entirely against it.

Erotic Ontologies

In terms of our imagined dialogue between Tantra and psychoanalysis, few would argue that human sexuality and religious experience can be easily separated. As the Nāth Siddhas claimed, there is a direct channel running from the tip of the penis to the top of the head, where mystical consciousness blooms: confessions of sexual-mystical connection do not get much clearer than that. The question, however, remains: *how* are these two areas of the human being related? When we examine erotic forms of mysticism, are we dealing with a conscious energy seeking greater and greater levels of organization, awareness, and bliss, or simply the blind and mechanical workings of an all too predictable universe that has 'displaced' a properly 'sexual' experience into a falsely imagined 'religious' one? As I have argued before, everything depends upon one's ontological commitments.

Volney Gay has shown that, because Freud was operating in a mechanistic universe, the impressive transformations of sublimation had to remain a mystery: his worldview ultimately could not adequately explain how higher forms of consciousness and creativity could be derived from lower forms.[117] Tantric ontologies are not restricted by such metaphysical assumptions. Indeed, they work from the *opposite* direction: because they assume that human sexuality is a potent manifestation of being (à la the ancient erotics of *ānanda*), they argue that, properly handled, sexual energies can be employed as a means toward greater and greater ontological realization. Contrary to what is often assumed, then, the sexual is not left behind or transcended for the spiritual. Doctrinally, physiologically, and ritually framed, the *deepest and most profound* of the five *kośas* or sheaths of the human being is the sheath of *ānanda*, the eros of Being itself (*Taittirīya Upaniṣad* 2.1–6), the sexual bliss of Śiva and Śakti is realized in the *last* and *final* stage of Śākta spiritual practice, not in the first, and intercourse with an actual female partner or 'seal' is needed in the *highest*, not the beginning, stages of Tantric yoga in Tibetan Vajrayāna. In Tantric language, both *mukti* or 'liberation' and *bhukti* or 'pleasure' are granted, hence Agehananda Bharati's epigrammatic dedication of one of his essays to the Goddess who grants both: '*bhukti-mukti-pradāyinyai ādiśaktyai namo, namaḥ*' (Salutations, salutations to the primordial power, to the giver of pleasure and liberation).[118] More radically still, the final thousand-petaled lotus drips with the nectar of Śiva and Śakti's love-play, which the Tantric poet in turn drinks.[119] From its roots in the *mūlādhāra* to its blooming in the *sahasrāra*, then, the Tantric lotus is sexualized, erotic, a thing of sublime beauty.

Despite its limiting, if perhaps methodologically necessary, ontological commitments, psychoanalysis can help us appreciate at least something of this both/and. The category of sublimation, after all, implies that the mystical *is and is not* the sexual. The mystical *is* the sexual because it is from sexual energies that the mystical is aroused, stimulated, even constituted. The mystical *is not* the sexual because through the processes of symbolization, displacement, repression, and sublimation these energies have indeed become 'something else'—they have organized themselves successfully on a 'higher' plane or level. We can well imagine a Freud, then, who would hardly argue Dasgupta's point with which I began this essay: 'though a Freudian explanation of the whole thing may not be absolutely inadmissible in such religious practices, one fundamental point, which we should never lose sight of even from the empirical point of view, is that though the lotus above the surface of the water may have its origin in the mud deep below, mud and lotus cannot surely be placed in the same scale in our general scheme of valuation'. Although he certainly privileged the muddy origins of the lotus over its eventual petals and denied any truly transcendent meanings of its bloom, Freud seldom confused these scales and, on the contrary, gave them each their due in his concept of sublimation, even if, ultimately, he could not explain how one could get from the muddy water to the shiny petal and delicate stamen.

Which is not to say that this solves everything. Far from it indeed. I would go so far as to say that what we should most likely be imagining is an entirely new dimension. To take a well-worn analogy used in the philosophy of science, it is as if we are trying to understand a three-dimensional reality while still trapped on its two-dimensional plane (here the warp and woof of our weave and its subsequent patterns). What we do not see is that the patterns we intuit or guess at are in actual fact a function of a three-dimensional perspective that can only appear to us as, well, as a mystery.

Along similar questioning lines, I think we must ask both ourselves and the texts if the sexual expression/repression dynamics we see explored in such detail and diversity in the traditions is really a zero-sum game. Does it, *really*, always follow what is essentially a logic of (libidinal) scarcity and hoarding: the more energy the male holds in, the more spiritual he becomes? If this is so, why is it, then, that so many of the texts enjoin a 'sacrifice' of the fluids and liken the mystical state to the release of orgasm? Such questions, which are perhaps nothing more (nor less) than our mechanistic and exclusive categories coming up against the paradoxical koan of the mystical and the erotic (or of sexual repression and expression), land us squarely in an epistemological crisis, which is also, I must add, an epistemological possibility. We would do well, then, to 'think outside the box' or, to stick to our original metaphor (for a box is already a three-dimensional space), 'outside the weave', outside even the warp and woof of the woven Tantra. I am not at all sure how to do this, but I am certain that it must be done.

NOTES

1. Sigmund Freud, *Introductory Lectures on Psychoanalysis*, trans. and ed. James Strachey (1966; New York: Norton, 1977), 284–85.
2. Sudhir Kakar, *Shamans, Mystics and Doctors: A Psychological Inquiry into India and Its Healing Traditions* (New Delhi: Oxford University Press, 1982), 153.
3. Volney P. Gay, *Freud on Sublimation: Reconsiderations* (Albany: State University of New York Press, 1992), 37.
4. David Bakan, *Sigmund Freud and the Jewish Mystical Tradition* (Boston: Beacon Press, 1958).
5. Quoted in David H. Wulff, *Psychology of Religion: Classic & Contemporary* (New York: Wiley, 1997), 265.
6. Wulff, *Psychology of Religion*, 266.
7. Suzanne R. Kirschner, *The Religious and Romantic Origins of Psychoanalysis: Individuation and Integration in Post-Freudian Theory* (Cambridge, Mass.: Harvard University Press, 1996).
8. Diana Hume George, *Blake and Freud* (Ithaca, N.Y.: Cornell University Press, 1980), 17.
9. Jeffrey J. Kripal, *Kālī's Child: The Mystical and the Erotic in the Life and Teachings of Ramakrishna* (1995; 2nd edn., Chicago: University of Chicago Press, 1998).
10. George, *Blake and Freud*, 17.
11. Michel de Certeau, *The Mystic Fable*, vol. 1: *The Sixteenth and Seventeenth Centuries* (Chicago: University of Chicago Press, 1992), 2.
12. Ibid., 9.
13. Ibid.
14. William B. Parsons, *The Enigma of the Oceanic Feeling: The Freud-Rolland Correspondence and the Revisioning of the Psychoanalytic Theory of Mysticism* (New York: Oxford University Press, 1999).
15. No Indian saint, with the possible exception of Gandhi, has received more psychoanalytic (and more controversial) attention than Ramakrishna.
16. Jeffrey J. Kripal, 'Pale Plausibilities,' preface to the second edition of *Kālī's*

Child; and 'Why the Tāntrika Is a Hero: Kālī in the Psychoanalytic Tradition,' in Rachel Fell McDermott and Jeffrey J. Kripal, eds., *Encountering Kālī: In the Margins, at the Center, in the West* (Berkeley: University of California Press, 2002), 196–222.

17. de Certeau, *Mystic Fable*, 8.
18. The last four sentences of this paragraph are taken from my 'Why the Tāntrika Is a Hero,' 196.
19. Shashibhushan Dasgupta, *Obscure Religious Cults* (1946; Calcutta: Firma KLM Private, 1976), 115–16.
20. Jeffrey J. Kripal, 'Psychoanalysis and Hinduism: Thinking Through Each Other,' Afterword to T.G. Vaidyanathan and Jeffrey J. Kripal, eds., *Vishnu on Freud's Desk: A Reader in Psychoanalysis and Hinduism* (New Delhi: Oxford University Press, 1999), 449.
21. Strictly speaking, the model I am developing here applies only to mystical traditions that employ sexual language to express the meaning and/or felt content of their sought-after states. It has little, if anything, to say about traditions that do not employ such language.
22. Kripal, *Kālī's Child*; see esp. 22–24, 317–28.
23. See Jeffrey J. Kripal, *Roads of Excess, Palaces of Wisdom: Eroticism and Reflexivity in the Study of Mysticism* (Chicago: University of Chicago Press, 2001).
24. This, by the way, is why I was originally drawn to Hinduism—I was convinced, and I am still convinced, that its traditions thought about sexuality and spirituality in richer, more diverse, and more subtle terms than my own Catholic heritage.
25. Leo Steinberg, *The Sexuality of Christ in Renaissance Art and Modern Oblivion* (1983; Chicago: University of Chicago Press, 1996).
26. Gay, *Freud on Sublimation*, 1. I am relying heavily on Gay for the following discussion, along with my own reading of Freud's *Three Essays on the Theory of Sexuality* (1905), vol. 7 (1901–1905) of *The Standard Edition of the Complete Psychological Works of Sigmund Freud* (London: Hogarth Press and Institute of Psycho-Analysis, 1953).
27. Gay, *Freud on Sublimation*, 4.
28. Something similar, of course, has happened in India over the centuries, and hence the 'scandal' of the erotic medieval temples of Konarak and Khajuraho and the consistent pious denial that the Śiva *liṅgam* is phallic. As the cultural constructions of sexuality and the sacred have changed, art forms and practices that once signaled a potent sacralization of sexuality have become cause for embarrassment or simple denial. And yet the ancient stones and the texts still celebrate.
29. Gay, *Freud on Sublimation*, 93–95.
30. Freud, *Three Essays*, 178.
31. Ibid., 170.

32. Peter Shabad, 'The Most Intimate of Creations: Symptoms as Memorials to One's Lonely Suffering,' in Peter Homans, ed., *Symbolic Loss: The Ambiguity of Mourning and Memory at Century's End* (Charlottesville: University Press of Virginia, 2000), 197–212.
33. Freud, *Three Essays*, 165.
34. Ibid., 238.
35. Gay, *Freud on Sublimation*, 105–6.
36. Ibid., 106.
37. Ibid., 107.
38. Ibid., 107–8.
39. In fact, Freud did not add the phallic stage until much later (1923) (see Freud, *Three Essays*, 199–200n.3), and the latency stage is, technically speaking, not a true stage, but I shall not detain our discussion here with such details.
40. Freud, *Three Essays*, 235; see also 155–56, 208.
41. Ibid., 205–6.
42. Ibid., 206. Freud defines sublimation in ibid., 238.
43. Ibid., 239.
44. Quoted in Gay, *Freud on Sublimation*, 110.
45. Gay, *Freud on Sublimation*, 111. 'Divine' and 'unconscious' are equally 'other' and so practically interchangeable in psychoanalytic thought.
46. Quoted in Gay, *Freud on Sublimation*, 111–12.
47. Ibid., 112.
48. Patrick Olivelle, 'Orgasmic Rapture and Divine Ecstasy: The Semantic History of "Ānanda",' *Journal of Indian Philosophy* 25 (1997): 153–80. Here Olivelle traces the uses of *ānanda* in early Vedic, middle Vedic (the Brāhmaṇas), late Vedic (the Āraṇyakas and Upaniṣads), and post-Vedic (primarily Buddhist and epic) literatures. What Olivelle finds is that there exists in the ancient Sanskrit texts an 'explicit and unambiguous connection between *ānanda* as orgasmic rapture and *ānanda* as the experience of *brahman/ātman*.' Put differently, it is the sexual meanings of *ānanda* that provide 'the foundation for its technical use within the theological vocabulary of the Upaniṣads,' which in turn of course became the basis for the later philosophical speculations of Advaita Vedānta and many other religio-philosophical traditions.
49. I borrow the phrase 'wave of genius' and the sixth-century dating from David Gordon White, *The Alchemical Body: Siddha Traditions in Medieval India* (Chicago: The University of Chicago Press, 1996), 1.
50. David Gordon White, 'Introduction' to *Tantra in Practice*, ed. id. (Princeton: Princeton University Press, 2000), 9.
51. White, *Alchemical Body*, Preface, ix–xiii.
52. Ibid., 353n.3.
53. Ibid., 204.

54. Ibid., 253. See also 207, 243, and 320.
55. See ibid., 147–252, for an elaborate description and analysis of these different chemical techniques.
56. Ibid., 301.
57. Ibid., 4.
58. Ibid.,
59. Ibid., 5.
60. 'Both historically and conceptually, yoga is in many ways an internalization of sexual intercourse between a man and a woman' (*Tantra in Practice*, ed. White, 15).
61. White, *Alchemical Body*, 138. It is in this context that I would read many contemporary accounts of *śaktipāt* at the hands, hugs, or touch of contemporary gurus with lineage relationships to Siddha systems (Swami Muktananda, Ammachi, and Ruchira Avatar Adi Da Samraj, for example) as sublimated forms of sexual fluid transfer. Along these same lines, devotees of Ammachi and Adi Da have shared with me accounts, some of them firsthand, in which the *śaktipāt* was accompanied by intense sexual arousal, sometimes lasting for days.
62. White, *Alchemical Body*, 138. See also 222, 241, and 279 for some descriptions of this Tantric nondual metaphysics and its relationship to the more dualistic systems of Advaita Vedānta.
63. This opting for a kind of Indic 'realization' over a psychoanalytic 'sublimation' was one of the conclusions of *Kālī's Child* (325–28). I borrow the expression 'always already' from the writings of Adi Da.
64. Edward C. Dimock, Jr., *The Place of the Hidden Moon: Erotic Mysticism in the Vaiṣṇava-sahajiyā Cult of Bengal* (1966; Chicago: University of Chicago Press, 1989), 153.
65. Ibid., 155.
66. This term from Catholic liturgical theology (the word is Thomistic and was used by medieval theologians to signal the miraculous transformation of bread and wine into the body and blood of Christ during mass) is a favorite of Tantric scholars, who routinely use it to capture something of the spirit and intent of Tantric practices of sublimation (see, for a start, Dasgupta, *Obscure Religious Cults*, 234, 244, 247, 248, 251, 252); and White, *Alchemical Body*, 171, 268, 314ff). White uses it as a translation of *śarīrayoga* (ibid., 268). I like it as well.
67. Dimock, *The Place of the Hidden Moon*, 163.
68. Ibid.
69. Ibid., 14–15.
70. Dasgupta, *Obscure Religious Cults*, 126, 130.
71. Dimock, *The Place of the Hidden Moon*, 168.
72. Ibid., 177.
73. Ibid., 171n.118.
74. Ibid., 177.

75. For a brilliant discussion of this distinction, see Peter Homans, 'Once Again, Psychoanalysis, East and West: A Psychoanalytic Essay on Religion, Mourning, and Healing,' *History of Religions* 24, no. 2 (1984): 133–54.
76. Agehananda Bharati, 'Techniques of Control in the Esoteric Traditions of India and Tibet,' in Agehananda Bharati, ed., *The Realm of the Extra-Human*, vol. 1: *Ideas and Actions* (The Hague: Mouton, 1976), 89–99.
77. For a discussion, see White, *Alchemical Body*, 134–35. White identifies the ninth-to-tenth-century *Kaulajñānanirṇaya* of Matsyendra as the earliest systematic discussion of the *cakra* model.
78. White, *Alchemical Body*, 134.
79. Weston La Barre, *They Shall Take Up Serpents: Psychology of the Southern Snake-Handling Cult* (Minneapolis: University of Minnesota Press, 1962).
80. For a fascinating Jewish analogue to this androgynous phallus, see Elliot Wolfson, *Through a Speculum That Shines: Vision and Imagination in Medieval Kabbalah* (Princeton: Princeton University Press, 1994).
81. Joseph S. Alter, *The Wrestler's Body: Identity and Ideology in North India* (Berkeley: University of California Press, 1992), 145.
82. Ibid.
83. Ibid., 146.
84. Ibid., 146.
85. Verse 10 of the *Ṣaṭcakranirupaṇa*, as translated and commented on in Sir John Woodroffe, *The Serpent Power: Being the Ṣaṭ-Cakra-Nirūpaṇa and Pādukā-Pañcaka* (1913; Madras: Ganesh, 1989), 346; the bracketed comments are my own, but they are based on Woodroffe.
86. David R. Kinsley, *Tantric Visions of the Divine Feminine: The Ten Mahāvidyās* (Berkeley: University of California Press, 1997), 243.
87. Per Kvaerne, *An Anthology of Buddhist Tantric Songs: A Study of the Caryāgīti* (Oslo: Universitetsforlaget, 1977).
88. Miranda Shaw, *Passionate Enlightenment: Women in Tantric Buddhism* (Princeton: Princeton University Press, 1994), 33.
89. John Powers, *Introduction to Tibetan Buddhism* (Ithaca, N.Y.: Snow Lion, 1995), 224.
90. Powers, *Introduction to Tibetan Buddhism*, 251.
91. Ibid., 253.
92. Jeffrey Hopkins, *Sex, Orgasm, and the Mind of Clear Light: The Sixty-four Arts of Gay Male Love* (Berkeley, Calif.: North Atlantic Books, 1998).
93. *Tibetan Arts of Love*, introduced and trans. by Jeffrey Hopkins (Ithaca, N.Y.: Snow Lion, 1992).
94. A shorter version of these 'Ruminations' appears as 'The Compatibility of Reason and Orgasm in Tibetan Buddhism: Reflections on Sexual Violence and Homophobia,' in Gary David Comstock and Susan E. Henking, eds., *Que(e)rying Religion: A Critical Anthology* (New York: Continuum, 1997), 372–83. I shall be referencing both versions.

95. Hopkins never explicitly mentions psychoanalysis, but its categories and insights are clearly working behind the scenes in: his general construal of Tantric thought as a 'psychology' (*Sex, Orgasm, and the Mind of Clear Light*, chap. 2) or even as a 'therapy' (98); his incisive discussion of the role of projection in homophobia (chap. 4); and, more specifically, the oedipal insights of n. 59, which reads, 'The female is called ômotherö (*yum*), and the male is called ôfatherö (*yab*). The terms are rich with suggestions (never made explicit in the tradition) of copulating with one's parents.' The same, of course, could be said of Śākta sexual ritual, in which the male's sexual partner is a manifestation of the mother-goddess.
96. Hopkins, *Sex, Orgasm, and the Mind of Clear Light*, 71.
97. Hopkins, 'Compatibility of Reason and Orgasm,' 382.
98. Hopkins, *Sex, Orgasm, and the Mind of Clear Light*, 72.
99. Ibid., 74.
100. Ibid., 72.
101. Ibid., 91. Such a position is uncannily close to that of the English romantic poet William Blake, who celebrated the scandalous 'hellish' powers and ontological revelations of mystical eroticism and ridiculed the conservative, stultifying prudishness of 'heavenly' religion in his *The Marriage of Heaven and Hell* (*c.* 1790). Pl. 4, entitled 'The Voice of the Devil,' for example, contains the following line: 'Energy is the only life and is from the Body[,] and Reason is the bound or outward circumference of Energy' (*William Blake's The Marriage of Heaven and Hell*, with an introduction and commentary by Geoffrey Keynes [New York: Oxford University Press, 1975]).
102. Hopkins, *Sex, Orgasm, and the Mind of Clear Light*, 99.
103. Hopkins, 'Compatibility of Reason and Orgasm,' 374.
104. Ibid., 376.
105. Ibid., 377.
106. Quoted in ibid.
107. Quoted in ibid., 379; bracketed glosses in original.
108. Hopkins, *Sex, Orgasm, and the Mind of Clear Light*, 78, 93.
109. Ibid., 103.
110. Ibid., 103.
111. Ibid., 102.
112. Ibid., 106.
113. Ibid., 105. Cf. 75: 'only the most compassionate are capable of using sexual bliss in the spiritual path'.
114. Ibid., 107.
115. Quoted in Gay, *Freud on Sublimation*, 111.
116. This, it seems to me, is a problem analogous to the one addressed by Wendy Doniger in her 'When a Lingam is Just a Good Cigar: Psychoanalysis and Hindu Sexual Fantasies,' reprinted in Vaidyanathan and Kripal, eds., *Vishnu*

on Freud's Desk, 279–303. In this essay, Doniger addresses the question of why the sexual is part of the manifest content instead of the latent content in Hindu mythology. If sexuality is so obvious, what is it that is being hidden? The manifestness of sexuality in Hindu mythology is analogous to the use of sexual expression (as opposed to repression) in certain Tantric rituals and meditative techniques.

117. Gay, *Freud on Sublimation*, 90.
118. Bharati, 'Śākta and Vajrayana,' 73.
119. See, e.g. the *Sākta Padāvalī* poems translated in Rachel Fell McDermott, *Singing to the Goddess: Poems to Kālī and Umā from Bengal* (New York: Oxford University Press, 2001), 103–17.

11

Magical Lovers, Sisters, and Mothers

Yakṣiṇī sādhana in Tantric Buddhism

MIRANDA SHAW

The early writings of Tantric Buddhism, dating from about the seventh through the tenth centuries CE, describe male Tāntrikas practicing in partnership with a range of mortal women and female spirits, known collectively as *ḍākinīs* and yoginīs. Scholars long assumed that the numinous females portrayed in Tantric annals as audacious, insightful, shape-shifting possessors of supernatural and enlightening powers must be figments of the male religious imagination, a literary screen erected to conceal the downtrodden prostitutes and low-caste unfortunates that Tantric yogis exploited in their sexual practices.[1] Before I ventured to India in 1986 to test my hypothesis that the spectrum of yoginīs and *ḍākinīs* included accomplished women who participated in the Tantric movement, my theory met with general resistance and skepticism on this side of the Pacific. Therefore, when I embarked upon my research in the legendary Tantric heartland of Bengal, I was surprised and gratified to encounter in Calcutta an ardent supporter of my theory in the erudite, immensely accomplished, irrepressibly charming Narendra Nath Bhattacharyya, who spared many precious hours to fortify me with tea while fostering my inquiries with his seemingly infinite fund of literary references, insights, anecdotes, and encouragement. I owe him a tremendous debt of gratitude and dedicate this essay to his profound and inspired mentorship.

My research, so generously supported by 'Narendra-ji', established that in many cases the yoginīs and *ḍākinīs* of Tantric lore were human women who variously practiced in solitude or met at gatherings of women where males were the companions, or adjuncts, not vice versa.[2] This finding in turn had implications for the interpretation of the sexual yoga described in Tantric texts, calling into question the presumption that the male Tāntrikas were the serious practitioners, while their female partners were characterized primarily by their sexual availability for nonmarital liaisons. Revising this misconception led to my now widely accepted claim that the women as well as the men celebrated in early Tantric Buddhist literature were serious practitioners, qualified for the yoga of sexual union (*karma mudrā* practice) by meditative training, philosophical study, and ritual and yogic proficiency.[3]

The present essay brings together two themes that long engaged Bhattacharyya, namely, the history of Śāktism and cultural roots of Tantra. I address a facet of Tantric Buddhism that is virtually undocumented in scholarship on the movement, namely, the phenomenon of *yakṣiṇī sādhana*, or invocation of *yakṣiṇī*s through Tantric rites. This little known strand of Tantric practice, briefly addressed in an article by Moti Chandra several decades ago,[4] otherwise finds no mention in studies of Tantric Buddhism. I first examine the roles and characterizations of *yakṣiṇī*s in early Buddhism, many of which resurface or appear in modified form in Tantric *yakṣiṇī* propitiation. The body of the essay introduces textual evidence for *yakṣiṇī sādhana*, focusing on the *Mañjuśrīmūlakalpa*, an early Tantric work from Bengal that treats the topic at length. Also considered here is the possible impact of the *yakṣiṇī* prototype upon the evolution of the *ḍākinī* figure that eventually came to the fore in Tantric symbology and practice.

*YAKṢIṆĪ*S IN EARLY BUDDHISM

Yakṣiṇī worship has a long history in the Buddhist tradition. The early Buddhist pantheon was replete with semi-divine beings whose presence and supernatural powers impinged on human life in various ways, both positive and negative. A popular genre was that of the *yakṣa* (male) and *yakṣiṇī* (female), a broad category that encompasses tree spirits, water sprites, local tutelaries, and a diverse range of beneficent and cannibalistic spirits. Buddhism inherited the belief in *yakṣas* and *yakṣiṇīs* as an integral part of the cosmology and cultic activity of the Indian populace. The Buddha and the generations who followed him did not call their existence into question or prohibit their worship, nor did they ignore their presence in the landscape and religious lives of the people. On the contrary, this class of beings is a recurrent theme in Buddhist art and literature. Indeed, a great deal of the evidence of *yakṣa* worship from the third century BCE through the second century CE is found in Buddhist sources.[5] Narratives of the teaching career of Śākyamuni Buddha consistently include *yakṣas* and *yakṣiṇīs* among his congregation and sphere of potential converts. It is not uncommon to find them cast in the role of guardians of Buddhist practitioners and monuments, bestowing blessings and offering protection against other supernatural beings—including *yakṣas*—of hostile intent.

Most relevant for the present study is the prominence of *yakṣiṇīs* in the iconographic programs of the earliest extant Buddhist monuments. Imposing carvings of voluptuous *yakṣiṇīs* were among the first images to greet those who came to worship at *stūpas* enshrining the relics of the Buddha. At the sites of Bhārhut (second century BCE) and Sanghol and Bhūteśvara (second century CE), *yakṣiṇī* images were prominently situated on the stone pillars of the *stūpa* balustrade surrounding the circumambulatory walkway. At Sāñcī (third century BCE to first century CE), *yakṣiṇīs* are sculpted in the round tower above those who pass through the massive gateways. The *yakṣiṇīs*, depicted as scantily clad and seductively posed dryads, are endowed with every gift of the female form, from lush curves to lavish adornment.

The conspicuous placement of the *yakṣiṇīs* and the artistic skill expended upon their feminine beauty attest to their active role in the imaginal world and devotional life of the Buddhists who commissioned and worshipped at the *stūpas*. Although Buddhism, in keeping with Indic religiosity at large, recognizes the existence of morally unevolved and dangerous *yakṣiṇīs*, the *yakṣiṇīs* portrayed on these monuments are beneficent figures, sometimes known as *mahāyakṣiṇīs*, or 'great *yakṣiṇīs*,' who have pledged loyalty to the Buddha and vowed to protect and bless his followers. Their effigies grace the *stūpa* railings not as decorative elements but as icons with ritual and symbolic significance. Symbolically, the *yakṣiṇīs* evoke the quality of auspiciousness (*maṅgala*), or life-enhancing energies that bring about fertility, growth, longevity, abundance, and material and spiritual well-being.[6] Their erotic quality expresses this life-enriching potency. As objects of ritual practice, their images probably received the forms of worship rendered at *yakṣa* shrines in general, such as prostration, prayer, and offerings of flowers, incense, lamplight, sandalwood paste, foods, oblations, garlands, and banners.[7] The benefits sought through their veneration, as described in Buddhist sources and other literature, were a spouse, progeny, wealth, bountiful crops, timely rainfall, safe travel by land and sea, and cure of epidemics.[8] In addition to their role in Buddhist devotionalism, the *yakṣiṇī* images may have served a talismanic function, being stationed at the gates and peripheries of monuments to radiate auspicious energies and ward off dangers and negative forces.[9]

There is evidence that *yakṣiṇīs* played a role in invocatory practices as well. One of the earliest recorded Buddhist magical techniques is the invocation of *yakṣas* and *yakṣiṇīs* with mantras. Scriptural sources divulge incantations, revealed by Śākyamuni Buddha, for eliciting the protection of these supernaturally potent beings. Most notably, the *Āṭānāṭiya Sutta* relates the spells that summon the guardian kings and their retinues of *yakṣas* and other spirits from the four quarters of the universe—east, south, west, and north, in turn—to protect whoever calls upon them, promising that they will rush to their aid and repel hostile *yakṣas* and other harmful spirits. The Buddha mentions several *yakṣiṇīs* in the company by name and recommends the recitation of these apotropaic chants by both laity and monastics.[10] Peter Skilling has drawn attention to Buddhist liturgical formulae, known as 'auspicious verses' (*maṅgala gāthā*), that could well have been recited during *stūpa* circumambulation to invoke the protective and prospering powers of the *yakṣas*, *yakṣiṇīs*, and other beings portrayed around the monuments.[11] The *Suvarṇabhāsottamasūtra* (*c.* late fourth to early fifth century) documents an ongoing interest in enlisting *yakṣas* and *yakṣiṇīs* as directional guardians. The scripture's readers are assured that the *yakṣiṇīs* 'Caṇḍā, Caṇḍālikā, . . . Caṇḍikā, Kuntī, and Kūṭadantī . . . possessed of supernatural powers, great strength and prowess, will give them protection everywhere in the four directions.'[12]

Another aspect of the *yakṣiṇīs* that finds expression in Buddhist literature is their role as seducers and lovers of mortal men. *Yakṣiṇīs* are reputed to be shape-shifters who can render themselves visible at will and adopt an irresistibly alluring guise in order to attract human paramours. The body that a *yakṣiṇī* manifests for this purpose is visible, tangible, and potentially mistakable for that of a mortal woman. The possibility of sexual union with a *yakṣiṇī* is recognized in the monastic code, which maintains that intercourse with a *yakṣiṇī* carries the same penalty as intercourse with a human woman, namely, expulsion from the order. Touching a *yakṣiṇī* with the intent of experiencing a pleasurable sensation is, on the same principle, an expiable offense.[13] (One imagines this rule was added to the code in part so that an erring monk could not evade the penalty for intercourse by claiming that he mistook the woman for a *yakṣiṇī*!) A *yakṣiṇī* might marry a human being and bear a child; the Buddha in one of his former lives was the offspring of such a union.[14]

The sexual charms of the *yakṣiṇīs* often take on a sinister cast in Buddhist legend. A number of narratives in the Pāli corpus describe *yakṣiṇīs* who prey upon men, hold them prisoner, and use them to fulfill their voracious erotic appetites. The men may well enjoy their captivity under such conditions, but the interludes usually end badly, for *yakṣiṇīs* of this breed eventually devour their hapless playthings, consuming everything but the bones.

One such account tells of an entire island of man-eating *yakṣiṇīs* who lie in wait for shipwrecked sailors and meet them at the shore disguised as young mothers with children on their hips, pretending to be widows of merchants who died at sea. They invite the men to marry them and even conjure up an illusory city in order to entice their would-be grooms to remain in their midst.[15] Another story describes how a group of *yakṣiṇīs* set a snare of captivating beauty for travelers on a remote forest path:

There . . . *yakṣiṇīs* make houses appear in the middle of the road and, having prepared a costly bed with a canopy painted overhead with golden stars and enclosed with silken curtains in many colors, they decorate themselves with celestial ornaments and go to sit down in the houses from which they ply men with sweet words, saying: 'You seem tired; come here, sit down, and have a drink of water before going.' When they have summoned them, they give those who come seats and seduce them with the charm of their wanton beauty. But, having excited their lust, they have intercourse with them and then they kill them and eat them while the warm blood flows.[16]

These *yakṣiṇīs* are said to have a full array of sensual enticements at their command; they charm lovers of music by singing and playing instruments, tempt gourmands with ambrosial repasts, seduce those fond of fragrance with sweet perfumes, and attract sybarites with heavenly couches. The account is accompanied by a warning that one who gazes upon the perfect beauty of the *yakṣiṇīs* falls under their spell and is doomed to be eaten. The *bodhisattva* passed safely through their midst because he was shielded by mindfulness and protected by consecrated thread and sand.[17] The amorous but bloodthirsty type of *yakṣiṇī* also has a range of malefic sisters who demand blood sacrifice, inflict disease and madness, and terrorize entire villages by kidnapping and devouring infants.[18]

What remains constant for the entire spectrum of *yakṣiṇīs* is their supernatural power. The beneficent *yakṣiṇīs* portrayed on Buddhist monuments and the man-eating sexual predators of written lore have in common a command of magical gifts and occult forces.[19] The *yakṣiṇīs* who have vowed their devotion to the Buddha are eager to bestow their blessings and protection upon his followers. Less morally evolved *yakṣiṇīs* exercise their superhuman powers in a harmful fashion but may be compelled by talismans, consecrated thread, or physical coercion to grant their assistance. For example, one Buddhist legend relates how the adventurer Vijaya journeyed to Laṅka and brought the man-eating *yakṣiṇī* Kuvaṇṇā under his power by capturing her in a noose and threatening her at sword-point. In exchange for her life, she transformed herself into a beautiful woman, became Vijaya's consort, bore him two children, and helped him conquer the *yakṣas* of the land and claim the throne of the country.[20] Kuvaṇṇā was not a benevolent *yakṣiṇī*, but she could nonetheless be compelled to use her sorcery to help Vijaya establish a dynasty. Thus, although some *yakṣiṇīs* are unquestionably dangerous, as a class they are regarded as a source of supernatural assistance, protection, and blessings.

These early Buddhist sources introduce several themes that resurfaced centuries later in Tantric *yakṣiṇī sādhana*. For example, the invocation of *yakṣiṇīs* with mantras evinces continuities with early Buddhist magical techniques. The conception of *yakṣiṇīs* as wondrously beautiful creatures with pronounced erotic appetites who moreover can unite with mortals persisted in the Tantric context and provided a major purpose for their conjuration. The characterization of *yakṣiṇīs* as controllers of occult powers and other gifts of a supernatural nature is another theme that bridges the earlier and later versions of the *yakṣiṇī* cult.

YAKṢIṆĪ SĀDHANA IN TANTRIC BUDDHISM

When Tantric Buddhism begins to emerge to historical view in the seventh century CE, a range of magical techniques were incorporated into the burgeoning ritual repertoire of the movement. These methods included *yakṣiṇī sādhana*, or invocation of *yakṣiṇīs* by means of offerings, mantra recitation, ritual diagrams, burnt oblations, and the rendition of a drawing or painting of the *yakṣiṇī* or the preparation of a seat or bed for her. Solitary nocturnal practice in secluded settings is the rule. Central to this practice is the belief that, if successfully summoned, the *yakṣiṇī* manifests bodily in the presence of the hierophant, although she may not be visible to others. Early Buddhist sources seem convinced that a *yakṣiṇī* can assume a body indistinguishable from a human one if she wishes, and Tantric *yakṣiṇī sādhana* seeks by magical means to compel a *yakṣiṇī* to appear before the *sādhaka* in bodily form and serve him in various ways.

There is evidence that this practice was not a Buddhist innovation. The *Jayākhya Saṃhitā*, a Hindu Tantric text from around the fifth–sixth centuries, provides instructions for drawing a portrait of a beautiful, fully ornamented *yakṣiṇī* on silk, fasting, and burning *guggulu* incense before the canvas at midnight for seven days. On the seventh night, it promises, the *yakṣiṇī* will appear in person and offer herself to the supplicant as a wife, sister, or mother. If he chooses her as a mother, she will grant his every wish; acting as a sister, she will shower him with treasure. She can carry him to heaven or the underworld and bestow upon him medicinal herbs and divine elixirs (*rasa*).[21] This ritual procedure and its portended outcome so closely dovetail with the general outlines of Buddhist *yakṣiṇī sādhana* that there is little doubt that Buddhists were drawing upon an established branch of magic in their codification of the practice.

Evidence for *yakṣiṇī sādhana* in Tantric Buddhism is on the whole not abundant. The *Hevajra Tantra* mentions in passing that a male practitioner may take a human partner or conjure a female consort from among the gods, demigods, angelic beings, or *yakṣiṇī*s.[22] The ability to summon *yakṣiṇī*s may be named among the magical powers attainable through Tantric practice.[23] Among the virtually countless Tantric adventure stories is the tale of a yogi who happens upon a golden house in a woodland, in which a multicolored, profusely bejeweled *yakṣiṇī* called Blackie lives. She gives him a bowl of nectar that takes him a month to drink; upon swallowing the last drop, his body is endowed with immortality.[24] Somadeva's *Kathāsaritsāgara* (eleventh century) includes a story that places knowledge of *yakṣiṇī* conjuration in the hands of a Buddhist adept.[25] A Brāhmaṇa youth named Ādityaśarman aspired to obtain the *yakṣiṇī* Sulocanā (Beautiful Eyes) as his lover, so he asked his friend's *yakṣiṇī* wife for Sulocanā's spell. The *yakṣiṇī* directed the youth to Viṣṇugupta, a Buddhist recluse. Ādityaśarman served Viṣṇugupta for three years and in return received the desired spell and accompanying rites. When he performed them in a solitary place, 'the *yakṣiṇī* Sulocanā appeared to him in an air-chariot, with world-enchanting beauty, and said to him: "Come! Come! I have been won by you; but you must not make me your wife for six months, great hero, if you wish by me to have a son, who will be a favourite of fortune, marked with auspicious marks, all-knowing and invincible."'[26]

Ādityaśarman resisted his virtually overpowering desire to enjoy the pleasures of love with Sulocanā and, after six months, married her and remained with her in the *yakṣa* realm. Somadeva's compendium is fictional rather than explicitly historical in genre, but insofar as his characters reflect the cultural landscape of his day, his association of this form of ritual knowledge with a Buddhist adept supplements the evidence found in Buddhist sources.

One of the most intriguing references to *yakṣiṇī sādhana* occurs in association with Nāgārjuna, one of the foremost adepts of Indian Buddhist Tantra, credited with mastery of a wide range of practices and authorship of treatises on philosophy, alchemy, and numerous deities. According to Abhayadatta's biographical sketch, Nāgārjuna's involvement with *yakṣiṇīs* spanned many years. Nāgārjuna had made significant progress in meditation and had even been granted a vision of Tārā, his tutelary goddess, when he decided that he wanted to do more to benefit living beings. In pursuance of this goal, he went to Rājagṛha and there propitiated twelve supreme *yakṣiṇī* consorts with mantras. On the first day of his practice, they shook the earth; on subsequent days they raised a flood, fire, whirlwind, shower of weapons, and rain of stones. On the seventh day they descended upon Nāgārjuna in tumultuous, threatening array. When the *yakṣiṇīs* saw that they could not distract the yogi from his meditation, they offered to do his bidding. Nāgārjuna requested only sufficient food to sustain him on his retreat; for the next twelve years they provided him with a daily supply of rice and vegetables. During that time, he gathered 108 *yakṣiṇīs* under his power, and when he died, eight *yakṣiṇīs* stood guard around his body and remain there to this day.[27] In light of Nāgārjuna's legendary versatility, it is fascinating that the only practice featured in Abhayadatta's hagiography is *yakṣiṇī sādhana*. Although *yakṣiṇī* conjuration is not mentioned in any of the other eighty-four biographies in Abhayadatta's compendium, its association with an adept of Nāgārjuna's stature suggests it was accepted as a valid genre of ritual practice.

These isolated references, culled from an extensive literary survey, attest to the inclusion of *yakṣiṇī sādhana* in the spectrum of Tantric methods but yield little information about the ritual procedure or goals of the practice. Thus, it is not surprising that *yakṣiṇī sādhana* finds little place in scholarly studies of the movement. Indeed, one could conclude that *yakṣiṇī sādhana* never figured significantly among Tantric Buddhist techniques were it not for the evidence to the contrary provided by the *Mañju-śrīmūlakalpa*.

The *Mañjuśrīmūlakalpa*, large portions of which date from the seventh and eighth centuries CE, is a vital document of early Buddhist Tantra in Bengal. The chapter colophons identify the work as a Mahāyāna text on the *bodhisattva* theme, but its Tantric contents place it at the transitional phase between the two movements, a historical location confirmed by its emphasis upon magical rather than yogic practices.[28] This voluminous work introduces an extensive pantheon whose centerpiece, as indicated by the title, is Mañjuśrī, the celestial *bodhisattva* of wisdom. Six chapters describe the ritual construction and artistic depiction of his *maṇḍala*.[29] The *Mañjuśrīmūlakalpa* has not been studied or translated in its entirety, not only because of its length, but because of the obscure vocabulary and grammatical irregularities in the text, which pose many problems of translation and interpretation.[30] What will be examined here are the general principles of *yakṣiṇī sādhana* expressed in the work, the pantheon of *yakṣiṇī*s that it introduces, the methods and purposes of their conjuration, and some conclusions that may be drawn regarding *yakṣiṇī sādhana* during the formative phase of Buddhist Tantra.

The *Mañjuśrīmūlakalpa* voices a number of beliefs regarding *yakṣiṇī*s that supplement the specific instructions for their conjuration. The work asserts that among *yakṣa*s and *yakṣiṇī*s, as among all deities invoked by mantra, there are higher and lower types.[31] The *yakṣiṇī*s who are advanced for ritual propitiation belong to the superior category and are characterized as *maharddhikā*, or 'ladies of great magical power' who bestow good fortune, abundance, accomplishment, and supernatural powers.[32] The assistance and blessings of these great *yakṣiṇī*s are integrated into a Buddhist soteriological framework. They are said to work under the direction of the *bodhisattva* Mañjuśrī and to be motivated by compassion to relieve the suffering of the world:

> They traverse the entire world and ascend to the realm of the gods in a fraction of a second. These *yakṣiṇī*-chiefs fight in the battle between gods and demons. They are pious, compassionate, benevolent toward beings, full of mother-love.

They roam the surface of the earth for the purpose of doing good to humanity. There is nothing they cannot achieve. They are auspicious ones, accomplishing all activities. They have been directed by the *bodhisattva* (Mañjuśrī) to increase the happiness of humankind.[33]

The ritual instructions regarding these 'compassionate, benevolent *yakṣiṇīs*' are in some cases attributed to Mañjuśrī and in others to Vajrapāṇi, who is characterized as lord of the *yakṣas* in this work,[34] thereby endowing the practices with a distinguished Buddhist pedigree.

The general benefits of propitiation of these great *yakṣiṇīs* are touted throughout the text. For example, they are said to grant many enjoyments and pleasures, success in mantra practice, wisdom, knowledge of the future, and lordship on earth.[35] Other benefactions recur among the blessings of individual *yakṣiṇīs*. For example, *yakṣiṇīs* enjoy the power of flight, especially at night, and can transport their mortal companions into the sky and across vast distances. One of their customary gifts is *rasarasāyana*, a magical elixir that bestows health, strength, luster, and immortality. Another common boon is wealth in the form of gold coins, gems, and precious jewelery, on the condition that the riches be spent on the same day they are received. After she has been invoked and appears before the practitioner in tangible, bodily form, a *yakṣiṇī* may serve the hierophant as a wife, mother, or sister, roles that are explained later in this section.

The practitioner is warned, however, against the inferior, or dangerous, type of *yakṣiṇī*. The *Mañjuśrīmūlakalpa* asserts that some *yakṣiṇīs* are deeply deluded (*mūḍhā*) and acknowledges:

Others roam at night, ravenous as lions, bloodthirsty, destroyers of children, avaricious, eaters of flesh. Such *yakṣiṇīs*, having been drawn to Rose Apple Island (i.e., India) by the smell of blood, are destroyers of life and fond of blood. They visit houses where there are corpses of children. It has been taught that this type of *yakṣiṇī* is to be subjugated. . . . How to subdue them has been taught here for the benefit of living beings.[36]

Here the text concurs with popular beliefs regarding dangers posed by morally unevolved *yakṣiṇīs*, namely, their taste for the blood of the living and the dead, their penchant for the flesh of children, and their custom of roaming at night in search of prey.

Yakṣiṇīs of predatory inclination also found berth in earlier Pāli Buddhist texts and have been a mainstay of Indian folklore down through the ages to the present day.[37] Tantric practitioners are urged to avoid places that are densely inhabited by *yakṣiṇīs* because of the likelihood that there will be dangerous representatives of the sisterhood among them. Along this line, the text expresses the belief, which I have not encountered elsewhere, that *yakṣiṇīs* govern meteors and therefore that a practitioner should vacate any locale where a meteor shower has occurred.[38]

Tantric practices in general are surrounded by secrecy, and this holds true in the case of *yakṣiṇī sādhana* as well. The *yakṣiṇīs* themselves are said to punish anyone who reveals the methods of their invocation by revoking whatever success that person may have attained in the practice. The admonition to secrecy is expressed in rather exacting terms: 'Because they [*yakṣiṇīs*] are supremely secretive, they do not pardon discussion with a second person. [This practice] is not to be discussed with a mother, father, friend, master, or even intimates. [It is] not to be disclosed even to an animal or a crawling creature. It is most secret. This is the rule for . . . all the *yakṣiṇīs*. If one discloses [their practices], even if one has been successful, one becomes unsuccessful.'[39]

Elsewhere the text asserts that the mantras are not to be divulged. If one reveals them to another person, one's knowledge is destroyed and one's magical powers are transferred to that person; therefore, maintaining secrecy assures that one's attainments will not be diminished or lost: '[As long as] one practices secretly, whenever and wherever one likes, in a secret place, one's supernatural powers [*siddhis*] do not depart or change. One may be pleasant to others but should not take them into confidence.'[40]

In addition, one's success in *yakṣiṇī sādhana* should not be revealed, or the *yakṣiṇī* 'will not return or may even cause disaster leading to death'.[41] It may seem disingenuous to insist upon secrecy in a text that records the practices and incantations in writing, but there is presumably an underlying assumption that the work will circulate only among those who are qualified by initiation for access to its contents.

Another warning is offered for those who do not want to anger the *yakṣiṇīs*, namely, that these supernatural ladies are possessive and will not share a lover with another. Therefore, one who has a *yakṣiṇī* consort 'should always shun copulating with another woman'.[42] The consequences can be quite serious. A man who has a *yakṣiṇī* consort 'should live only with her; if he has sexual relations [with another], she gives him death or madness'.[43] Additional restrictions or conditions are imposed by some of the *yakṣiṇīs* discussed subsequently in this essay.

Many of the standard elements of *yakṣiṇī sādhana* appear in the instructions for the invocation of Guhyavāsinī ('Lady Clothed in Secrecy'), a *yakṣiṇī* who acts as mother to one who successfully summons her:

The mantra of Guhyavāsinī: *Oṃ guhile guhamati guhavāsi ānaya bhagavati mamāntikam samayam anusmara svāhā!*

Igniting a fire with acacia wood, one should offer 8,000 *priyaṇgu* flowers smeared with ghee in the morning, at midday, and in the evening for one month. The first offering-service thus completed, one should begin the *sādhana*. On a board, cloth, or mud surface, with a new brush and paint pots and unmixed colors, first draw Sumeru, the king of mountains, four-cornered, with four raised peaks, encircled by a row of seven mountains. At the end of these mountains, draw a cave issuing from the mountain.

Portray, residing there, a solitary *yakṣiṇī* of divine beauty, adorned with every ornament, Guhyavāsinī by name, golden-hued, wondrously beautiful, wearing a silken garment. Drawing her on a cloth in that way, at a pure place, [subsisting on] pure foods of milk, one should chant 100,000 mantras, or stage a grand worship-ceremony to the extent within one's power.

When the recitation is completed, the divinely lovely *yakṣiṇī* herself appears, radiating immense luster. When she arrives, offer jasmine flowers generously mixed with white sandalwood paste. Then she'll say, 'Child, what would you have me do?' Reply, 'Be my mother!' That having been done, she vanishes!

One's mind should not become sullied with regard to her. One should not supplicate [her] with erotic intent. She is a noble lady of great magical power. One who has sexual pleasure [with her] as one's object will not succeed.

Thereafter, she accomplishes everything, like a mother. She provides rice and shelter for 800 families. She rescues one who is in danger, performs all tasks even for one who stays on a great wild mountain, and gives the food desired. She bestows everything, such as magical elixir [*rasarasāyana*] and so forth, and follows [the practitioner], as desired. She builds a hut, cottage, etc., and each day confers 1,000 gold coins, all of which must be spent that very day. If [that] is not done, it [the flow of coins] is severed.[44]

Many of the basic elements of *yakṣiṇī sādhana* are present here.

The execution of a portrait of the *yakṣiṇī* is a recurrent feature. Mental visualization is not explicitly enjoined, although the importance placed upon the physical description of the *yakṣiṇī* and the act of envisioning her that is implicit in the process of portraiture represent a rudimentary version of the deity visualization that became a mainstay of Tantric praxis. In this text, however, it is the ritual procedure rather than mental envisioning that conjures the presence of the *yakṣiṇī*. Mantra recitation accompanied by flower offerings is commonly prescribed, although the flowers to be offered and substances to be mixed with the blossoms vary in accordance with the preference of the individual *yakṣiṇī*, as does the type of wood used for the fire offering. The manner of arrival of the *yakṣiṇī* is foretold, and the aspirant is instructed how to address her and told whether there are any stipulations associated with her *sādhana*. In the case of Guhyavāsinī, she will not become a consort, or 'wife', but will only serve as a mother. Therefore, the aspirant must not summon her with erotic intent or respond to her beauty with lustful feelings. The maternal role is to provide food, shelter, protection, wealth, and other blessings. As is typical, any wealth that is bestowed must be spent on the day that it is received or no more will be forthcoming.

We also find reference in Guhyavāsinī's *sādhana* to the magical elixir that may be obtained from *yakṣiṇīs*, namely, *rasarasāyana*, which David White characterizes as 'a mercurial elixir cum philosopher's stone . . . won or wrested from gods, demigods, or demons rather than produced in a laboratory', for it is prepared and imbibed by supernatural beings such as *yakṣas* to secure eternal youth and perfect health.[45] This divine nectar is coveted by Hindu and Buddhist Tāntrikas as a source not only of an ageless, immortal body but also of strength, vigor, beauty, and luster. Other passages in the *Mañjuśrīmūlakalpa* confirm that by drinking *rasarasāyana* one 'lives for an aeon' and 'attains a divine form rivaling that of a great *yakṣa*'.[46]

Although Guhyavāsinī herself will not serve as a consort to the practitioner, one of her rituals may be used to procure a human consort. For this rite, the practitioner must know the name of the woman he desires to summon:

Before the selfsame cloth, ignite a fire with acacia branches. When the flames and smoke are gone, take the charcoal and red arsenic and paint a figure on the right palm and the name of the man and the woman on the left palm. [Hold one's hand] in the heat, over the same heap of charcoal, while reciting the mantra. One draws the woman from as far away as 100 *yojanas*. All that one speaks will be accomplished. This ritual [is to be done] at night, not by day.[47]

By performing this ceremony, a male practitioner can draw the object of his desire from a long distance away, and she will suddenly find herself in his presence and under his power. This type of rite is well known in the Indian magical corpus as *strīvaśīkaraṇa*, 'bewitchment of women' or 'compulsion of women'. The usual purpose of such a ritual, left unstated here, is either to enjoy the woman as a sexual partner or to engage in yogic union (*karma mudrā* practice) with her. Because the practice of yogic union does not fall within the purview of the *Mañjuśrīmūlakalpa*, it may be assumed that the objective of this rite is to obtain a desired sexual partner.

It is unusual to find the magical procuration of women among the ministrations of a *yakṣiṇī* acting as a mother. In the *Mañjuśrīmūlakalpa*, the primary role of a *yakṣiṇī* acting as a sister (*bhaginī*) is to provide women for her mortal 'brother'. We see this in the instance of Naravīrā, a *yakṣiṇī* sister whose *sādhana* immediately follows and is patterned upon that of Guhyavāsinī:

Naravīrā's mantra: *Oṃ naravīrā svāhā!*

Render her painting in the same manner, except for the cave residence. She is to be drawn residing in an *aśoka* tree; this is her special feature. All the rites are the same as in the case of Guhyavāsinī. Say [to Naravīrā, however,] 'Be my sister!'

She has another rite: During an eclipse of the moon, wrap a [piece of] golden red chalk with a birch leaf and, casting it in one's mouth, recite until the moon is freed. Then Naravīrā will deliver any woman whose name one writes with the golden red chalk, even if she lives 100 *yojanas* away. In the morning, she returns her back there. She acts like a sister and offers great protection from calamities. Merely chanting [her] mantra overpowers all women.[48]

Naravīrā, who acts only as a sister, is thus invoked primarily for the performance of *strīvaśīkaraṇa*. The fact that Naravīrā resides in an *aśoka* tree is telling in this respect, for the red-flowering *aśoka* is associated with the stimulation of sexual desire in India's arboreal lore and magical practice.

Several *yakṣiṇīs* in the *Mañjuśrīmūlakalpa* pantheon may be requested to serve as a mother, sister, or wife. One of the *yakṣiṇīs* of this type is Yakṣakumārikā (Yakṣa-Girl), whose *sādhana* provides a useful overview of the salient differences among the three roles:

The mantra of Yakṣakumārikā: *Oṃ yakṣakumārike svāhā!*

This is her procedure: The *kumārī* is to be drawn on a birch leaf with *gorocana* (yellow pigment made of bovine bile), with half a head of curly hair, adorned with all ornaments, wearing a one-piece garment, holding a citron and bearing in her left hand an *aśoka* branch. The birch leaf should be placed over [one's] head, and one should sleep alone in a secret place. Making a circle [*maṇḍala*] with white sandalwood paste, one should recite 8,000 mantras for a month at the three junctures [morning, midday, and evening], scattering flowers and burning *guggulu* incense.

Then, on a full-moon night, performing a great worship ceremony with jasmine flowers, offering lamps full of ghee and other gifts, sitting on a seat of *kuśa* grass, one should recite at night until the *kumārī* appears. Encircled by a retinue of 500, the daughter of Vaiśravaṇa appears in her own form. Having gazed in every direction, she hovers in the air in her own form. She speaks thus: 'What shall I do?' Then the practitioner should specify one of the three boons. Only one boon is to be requested—motherhood, sisterhood, or wifehood.

If she becomes a mother, the mind should not be sullied. If one pollutes oneself [with lust], it leads to destruction. She should remain a mother, and that mother, always and at a mere thought, supplies food, shelter, and varied adornments to 500 families. She gives 1,000 gold coins daily. She remains there and accomplishes everything for one who lives on Rose Apple Island.

If she becomes a sister, she brings a woman from even 100 *yojanas* away and returns [her] there again. Like a sister, she performs all tasks.

Now, if she becomes a wife, she takes [one] to her own house. One lives for thousands of divine years. When one dies, one is born into a rich family. She accomplishes all that one commands, like a wife.[49]

Yakṣakumārikā must not be regarded with lust when she fulfills her maternal role. In her sisterly guise, she procures sexual partners from afar for her conjurer. Chosen as a wife, however, she takes the hierophant to her own home and wifely obedience is reflected in the claim, reiterated in the case of every *yakṣiṇī* wife, that she will carry out all that one orders, like any wife.

Another *yakṣiṇī* who, once summoned, will serve as a wife, sister, or mother is Jayā (Victorious Lady). Her relatively short *sādhana* provides a summary overview of the three roles. The description of Jayā's appearance conveys the luminous beauty that a *yakṣiṇī* might possess:

The mantra of Jayā: *Oṃ jaye sujaye sarvakāryāṇi kuru me svāhā!*

Golden-hued, with bright limbs and curly blue hair, a goddess [*devī*] perfect in every limb, fit to be enjoyed, rich, auspicious, speaking words one likes to hear, infatuating, exquisite, lovely, pleasurable to gaze upon, inspiring praise, effulgent, well-worshipped in all the worldsùone should recognize this one, wearing a reddish cloth, as Jayā.

Her ritual: First one should recite [the mantra] 1,000 times and do the preliminary service. Then, entering a great forest, eat fruits and chant until she arrives in her own form. After arriving, she says, 'What shall I do?'

If she becomes a mother, she fulfills all hopes, like a mother. She grants a kingdom, makes one a great lord of riches, and establishes [one] in the state of long life.

If a sister, she brings a coveted woman from a distance of 1,000 *yojanas*. Day after day, she gives 100,000 gold coins, which must be spent. Now then, if she becomes a wife, she takes [one] to her own home. Ascending in a divine aerial car, one makes love with her for a long time—30,000 years—roaming at will. One attains the form of a great *yakṣa*.[50]

The preliminary service (*pūrvaseva*) of Jayā is unspecified, leaving to the practitioner the choice of flowers, foods, and gifts to be offered. The simple method of invoking her devolves upon mantra recitation in a forest setting. The resplendent presence of Jayā, described here with laudatory prose, clearly conveys the appeal of having such a wondrous creature as a 'wife'. Enticing, too, must be the prospect of enjoying her sexual favors while floating through the sky in an airborne chariot for a veritable eternity.

The pleasures and blessings that *yakṣiṇīs* bestow upon their human paramours leave little doubt regarding why these supernatural creatures are desired companions. Consider, for example, the benefits of conjuring Bhaṭṭā, who acts only as a wife (*bhāryā*). Bhaṭṭā's appearance is not described and the rendition of a portrait does not figure in her *sādhana*:

Bhaṭṭā's mantra: *Oṃ bhaṭṭe bhaṭṭe ālokini kiṃ cirāyasi ehyehi āgacchāgaccha mama kāryaṃ kuru svāhā!*

This can be done even without a canvas. Make a circle [*maṇḍala*] at the place of the head. While *guggulu* incense is burning, one should utter the mantra 8,000 times, silently, while alone and purified, with the door closed.

Within a month, she definitely comes at night. When she has come, asked for as a wife [*bhāryā*], she becomes a bestower of every pleasure. If one enters her house, one lives for 5,000 years. If not, one roams here on Rose Apple Island, lives for 500 years, and frolics with her. [She carries out] all one's orders. She goes with one wherever one wishes and gives one *rasāyana*.[51]

Bhaṭṭā's mantra is translatable as 'O Bhaṭṭā, O Bhaṭṭā, one full of light, why are you delaying? Come, come! Arrive, arrive! Do my bidding!' Bhaṭṭā, as is typical of *yakṣiṇī* wives, may take one to live with her in her own home. Life with a *yakṣiṇī* in her own realm, although not described, is apparently an idyllic prospect, which is not surprising in view of the food, wealth, long-life nectar, and sexual enjoyment in store for the human consort of one of these numinous ladies. The desirability of living with a *yakṣiṇī* may also be enhanced by the popular belief that *yakṣas* live in fabulous cities full of pleasure gardens, jewel-laden palaces, and numinous beings who engage in amorous pastimes and partake of intoxicating libation night and day.

Naṭikā (Dancer) is another *yakṣiṇī* who acts only as a wife. Her portrait is to be painted on a canvas or hard surface. She is described as 'black and white, adorned with all ornaments, reclining on a tree, wearing a single garment, with disheveled hair, red-eyed, with a slight smile on her face, threatening the devotee, holding a tree branch with her right and left hands, graceful in every limb, wearing multicolored cloth.'

After her portrait is drawn, her mantra is to be intoned 8,000 times. Naṭikā has two mantras. One, *Oṃ naṭi mahānaṭi āgacchāgaccha divyarūpiṇi svāhā*, is translatable as 'O Naṭi, great Naṭi, come, come, O you of divine beauty.' The other, *Oṃ nāṭṭe śuklāmbaramālyadhāriṇi maithunapriye svāhā*, means 'O Naṭā, wearing white garlands and garments, O one fond of love-making!' Thus invoked, Naṭikā manifests in bodily form, dazzling in appearance, and 'becomes a wife who fulfills all desires. She takes one to her own house and gives *rasāyana*, by drinking which one attains a divine form, rivaling that of a great *yakṣa*.' One of the particularities of Naṭikā is that, once summoned, she must come every day or she dries up and dies.[52]

Another *yakṣiṇī* wife is Tamasundarī, 'Dark Beauty'. No physical description of Tamasundarī is provided, for she is an invisible, nocturnal presence. Her mantra is *Oṃ ghuṇu guhyake ghuṇu ghuṇu guhye ehyehi guhyake svāhā!* The practitioner is to be clean, wear pure garments, and perform all the mantra recitations at night, in total darkness, beginning on a full moon night and continuing to the next full moon. On the first night, the mantra is to be recited 10,000 times. Thereafter, 'at night, in bed, while going to sleep, in a lonely, solitary, secluded place, alone, close the door and cleanse one's hands and feet with dried *karṇikā* flowers mixed with pungent oil. Having uttered the mantra 800 times over one's right hand, one should sleep and keep total silence.'[53]

It is not clear how the *sādhaka* is to discern the arrival of the invisible *yakṣiṇī*, but she comes in the middle of the night, and no mantras are to be intoned in her presence. After Tamasundarī has arrived, the practitioner must submit to a lengthy waiting period before claiming her as a wife:

> She should be desired silently for six months. . . . After that, she is obtained. She becomes a wife, a bestower of every pleasure, and her blissful touch is divine. Even unseen, she performs all that one commands. She gives the elixir of eternal youth [*rasarasāyana*] and carries one on her back to the cosmic mountain, Sumeru. At night she takes one on a tour throughout India. From a distance of 100 *yojanas* she kills one's enemies. She performs everything as ordered, with the exception of [helping one] have sex with another woman.[54]

The moral neutrality of *yakṣiṇī sādhana*—that is, its operation in the realm of magical power rather than of explicitly soteriological aims—is seen in the promise that Tamasundarī will kill her conjurer's enemies. There is, however, one thing that she refuses to do, and that is to procure for the *sādhaka* another woman, which is consistent with the *yakṣiṇīs'* possessiveness toward their human lovers.

Although *yakṣiṇī* wives bestow a similar range of benefactions, each one has an individual cast in terms of her invocatory ritual, requirements, and/or blessings. Consider the example of Padmoccā.

Her physical appearance is not described, and no portrait is drawn. Rather, the practitioner prepares a bed for her and chants her mantra daily for a month:

Padmoccā's mantra: *Oṃ padmocce svāhā!*

Her ritual: On the bank of the Ganges, or on a seashore, or in a flower-house in a garden. . . . make an image of a slab of stone out of clay. There only, at night, having closed the door, arrange all the articles of desire and enjoyment. One should make a bed for the *yakṣiṇī* near oneself, at that very spot.

Then one should chant the mantra 10,000 times. [Continue] in this way until, after a month, she comes regularly. After arriving, she becomes one's wife, to be enjoyed with sexual desire. She goes away [in the morning], leaving a divine pearl necklace on the bed. Thus, for six months, as she stays continually, day after day, that pearl necklace should not be accepted. If one takes it, that alone is all one will receive—that necklace worth 100,000 gold pieces, shining with pearls and gems. After six months have passed, she becomes a wife, staying permanently, granting every pleasure. She assumes whatever form one desires. She transforms herself as desired by the practitioner, at the wish of the practitioner. This principle applies to all *yakṣiṇīs*.[55]

Padmoccā, as is typical of many *yakṣiṇī* wives, visits the practitioner at night and leaves each morning. The condition associated with her visitations is that the necklace that she leaves behind each day should not be accepted, or she will not return or bestow further riches. If, however, her conjurer can resist the fabulously valuable necklace for six months, Padmoccā will stay permanently with him, living as his wife night and day. Few of the *yakṣiṇīs* who serve only as wives are given a physical description in the text. The reason for what otherwise seems to be a puzzling omission may be elicited from Padmoccā's *sādhana*, namely, that these shape-shifting spirits can assume whatever form they choose and use this ability to suit the tastes of their fortunate paramours.

Another *yakṣiṇī* who serves only as a wife is Vadhuyakṣiṇī, whose name simply means '*Yakṣiṇī* Wife'. Her appearance, too, is not described. The invocatory ritual, as is customary, is to be performed in a secret place, behind closed doors, and involves periods of total silence:

Vadhuyakṣiṇī's mantra: *Oṃ niḥ!*

Her ritual: Smear one's right hand with white sandalwood paste. Recite the mantra 1,000 times over the left [hand smeared] with vermilion powder. Then at night, alone, without speaking a word, in a secret place, having bolted the door, one should throw five or eight pieces of fruit in sesame oil and cook them. Remove the fruit and place the oil in a new pot of gold, silver, copper, or clay. Recite the mantra 1,000 times over [that]. . .

Sleep in darkness on a solitary bed strewn with flowers. Arriving there, the *yakṣiṇī* massages one's legs, [giving] divine pleasure with her palms, very soft to the touch, the mere caress of whose divinely soothing touch puts one to sleep. Because of this, at sunrise, at the end of the night, one wakes up sorrowfully [i.e., longing for her divine touch].

After waking up, one should think only of that [massage]; she is neither to be desired nor recited over. Within six months, one attains success. The divinely beautiful one, equal in age to a newly married wife, with a lamp in her hand, attended by maidservants, sparkling and flashing with her own radiance, accepts the bed and seat [prepared for her]. When she has arrived, shining with various ornaments, and accepted the offering materials of love and enjoyment, recite the mantra over her.

Having arrived, she embraces the *sādhaka* around the neck. From that time forward, she follows [one] as a cherished wife. Once she has appeared, she is to be desired with lust. Serving at night, she vanishes in the morning, leaving on the bed a pearl necklace and a thousand gold pieces. Day after day she departs, leaving that. All should be spent without remainder. If one saves something, it doesn't happen again. One should not speak about it to anybody. If one does, she won't return or causes disaster leading to death.[56]

The aspirant awaits the arrival of Vadhuyakṣiṇī in a flower-strewn bed. The stricture of total silence before she arrives is seen also in the case of Tamasundarī. A special feature of Vadhuyakṣiṇī's visitation is that before she manifests in bodily form, she massages the practitioner's legs with her celestially soothing touch, easing him gently into slumber. For the first six months, he must be content with the massage and not engender lust toward her. After this, she manifests in all her divine beauty and remains with him every night, leaving behind each morning pearls and gold whose source he must disclose to no one.

Manojñā (Lovely One) is another *yakṣiṇī* wife introduced in the *Mañjuśrīmūlakalpa*. For her conjuration, the practitioner constructs the hut in which she will join him and leaves a cloth outside the door in which she can drape herself when she arrives:

The mantra of Manojñā: *Oṃ manohare madonmādakari vicitrarūpiṇi maithunapriye svāhā!*

Her ritual: Under an *aśoka* tree, in a garden pavilion, build a hut with room divisions, not very hidden, with raised doors, bolts, and a wall. One should chant 100,000 times in a pure manner. Then one should start the rite. Collect great [i.e., cow] fat, make a wick out of cremation rags, close the door, and light the lamp. One should place a cloth outside the door. . . . At night, she arrives there naked. Donning that cloth, she enters [the hut] in the form of a human woman. Then the practitioner makes love with her as long as the light burns.

When the lamp goes out, she vanishes. Tying a piece of gold in that cloth and leaving the cloth on the bed, she departs. The practitioner should take that in his hand, as she removes her ornaments one by one with her finger: the divine pearl necklace from her neck, the armlets from her arms, the girdle from her waist, the anklets from her feet, the jewel from atop her head. . . . It should be spent completely every day. In this way, for whatever months one recites mantras, she becomes an ever-staying wife and gives *rasāyana*, drinking which one lives for a long time.[57]

The desirability of Manojñā as a wife is foreshadowed by her mantra, which is translatable as 'O lovely one, O one causing the intoxication of infatuation, O one of varied forms, O enjoyer of love-making!' Manojñā is a prototypical *yakṣiṇī* wife, for the fruits of her conjuration are nights of connubial bliss, days devoted to spending the wealth she bestows, and access to the nectar of long life. She also presides over special magical powers. For example, if her conjurer plants a peg of *khadira* wood in the ground, a divine chariot for his aerial conveyance will appear and remain until the peg is removed. Her second mantra, *Oṃ mahānagni nagnije svāhā* (O great naked one! Naked-born!) is to be recited while kindling a lamp and planting a peg in the ground. When the lamp burns out, the practitioner and the peg become invisible. If he then repairs to a cremation ground carrying a wick of cloth on a buffalo or gayal horn, she will procure objects for him from other countries. Moreover, if he cherishes a desire for another woman, Manojñā accommodates him by adopting the appearance of that woman.[58]

YAKṢIṆĪ CONSORTS AND *ḌĀKINĪS*

Five *yakṣiṇīs* in the *Mañjuśrīmūlakalpa* pantheon may be requested to serve as a mother, sister, or wife, while eight are to be summoned solely as wives. Therefore, the wifely role is more fully delineated than the others, and the emphasis upon this theme clearly reflects a belief that *yakṣiṇīs* are highly to be desired as companions and lovers. Indeed, this emerges as the primary reason for their conjuration in this early Tantric work. The desirability of *yakṣiṇīs* as sexual partners is emphasized, for they are repeatedly said to 'bestow every pleasure' (*sarvakāmadā*) and to be 'fond of making love' (*maithuna-priyā*), in keeping with popular lore regarding their pronounced libidinous appetites. A man who has been kidnapped by predatory *yakṣiṇīs* becomes their sexual plaything until, having served his purpose, they drink his blood and consume his flesh. Tantric *sādhana*, however, brings a *yakṣiṇī* under a *sādhaka's* power so that he can enjoy her without the usual peril, unless he violates the requirements of secrecy and fidelity. The renowned beauty of the *yakṣiṇīs* enhances their repute as ideal lovers, as does their ability to assume any form the practitioner wishes. Some *yakṣiṇī* wives make nightly visitations and leave each morning, providing for the sustenance of the *sādhaka* in the process, a pattern with obvious appeal. In other cases, a *yakṣiṇī* wife may take her lover to her own supernal realm or fly with him in a divine chariot, both delightful prospects. The fact that a *yakṣiṇī* will accomplish nearly anything her mortal lover requests endows him with virtually limitless magical powers.

The emphasis upon the conjuration of *yakṣiṇīs* to serve as a wife, or lover, of the *sādhaka* naturally invites comparison with the role of human *ḍākinīs* as consorts in the practice of sexual yoga (*karma-mudrā*) that became central to the Tantric Buddhist paradigm. The latter practice figures in the fully developed form of Buddhist Tantra known as *anuttara yoga tantra*, whose aims are explicitly yogic and soteriological. In the *anuttara yoga* framework, the practice of sexual union is a spiritual discipline in which a man and woman unite in order to combine their subtle energies and channel them in specific ways to cultivate the nondual wisdom and transcendent bliss of supreme enlightenment. The *yakṣiṇī sādhana* of the *Mañjuśrīmūlakalpa* is, in contrast, a magical rather than yogic practice. The mantra recitation and ritual procedures are characteristic of the emergent phase of Tantra that was later codified as *kriyā* and *cārya tantra*, designating practices geared toward the mastery and manipulation of supernatural forces. These magical techniques and resultant occult powers were integrated into a hierarchy of practices and goals in the *anuttara yoga* paradigm. For example, the powers of flight and invisibility, the acquisition of *rasarasāyana*, the ability to procure objects from a distance, and the manifestation of food and wealth were eventually classed as mundane, or worldly, accomplishments (*siddhi*), in contrast to the ultimate attainment, *mahāmudrā siddhi*, or Buddhahood. In transitional works such as the *Mañjuśrīmūlakalpa*, however, an explicit ranking principle is not articulated, and magical powers are treated largely as ends in themselves. Accordingly, the purpose of attaining a *yakṣiṇī* as a consort in this context is not for engagement in yogic practice but rather to gain entré to the realm of magical manifestation the *yakṣiṇī*s inhabit.

Another theme that is altogether absent from the *Mañjuśrīmūlakalpa* is the positive valuation of women that undergirds the practice of yogic union as a mutually enlightening enterprise. *Yakṣiṇī*s are advanced as sexual partners not only because of their suitedness for this role but because they are preferable to human women. The practitioner should ideally be free from carnal desire, for 'the mantras of one who is dispassionate regarding sexual pleasure will be successful'.[59] As a concession to those practitioners who are not yet free from sexual desire, union with *yakṣiṇī*s and other supernatural females is recommended:

A mantra-practitioner who is desirous of copulation, blind with lust, with a deluded heart, should enjoy, attracting [her] by mantras, a *yakṣiṇī*, fiendess [*rākṣasī*], serpent maiden [*nāgī*], angel [*gandharvī*], demoness [*daityā*], or fairy [*kiṃnarī*]. . . . He should enjoy, attracted by mantras, divine maidens [*surakanyā*], demigoddesses [*asurī*], and excellent enchantresses [*vidyādharī*]. Then there is enjoyment of divine pleasure.[60]

The same lust that is to find fulfillment in 'divine pleasure' should not, however, drive the practitioner into the arms of a human woman:

One should not touch a female body, drenched with feces, urine, and blood, as well as worshipped, [marked by] old age, death, and great sorrow—one should not enjoy copulation there, blinded by delusion, with a lustful heart. The mantras of one who, ever impure, enjoys these [human women] will not yield success.[61]

The text elaborates, in an astonishingly misogynistic vein, that 'excellent attainment [*siddhi*] is seldom produced by an impure place of feces and urine, ever foul-smelling and disgusting in odor, [the cause of] disease, sorrow, and mourning, the receptacle of misery leading to death and separation, attached to pleasure—one should not touch human women, impermanent, suffering, empty, insubstantial, insignificant, transitory, childish in speech'.[62]

The condemnatory language of this diatribe tallies comfortably with earlier Buddhist vilifications of the female body, issued largely to curb the sexual lust of male monastics, and a similarly motivated strand of misogynism that persisted in the Mahāyāna movement alongside a gender-neutral, nondualistic outlook. The appearance of such pronouncedly anti-female sentiments in the *Mañju-śrīmūlakalpa* accords with its historical and ideological location as a work with one foot in the Mahāyāna value system and the other in the earliest magical strand of Tantric practice, distancing it from the explicitly woman-affirming stance of the *anuttara yoga* ethos.[63] Thus, it is not surprising that sexual union with an apparitional *yakṣiṇī* is deemed preferable to union with a human woman in this work.

The *yakṣiṇī sādhana* described and indeed promoted by the *Mañjuśrīmūlakalpa* did not secure a permanent or prominent niche in the Tantric repertoire, if we are to judge by its absence from the broader Tantric literary corpus. Although *yakṣiṇīs* loom large in the magico-religious universe of the *Mañjuśrīmūlakalpa*, they virtually disappeared from the classical Tantric paradigm as formulated in such Tantras as the *Cakrasaṃvara*, *Hevajra*, and *Guhyasamāja*, in which a comparable and expanded role is filled by women and female spirit beings known collectively as *ḍākinīs*.

A possible connection between *yakṣiṇīs* and *ḍākinīs* is suggested by a number of parallels between them. For instance, the shape-shifting capacity of *yakṣiṇīs* is shared by the protean *ḍākinīs*, who can transform themselves at will in order to challenge, instruct, and enlighten Tantric practitioners. The conception of *yakṣiṇīs* as bestowers of magical powers is echoed by the role of *ḍākinīs* as guardians and transmitters of Tantric knowledge. The long-life nectar (*rasarasāyana*) conferred by *yakṣiṇīs* foreshadows the bliss-bestowing nectar that many a *ḍākinī* sups and serves from her skull-bowl. The invocation of *yakṣiṇīs* by incantations calls to mind the category of the 'mantra-born' (*mantrajā*) *ḍākinī* who is made to materialize through mantra recitation. The envisioning of *yakṣiṇīs* as aerial creatures who can rapidly traverse vast distances and transport persons and objects through space accords with the understanding of *ḍākinīs* as 'sky-goers' and 'enjoyers of flight' (*khecarī*) whose natural habitat is space, although their flight is understood primarily in metaphorical terms as inner freedom and understanding of emptiness. Just as one of the benefits of *yakṣiṇī sādhana* is to be taken by a *yakṣiṇī* to her own home, to enjoy celestial pleasures with her, there is in *anuttara yoga* sources the concept of *ḍākinī*-paradise as a realm of visionary experience during one's life and desirable destination after death. Thus, the *Cakrasaṃvara Tantra* issues the promise to one who has found favor with the *ḍākinīs* that they will take him by the hand 'and carry him to their own realm and cavort with him, and that place will become like paradise'.[64] Another suggestive parallel is the characterization of *ḍākinīs* as mothers, daughters, wives, and sisters of the *sādhaka*.[65] This somewhat awkward classificatory scheme, which gave rise to a range of creative exegeses, may take its inspiration from the belief that *yakṣiṇīs*, once invoked by magical rite, typically serve as mothers, sisters, or wives.

The features shared by *yakṣiṇīs* and *ḍākinīs* draw attention to what may be the mutual development of this pair of figures. These parallels suggest that the Tantric formulation of the *ḍākinī* figure may to some degree have been patterned upon that of the *yakṣiṇī*, which in turn may help to explain why interest in *yakṣiṇīs* receded as *ḍākinīs* came to the fore and received elaboration and reformulation. Initially, the *ḍākinī* had a purely negative association in the Buddhist context, designating a type of demoness, or spirit being of flesh-eating and blood-drinking tendency. Possibly the earliest occurrence of the term in a Buddhist work is its appearance in the *Laṅkāvatāra Sūtra* (*c.* fourth century CE), wherein, to promote its vegetarian viewpoint, the text avows that one who eats meat will be reborn as the carnivorous child of a *ḍākinī*, then as the child of a type of flesh-eating demoness (*rākṣasī*), and finally as a cat, another creature with a meat diet.[66] The *Bodhicaryāvatāra* (eighth century CE) includes a prayer that *ḍākinīs* and *rākṣasas* might become compassionate.[67] The *Mañjuśrīmūlakalpa* itself offers protective mantras and rites for controlling fearsome *ḍākinīs* who inflict disease and cause madness.[68]

It remains possible that the *ḍākinī* figure had a historical trajectory independent of that of the *yakṣiṇī*. However, the fact that the *yakṣiṇī* figure had a positive significance long before the similarly positive elaboration of the *ḍākinī* figure leaves open the possibility that the favorable associations and roles originally vested in the *yakṣiṇī* were at some point transferred to that of the *ḍākinī*. I suggest that the *yakṣiṇī*, as a well-known type of supernatural being with a long-established association with fertility, abundance, and magic in Indic religiosity, could less convincingly be reformulated into a figure associated with the higher metaphysical principles and aims of the Tantric movement. The *ḍākinī*, on the other hand, as a more obscure and vaguely defined class of spirit, was thus arguably more suitable for reinvention along the lines of the Tantric ethos and could more easily be expanded to include human women. Moreover, the revalorization of the *ḍākinī*, originally conceived as a negative and feared creature, was consistent with the Tantric emphasis on confronting that which is normally regarded as dangerous, impure, or taboo as a means to cultivate self-mastery and nondual awareness. In the process of reformulation, the *ḍākinī* by all evidence absorbed many characteristics of the *yakṣiṇīs*. What initially may have been a matter of terminological preference between two analogous classes of beings may eventually have given rise to a clear metaphysical distinction, as *ḍākinīs* became associated with the higher yogas and pursuit of supreme liberation.

Another shift that took place in this transition is that the *yakṣiṇī*, an unambiguously supernatural figure, was replaced by a figural type that encompasses human women. In the case of *yakṣiṇīs*, the divine-human boundary is clearly demarcated, while in the case of *ḍākinīs* it is fluid and shifting. That is, when reading Buddhist sources, care must be taken to determine whether a given *ḍākinī* is simply a female practitioner of Tantra, a spiritual being who operates on the visionary plane of experience, or a woman whose lofty metaphysical attainments have endowed her with divine qualities. That *ḍākinīs* may be spirit beings or mortal women, however, does not obviate the many parallels between *yakṣiṇīs* and *ḍākinīs*. The suggested continuity between the two types of figures is reflected in the fact that human *ḍākinīs* are often attributed with a range of magical and supernatural powers once vested in the *yakṣiṇīs*, in addition to inheriting their role as sexual partners of male Tāntrikas. That the category of *ḍākinī* includes and in some contexts refers primarily to human women accords with the explicitly female-affirming *anuttara yoga* value system, which esteems the human body in general and the female body in particular as a pure, divine abode of bliss and locus of Buddhahood.

The hypothesis presented here has the virtue of explaining why the *yakṣiṇī* figural type virtually disappeared from the view at the same time that the *ḍākinī* concept was on the ascendant, in the eighth and ninth centuries. A detailed juxtaposition of the chronological development of the two figures may shed more light on this issue.

In conclusion, the practice of *yakṣiṇī sādhana* as articulated in the *Mañjuśrīmūlakalpa* is an intriguing phenomenon, historically and religiously, for it represents an important magical technique of early Buddhist Tantra in Bengal and, upon closer examination, may be discovered to have had an impact on the evolution of the *ḍākinī* figure that became the primary female figure of Tantric Buddhist symbology and practice.

This study demonstrates the need for more focused scholarly attention to the divine females of the Buddhist tradition. Extensive documentation and analysis of individual figures and figural types will make it possible more fully to identify historical continuities and divergences among them. Charting their historical evolution will in turn inform our understanding of the Buddhist tradition as a whole, in such areas as devotional practice, ritual, meditation and doctrinal development. Moreover, visual and written expressions of the female pantheon represent a domain of gender discourse and ideology. Mapping this metaphorical terrain will enhance the increasingly substantive and nuanced analyses of Buddhist attitudes toward and roles of human women in different social, institutional, geographical, cultural, and historical settings. Finally, serious attention to the vital stream of goddess worship within Buddhism will promote discussion of Buddhist participation in broader currents of Śākta worship in Indian culture—an undertaking that would surely gratify our beloved mentor, Narendra Nath Bhattacharyya.

NOTES

1. For citations, see Miranda Shaw, *Passionate Enlightenment: Women in Tantric Buddhism* (Princeton: Princeton University Press, 1994), 7–8, 59, 209nn.21–30, 219nn.76–78.
2. Ibid., chaps. 4–5, 7.
3. Ibid., chaps. 5–6.
4. Moti Chandra, 'Some Aspects of Yaksa Cult,' *Bulletin of the Prince of Wales Museum* 3 (1954): 55–57.
5. This topic has been treated at length elsewhere, most notably, Ananda K. Coomaraswamy's pioneering *Yakṣas: Essays in the Water Cosmology*, ed. Paul Schroeder (1928–1931; Delhi: Indira Gandhi National Centre for the Arts, 1993). For an extensive survey of characterizations of *yakṣas* and *yakṣiṇīs* in the Jātakas and other Pāli literature, see Ram Nath Misra, *Yaksha Cult and Iconography* (New Delhi: Munshiram Manoharlal, 1981), 24–26, 35–45, 147–60, and passim.
6. Thomas Donaldson, 'Propitious-Apotropaic Eroticism in the Art of Orissa,' *Artibus Asiae* 37 (1975): 76–77, 85, 96. For a detailed analysis of the symbolism and religious roles of these early *yakṣiṇī* images, see Miranda Shaw, *Buddhist Goddesses of India, Tibet, and Nepal*, forthcoming from Princeton University Press.
7. For literary references to these and additional practices, see Coomaraswamy, *Yakṣas*, 57, 60, 66–67, 73–77, 80; and Misra, *Yaksha Cult and Iconography*, 40, 98–100.
8. Coomaraswamy, *Yakṣas*, 74, 76, 78–79; and Misra, *Yaksha Cult and Iconography*, 41, 99–100, 151–52, 156–60.
9. Donaldson, 'Propitious-Apotropaic Eroticism,' 77–78, 85–86.
10. *The Long Discourses of the Buddha: A Translation of the Dīgha Nikāya*, trans. Maurice Walshe (1987; Boston: Wisdom, 1995), 471–78, esp. 475.
11. Peter Skilling, 'The Rakṣā Literature of the Śrāvakayāna,' *Journal of the Pali Text Society* 16 (1992): 129–34, 163. The retinues of the Four Guardian Kings, a recurrent element of these *maṅgala gāthā*, implicitly include the *yakṣas* and *yakṣiṇīs* in the train of the *mahāyakṣa* Vaiśravaṇa (alias Kubera), guardian king of the north.
12. *The Sūtra of Golden Light: Being a Translation of the Suvarṇabhāsottamasūtra*, trans. R.E. Emmerick (London: Pali Text Society, 1970), 68.

13. *The Book of the Discipline (Vinaya-Piṭaka)*, trans. Isaline B. Horner (1949–66; rpt., Oxford: Pali Text Society, 1992–96), 1: 48–49, 57–58, 211–12; extenuating circumstances that lessen the penalty for intercourse are specified on 211.
14. *Padakusalamāṇava-jātaka*, no. 432; *The Jātaka or Stories of the Buddha's Former Births*, ed. E.B. Cowell (1895–1913; Delhi: Munshiram Manoharlal, rpt. 1990), 3: 298–300.
15. *Sakuṇa-jātaka*, no. 196; *Jātaka,* ed. Cowell, 2: 89–91.
16. *Telapatta-jātaka*, no. 96; trans. by Gail Hinich Sutherland, *The Disguises of the Demon: The Development of the Yakṣa in Hinduism and Buddhism* (Albany: State University of New York Press, 1991), 138, with minor emendations.
17. For the entire story, see *Jātaka,* ed. Cowell, 1: 233–36.
18. For a survey of this type of characterization in Pali literature, see Misra, *Yaksha Cult and Iconography*, 152–55, 160.
19. Gail Sutherland draws attention to this distinction between artistic and literary characterizations in *Disguises of the Demon*, 106–7, 137–38.
20. *Mahāvaṃśa* chaps. 6–7; cited in Coomaraswamy, *Yakṣas*, 50.
21. *Jayākhya Saṃhitā*, ed. Embar Krishnamacharya (Baroda: Oriental Institute, 1967), 294–95, vv. 77–85.
22. David L. Snellgrove, *The Hevajra Tantra: A Critical Study* (London: Oxford University Press, 1959), 1: 90–91.
23. See, for example, the list excerpted in Stephan Beyer, *The Cult of Tārā: Magic and Ritual in Tibet* (Berkeley: University of California Press, 1973), 252–53 (*yakṣiṇīs* designated here as 'nöjin-spirits').
24. Jonanpa Tāranātha, *The Origin of the Tārā Tantra*, trans. David Templeman (Dharamsala: Library of Tibetan Works and Archives, 1981), 31.
25. Somadeva Bhaṭṭa, *The Ocean of Story; Being C.H. Tawney's Translation of Somadeva's Kathāsaritsāgara; or, Ocean of Streams of Story*, ed. N.M. Penzer (1880, 1923; Delhi: Motilal Banarsidass, 1984), 4: 96–98, 102.
26. Ibid., 97.
27. Keith Dowman, *Masters of Mahāmūdra: Songs and Histories of the Eighty-Four Buddhist Siddhas* (Albany: State University of New York Press, 1985), 114–17.
28. These chapters are available in French translations: chaps. 2–3 in Ariane MacDonald, ed., *Le Maṇḍala du Mañjuśrīmūlakalpa* (Paris: Adrien-Maisonneuve, 1962), and chaps. 4–7 in S.K. Pathak, 'The Language of the Ārya Mañjuśrīmūlakalpa,' in *Aspects of Buddhist Sanskrit: Proceedings of the International Symposium on the Language of Sanskrit Buddhist Texts, Oct. 1–5, 1991,* ed. Kameshwar Nath Mishra (Sarnath: Central Institute of Higher Tibetan Studies, 1993), 279.
29. Marcelle Lalou, *Iconographie des étoffes peintes (pata) dans le Mañjuśrīmūlakalpa* (Paris: P. Geuthner, 1930). Some passages appear in English

translation in David L. Snellgrove, *Indo-Tibetan Buddhism: Indian Buddhists and Their Tibetan Successors* (London: Serindia, 1987), 191–94, 225–27.

30. Pathak, 'Language of the Ārya Mañjuśrīmūlakalpa,' 287–98. I would not have been able to decipher many of the passages translated in this essay were it not for the able assistance of the master Sanskrit philologist and linguistic historian, Abhijit Ghosh, presently of Jadavpur University, Calcutta.
31. *Āryamañjusrimūlakalpa*, ed. P.L. Vaidya (Darbhanga: Mithila Institute, 1964), 387, v. 68.
32. Ibid., 442, line 16; 446, line 29; 490, v. 569; 508, v. 834.
33. Ibid., 442, vv. 3–5.
34. Ibid., 436, v. 72; 445, line 19; 508, v. 834, and, on Vajrapāṇi in the *Āryamañjusrimūlakalpa*, Snellgrove, *Indo-Tibetan Buddhism*, 135–37.
35. *Āryamañjusrimūlakalpa*, 93, v. 48; 448, v. 4; 478, v. 395; 478, vv. 397–98; 490, v. 569; 508, v. 834.
36. Ibid., 445, lines 22–30.
37. For example, when I was doing fieldwork in Calcutta in the autumn of 1999, a history professor told me about a family friend in Tamil Nadu who—despite his guru's warning that he was not sufficiently ready—conjured up a *yakṣiṇī* and was found covered with semen at the site of his *sādhana*, in a coma from which he never recovered. One of my research assistants told me of his fear of walking in certain areas at night because of the danger of being kidnapped or driven mad by a predatory *yakṣiṇī*.
38. *Āryamañjusrimūlakalpa*, 153, vv. 57–58.
39. Ibid., 444, lines 22–25.
40. Ibid., 445, lines 11–13.
41. Ibid., 444, line 22.
42. Ibid., 444, lines 25–26. The term *anyāstrī*, translated here as 'another woman,' may alternately be construed as 'the wife of another.' The contexts of usage provide little basis for determining which meaning is intended, but a concern for married women to my mind suggests an ethical stance that is inconsistent with the general moral neutrality of the *yakṣiṇīs*.
43. Ibid., 442, line 14.
44. Ibid., 442, line 29, 443, line 13.
45. White, *Alchemical Body*, 58, and quotation on 53.
46. *Āryamañjusrimūlakalpa*, 557, lines 26–27; 441, line 11.
47. Ibid., 443, lines 14–17.
48. Ibid., lines 18–24.
49. Ibid., 443, line 25; 444, line 7.
50. Ibid., 447, lines 8–19.
51. Ibid., 441, lines 18–20.
52. Ibid., lines 1–14, quotations of lines 3–5 and 11.

53. Ibid., 442 lines 3–6, quotations of lines 4–6.
54. Ibid., lines 8–13, quotations of lines 9–13.
55. Ibid., 446, line 30; 447, line 6.
56. Ibid., 444, lines 8–22.
57. Ibid., line 27; 445, line 6.
58. Ibid., 445, lines 7–10.
59. Ibid., 446, line 21.
60. Ibid., lines 1–3 and 9–10.
61. Ibid., lines 23–25.
62. Ibid., lines 13–16.
63. On views of women in *anuttara yoga* sources, see Shaw, *Passionate Enlightenment*, chap. 3.
64. Cited in Shaw, *Passionate Enlightenment*, 55.
65. Ibid., 58.
66. On this and an analogous usage of the term in the same work, see Adelheid Herrmann-Pfandt, 'The Good Woman's Shadow: Some Aspects of the Dark Nature of Ḍākinīs and Śākinīs in Hinduism,' in *Wild Goddesses in India and Nepal: Proceedings of an International Symposium, Bern and Zurich, November 1994*, ed. Cornelia Vogelsanger et al. (Bern: Peter Lang, 1996), 51–53.
67. *Bodhicaryāvatāra* 10.40. See Shantideva, *A Guide to the Bodhisattva's Way of Life*, trans. Stephen Batchelor (Dharamsala: Library of Tibetan Works and Archives, 1979), 185.
68. *Āryamañjusrimūlakalpa*, 421, lines 1–13; 440, line 10; 539, line 10; 541, line 9.

12

The Power of Creation

Śakti, Women, and the Goddess

CYNTHIA ANN HUMES

Narendra Nath Bhattacharyya's *History of the Śākta Religion* begins by explaining how the primitive Mother Goddess cult in India centered on women as both the symbol and the actual generators of life. Prehistorical society was organized in a mother-right system. However, subsequent changes in the mode of food gathering and production led to father-right elements being imposed on it, and increased knowledge about the male's role in procreation led to the introduction of a male element in the cult of the Mother Goddess. With the advent of agriculture, Bhattacharyya argues, women's generative power eventually came to be linked, not only with Mother Earth, but also with the fertility of the soil in general. This linkage increased women's status and revived the ancient mother-right. When the influence of the life-producing Mother was extended to the vegetable kingdom, Mother Earth became imagined as the 'womb' in which crops were sown. The Goddess enjoyed a glorious career among the agricultural peoples, until fundamentally male-oriented religions appeared—such as those preserved in the Vediç texts of the Aryans—and her position declined. The connection of goddess worship and agriculture is so integral that despite attempts to establish male superiority, mother-right elements among rural Indian people remain strong. '[S]tories of Virgin Goddesses are the relics of an age when the father had no significance at all and of a society in which man's contribution to the matter of procreation was hardly recognised,' NNB ventured.[1]

Many of NNB's insights are helpful even today in examining concepts of fertility, creation, and the feminine power known as *śakti* in modern Indian goddess traditions. During my fieldwork, I had the great privilege of meeting and consulting with him in Banaras, India. We talked in detail about his theory of virgin goddesses, especially in connection with questions that I asked pilgrims to the Vindhyachal Temple about both the Great Goddess Vindhyavāsinī worshipped there and the scripture *Devī Māhātmya*, which is inscribed on the temple walls and commonly recited within the temple environs. He was especially interested in my findings that modern devotees did not avail themselves of the concept of *śakti* to link women with the Virgin Goddess, Vindhyavāsinī.

A Sanskrit term, *śakti* is grammatically feminine and connotes potency, energy to act, capacity, power, strength, or skill. *Śakti* may be used in the sense of the activating power source of a male deity, often understood as a female energy, or the divine force that may reside in all human beings. The word also functions as a proper noun to refer to a goddess who is the consort of a male deity, or to an independent goddess who endures as the embodiment and source of power itself. The Ādiśakti, the 'Original' or 'Primordial power', is a common name in various Hindu philosophies for the Great Goddess who is understood as the divine creatrix. In modern north Indian languages, *śakti* is often understood to be a preeminently moral and creative power, and a psycho-physiological energy possessed primarily by women and/or by individuals of moral purity and feeling, developed through selfless devotional service.[2]

This chapter focuses on three major themes NNB raised that have interesting connections to findings from my fieldwork and that problematize how Hindus may believe that women, *śakti*, and the Goddess can be connected.[3] First, in the section 'Creation: Oblations, Seed, Womb, and Field', I explore some of the agricultural metaphors in early Hindu texts that draw comparisons between soil and woman and link procreative power with social power, and about which NNB wrote so much. In the next section, 'Creation Symbolism in the *Devī Māhātmya*', I quickly sketch out specific instances in this Śākta scripture to show how it is continuous with the phenomenon of the Virgin Goddess and NNB's hypothesis that such deities hearken back to an age 'when the father had no significance at all'. In particular, I demonstrate the relevance of NNB's insights on *śakti*, the 'generative power of women', in the modern cult of the goddess Vindhyavāsinī, specifically as she is worshipped in Vindhyachal, Uttar Pradesh, a north Indian site of pilgrimage. In the third section, '*Śakti*, the Goddess, and Women', I discuss fieldwork at Vindhyachal among pilgrims (including a specific question that NNB suggested that I ask). I share responses to a question on how one might compare and contrast women with the Goddess. Most pilgrims predictably emphasized there to be a great gulf between them. To justify their opinions, some used metaphors of the field and motherhood, as well as of *śakti*, to highlight differences between them, in many cases underscoring NNB's thesis that it is the perception of the Virgin Goddess's lack of need for a male that demonstrates her transcendence.

CREATION: OBLATIONS, SEED, WOMB, AND FIELD

Although the Indian Aryan people were patriarchal (for example, elevation of males, patrilineality, and patrilocality), in their earliest Sanskrit 'collections' or Saṃhitās, women as wives and mothers were important to religious goals. Both domestic and public rituals depended on the co-presence of husband and wife, and life-affirming references depicted the way to salvation as a joint venture. A woman's gender, while it defined her contributions, did not render her incapable of salvation per se, nor did it preclude her from uttering sacred mantras and acting in the salvific sacrifice.

The Brāhmaṇas (*c.* 1000–700 BCE) posited disparities between birth-groups (*jāti*, *varṇa*) and the increasing importance of having a son to deliver his father to heaven through ritual. The Brāhmaṇas also promoted belief in the necessity for one to be 'born again' through initiation into Vedic ritual so as to be saved, an initiation that was reserved for the top three classes or *varṇas*, thereby excluding the fourth *varṇa*: the Śudras. Greater emphasis was laid on female chastity, and eventually 'purity', defined as chastity, because of the prerequisite for sons in the quest for heaven. Chastity—understood as appropriate marriage and controlled sexuality—came to be viewed as a proper substitute for education in women, yet emphasis was laid on males gaining an education at the home of a teacher after initiation, resulting in the widening gulf between men's and women's educational levels. The earlier view of different but complementary roles served eventually to legitimatize gender role definitions. Since a man's status was closely related to his wife's purity/chastity, greater control of women's sexuality was considered necessary. These developments contributed to the increasingly more common view that women were ignorant and by their very nature incapable of Vedic study, even if chaste and honored. By the late Brāhmaṇas, menstruation and childbirth came to be viewed as taboo; thus, women's inferior nature was intellectual as well as biological.

NNB argued that together with the lowering of women's status, the devaluation of non-Brāhmaṇical religious phenomena also occurred in India, leading to the eventual acceptance of tamed goddess traditions that he called 'dependent Śāktism'.[4] Dependent Śāktism, NNB continued, stood in contrast to the 'independent Śāktism' evidenced by those traditions privileging the Virgin Goddess.

Brian K. Smith's work, while not specifically concerned with gender issues in Brāhmaṇical religion, offers a means of explaining the philosophical and ritual underpinnings of the trends noted by NNB, including its male-oriented pantheon, progressive devaluation of women and the non-Brāhmaṇical, and the eventual rise of 'dependent Śāktism'.[5]

Vedism, Smith explains, posits that the philosophical center around which Vedic thought revolves is resemblance (*sāmānya*). Vedism turns on the assumption that it alone can correlate corresponding elements lying on three discrete planes of reality. These planes include the macrocosmos (*adhidevatā*, 'relating to the godly'), the ritual sphere (*adhiyajña*, 'relating to the sacrifice'), and the microcosmos (*adhyātman*, 'relating to the self'). Connections between cosmos, ritual, and self were not designed to reduce these levels to any specific one, nor were they metaphors: these homologies expressed metaphysical truth and made all three levels mutually explicative.[6]

While there are many creation myths in the Saṃhitās, the

foremost Vedic story posits Prajāpati (the Lord of creatures and of procreation) and the sacrificial ritual bringing each other into existence. In regard to this important figure, NNB commented, 'the Vedic tribes who developed a pastoral economy and a patriarchal form of social organization, were not willing to give a minimum recognition to this old mother of the gods [Aditi]. In her place they were gradually developing the idea of a male creator which was later finalized in the form of Dakṣa-Prajāpati.'[7] Rather than a female creative model, Smith explains, the procreative act of Prajāpati becomes the prototype of all procreative acts, including the sexual act, which engenders new human life.[8] Prajāpati emits creatures, but they are not fully formed; they are characterized by having either an excessive resemblance or uniformity which prohibits production (*jāmi*), or they are 'separate' or isolated (*pṛthak*), not having enough resemblance.[9] To give the chaotic creation structure and order, a secondary operation of ritual is necessary. In Vedism, the ritual is the workshop in which all true reality is forged: 'birth and anthropogony are distinct and separate moments, the first being only the necessary precondition for the second. As cosmic creation is not cosmogony, biological reproduction is not the production of a true human being.'[10] This understanding of humanity and ritual assumes that what is 'natural', that is, that which is not ritually constructed, is inherently defective, chaotic, disorganized, and unformed.

Prajāpati's cosmic emission is 'replicated by the emission of semen in the act of human procreation. Semen is considered the "essence" of the "life sap" (*rasa*) of the man, his condensed representative'.[11] When the concentrated identity of man (semen) is emitted into the womb of the woman, it is 'as if the very self of the procreator has been reproduced in the form of the new embryo'.[12] The later texts called the Upaniṣads continue to equate a man's seed with his offspring.[13] But this vision of reproduction, in which the embryo is an exact replica of the father, introduces the macrocosmic error of excessive resemblance (*jāmi*). The fetus is undifferentiated from the father until it is recast and individually shaped in the womb of the mother through the application of ritual. The transcendental self (*daiva ātman*) is still not the biological self that emerges out of the woman's womb, however; the divine self is 'born out of the sacrifice', in a second birth through the 'divine womb' of the *āhavanīya* fire, which brings forth superior fruit when compared to the 'natural' (and thus inferior) womb of women.[14] Those unable or unqualified to perform the rituals remain inferior, not as fully human as those who do perform the rituals, and who thus experience second, fully human and Aryan, birth.

The creation of human bodies is often depicted as a process of sacrificial oblations of male seed into the 'fire' that is woman. First, the gods make an 'offering of food' into the 'fire' that is man, from which semen is produced, which is then 'poured' into the woman to produce a new life. 'Woman, Gautama, is a sacrificial fire. The vagina is her fuel, foreplay her smoke, the womb her flame, the penetration her coals, and pleasure her sparks. Into this fire the gods make an offering of semen, and from that oblation the embryo is born.'[15] The term *tejas* is directly associated with semen.[16] 'In a person, this one [the *ātman*] first becomes an embryo. That which is semen is the luminous power (*tejas*) extracted from all the parts [of the man]. In the self, truly, one bears another self. When he emits this into a woman, he then begets it. This is one's first birth.'[17] This sense of the term *tejas* is continuous in later times, where in myth cycles of Śiva, too, his *tejas* is equated with his seed.[18]

This ritual model presumes the male seed to be unilaterally effective. The common 'field' metaphor, for example, presupposes that the woman is merely a receptacle, not an active partner in the process. Some Saṃhitā passages suggest that the woman has seed (*vṛṣṇyam payas*, 'virile milk') just as the man does (*Ṛg Veda* 1.105.2bc), and that both mother earth and father sky have seed (*retas*).[19] The prevailing portrayal of birth, however, features the woman serving merely as a birthing courier, so to speak, passively 'seeded' by her husband. Her contribution to the child is merely nourishment through her uterine blood, which was believed to be eventually transformed into milk. Women's milk, not her ovum, corresponds to men's seed.

Although the Vedas contain conventional observations on the predictable interdependence of phallus and womb, they also hold to a correspondence of the phallus and the breast, and the notions that men's semen can create without a woman at all, and a woman without a man through her milk.[20] Since milk is not literally procreative, there is a tendency to emphasize the male's role, so that semen is the 'more equal' of the pair: 'Thus a man may become an androgyne, but a woman seldom does.'[21] Hence although milk is the primary Vedic procreative symbol, the gods are the primary actors, and as their semen is identified with milk, it becomes a male fluid. 'The corresponding identification, which credits women with seed, is far less common in the Ṛg Veda; yet the fact that this identification occurs at all lays the groundwork for the later development of a more egalitarian view of the relative importance of women in procreation.'[22]

A major new philosophical system that would come to hold great import for the eventual development of Śāktism is Sāṃkhya dualism (*c.* 500 BCE). In Sāṃkhya, *prakṛti*, the feminine material cause of the universe, existed and functioned independently of the male principle of spirit. As NNB commented,

> The cult of the Mother-goddess is intimately associated with the *Sāṅkhya* concept of *Prakṛti*. The *Sāṅkhya* identifies *Puruṣa* and *Prakṛti* respectively with the male and female principles, man and woman. Just as the offspring is produced by the union of man and woman, so also this universe is produced by the union of *Puruṣa* and *Prakṛti*. But the same *Sāṅkhya* holds that *Puruṣa* is subordinate and nothing but a passive spectator; *Prakṛti* is all in all. . . . The problem regarding the role of husband in a matriarchal society perhaps finds its expression in the *Sāṅkhya* philosophy. In a matriarchate, father has something to do in the matter of creation; but his role is that of a passive spectator. It is *Prakṛti* that is supreme and her partner is not only subordinate, but also indifferent, inactive and insignificant.[23]

Eventually, however, dominant philosophical systems came to understand *prakṛti* as controlled by the *puruṣa*, which was, in turn, identified with the *ātman*, that is, the individual soul identical with Brahman or the essence of the universe, through 'a deliberate contamination of genuine Sāṅkhya with Upaniṣadic Vedānta'.[24] The ascetic Upaniṣads that claim neuter Brahman to be an all-pervasive, eternal, and fully real principle also view the world as temporary and ultimately illusory. Fertility in women was equated with sexuality, which if left uncontrolled, obstructs the path to enlightenment.[25] This spirit/matter, male/female, knowledge/illusion dichotomy—so common in world religions, and presupposed in the Vedic portrayals of reproduction already described—pictures the male as providing the essence to life and the female merely material fabric to sustain it. To destroy embodiedness but retain life, one must destroy the female and become fully male, the *puruṣa*.[26] Thus, while the ultimate Brahman may be a neuter noun, the epitome of human behavior, that is, the divine spirit, is clearly modeled on the male.

Having laid out how the philosophy of divine creativity has been imagined in a gendered manner, and how such dominant ritual interpretations of creation have been incorporated into later gender concepts in the development of Śāktism, I turn now to the implications of such ideas for the *Devī Māhātmya*.

CREATION SYMBOLISM IN THE *DEVĪ MĀHĀTMYA*

In approximately the third or fourth century of the Common Era, the worship of the Goddess came to be incorporated in the Sanskrit canon.[27] Paramount among these early sources on the Goddess is the *Devī Māhātmya* (*c.* fifth–sixth centuries), found in the *Mārkaṇḍeya Purāṇa*. Even today, the *Devī Māhātmya* functions as the single most important Sanskrit source on goddess worship.

The *Devī-Māhātmya* is commonly conceptualized as being divided into three episodes or *caritas*, tales of the Goddess's 'actions', some of which retell mythological history to privilege the Great Goddess's might. Viṣṇu, for example, is credited in earlier literature with having defeated the two twin demons Madhu and Kaiṭabha, yet in the *Devī Māhātmya*'s first episode, the 'Great Deluding', Māhāmāyā is shown as truly responsible. Brahmā Prajāpati's hymn of appeal to the Goddess to waken Viṣṇu from slumber so that he can fight makes clear that Devī is greatest of, and subsumes, all deities, including the male gods, whom she can subdue at will. In her role as Tamasī, the goddess presiding over the dark quality of inertia, deception, and darkness, the Goddess renders the two 'tremendously virile' (*ativīrya*) demons 'intoxicated' and 'deluded' by an excess of power (*atibala*) generated in battle (1.71, 73). The demons foolishly agree to a boon requested by Viṣṇu that tips the balance against them. This *carita* asserts that the Goddess controls virile power, an excess of which can result in braggadocio and foolish overconfidence that can lead to defeat.

In contrast with the dark, shadowy presence of the Goddess in the first *carita*, the second episode portrays her as a latent luminosity that is evoked from the gods and takes female form to defeat the shape-shifting male buffalo demon, Mahiṣa. Here, too, earlier myth cycles credit the victory over the demon to another male god: either Śiva or his son, Skanda. In our text, after Mahiṣa defeated the gods, the discouraged deities (led once again by Creator Brahmā Prajāpati) appeal to Śiva and Viṣṇu, urging them to 'set their minds on destroying the demon'. Immediately, Śiva's and Viṣṇu's countenances become furrowed and twisted with rage. *Tejas* streams from the faces of Śiva, Viṣṇu, and Brahmā, and from the bodies of all the other gods. The *tejas* coalesces first into a shimmering mass, and then a refulgent Goddess, whose form is shaped in the likeness of the male gods: her mouth is shaped from Śiva's *tejas*, her arms from Viṣṇu's splendor, and so on. The gods rejoice on seeing her. Mirroring the Goddess's origin from within them, each of the deities draws out from his characteristic weapon or totem an immanent but now manifested duplicate, and hands it to the Goddess.

From the breaths she releases in the heat of battle, hundreds and thousands of troops appear. Sustained by her *śakti*, the Goddess's multiforms assist in destroying the buffalo demon's many legions. With his snout, hooves, tail, and horns, Mahiṣa casts down her many troops. After summoning the necessary anger to kill him, 'the shining' Caṇḍikā at last turns her attention directly to Mahiṣa. The shape-shifter successively assumes the form of a lion, man, elephant, and buffalo again in their fight. Mounting him, Caṇḍikā kicks Mahiṣa so hard that she literally kicks him inside out; half of his human torso is projected through the mouth of his buffalo form by the force of her foot. Then, completely surrounding him with her virile power (3.38, *devyā vīryeṇa saṁvṛtaḥ*), the Goddess slices the demon's head off with her great sword (3.39). Thus, before the demon can transform or give birth to himself again, the Goddess uses her own *vīrya* to initiate his transformation—which she herself aborts. This expresses a central truth: the immanent, refulgent Goddess is Queen of Creation. The 'Crusher of Mahiṣa' (Mahiṣamardinī) is often viewed as the manifestation of the Great Goddess when predominated by *rajas*. *Rajas* is *prakṛti*'s quality of passion, emotion, and affection, which is said to predominate as an active, diffuse force in air or the atmosphere of vapor and mist. The interrelated themes of fiery liquid *tejas*, shifting power, and mutability are deliberately exploited in this *carita* to express the central truths of the immanent, shining, angry Goddess's ability to take various forms and control development of matter and moral conflict.

In the last episode, Devī faces Śumbha and Niśumbha.[28] This time, the star of the myth is portrayed as the goddess Ambikā, also known as Kauśikī, the text explains, for having come forth from the sheath (*kośa*) of Pārvatī. In the story, Pārvatī does not recognize Ambikā or her origin. Indeed, Pārvatī must be told Ambikā's true identity by the mysterious goddess who emerges from Pārvatī herself. The twin demons Śumbha and Niśumbha view Ambikā as a jewel to be possessed through marriage, but she has other ideas. She refuses their proposal, explaining to their messenger that she had vowed long before to marry only the man who conquers her in battle. The messenger scoffs at the 'haughty' woman: 'All the gods, led by Indra, were no match in battle for Śumbha and the others. How can you, a lone woman, go into battle with them?' (5.73) All demonic attempts to conquer and control her fail, of course, for despite appearing from the sheath of Pārvatī (understood in contemporaneous literature as Śiva's wife), Ambikā is not a married or marriageable goddess.

To subdue her, Śumbha and Niśumbha send Raktabīja—literally 'red-seed/semen' or 'blood drop'—a demon who regenerates identical forms of himself when any of his blood 'seeds' the earth. From the Goddess's forehead, 'black as ink in anger', Kālī emerges directly. The site of this next goddess's manifestation is the third eye, as in the Mahiṣa story, but here Kālī is, in a sense, sloughed off or out of the Goddess's eyebrows, rather than appearing and being shaped out of *tejas*/seed. When the Goddess, her lion vehicle, and Kālī are surrounded on all sides, *śaktis* or separate female 'powers' emerge just as Kālī did from the bodies of a group of seven *ativīryabalānvitāḥ* (literally, 'extremely virile and strong') male gods. Seven *śaktis* appear in femininized forms of their male progenitors, with the same vehicles, weapons, and ornaments, and an eighth *śakti* emerges from the Great Goddess herself. When the *śaktis* wound Raktabīja, even more demons arise from his blood when it hits the soil. On Ambikā's orders, Kālī eats the demons and laps up any blood before it hits the ground, sapping Raktabīja's strength and ultimately devouring him. His blood-seed creates multiforms of himself, but only on touching the soil. The earth must adhere to its dharma as creatrix; it cannot exercise her own will. However, in our story, Ambikā forces the demon to shed his blood-seed, and when Kālī swallows the seed, she chooses not to give birth to Raktabīja's forms, unlike in other Hindu myths in which female ingestion of seed causes impregnation. After slaying Niśumbha, Devī cuts off the head of yet another 'man of great strength and great virility' (*mahābalo mahāvīrya*) who emerges from a male demon in another fashion: springing from the heart of the fallen demon (9.33–34). This *carita* explicitly refutes masculine, unilateral creation models in which the female Ultimate is merely an earth womb awaiting male seed, or the model that the male can replicate himself on his own.

The Raktabīja myth resonates with earlier themes in the Upaniṣads that expressly identify virility and seed and view semen as an instrument of power that males should attempt to reclaim from women. A *Bṛhadāraṇyaka Upaniṣad* (6.4.4–5) prayer requests: 'Let virility return to me, and energy and strength. Let the fire be put in its right place, on the fire altar' (this last noun here is feminine). On saying this, the ritualist should take semen with his thumb and fourth finger and rub it between his breasts, at his heart, or between his eyebrows[29]—the same sites from which the male warrior from Niśumbha, Kālī from the Goddess, and luster, or *tejas,* from the gods emerge.

The power of the *Devī Māhātmya* myths stems in part from its exploitation of contemporaneous procreative symbolism. Recall that the *tejas* story describes the 'birth' of the Goddess in the world in a fashion similar to that of humans as propounded in the Āraṇyakas above. Her 'first birth' is the collection of luminous power, visible as a fiery mountain, which only subsequently becomes an ordered female form, reminiscent of myths of fiery mountains of semen in the Agni, Śiva, and Skanda cycles, for example, which require no field or womb.[30]

Some contemporary informants and various scholars interpret the Goddess's creation from *tejas* in the Mahiṣa myth as proof that she is derivative of (and a few male respondents add that this means she is subordinate to) the male gods. They then use this passage as an explanation and justification for male dominance in transcendent and domestic hierarchies. Yet according to the text, what is the source of the gods' *tejas*? The Goddess's origin proceeds precisely along the lines of the ancient Vedic theory of procreation, namely, the divine substance is first poured into the male deities, and only subsequently emitted in the form of *tejas*/semen. This divine, fiery, fluid-like inner power of the gods is the Goddess herself. The first episode confirms that she abides as *śakti* in whatever and wherever anything exists (1.63). Although dwelling within Viṣṇu, for instance, she precedes him, for he, Śiva, and Brahmā have been made to assume bodily form by her (1.64–65). The *Devī Māhātmya* also specifies that the Goddess 'vanishes' after being praised for slaying Mahiṣa.[31] Thus, while it may be said that the body parts of the Shining Goddess appear just as the body parts of the various gods, the gods are her multiforms, not she theirs, because they have previously been made to assume bodily form by her. Furthermore, no ritual is necessary to effect the transformation of the *tejas*; thus, while the two-step process is retained, this myth exalts the agency and primacy of the Goddess as the Great Creatrix, who, immanent within her creation as *tejas*, also gives it its shape. This model of the Goddess's origin proceeds precisely along the lines of the ancient Vedic theory of origin: the divine substance is first poured into the male deities, and subsequently emitted in the form of *tejas*/semen. Thus the Goddess, already immanent in the gods, takes specific incarnate form from the *tejas*/semen/energy drawn out of their anger. This is reminiscent of a story in the *Taittirīya Brāhmaṇa* that describes how Prajāpati can be reinvigorated by collecting together the *tejas* from beings whom he has emitted: 'the revivification of Prajāpati is depicted as a cosmic healing, performed by collecting together the luminous energy (*tejas*) and life essence (*rasa*) of all the emitted creatures, thereby simultaneously reuniting the dispersed creation (the *sṛṣṭi*) into a reconstituted unity and reinvigorating Prajāpati (the *atisṛṣṭi*) who is that unity.'[32]

Thomas Coburn asserts that a major intention of the *tejas* episode in the second *carita* is to show not only that the Goddess is operative in the world, but that she is the supreme ruler of all creatures. Coburn notes that it draws on *Manu*'s classical Indian model of kingship:

> When these creatures, being without a king, through fear dispersed in all directions, the Lord created a king for the protection of this whole (creation), Taking (for that purpose) eternal particles [of the various deities, namely,] of Indra, of the Wind, of Yama, of the Sun, of Fire, of Varuna, of the Moon, and of the Lord of Wealth (Kubera). Because a king has been formed of particles of those lords of the gods, he therefore surpasses all created beings in lustre [*tejas*]; And, like the sun, he burns eyes and hearts; nor can anyone on earth even gaze on him.[33]

Coburn concludes they have a shared image of origin, a common ability to assume a variety of forms, and a like character as both valorous and irascible, but he notes that what had previously been affirmed of the king on a mundane scale is affirmed in the *Devī Māhātmya* on a cosmic scale.[34]

The king is terrifying because of his alliance with the Lord's son, Daṇḍa, the great 'stick' symbolizing brute punishment. Various male gods are said to be lords of punishment, just as, through ritual, kings become human wielders, or even divine embodiments, of Daṇḍa.[35] These two myths are indeed cousins, but the *Devī Māhātmya* also bears a likeness to scriptures privileging feminine imagery in establishing leadership that predate the masculine imagery of *Manu*.

NNB wrote an interesting and informative corrective to the concept of *rājā* in the Vedas, and in particular the *Atharva Veda*.[36] He explains that in its original usage, *rājā* was the term for 'war-chief', and only later came to mean 'king'.[37] War-chiefs in the time of the *Atharva Veda* were elected by the consent of the tribe, and underwent royal consecration.[38] The royal consecration was critical in establishing the authority of the war-chief. One of the features of royal consecration was investing glowing power within the would-be leader. Several Saṃhitās describe an inner, shining power in male gods; others claim such a power resides in a goddess, or the Goddess. Incantations from portions of the *Atharva Veda* portray divine splendor as fluids from, or constituting, the body of the Goddess—golden waters, honey, sap, and milk. In some sections, these liquids are sprinkled or rained down (*abhiṣeka*) upon a would-be *rājā*, within whom they become a powerful, inner fluid energy source.[39]

Since the luster of the goddess is believed to infuse the beseecher with strength and authority, these passages share remarkable continuity with later Śākta and Tantric philosophies. For example, in *Atharva Veda* 6.38.1–4 the goddess Tviṣi (brilliance) gives birth to all that is resplendent, and abides as *varcasā* or *tviṣiṁ*, 'brilliance', within various beings and animals who are known for their lustrous power, including tribal leadership or royalty (*rājanye*). The same root word, *tviṣā* is used synonymously for the luster of the female produced from the gods' *tejas* in the second *carita* of the *Devī Māhātmya*. In *Atharva Veda* 6.8.1–7, the prominent Vedic water goddess—or more abstractly, the shining, celestial waters, made up of seventeen kinds of liquids[40]—consecrates (*abhiṣeka*) the *rājā* with luster (*varcasā*, viz., vigor, energy, illuminating power) on his coronation. *Atharva Veda* 1.33 and 1.35, too, draw connections between rulers, luster, milk/semen, and the celestial water goddess, as well as the practice of *dig-vijaya*, the newly consecrated *rājā*'s martial 'conquest [victory] of the directions', or bid for world conquest, which almost always involves worship of goddesses, even up to and including the modern era.[41]

By the time of *Manu* and the *Devī Māhātmya*, the term *rājā* had gained the sense of a monarchical king, but to become a *rājā* still required the ceremony of *abhiṣeka*, drawing glowing, powerful liquid energies from many sources. In the *Devī Māhātmya*, the Goddess is lauded many times as Caṇḍikā in the middle episode, as well as whenever she acts outs of passion, emotion, and affection elsewhere in the text. The meanings of the adjective *caṇḍa/ā/ī* (viz., burning, violent, impetuous, passionate, enraged, wrathful, and fierce) share the same qualities denoted by the noun *tejas*, except that *tejas* lacks the emotive qualities of anger and impetuousness, which require anthropomorphic form.[42] The feminine nominative ending (*ikā*) functions to personify the heated anger of the gods, which we know to be the agent that evokes their indwelling power (*tejas*). In 3.27, even Caṇḍikā herself must become enraged to summon the strength to slay the buffalo demon, illustrating that rage against wrong is a powerful catalyst for action to restore dharma; Daṇḍa acts as a ferocious, dark, drunken, and genocidal creature whose pure rage exhibits nothing less than the very antithesis of dharma, yet this is the paradoxical condition for its restoration.[43] The concept of a goddess or the Goddess existing within beings as mutable, indwelling, bright, and fiery power, and closely connected with sovereignty and glorious burning power that allows kings to vanquish opponents is at least a millennium older than the *Devī Māhātmya*'s characterization of 'Caṇḍikā.' What has shifted in our text is that rather than a human *rājā* infused with *tejas*, the Goddess manifests herself from *tejas* at times to restore divine order. The authors of the text thus restore an ancient conflation of the goddess and powerful, immanent brilliance, the term for which has been variously labeled *tviṣā*, *varcasā*, *tejas*, and *śakti*, but the authors also affirm an anthropomorphic, concerned personal Goddess, adding a new dimension to the more abstract concept of divine feminine force in the Saṃhitās.

As shown in Table 12.1, if one places the three myths side by side, further comparisons are possible. In *Manu*, that which makes the king so terrifying is his alliance with the Lord's son, Punishment, who is born of Brahman's *tejas*. Caṇḍikā/*Tejas*, like Punishment/*Tejas*, takes birth in the world of action herself precisely to restore order and establish dharma. Thus, in *Manu*, we do have a divine king model distinctly similar to that of the goddess queen in the *Devī Māhātmya*; however, the male embodiment of *tejas* in 7.17 is described as progeny of the Lord, not the embodiment of the supreme itself. In recognizing that feminine Padmā ('lotus', probably referring to Śrī) and victory dwell in the king, *Manu* draws

Table 12.1: Comparison of Mythical Structures Involving Divine Brilliance and Rule

Theme	*Atharva Veda*	*Manu Smṛti*	*Devī Māhātmya*
Agent of Transformation	G/goddess, seeking to support a supplicant's bid for rule	Lord, seeking to create a being fit for kingship	Gods' concentration seeking victory, notably, the three Great Gods
Underlying Emotions, Motives	Deliberate ritual conjuring by devotee; G/goddess's kindness	People's fear, Lord's kindness	Anger in gods who seek to conjure power; Goddess's kindness, but righteous anger toward demons
Common Source of Power	Brilliance, which is the G/goddess, is consciously installed in the person to become leader, *rājā*	Gods' *tejas*, which they 'possess', is drawn from them; the Lord's Son, Daṇḍa, 'Punishment,' is brilliance itself	Gods' *tejas*, which is the Goddess Herself
Who is Fashioned from *Tejas*	Divinized but human *rājā*	Divinized but human king; he rules with Punishment/ luster, the Lord's son	Cosmic Queen, who is herself luster, and who may intervene to ensure justice
Relation between Agent and Created Being	The celestial waters affectionately embrace the *rājā*	No intrinsic connection between Lord and king, but fierce son helps the good king	Gods' fiery anger is embodied in the Goddess, who fiercely protects gods

Characteristics of Brilliance within the Created Being	The *rājā* moves about, shining by himself	Like the sun, the king burns hearts and eyes; nor can any on earth gaze on him	The Goddess moves about, shining; demon is destroyed upon looking at her lustrous face (4.19)
Gender implications	G/goddess infuses her own brilliance within a male *rājā* for his welfare (*saubhagā*)	Male God uses *tejas* from male gods to create a male king who rules with the Lord's Son, Male Punishment, yet in 7.11, the king is he in whom the goddess Padmā dwells	Female Goddess uses power source already within male kings to take female form and restore righteousness over evil shape-shifting male

on earlier watery female symbolism of inner power vested in royalty, and the text seems to be especially concerned with vesting patriarchy with authority. For example, 7.17: 'Punishment [*daṇḍa*] is the king [*rājā*], the male [*puruṣa*], the applier [of the stick, i.e., the law], the ruler, and he is regarded as the equal of the dharma of the four *āśrama*s.' In 7.28–29, 'Punishment [possesses (just as easily read, 'is')] a very bright luster, and is hard to be administered by men with unimproved minds; it strikes down the king who swerves from his duty, together with his relatives. Next it will afflict his castles, his territories, the whole world together with the movable and immovable [creation], likewise the sages and the gods, who [on the failure of offerings] ascend to the sky.' In contrast with the righteous anger of the Goddess rightfully directed towards demons, the presiding emotion in *Manu* is mortal fear of Punishment/*Tejas*: 'Through fear of [Punishment] all created beings . . . swerve not from their own duties [*svadharma*]' (7.15).

A less obvious but equally significant factor is precisely who can evoke power and create from or conjure up *tejas*. In *Manu*, both gods and humans are dependent upon the will of the Lord, and neither have voices in the construction of the king; the frightened beings do not ask for intercession, and the *tejas* is removed from the gods without their express permission or knowledge. Unlike *Manu*, in the *Devī Māhātmya*, the Goddess grants the gods' request after Mahiṣa is killed that whenever they remember her, she might destroy their misfortunes, and when mortals praise her, the Goddess will be concerned with their welfare. In the third *carita*, the Goddess goes so far as to promise that she will appear directly in gynemorphic form whenever her devotees are threatened, suggesting greater immediacy between the Goddess, deities, and humans.

The *Devī Māhātmya* seeks to convince its audience that although she may have what humans may perceive to be mysterious and negative qualities, she only enters conflicts to effect the greatest good. Her various stories reveal that she is the Great Goddess of both wisdom and delusion, who acts at times by kindly withdrawal or punitive excessive saturation; she may manifest herself as a brilliant Queen from combined powers, the form in which she exists in all creation; she may appear in specific lesser manifestations, which even themselves may not understand their connection to the transcendent Great Goddess; and she can also appear as a multitude of separate *śaktis*, or manifested 'powers', not just from subsidiary male deities, but also herself. None of the ways in which the Goddess creates resemble ordinary human reproductive techniques: she is not a 'mother' in any anthropomorphic understanding of the term.

The variety of ways the Goddess manifests herself and the deliberacy with which she is portrayed as eschewing marriage and dependence on others all reveal that unlike human females, this divine feminine force is entirely self-sufficient and creates by her own power. Thus, while one of the *Devī Māhātmya*'s verses commonly quoted to support women's status affirms that 'each and every woman' is a 'portion' of her, the verse does not mention women as mothers, and indeed, the rest of the verse deliberately minimizes women's role in procreation: 'by you [Goddess] alone as mother has this world been filled up' (11.5).

The theology of the *Devī Māhātmya* accords well, then, with NNB's description of the early Śākta scheme of cosmogonical evolution: 'the unmanifested *Prakṛti* alone existed before creation. She wished to create, and having assumed the form of the Great Mother, she created Brahmā, Viṣṇu and Śiva out of her own body'.[44] The *Devī Māhātmya* is an example of NNB's independent Śāktism.[45] The depiction of ultimate reality is quite deliberately female, and its concomitant understanding of the world refutes Vedic arguments that what is 'natural'—that is, that which is not ritually constructed—is inherently defective, chaotic, disorganized, and unformed. Developing from and abiding within the body of the Goddess, even if beings are unaware of their true nature, they yet have divine purpose and meaning.

From a historical perspective, seed—and even semen—have been gendered as female in Sanskrit texts at one time or another preceding our work.[46] In the *Devī Māhātmya*, seed, *tejas*, and semen become female substance/s and fluids, as do power and strength. Even *vīrya*, literally, virile strength, becomes the very hallmark of the Goddess; indeed, her 'virility' is extolled in every one of the *caritas*. This appropriation of masculine imagery by the Goddess is obvious in the Sanskrit original, but is obscured in most English translations because their authors intuitively translate the same words selectively, both to render the translation less repetitive but also to reflect differences depending on the gender of the signified.[47] In Purāṇas composed several centuries after the *Devī Māhātmya* (the *Garuḍa Purāṇa*, for instance), *vīrya* is shown to be an important term that is deliberately portrayed as a creative power possessed by the supreme male deity, not a goddess.[48]

Finally, the *vīrya* of Devī differs from that of simple male power, reflecting the fact that the authors were moved to situate it within their view of her female gender. In a hymn to the Goddess, the gods marvel at how her *vīrya* destroys enemies, yet acts as a salvific device; it is simultaneously compassionate. This leads them to wonder (4.21), 'What comparison can there be to your bold acts? Where [else] is there such a lovely form, yet one that strikes such fear among foes?' Thus, the Goddess is female because of her embodiedness and creative power, but she is also female because of her wondrous, compassionate use of virile power in service to others.[49]

The Goddess's battles prove that she is not 'a mere woman', as taunted by her opponents. Indeed, after defeating the demons, the gods extol her in feminine but also explicitly masculine terms in verses 11.3–11.4ab: 'You have become the sole support of the world, for you abide in the form of the earth. By you who exist in the form of water, all this universe is filled up, O one of inviolable valor [*ativīryā*: literally, our cognate, great 'virility'], You are the power [*śakti*] of Viṣṇu, of boundless valor [again, *vīryā*], you are the seed [*bīja*, also 'semen'] of all, the supreme illusion [*māyā*].' The linking here of the heaven and earth dyad, virility, and semen, resonate with the unilateral portrayals of creation that I have discussed above. The Goddess is not merely field; she is seed as well, which explains why verse 11.5 takes pains to acknowledge women being 'particles' of her, but attributing true creation to the Goddess alone.

Clearly, the feminine qualities ascribed to the Great Goddess and to women in the *Devī Māhātmya* are not isomorphic: her nature as 'mother' or creatrix is different, her relation to men is different, and her strength and abilities are different.[50] These differences between women and the Goddess continue to be recognized, and emphasized, by her devotees today.

ŚAKTI, THE GODDESS, AND WOMEN

In this section, I shall list and discuss specific responses from pilgrims to questions about how to understand *śakti*, the Goddess, and women. Over a period of a year, I asked fifty-four male and twenty-five female pilgrims to Vindhyachal a question that NNB had encouraged me to pose: 'How does the goddess Vindhyavāsinī compare to the ordinary woman? What are the differences, and what are the similarities?' The most surprising result is that only one of these seventy-nine pilgrim respondents claimed that women and the Goddess were alike because of *śakti*: on the contrary, twenty per cent of the men—but no women—used the concept to emphasize their difference. Furthermore, motherhood was used more often to distinguish, rather than to show similarity between, women and the Goddess.

I also posed my query to persons whom I had identified in advance as lay reciters of the *Devī Māhātmya*, that is, people who recited the scripture but did not do so for hire, as professional *paṇḍits* do.[51] I have not included their responses here, both for the sake of brevity and, more important, for the purpose of showcasing the understandings and interpretations of 'average', nonelite devotees of the Goddess. I would note, however, that unlike the pilgrim sample, some reciters—both male and female—did use the concept of *śakti* to indicate similarity between women and the Goddess, although an even greater percentage of men—12 of 34, or 35 per cent—used the concept to differentiate. I shall periodically provide relevant counterparts to the pilgrim sample from this lay reciter sample.

When asked how the goddess Vindhyavāsinī compares with ordinary women, fourteen of seventy-nine pilgrims (Pilgrim Sample ID ## 1–14) responded that they did 'not know'. Gender seemed to influence who felt capable of answering; only two of fifty-four male pilgrims responded that they did not know, and just two others declined to answer, whereas ten of twenty-five female pilgrims, or forty per cent, responded, 'I do not know'. Caste and education level were also significant.[52]

The single most common explanatory response was that there is an obvious, insuperable gulf between the nature of women and the Goddess. This is not surprising; the stance of adoration, wonder, and awe that devotees report toward a supreme divine being, who they believe transcends all humans, even if immanent, should not be underestimated or minimized. Metaphorical and symbolic imitation of goddesses by women may indeed lead to human ennoblement, but most pilgrims drew distinct boundaries between the divine and human beings from the stance of devotion. Twenty-four men and nine women of the seventy-nine pilgrims who responded (forty-two per cent) answered in one form or another that women are simply women, and the Goddess is the Goddess; that they are simply different; or that no comparison is possible. In doing so, a few denigrated women, but most merely said women were ordinary or human. Following each statement, I give the age, caste status, degree of education, and, where known, religious orientation of the interviewee.

ID # 15 'There is this much difference—that not every human is human, and every stone is not God. This much difference is there—there is one stone on which you offer flowers, and there is another stone on which you shit. There is that much difference.' Age 30, Caurasiya Vaiśya (betel seller) male, 12th standard, Śaiva.

ID # 16 'There is a big difference, because the ordinary women are those of the Kali Yuga—Kali Yuga women—(in contrast,) she has a good nature, and she is the Goddess.' Age 32, Brāhmaṇa male, 10th standard.

ID # 17 'There's no special difference between the ordinary woman and the Goddess, the Goddess is simply Goddess.' Age 47, Kṣatriya male, BA, Śaiva/Sanātana Dharma.

ID # 18 'The Goddess is the creator of the world, and women are just women.' Age 68, Bhumihar Brāhmaṇa male, 12th standard, Śākta.

ID # 19 'There's a great difference between them; she is a goddess, women are not.' Age 51, Kṣatriya male, 8th standard, Vaiṣṇava.

ID # 20 'Vindhyavāsinī is one of the seven sisters, and she is also the direct incarnation of Durgā [*sakṣāt Durgā ki avatāra*]. She is the direct Goddess, Bhagavatī; women are just ordinary.' Age 45, Bhumihar Brāhmaṇa male, 11th standard, Vaiṣṇava.

ID # 21 'She is Māyā and we are ordinary.' Age 56, male Brāhmaṇa, 10th standard, Vaiṣṇava.

ID # 22 'She is an Ādi [Primeval] Devī, and she appeared from the portions of all the gods; she is everything, and does the welfare of all. . . . Women are merely humans and she is a goddess. She doesn't change at all.' Age 45, male Kṣatriya, 10th standard, Tantric.

ID # 23 'The ordinary woman remains ordinary; even as a *pativrat* [wife dedicated to her husband], she can never truly compare with the Goddess.' Age 64, Brāhmaṇa male, 10th standard, none expressed.

ID # 24 'Oh, there is a huge difference between the Goddess and women—they are just women and she is Vindhyavāsinī.' Age 60, Brāhmaṇa male, 10th Standard.

ID # 25 'While everything is not being worshipped, Vindhyavāsinī is like this, that she is worshipped by men, and all come here, and salute her and then leave' (in English). Age 25, Dhobi male (English-medium high school, born in Lucknow, Unnau district, but raised in Dubai, United Arab Emirates), 'simple Hinduism'.

ID # 26 'There is a big difference; women are just ordinary. That is the difference.' Age 35, Nayi (barber) male, 12th standard, Śaiva.

ID # 27 'I can't say anything about this . . .' (this man was with a number of friends, and after he looked around at them for their opinion, one interjected helpfully, 'there is a big difference: she is a goddess', and the respondent nodded, smiled, and affirmed.) Age 25, uneducated, Yādava male, none expressed.

ID # 28 'Brother, she is Devī. What can I tell you? There is a huge difference.' Age 40, uneducated Pāśi Scheduled Caste male, Śākta.

ID # 29 'There's no difference, and yet no comparison. She is a deity and ordinary women are just ordinary.' Age 40, uneducated, Pāśi Scheduled Caste male, Śākta.

ID # 30 'She is the Mahāśakti, and ordinary women are just ordinary women.' Age 35, Brāhmaṇa, 5th standard, 'Hindu dharma'.

Four male respondents (ID ## 31–34) simply stated that the two were very different,[53] and two male respondents (ID ## 35–36) claimed there to be nothing that could even allow a comparison between the Goddess and women.[54] One other informant compared women and the Goddess by their ability to aid, and another hinted at an identity between women and the Goddess, but affirmed their difference.

ID # 37 'A general woman can only serve her husband, but this Goddess does the welfare of all; women and the Goddess are as different as the sky and the earth.' Age 35, Vaiśya male, BS, Vaiṣṇava.

ID # 38 'A general woman and Mother Vindhyavāsinī—there is no true comparison. We cannot compare them. Vindhyavāsinī is in the very form of motherhood; and in family life, the form of woman is in the form of mother, wife, and sister; Vindhyavāsinī has only one form, of Mother.' Age 40, Kṣatriya male, MA, LLB, Śaiva.

Four female respondents (ID ## 39–42) repeated that women are women and the Goddess is a Goddess,[55] and a number of others replied the same almost verbatim.

ID # 43 'She is divine. Women are just human beings.' Age 23, Bhumihar Brāhmaṇa female, BA, MA, Śākta.

ID # 44 'We are humans, she is a deity; she is greater than us.' Age 32, Brāhmaṇa female, 5th standard, Śākta.

ID # 45 'There is a big difference between us and her; she is a different type of female.' Age 18, Bhumihar Brāhmaṇa female, doing her BA, 'all gods and goddesses'.

ID # 46 'Ordinary women are women, and she is the form of a deity.' Age 40, Brāhmaṇa female, 10th standard, 'Hindu dharma'.

ID # 47 'She does kind things—she gives long life to husbands, protects children, so she is famous as a goddess.' Age 60, Brāhmana female, uneducated, 'repeats Rām nām'.

Eleven males, but no females, used the concept of *śakti* to stress difference. Their comments ranged from simply implying that she has special or far greater powers in her capacity as Ādiśakti to denying explicitly that women have any *śakti* whatsoever.

ID # 48 'There is no comparison, because she is Ādīśakti and ordinary women are involved in worldly things.' Age 43, Brāhmana, 10th standard, Vaiṣṇava.

ID # 49 'Her *śakti* is incomparable.' Age 25, Hela (Scheduled Caste sweeper), 8th standard, 'Hindu dharma'.

ID # 50 'The difference is that she [Vindhyavāsinī] has great *śakti*, that's the difference.' Age 34, Vaiśya, 7th standard, 'all gods'.

ID # 51 'There is as much difference as the earth and sky. She is without beginning, indestructible. [Women] don't have the power [*śakti*] of beginninglessness. They don't have the *śakti* to live 100 years, or the *śakti* to perform miracles. She gives fruits according to the devotees's desires.' In his visions, he noted, 'I have never seen any woman in the world so beautiful, with a wondrous character, or so divine, and with such an expression.' Age 52, Brāhmaṇa, graduate degree in medicine, Sanātana Dharma.

ID # 52 'Ādiśakti Great Queen Vindhyavāsinī has incomparable power [*śakti*], and there is [not even a] goddess to compare with her. . . . There is a big difference [between women and the Goddess].' Age 37, Gond (Scheduled Caste), 5th standard, Vaiṣṇnava.

ID # 53 'The Goddess has the capacity to offer peace within the heart; women cannot.' Age 45, Kṣatriya, 10th standard, Sanātana Dharma.

ID # 54 'Vindhyavāsinī has never appeared to me directly, but she has this invisible *śakti* to give us mental peace—a cool and calm life, she gives peace.' Age 45, Jaisaval, 10th standard, Sanātana Dharma.

ID # 55 'There is a big difference, like sky and land. She is Ādiśakti, and they are general women, so there is no comparison.' Age 57, Brāhmaṇa, BA, MA, Śaiva/Śākta.

ID # 56 'Women do not have any *śakti*, and Devī has *śakti*.' Age 46, Baniya, unschooled but literate, Vaiṣṇava.

ID # 57 'There is a major difference. It is this way: she is the Ādiśakti, and Kaṁsa struck her when she was small' (he went on to explain one of her great myths). Age 45, Brahmabhakta (type of priest), 5th standard, not expressed.

ID # 58 'She is famous for her place of power [*śakti pītha*], and she is our protector; general women worship her.' Age 42, Thakur, 12th standard, not stated.

In contrast with the many pilgrims introduced thus far, men and women who emphasized the dissimilarity between the human and divine feminine, there were some who preferred to think in terms of parallel, or similitude—or who were willing to nuance their answers in some fashion, admitting that the answer to my question might depend on circumstance. The most straightforward respondents in this group, five men and one woman, claimed simply that women and the Goddess are not different, although they did not qualify their answer.

ID # 59 'There is no difference.' Age 25, Brāhmaṇa male, BA, 'Hindu'.

ID # 60 'They are both the same: mother, girl.' Age 50, Brāhmaṇa male, 4th standard, Śākta.

ID # 61 'There is no difference, they are both the same.' Age 55, Lodh jalapait (water-bearer) uneducated male, 'Hindu'.

ID # 62 'No difference at all.' Age 45, uneducated Harijan male, 'Kālī, Śiva, Rām'.

ID # 63 'There is no difference between women and Devī.' Age 30, Harijan female, literate, but not formally educated, 'Hindu'.

ID # 64 'What is the difference? There's no difference.' Age 33, Yādava male, 4th standard, 'Bhagavān and Vindhyavāsinī'.

Fifteen respondents offered more subtle comments, giving both comparisons and contrasts between the Goddess and women. They suggested that certain women can indeed be linked in some ways to the Goddess; this they explained in terms of the women's behavior, or the category of motherhood itself, or even the attitude of the outside interpreter making the judgment.

For instance, two women made distinctions between the types of women in the world based on their behavior and people's perceptions of them. They identified certain qualities that are divine in female humans and noted how the Goddess differs in her capacity to protect and assume multiple forms.

ID # 65 'Women are goddess and demoness [*rākṣasī*] both: she who sees everybody in the same way, she is a goddess, and she who is jealous is a demoness. The Mother takes care of everybody.' Age 50, Brāhmaṇa female, 10th standard, Śaiva.

ID # 66 'She is the Ādiśakti, and there is a portion of her in every woman; there is some of her nature in every woman. And if a woman lives in a proper manner, protecting people, and she does that, then it means she will be worshipped as the Goddess. She has different forms.' Age 32, Brāhmaṇa female, 10th standard (she reads the *Devī Māhātmya* in Hindi translation), Śākta.

Six persons drew on the concept of motherhood to differentiate or identify Vindhyavāsinī and women. Their responses ranged from blank disjunctions or identifications to highly subtle comments. One woman and three men used the concept to emphasize difference; one woman and one man used the concept to emphasize similarity. The male who emphasized similarity specifically noted that this perception was due to his attitude. The differences in human mothers center on two issues: women are not merely mothers, but have different social relations; and women can only give birth to several children, but the Goddess gives birth to all. The four stressing difference spoke as follows:

ID # 67 'This Goddess is the mother of all of the universe; the general woman is the mother of just one-two-four children, or a family.' Age 49, Kṣatriya male, 10th standard, Śaiva/Śākta.

ID # 68 'On Mother and ordinary women—ordinary women are female, but [the human woman] has many positions: mother, wife, sister, daughter, daughter-in-law. So, she has many separate roles, and she plays them.' Age 33, Brāhmaṇa male, Ācārya (Sanskrit BA), 'Hindu'.

ID # 69 'The general woman appears in four ways: there is the form of one's mother, as a servant, as a wife, and as an advisor. But the Mother's form is the form of the Mother. In her, there is no difference. She has only one form of [Mother].' Age 40, Brāhmaṇa male, Śāstri degree (Sanskrit MA), Vaiṣṇava.

ID # 70 'There is a big difference; she is Mother.' Age 42, Kaśyapa Dhobi Scheduled Caste female, uneducated, none expressed.

By contrast, one male and one female identified women and goddesses through the concept of mothering. In making this comparison, both spoke of how the Goddess is perceived, rather than how she exists ontologically.

ID # 71 'For me, they are all equal; all women look like mothers, and all mothers look alike.' Age 45, Khatri male, 9th standard, Vaiṣṇava.

ID # 72 'Oh, there is no difference; it is her fate for all to think, "she is a mother".' Age 30, uneducated Yādava female, Śākta.

Some respondents explained that the answer depends on depth

of perception or faith; if the observer has the proper mental stance, then there is no difference.

ID # 73 'If your thinking is pure, then there is no difference.' Age 49, Agrawala Vaiśya male, MBBS (bachelors of medicine and of surgery), Sanātana Dharma.

ID # 74 'Who you see depends on your perception. If you see someone as a sister, she is a sister, a goddess as a goddess, and a mother as a mother; in whatever way you view them, she will appear that way.' Age 22, Brāhmaṇa male, BA, 'Hindu dharma'.

ID # 75 'There is no difference between them if you worship her with faith: it depends on one's faith.' Age 37, Rajput female, 5th standard, Śākta.

ID # 76 'General women are also in the form of Devī, and this is my opinion.' Age 30, Svarnaka Vaiśya male, 10th standard, Vaiṣṇava.

ID # 77 'There is no difference. She is an incarnation of Lakṣmī, and women are also an incarnation of Lakṣmī.' Age 45, Yādava male, fifth standard, 'Hindu'.

Finally, two respondents offered philosophical explanations that accepted a limited degree of similarity between women and the Goddess.

ID # 78 'There is only a difference in terms of the ideal—and there is some difference in their *guṇas* [qualities].' Age 29, Kṣatriya male, LLB, none expressed.

ID # 79 'It is written in the *Durgā Saptaśatī* (another name for the *Devī Māhātmya*) that all the women of the world are incarnations of Vindhyavāsinī. She pervades all of them, but she is in the masculine forms also.' Age 40, Rajput male, 12th standard, Śākta. He explained earlier in his interview that Vindhyavāsinī is Ādiśakti, who is *nirguṇa* [without qualities] and *nirākār* [without manifestation], but she is also *saguṇa* [with qualities] with the nature of all three *guṇas*, and *sākār* [in manifestation].

REFLECTIONS

The majority of pilgrim respondents—of both genders—held that there was a great difference between women and the Goddess. Put simply, they identified the Goddess as a divine being whose power is immeasurably beyond that of human females: and, as many note, beyond that of human men. Such a reverential attitude on the part of ordinary devotees should not be glossed over by undue emphasis on elite monistic philosophies and academic truisms positing little, or less, distinction between humans and deities in Hinduism.

As mentioned earlier, only one (ID # 66) of the seventy-nine pilgrims claimed that women and the Goddess were alike because of *śakti*—and the woman who reported this similarity, though not a lay reciter, reads the *Devī Māhātmya* and hence is influenced by the text's theological position.[56] By contrast, eleven men used the concept to show their difference. Although it may be intellectually or personally stimulating to posit that women are *śakti*, and therefore can be seen as divine, and some people do report such a belief, my own experience at Vindhyachal demonstrates this to be an unusual and exceptional response.

Most pilgrim women—sixteen out of twenty-two—were unable or unwilling to draw any parallel between the Goddess and themselves. If they secretly identified with her, they did not show or admit it. In their interviews, although they confidently answered virtually all of the dozens of other questions posed, many of these women deferred to their husbands in knowledge about the divine and their own nature. The feminine qualities ascribed to the Great Goddess and to women were not seen as isomorphic: her nature as 'mother' or creatrix is different, her relation to men is different, and her strength and abilities are different. And those differences are recognized, and emphasized, by her devotees today.

On the other hand, five of the twelve women pilgrims who did respond to the question saw similarity. Again, to provide a touchstone of comparison, the second data sample of reciters suggests some interesting gender patterns. As stated above, one of the five females in my pilgrim sample who saw similarity reported that she reads the *Devī Māhātmya*. In the lay reciter sample, that is, those of whom I had noted in advance that they recited the text, all four women who felt sufficiently confident to comment suggested similarities between women and the Goddess rather than difference.[57] The demographic information hints that women's education and active engagement in Goddess worship may translate to a greater perceived connection with the Goddess. Seeing divine attributes in oneself may also be related to class and caste, demonstrating that if women are empowered through education and social opportunity, they may be more likely to see connection than difference.

Cult orientation did appear to be a significant factor in the responses. Twelve of the forty reciters claimed to be Śākta or Tantric in orientation; sixteen said they were Vaiṣṇava. Of the eleven Śāktas or Tāntrikas who gave a response, six emphasized similarities between women and the Goddess, and the others explained that the Goddess differs because she created the world as the Primordial Power or World Mother. Four Vaiṣṇava reciters simply stated that women were women, the Goddess was the Goddess. In the pilgrim set, twenty-two claimed to be Śākta, Śaiva, Tantric, or some combination thereof; of these three did not answer the question, twelve saw difference between human women and the Goddess, and seven asserted similarity or nuance in their answer. Of the thirteen pilgrims who self-identified as Vaiṣṇava, ten distinguished between women and the Goddess, and three saw similitude. Among the forty-four remaining pilgrims, those who stated that they were 'Hindu', worshipped all gods, were adherents of Sanātana Dharma, or gave no sectarian affiliation, a full half said that there was a big gulf between human women and the Goddess, whereas a quarter were willing to conceive of some parallel or connection. Thus, while overall the pilgrims did not see women as sharing many of the Goddess's characteristics, those who did make theological connections tended to be Śākta, Tantric, or Śaiva (31 per cent), rather than Vaiṣṇava (23 per cent) or generically 'Hindu' (25 per cent).

Some Hindu rituals involve the direct worship of women, symbolizing some kind of ongoing correspondence with the Goddess. Most respondents agree that it is the Goddess's control over all of life that differentiates her from human females: dominance over other beings and the ability to protect, dispense favors, and unilaterally create. Men used the concept of motherhood or the ability to give birth as a point of contact between the Goddess and women, but in doing so, most used it to show how women are less complete, less capable, and less powerful than the Goddess, unless one adopts a particularly enlightened emotional stance.

Among reciters, on the other hand, women emphasized appropriate mental attitudes, caring for others, doing good deeds, and working in the world as divine qualities in human women, and closely related them to *śakti*. Rather than seeing *śakti* as a generative power, female respondents who connected women and goddesses through *śakti* saw it as power to effect change, to protect, and to excel within the limits of—or transcend—their embodied human condition. In sum, power and the powerful are in the eyes of the beholder.

The *Devī Māhātmya* takes pains to prove that unlike human women, the Virgin Goddess is powerful and authoritative—that is, she can righteously use that power herself, like a man—and, furthermore, that she controls all fertility. The scripture seems to be a living proof text of Narendra Nath Bhattacharyya's observation regarding stories of the Virgin Goddesses: the *Devī Māhātmya* is a living relic 'of an age when the father had no significance at all and of a society in which man's contribution to the matter of procreation was hardly recognized'[58]—or perhaps in which man's contributions to procreation are vigorously contested as ultimately real and significant. Mere physical ability to procreate appears in the voices of devotees to be a quite limited power indeed.

The Virgin Goddess Vindhyavāsinī does seem to carry into the present ancient ideas of generative power, and as the influence of one's religious orientation and education reveals in our sample, the status of woman and her relationship to the divine feminine depends a great deal on who is in the position of interpreting.

While women may resemble the Divine Mother in giving birth, because they do not control their own fertility, or impart their essence to their children, most devotees of Vindhyavāsinī, especially those self-reporting as Vaiṣṇava, consider them to be weak counterparts 'standing for' or 'representing' the original, that is, the unilaterally creative Goddess. They are, if one adopts Brian Smith's language, 'more or less incomplete images or emanations' of the Goddess.[59] However, for those who continue to honor the Virgin Goddess Vindhyavāsinī, self-report as espousing a Śākta, Tantric, and/or Śaiva view, and familiarize themselves with the *Devī Māhātmya* scripture, women can still resemble the Goddess in a significant way in India today, despite their purported incompleteness. NNB's insights—penned nearly forty years ago—remain vibrant contributions to the field of religious studies in India.

NOTES

1. Narendra Nath Bhattacharyya, *History of the Śākta Religion* (1974; New Delhi: Munshiram Manoharlal, 1996), 6.
2. For a discussion of various taxonomies I elicited regarding the many indigenous terms related to the English word 'power,' and how gender inflects them, see my 'Is the *Devi Mahatmya* a Feminist Scripture?' in *Is The Goddess a Feminist? The Politics of South Asian Goddesses*, eds. Alf Hiltebeitel and Kathleen M. Erndl (Sheffield: Sheffield Academic Press, 2000), 123–50.
3. The data sets I use here stem from research that I conducted in 1987–1989 at Vindhyachal, a north Indian village on the Ganges River located just outside of Mirzapur. Narendra Nath Bhattacharyya kindly suggested a number of research avenues. For one, he was helpful in linking me to other sites associated with the goddess Vindhyavāsinī. For another, he offered several of the specific questions that I eventually incorporated into the questionnaire schedules that I used to collect the ethnographic data that I cite here. The first draft of this paper was written four years after my return from fieldwork and my initial conversations with NNB. While my research today centers in large part on the phenomenon of the guru and Western meditative practices, I am very pleased to see the publication of this essay on Śāktism, which has been so greatly influenced by NNB, and so directly interacts with his research. NNB was a kind and generous mentor, who profoundly influenced me in becoming a scholar of Indian history and religion.
4. Bhattacharyya, *History of the Śākta Religion*, 96.
5. Brian K. Smith, *Reflections on Resemblance, Ritual, and Religion* (Delhi: Motilal Banarsidass, 1988).
6. Smith, *Reflections on Resemblance, Ritual, and Religion*, 46. Wendy Doniger O'Flaherty notes that when an actual birth model is finally constructed in the Sanskrit literature, beginning in the Upaniṣads, the model is an almost

literal application of the ritual metaphors. O'Flaherty, *Women, Androgynes, and Other Mythical Beasts* (Chicago: University Press, 1980), 31.

7. Narendra Nath Bhattacharyya, *The Indian Mother Goddess* (1970; New Delhi: Munshiram Manoharlal, 1999), 95–96.
8. Smith, *Reflections on Resemblance, Ritual, and Religion*, 82.
9. Ibid., 63.
10. Ibid., 51.
11. Ibid., 83.
12. Ibid.
13. Ibid., 26.
14. Ibid., 116.
15. Ibid., 205–6
16. *Aitareya Upaniṣad* 2.4.1, *Aitareya Brāhmaṇa* 7.13, and *Aitareya Āraṇyaka* 2.5, as referenced in Smith, *Reflections on Resemblance, Ritual, and Religion*, 84.
17. *Aitareya Upaniṣad* 2.4.1, as quoted in Smith, *Reflections on Resemblance, Ritual, and Religion*, 84.
18. Even *Ṛg Veda* 1.71.8 seems to suggest the identity of *tejaś* and *retas*. O'Flaherty, *Śiva: the Erotic Ascetic* (Oxford: University Press, 1981), 283–86.
19. O'Flaherty, *Śiva: the Erotic Ascetic*, 21.
20. Ibid., 32.
21. Ibid.
22. Ibid., 33.
23. Narendra Nath Bhattacharyya, 'Śāktism and Mother Right,' in *The Śakti Cult and Tārā*, ed. D.C. Sircar (Calcutta: University of Calcutta, 1967), 69–70.
24. Bhattacharyya, *History of the Śākta Religion*, 115.
25. Rajeshwari Pandharipande, 'Spiritual Dimension of Fertility Cult and Power in Woman,' *Journal of Dharma* (Bangalore) 13 (July–September 1988): 271.
26. For an extended discussion of this process working through various texts, see Cynthia Ann Humes, 'Becoming Male: Salvation Through Gender Modification in Hinduism and Buddhism,' in Sabrina Petra Ramet, ed., *Gender Reversals and Gender Cultures: Anthropological and Historical Perspectives* (New York: Routledge, 1996), 123–37.
27. Bhattacharyya, *History of the Śākta Religion*, 100; and C. Mackenzie Brown, *God as Mother: Feminine Theology in India—An Historical and Theological Study of the Brahmavaivarta Purāṇa* (Hartford, Vt.: Claude Stark, 1974), xv.
28. For more detailed interpretation and feminist exegesis of this episode, see Humes, 'Is the *Devi Mahatmya* a Feminist Scripture?', 135–38.
29. See Wendy Doniger O'Flaherty, 'Sexual Fluids in Vedic and Post-Vedic India,' in *Women, Androgynes, and Other Mythical Beasts*, 30–31.

30. Earlier myth cycles credit the victory over Mahiṣa to either Śiva or his son Skanda; Śiva is often called Hiraṇyagarbha, or 'Golden Womb/Fetus', capable of unilateral creation as the combined seed[gold/fire]-womb. Skanda's birth is portrayed variously; it was the result of the combined effort/semen of multiple fathers (usually Agni [fire] and/or Śiva), and bearing and tending by multiple mothers, none of whom could keep the fiery seed within her womb.
31. In an earlier Mahiṣa story in the *Varāha Purāṇa*, the goddess remains where she is, and in the contemporaneous or earlier *Vāmana Purāṇa*, she 'reenters the gods'. See C. Mackenzie Brown, *The Triumph of the Goddess* (Albany: State University of New York Press, 1990), 96–101.
32. Smith, *Reflections on Resemblance, Ritual, and Religion*, 65.
33. Quoting Buhler's translation, 216–17; Thomas B. Coburn, *Encountering the Goddess: A Translation of the Devī Māhātmya and a Study of Its Interpretation* (Albany: State University of New York Press, 1991), 25–26.
34. Coburn, *Encountering the Goddess*, 25–26. Although Coburn does not reference the *Atharva Veda*, he rightly recognizes that 'the interplay of female deity and masculine secular authority may prove to be one of the important continuities in Indian religion' (202–3n35).
35. For a description of how kings become embodiments of Daṇḍa, see Ariel Glucklich, *The Sense of Adharma* (Oxford: Oxford University Press, 1994), esp. 223–25.
36. *Ancient Indian Rituals and Their Social Contents* (New Delhi: Manohar, 1975), 29ff.
37. Ibid., 29.
38. Ibid., 31.
39. *Atharva Veda* 1.33, 35; 4.8.1–7; 6.38.1–4.
40. *Ancient Indian Rituals and Their Social Contents*, 26.
41. The *Dig-vijaya* is described in connection with the/a goddess in *Atharva Veda* 4.8.4. In *Mahābhārata* 6.23.4 and 8, Durgā is called Siddhasenānī (general of the *siddhas*), and *raṇa-priyā* (fond of war).
42. Arthur Anthony Macdonell, *A Practical Sanskrit Dictionary* (1924; rpt., Oxford: Oxford University Press, 1965), 90, 112.
43. Glucklich, *Sense of Adharma*, 231.
44. Bhattacharyya, *The Indian Mother Goddess*, 28.
45. Ibid., 96.
46. See Doniger, 'Sexual Fluids in Vedic and Post-Vedic India,' 17–61, esp. 21–25.
47. For example, in *Encountering the Goddess*, Coburn translates *ativīrya* as 'tremendously virile' in 1.71 when the term modifies the demons (p. 38), but at no point does he translate the Goddess as being extolled as 'virile,' although the same word is used for both the demons and the Goddess throughout the text, demonstrating the challenges of translation.
48. Tracy Pintchman, *The Rise of the Goddess in the Hindu Tradition* (Albany:

State University of New York Press, 1994), 133–34 on the *Bhāgavata* (*c.* 800–1000 CE), and 152–54 on the *Garuḍa* (*c.* 850–1000 CE). These texts depict the Goddess as a field, and the male god as the outside agent who 'inserts his *vīrya* into her' and thus is the efficient cause of creation. See 130–31.

49. The feminized *vīrya* of Devī has significant symbolic ramifications: it is a compassionate, righteous, self-controlled power used in service for the good. Kathryn Hansen reports that narrative traditions have celebrated warrior women as agents of heroic action (*vīrāṅganā*), often likening them to the goddess Durgā or Kālī. They share iconographic and moral links; their 'defeat of threatening enemies is comparable to the warring goddesses' punishment of evil demons'. Hansen, 'Heroic Modes of Women in Indian Myth, Ritual, and History: The *Tapasvinī* and the *Vīrāṅganā*,' in Arvind Sharma and Katherine K. Young, eds., *The Annual Review of Women in World Religions* (Albany: State University of New York Press, 1992), 2: 35.
50. Reciters of the *Devī Māhātmya* found it amusing that the twin demons so misunderstand the Goddess's nature: they misinterpret her as an ordinary, haughty female with a bad attitude, and conclude that subjugation by a male will make her a good female.
51. This sample set included six women and thirty-four men. These interviews included both a schedule of demographic and thematic questions and extensive, undirected interview time, commonly lasting an hour and longer.
52. The following responded that they did not know how women and the Goddess compared: ID # 1, age 50, uneducated, Paśi Scheduled Caste female, 'Hindu'; ID # 2, age 40, uneducated, Harijan female, Śākta; ID # 3, age 35, Kunabi Scheduled Caste female, 8th standard, 'all gods honored'; ID # 4, age 60, uneducated, Rajput female, none expressed; ID # 5, age 25, uneducated, Kasera (Vaiśya) female, 'Vindhyachal'; ID # 6, age 55, Khatri female, 8th standard, Sanātana Dharma; ID # 7, age 18, Thakur female, 5th standard, Śākta; ID # 8, age 25, uneducated, Yādava female, none expressed; ID # 9, age 30, Brāhmaṇa female, 5th standard, 'Hindu'; ID # 10, age 50, uneducated, Khatri female, 'all gods honored'; ID # 11, age 32, Brāhmaṇa male, with a law degree, Tantric; ID # 12, age 30, uneducated, Paśi Scheduled Caste male none expressed; ID # 13, age 37, Brāhmaṇa male, with a BA and LLB none expressed; and ID # 14, age 41, Brāhmaṇa male, with BS none expressed.
53. ID # 31, age 27, Kṣatriya male, 12th standard, 'Hindu dharma'; ID # 32, age 35, Kṣatriya male, 10th standard, 'Hindu dharma'; ID # 33, age 22, Brāhmaṇa male, B. Comm., Vaiṣṇava; ID # 34, age 58, uneducated Brāhmaṇa male, 'Bhagavān and Karma.'
54. ID # 35, age 45, Brāhmaṇa male, 10th standard, Śaiva; ID # 36, age 38, Kṣatriya male, 12th standard, Vaiṣṇava.
55. ID # 39, age 16, Kahara (water-bearer) female, 10th standard, Śaiva; ID # 40, age 32, Vaiśya (Agrawala) female, education not listed, Vaiṣṇava; ID #

41, age 25, Kāyasth female, Hindu dharma; ID # 42, age 35, Thakur female, no education, 'all gods respected'.

56. In contrast with the pilgrims whom I inteviewed, many of the forty lay reciters with whom I spoke provided explanations of *śakti* and how it relates to women with significant sophistication, and careful, subtle efforts to distinguish layers of interpretation.
57. Two of six women declined to reply, although they answered all other questions in depth.
58. Bhattacharyya, *History of the Śākta Religion*, 6.
59. Smith, *Reflections on Resemblance, Ritual, and Religion*, 75.

Select Bibliography

PRIMARY TEXTS, IN BENGALI, SANSKRIT, AND TAMIL

Adbhuta Rāmāyaṇa. Sanskrit text with Hindi translation by Camanlal Gautam. Bareilli: Samskrti Samsthan, 1990.

Adbhuta Rāmāyaṇa. Sanskrit text with Hindi translation by Jvalaprasad Misra. Bombay: Venkatesvara Press, 1990.

Adbhuta Rāmāyaṇa. Sanskrit text with Hindi translation by Rām Kumār Rai. Varanasi: Prachya Prakashan, 1989.

Adbhuta Rāmāyaṇa. Sanskrit text with Hindi translation by Urvasi Jayantilal Surati and Jasvanti Hasmukh Dev. Lucknow: Bhuvan Vani Drast, 1983–84.

Adigal, Prince Ilangô. *Shilappadikaram*. Translated by Alain Daniélou. New York: New Directions, 1965.

Āgamavāgiśa, Kṛṣṇānanda. *Bṛhat Tantrasāra*. Edited by Rasikmohan Caṭṭopadhyāy and translated from Sanskrit to Bengali by Candrakumār Tarkālaṅkār. Calcutta: Nababhārat, 1982.

Aitareya Brāhmaṇa. Edited by Kasinatha Sastri Agase. 2 vols. Poona: Hari Narayana Apte, 1986.

Aitareya Brāhmaṇa. Edited by Satyavrata Samasrami. 4 vols. Calcutta: Bibliotheca Indica, 1895–98.

Āpastamba Śrauta Sūtra. Edited by Richard Garbe and Chintaman Ganesh Kashikar. 3 vols. Calcutta: Bibliotheca Indica, 1882, 1885, 1902.

Āryamañjusrimūlakalpa. Edited by P. L. Vaidya. Buddhist Sanskrit Texts No. 18. Darbhanga: Mithila Institute, 1964.

Atharva Veda. Edited and translated by Devi Chand. New Delhi: Munshiram Manoharlal, 1982.

Atharva Veda Samhitā. Translated by W.D. Whitney. 2 vols. Cambridge, Mass.: Harvard University Press, 1905.

The Book of the Discipline (Vinaya-Piṭaka). Translated by Isaline B. Horner. 6 vols. Sacred Books of the Buddhists, vols. 10–11, 13–14, 20, 26. London: Luzac, 1949–66. Reprint. Oxford: Pali Text Society, 1992–96.

Baudhāyana Śrauta Sūtra. Edited by Willem Caland. 3 vols. Calcutta: Asiatic Society, 1904, 1907, 1913.

Bhaṭṭa, Somadeva. *The Ocean of Story; Being C. H. Tawney's Translation of Somadeva's Kathāsaritsāgara; or, Ocean of Streams of Story.* Edited by N.M. Penzer. 1880, 1923. 2nd rev. ed. 10 vols. Reprint. Delhi: Motilal Banarsidass, 1968–84.

Bhattacharya, Sriyukta Siva Candra Vidyarnava. *Tantra Tattva.* Edited by Sir John Woodroffe as *Principles of Tantra.* 1914. 5th edn. 2 vols. Madras: Ganesh, 1978.

Brahmavaivarta Purāṇam. Sanskrit with Bengali translation. Edited by Pañcānan Tarkaratna. Calcutta: Nababhārat, 1386 [1979].

Cakrabartī, Mukundarām. *Kabikañkaṇ Caṇḍī.* Calcutta: Basumatī-Sāhitya-Mandir, 1963.

Cāttaṉār. *Manimekhalai (The Dancer with the Magic Bowl) by Merchant-Prince Shattan.* Translated by Alain Daniélou, with the help of T.V. Gopala Iyer. New York: New Directions Books, 1989.

Chatterjee, Bankimcandra. *The Abbey of Bliss.* Translated by Nares Candra Sengupta. Calcutta: Cherry Press, 1902.

Coburn, Thomas B. *Encountering the Goddess: A Translation of the Devī-Māhātmya and a Study of Its Interpretation.* Albany: State University of New York Press, 1991.

Deśika, Lakṣmaṇa. *Śāradātilakam.* With the commentary of Śrī Rāghava Bhaṭṭa. Edited by Ācārya Karuṇāpati Tripāṭhī. 2 vols. Varanasi: Sampurnanand Sanskrit University, 1997.

Devī Purāṇam. Sanskrit with Bengali translation. Edited by Pañcānan Tarkaratna. Calcutta: Nababhārat, 1384 [1977].

The Hymns of the Ṛgveda. Translated by Ralph Griffith. 4th edn. 2 vols. 1889; Varanasi: Chowkhamba Sanskrit Series Office, 1963.

The Hymns of the Rig Veda. Edited by F. Max Müller. 2nd edn. 2 vols. 1877. Varanasi: Chowkhamba Sanskrit Series Office, 1965.

The Jātaka, or, Stories of the Buddha's Former Births. Edited by E.B. Cowell. Delhi: Munshiram Manoharlal, 1990.

Jayākhya Saṃhitā. Edited by Embar Krishnamachaya. Gaekwad's Oriental Series, no. 54. Baroda: Oriental Institute, 1967.

Kālī Tantra. Edited by Paṇḍit Nityānanda Smṛtitīrtha. Calcutta: Nababhārat, 1388 [1981].

Kālikā Purāṇam. Sanskrit text edited with an English translation by Biswanarayan Shastri. 3 vols. Delhi: Nag, 1991.

Kālikā Purāṇam. Sanskrit text with Bengali translation. Edited by Pañcānan Tarkaratna. Calcutta: Nababhārat, 1384 [1977].

Kāmākhyā Tantram. Sanskrit text edited with a Bengali translation by Jyotirlāl Dās. Calcutta: Nababhārat, 1978.

Kubjikā Tantram. Sanskrit text edited with a Bengali translation by Jyotirlāl Dās. Calcutta: Nababhārat, 1978.

Lakṣmī Tantra: A Pāñcarātra Text. Translated and edited by Sanjukta Gupta. 1972. 2nd edn. Delhi: Motilal Banarsidass, 2000.

The Long Discourses of the Buddha: A Translation of the Dīgha Nikāya. Translated by Maurice Walshe. Boston: Wisdom, 1987. Reprint, 1995.

Mahīdhara, *Mantramahodadhih*. Translated by a board of scholars. No. 12 of the Sri Garib Dass Oriental Series. Delhi: Sri Satguru, 1985.

Mahīdhara's Mantramahodadhiḥ. Text in Sanskrit and Roman along with English translation and commentary by Rām Kumār Rai. 2 vols. Varanasi: Prachya Prakashan, 1992.

Matsubara, Mitsunori. *Pāñcarātra Saṃhitās and Early Vaiṣṇava Theology: A Translation and Critical Notes from Chapters on Theology in the Ahirbudhnya Saṃhitā*. Delhi: Motilal Banarsidass, 1994.

Nīlatantram. Edited by Jyotirlāl Dās. Calcutta: Nababhārat, 1388 [1981].

Pañcaviṁśa Brāhmaṇa. Translated by Willem Caland. Calcutta: Asiatic Society, 1913.

Pañcaviṁśa Brāhmaṇa. Edited by Ananda Candra Vedantavagisa. 2 vols. Calcutta: Bibliotheca Indica, 1870, 1874.

Pauṣkara Saṃhitā. Edited by His Holiness Sree Yatiraja Sampathkumara Ramanuja Muni of Melkote. Bangalore: A. Srinivasa Aiyangar and M.C. Thirumalachariar, 1934.

Rāmānuja. *Vedārthasaṃgraha*. Translated by S.S. Raghavachar. Mysore: Sri Ramakrishna Ashrama, 1968.

The Ramayana of Valmiki. Translated by Hari Prasad Shastri. London: Shanti Sadan, 1952–59.

Rig Veda Brāhmaṇas. Translated by Arthur Berriedale Keith. Vol. 25 of the Harvard Oriental Series. Cambridge, Mass.: Harvard University Press, 1920.

Saṃvit-Prakāśa by Vāmanadatta. Edited with an English introduction by Mark S.G. Dyczkowski. Varanasi: Ratna, 1990.

Śāṅkhāyana Śrauta Sūtra. Edited by A. Hillebrandt together with the commentary of Varadattasuta Ānartīya and Govinda. 2 vols. 1888-89. Reprint. New Delhi: Meharchand Lachhmandas, 1981.

Śāṅkhāyana Śrauta Sūtra. Translated by Willem Caland and edited with an introduction by Lokesh Chandra. Delhi: Motilal Banarsidass, 1980.

The Śatapatha Brāhmaṇa: According to the Text of the Mādhyandina School. Translated by Julius Eggeling. Reprint in 5 vols. of *The*

Sacred Books of the East, vols. 12, 26, 41, 43, 44. Delhi: Motilal Banarsidass, 1963–78.

The Śatapatha Brāhmaṇa. Edited by Albrecht Weber. Varanasi: Chowkhamba Sanskrit Series Office, 1964.

Sāttvata Saṃhitā, with a Commentary by Alaśiṃha Bhaṭṭa. Edited by Vraja Vallabha Dviveda. Varanasi: Sampurnanand Sanskrit University, 1982.

Shantideva. *A Guide to the Bodhisattva's Way of Life*. Translated by Stephen Batchelor. Dharamsala: Library of Tibetan Works and Archives, 1979.

Srimad Devi Bhagawatam. Translated by Swami Vijnanananda. 2nd edn. 1921–23. Reprint. Delhi: Oriental Books, 1977.

Śrīvacana Bhūṣaṇa of Pillai Lokācārya. Translated and edited by Robert C. Lester. Madras: Kuppuswamy Sastri Research Institute, 1979.

The Sūtra of Golden Light: Being a Translation of the Suvarṇabhāsottamasūtra. Translated by R.E. Emmerick. London: Pali Text Society, 1970.

Taittirīya Āraṇyaka. Commentary by Bhaṭṭa Bhāskara Miśra. Edited by A. Mahadeva Sastri and K. Rangacarya. Delhi: Motilal Banarsidass, n.d.

The Tāṇḍyamahā Brāhmaṇa According to the Sāmaveda. Edited by A. Cinnasvami Sastri. 2 pts. Banaras: Chowkhamba Sanskrit Series Office, 1935, 1936.

Tāranātha, Jonanpa. *The Origin of the Tārā Tantra*. Translated by David Templeman. Dharamsala: Library of Tibetan Works and Archives, 1981.

Two Tamil Folktales: The Story of King Matanakama and The Story of Peacock Rāvaṇa. Translated by Kamil V. Zvelebil. Delhi: Motilal Banarsidass, 1987.

Upaniṣads: A New Translation. Translated with an introduction by Patrick Olivelle. New York: Oxford University Press, 1996.

Vāmanadatta. *Saṃvitprakāśa*. Edited by Mark S.G. Dyczkowski. Varanasi: Ratna, 1990.

The Veda of the Black Yajus School Entitled Taittirīya Saṃhitā. Translated by Arthur Berriedale Keith. 2 vols. Vols. 18–19 of the Harvard Oriental Series. Cambridge, Mass.: Harvard University Press, 1914.

Woodroffe, Sir John. *The Serpent Power: Being the Ṣaṭ-Cakra-Nirūpaṇa and Pādukā-Pañcaka*. 1913. 14th edn. Madras: Ganesh, 1989.

Yāmunācārya. *Āgamaprāmāṇyam*. Edited by M. Narasimhachary.

Gaekwad's Oriental Series, no. 160. Baroda: Oriental Institute, 1976.
———. *Yāmuna's Āgama Prāmāṇyam; or, Treatise on the Validity of Pāñcarātra.* Sanskrit text and English translation by J.A.B. van Buitenen. Madras: Ramanuja Research Society, 1971.

SECONDARY TEXTS, IN BENGALI, ENGLISH, FRENCH, GERMAN, ITALIAN, AND RUSSIAN

Agarwala, Prithvi K. 'Notes on Two Problematic Images from Bengal.' In *Studies in Art and Archaeology of Bihar and Bengal: Nalinikanta Satavarsiki, Dr. N.K. Bhattaasali Centenary Volume, 1888–1988*, eds. Debala Mitra and Gouriswar Bhattacharya. Delhi: Sri Satguru, 1989.
Alter, Joseph S. *The Wrestler's Body: Identity and Ideology in North India.* Berkeley: University of California Press, 1992.
Appadurai, Arjun, Frank J. Korom, and Margaret A. Mills, eds. *Gender, Genre, and Power in South Asian Expressive Traditions.* Philadelphia: University of Pennsylvania Press, 1991.
Ayyar, P. V. Jagadisa. *The Legends of Vikramaditya.* Calcutta: D. Bose, 1924.
Azarpay, Guitty. *Sogdian Paintings: The Pictorial Epic in Oriental Art.* Berkeley: University of California Press, 1981.
Bakan, David. *Sigmund Freud and the Jewish Mystical Tradition.* Boston: Beacon Press, 1958.
Bandyopādhyāy, Jitendra Nāth. *Pañcopāsanā.* In Bengali. Calcutta: Firma K.L. Mukhopādhyāy, 1960.
Banerjea, Jitendra Nath. *The Development of Hindu Iconography.* 1956. 4th edn. New Delhi: Munshiram Manoharlal, 1985.
Banerjea, S.C. *A Brief History of Tantric Literature.* New Delhi: Naya Prakash, 1988.
Banerjee, P. 'Some Inscriptions from Bihar.' *Journal of Ancient Indian History* 7, pts. 1–2 (1973–74): 102–11.
Banerji, Rakhal Das. *Eastern Indian School of Mediaeval Sculpture.* Archaeological Survey of India, New Imperial Series, 47. Delhi: Manager of Publications, 1933.
Barthakuria, Apurba Chandra. *The Kapalikas: A Critical Study of the Religion, Philosophy and Literature of a Tantric Sect.* Calcutta: Sanskrit Pustak Bhandar, 1984.

Basham, A.L. *The Wonder That Was India*. 2nd edn. 1954. Calcutta: Rupa, 1981.

Behera, D.P. 'Eradication of Meriah or Human Sacrifice from the Social Life of the Kondhs of Orissa in the Nineteenth Century.' In *Tribals of Orissa: The Changing Socio-Economic Profile*, ed. B.C. Ray, 67–76. New Delhi: Gian Publishing House, 1989.

Belenitsky, Alexander. *Central Asia*. Translated by James Hogarth. Cleveland: World, 1968.

Beyer, Stephan. *The Cult of Tārā: Magic and Ritual in Tibet*. Berkeley: University of California Press, 1973.

Bharati, Agehananda. 'Śākta and Vajrayāna: Their Place in Indian Thought.' In *Studies of Esoteric Buddhism and Tantrism*, ed. Gisho Nakano, 73–99. Koyasan: Koyasan University, 1965.

Bharati, Agehananda. 'Techniques of Control in the Esoteric Traditions of India and Tibet.' In *The Realm of the Extra-Human*, vol. 1: *Ideas and Actions*, ed. Agehananda Bharati, 89–99. 2 vols. The Hague: Mouton, 1976.

Bhaṭṭācārya, Haṁsanārāyaṇ. *Hinduder Debadebī: Udbhav o Kramabikāś*. 3 vols. Calcutta: Firma KLM, 1986.

Bhattacharya, Asutosh. 'The Cult of Sasthi in Bengal.' *Man in India* 28, no. 3 (1948): 152–62.

Bhattacharya, A.K. 'A Nonaryan Aspect of the Devī.' In *The Śakti Cult and Tārā*, ed. D.C. Sircar, 56–60. Calcutta: University of Calcutta, 1967.

Bhattacharyya, Narendra Nath. *A Dictionary of Indian Mythology*. New Delhi: Munshiram Manoharlal, 2001.

———. *A Glossary of Indian Religious Terms and Concepts*. New Delhi: Manohar, 1990.

———. *Ancient Indian History and Civilization: Trends and Perspectives*. New Delhi: Manohar, 1988.

———. *Ancient Indian Rituals and Their Social Contents*. 1975. 2nd edn. New Delhi: Manohar, 1996.

———. *Bhārater Svādhīnatā Saṁgrāmer Itihās*. Calcutta: General Printers, 1972.

———. *Buddhism in the History of Indian Ideas*. New Delhi: Manohar, 1993.

———. *Cultural Index to Vedic Literature*. New Delhi: Manohar, 2007.

———. *Encyclopaedia of Jainism*. New Delhi: Manohar, forthcoming.

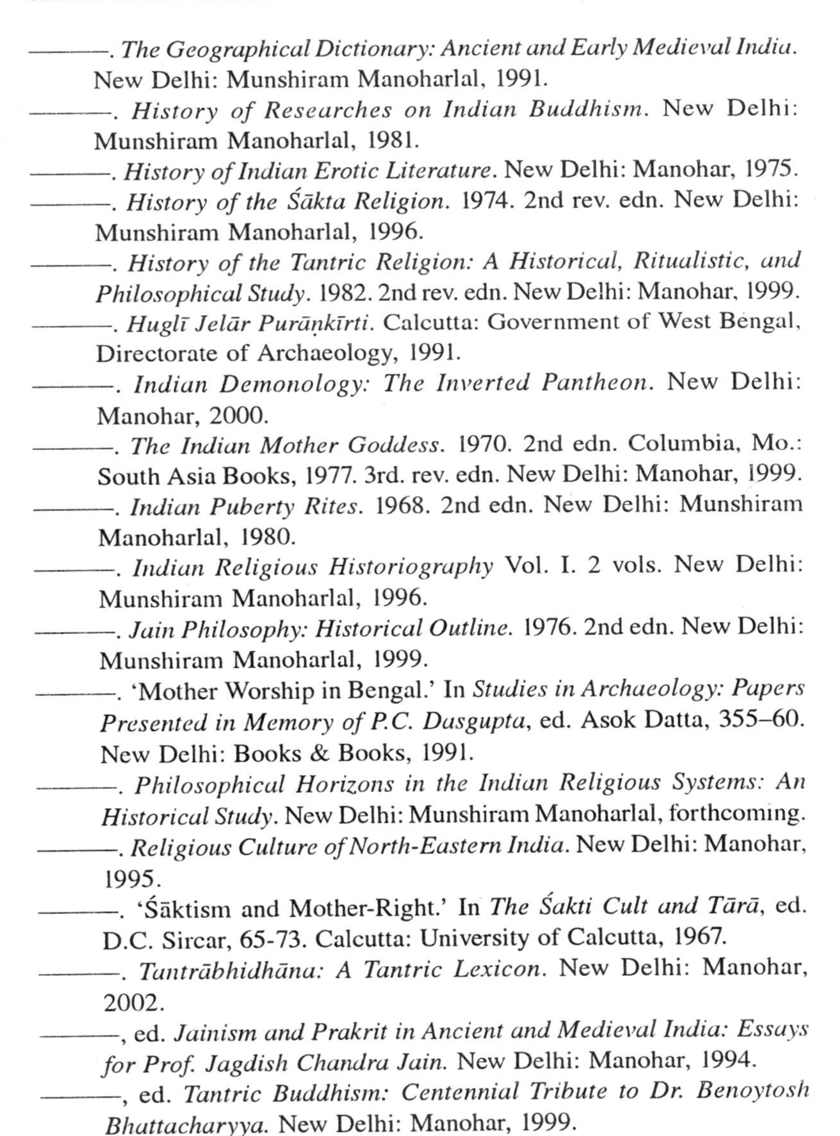

———. *The Geographical Dictionary: Ancient and Early Medieval India*. New Delhi: Munshiram Manoharlal, 1991.
———. *History of Researches on Indian Buddhism*. New Delhi: Munshiram Manoharlal, 1981.
———. *History of Indian Erotic Literature*. New Delhi: Manohar, 1975.
———. *History of the Śākta Religion*. 1974. 2nd rev. edn. New Delhi: Munshiram Manoharlal, 1996.
———. *History of the Tantric Religion: A Historical, Ritualistic, and Philosophical Study*. 1982. 2nd rev. edn. New Delhi: Manohar, 1999.
———. *Huglī Jelār Purāṇkīrti*. Calcutta: Government of West Bengal, Directorate of Archaeology, 1991.
———. *Indian Demonology: The Inverted Pantheon*. New Delhi: Manohar, 2000.
———. *The Indian Mother Goddess*. 1970. 2nd edn. Columbia, Mo.: South Asia Books, 1977. 3rd. rev. edn. New Delhi: Manohar, 1999.
———. *Indian Puberty Rites*. 1968. 2nd edn. New Delhi: Munshiram Manoharlal, 1980.
———. *Indian Religious Historiography* Vol. I. 2 vols. New Delhi: Munshiram Manoharlal, 1996.
———. *Jain Philosophy: Historical Outline*. 1976. 2nd edn. New Delhi: Munshiram Manoharlal, 1999.
———. 'Mother Worship in Bengal.' In *Studies in Archaeology: Papers Presented in Memory of P.C. Dasgupta*, ed. Asok Datta, 355–60. New Delhi: Books & Books, 1991.
———. *Philosophical Horizons in the Indian Religious Systems: An Historical Study*. New Delhi: Munshiram Manoharlal, forthcoming.
———. *Religious Culture of North-Eastern India*. New Delhi: Manohar, 1995.
———. 'Śāktism and Mother-Right.' In *The Śakti Cult and Tārā*, ed. D.C. Sircar, 65-73. Calcutta: University of Calcutta, 1967.
———. *Tantrābhidhāna: A Tantric Lexicon*. New Delhi: Manohar, 2002.
———, ed. *Jainism and Prakrit in Ancient and Medieval India: Essays for Prof. Jagdish Chandra Jain*. New Delhi: Manohar, 1994.
———, ed. *Tantric Buddhism: Centennial Tribute to Dr. Benoytosh Bhattacharyya*. New Delhi: Manohar, 1999.
Bhattasali, Nalini Kanta. *Iconography of Buddhist and Brāhmaṇical Sculptures in the Dacca Museum*. Dacca: Rai S.N. Bhadra Bahadur, 1929.

Biardeau, Madelaine. 'The Śamī Tree and the Sacrificial Buffalo.' *Contributions to Indian Sociology*, n.s., 18, no. 1 (1984): 1–23.

Biasutti, Renato, et al. *Le razze e i popoli della terra*. 1941. 4th rev. edn. 3 vols. Turin: Unione tipografico / Editrice torinese, 1967.

Boal, Barbara M. *The Konds: Human Sacrifice and Religious Change*. Warminster, U.K.: Aris & Philips, 1983.

Briffault, Robert. *The Mothers: A Study of the Origins of Sentiments and Institutions*. 3 vols. New York: Macmillan, 1927.

Brighenti, Francesco. *Śakti Cult in Orissa*. New Delhi: D.K. Printworld, 2001.

Brown, C. Mackenzie. *God as Mother: Feminine Theology in India—an Historical and Theological Study of the Brahmavaivarta Purāṇa*. Hartford, Vt.: Claude Stark, 1974.

———. *The Triumph of the Goddess: The Canonical Models and Theological Visions of the Devī-Bhāgavata Purāṇa*. Albany: State University of New York Press, 1990.

Bühnemann, Gudrun. *The Iconography of Hindu Tantric Deities*. Vol. 1: *The Pantheon of the Mantramahodadhi*. Vol. 2: *The Pantheon of the Prapañcasāra and the Śāradātilaka*. Gonda Indological Studies, vol. 9. Groningen: Egbert Forsten, 2000.

Burwick, Frederick. *Mimesis and Its Romantic Reflections*. University Park: Pennsylvania State University Press, 2001.

Busquet, G. and C. Delacampagne. *Les Aborigènes de l'Inde*. Paris: Arthaud, 1981.

Carman, John Braisted. *The Theology of Rāmānuja*. New Haven: Yale University Press, 1974.

Certeau, Michel de. *The Mystic Fable*. Vol. 1: *The Sixteenth and Seventeenth Centuries*. Chicago: University of Chicago Press, 1992.

Chakravarti, Chintaharan. *Tantras: Studies on Their Religion and Literature*. Calcutta: Punthi Pustak, 1963.

Chandra, Moti. 'Some Aspects of Yaksa Cult.' *Bulletin of the Prince of Wales Museum* 3 (1954): 43–62.

Chandra, R. P. *The Indo-Aryan Races: A Study of the Origins of Indo-Aryan People and Institutions*. 1916. Reprint. New Delhi: Indological Book Corp., 1976.

Charbonneaux, Jean, Roland Martin, and François Villard. *Hellenistic Art (330-50 B.C.)*. Translated from the French by Peter Green. New York: Braziller, 1973.

Chaudhuri, Buddhadeb. *The Bakreshwar Temple: A Study of Continuity and Change*. Delhi: Inter-India, 1981.

Chilli, Shaikh. *Folk-Tales of Hindustan*. Bahadurganj: Bhuwaneswari Asrama, 1920.

Coburn, Thomas B. *The Devī-Māhātmya: Crystallization of the Goddess Tradition*. Delhi: Motilal Banarsidass, 1985.

———. 'Sītā Fights While Rāma Swoons: A Śākta Perspective on the *Rāmāyaṇa*.' *Manushi: A Journal About Women and Society* 90 (1995): 5–16.

Connolly, Peter. *Vitalistic Thought in India: A Study of the 'prāṇa' Concept in Vedic Literature and Its Development in the Vedānta, Sāṃkhya and Pāñcarātra Traditions*. Delhi: Sri Satguru, 1992.

Coomaraswamy, Ananda K. 'Angel and Titan: An Essay in Vedic Ontology.' *Journal of the American Oriental Society* 55, no. 4 (December 1935): 373–419.

———. *Hinduism and Buddhism*. 1944. Edited by Keshavaram N. Iengar and Rama P. Coomaraswamy. 2nd rev. edn. New Delhi: Indira Gandhi National Centre for the Arts, 1999.

———. *Yakṣas: Essays in the Water Cosmology*. Edited by Paul Schroeder. 1928–31. New rev. edn. New Delhi: Indira Gandhi National Centre for the Arts, 1993.

Dalton, E.T. *Descriptive Ethnology of Bengal*. 1872. Reprint. Calcutta: Firma K.L. Mukhopadhyaya, 1960.

Daniélou, Alain. *Hindu Polytheism*. New York: Bollingen Foundation, 1964.

Dasgupta, Shashibhushan. *Obscure Religious Cults*. 1946. Reprint of 3rd edn. Calcutta: Firma KLM, 1976.

Dasgupta, Surendranath. *History of Indian Philosophy*. 5 vols. Cambridge: Cambridge University Press, 1940.

Das, M. N. 'Suppression of Human Sacrifice Among the Hill Tribes of Orissa.' *Man in India* 36 (1956): 21–48.

Datta, Mahendranāth. *Kalikātār Purātan Kāhinī o Prarthā*. 1973. 2nd edn. Kalikata: Mahendra, 1975.

The Days of John Company: Selections from the Calcutta Gazette, 1824–1832. Compiled and edited by Anil Chandra Das Gupta. Calcutta: Government Printing, 1959.

De, Premtoṣ. 'Candanagarer Jagaddhātrī Pujo.' *Sāptahik Bartamān* 12, no. 25 (13 November 1999): 8–10.

Dehejia, Vidya. *Yogini, Cult and Temples: A Tantric Tradition*. New Delhi: National Museum, 1986.

Dehon, P. 'Religion and Customs of the Uraons.' *Memoirs of the Asiatic Society of Bengal* 1 (1905–7): 121–81.

Dimock, Edward C., Jr. *The Place of the Hidden Moon: Erotic Mysticism in the Vaiṣṇava-sahajiyā Cult of Bengal*. 1966. Reprint with a new foreword by Wendy Doniger. Chicago: University of Chicago Press, 1989.

Dimmitt, Cornelia. 'Sītā: Fertility Goddess and *Śakti*.' In *The Divine Consort: Rādhā and the Goddesses of India*, eds. John S. Hawley and Donna Wulff, 210–23. Berkeley, Calif.: Berkeley Religious Studies Series, 1982.

Doniger, Wendy, ed. *Purāṇa Perennis: Reciprocity and Transformation in Hindu and Jaina Texts*. Albany: State University of New York Press, 1993.

———. 'When a Lingam is Just a Good Cigar: Psychoanalysis and Hindu Sexual Fantasies.' Reprinted in *Vishnu on Freud's Desk: A Reader in Psychoanalysis and Hinduism*, eds. T.G. Vaidyanathan and Jeffrey J. Kripal, 279–303. New Delhi: Oxford University Press, 1999.

Donaldson, Thomas. 'Propitious-Apotropaic Eroticism in the Art of Orissa.' *Artibus Asiae* 37 (1975): 75–100.

Dowman, Keith. *Masters of Mahāmūdra: Songs and Histories of the Eighty-Four Buddhist Siddhas*. Albany: State University of New York Press, 1985.

Dowson, J. *A Classical Dictionary of Hindu Mythology and Religion, Geography, History, and Literature*. 1891. Reprint. New Delhi: Oriental Books, 1973.

Dyczkowski, Mark S.G. *The Canon of the Śaivāgama and the Kubjikā Tantras of the Western Kaula Tradition*. Albany: State University of New York Press, 1988.

Eliade, Mircea. *A History of Religious Ideas*. Vol. 1: *From the Stone Age to the Eleusinian Mysteries*. Translated by Willard R. Trask. Chicago: University of Chicago Press, 1978.

———. *Patterns in Comparative Religion*. Translated by Rosemary Sheed. New York: New American Library, 1974.

———. *Rites and Symbols of Initiation: The Mysteries of Birth and Rebirth*. New York: Harper & Row, 1958.

———. *Yoga: Immortality and Freedom*. Translated by Willard R. Trask. 1958. 2nd ed. London: Routledge & Kegan Paul, 1969. Originally published as *Le Yoga: Immortalité et liberté: Patanjali et les Yoga-sutra* (Paris: Payot, 1954).

Elwin, Verrier. *The Muria and Their Ghotul*. Bombay: Oxford University Press, 1947.

———. *Myths of Middle India*. Madras: Oxford University Press, 1949.
———. *Nagaland*. Shillong: Research Department, Adviser's Secretariat, 1961.
———. 'Notes on a Kondh Tour.' *Man in India* 24 (1944): 40–58.
———. *The Religion of an Indian Tribe*. Bombay: Oxford University Press, 1955.
———. *Tribal Myths of Orissa*. Bombay: Oxford University Press, 1954.
Emeneau, M. B., trans. 'Jambhaladatta's Version of the Vetālapañcaviṃśati.' *American Oriental Society* 4 (1934): 59–63.
The Encyclopedia of World Art. 16 vols. New York: McGraw-Hill, 1959–87.
Erndl, Kathleen. 'The Mutilation of Śūrpanakhā.' In *Many Rāmāyaṇas: The Diversity of a Narrative Tradition in South Asia*, ed. Paula Richman, 67–88. Berkeley: University of California Press, 1991.
Ferguson, John P. 'The Great Goddess Today in Burma and Thailand: An Exploration of Her Symbolic Relevance to Monastic and Female Roles.' In *Mother Worship: Theme and Variations*, ed. James J. Preston, 283–303. Chapel Hill: University of North Carolina Press, 1982.
Filippani-Ronconi, Pio. *Miti e religioni dell'India*. 2nd edn. Rome: Newton Compton, 1992.
Frazer, Sir James George. *The Golden Bough: A Study in Magic and Religion*. 1890–1915. 12 vols. 3rd edn. London: Macmillan, 1912–30.
Freud, Sigmund. *Introductory Lectures on Psychoanalysis*. Edited and translated by James Strachey. 1966. New York: Norton, 1977.
———. *Three Essays on the Theory of Sexuality*. 1905. Vol. 7 (1901–5) of *The Standard Edition of the Complete Psychological Works of Sigmund Freud*. Translated under the General Editorship of James Strachey. London: Hogarth Press and Institute of Psycho-Analysis, 1953.
Frumkin, Gregoir. *Archaeology in Soviet Central Asia*. Leiden: E.J. Brill, 1970.
Fürer-Haimendorf, Christoph von. *The Konyak Nagas: An Indian Frontier Tribe*. New York: Holt, Rinehart & Winston, 1969.
———. *The Naked Nagas*. Calcutta: Thacker, Spink, 1933.
———. *The Raj Gonds of Adilabad: A Peasant Culture of the Deccan, Book I: Myth and Ritual*. London: Macmillan, 1948.
Gai, G.S. 'Umā-Maheśvara Image Inscription from Skandar.' *Studies in*

Indian Epigraphy. 3 vols. Vol. 1: 1–6. Mysore: Epigraphical Society of India, 1975–77.

Gait, E.A. 'Human Sacrifice (Indian).' In *Encyclopaedia of Religion and Ethics*, ed. James Hastings. 13 vols. Vol. 6: 853. Edinburgh, T. and T. Clark; New York: Scribner, 1913.

Gay, Volney P. *Freud on Sublimation: Reconsiderations*. Albany: State University of New York Press, 1992.

George, Diana Hume. *Blake and Freud*. Ithaca, N.Y.: Cornell University Press, 1980.

Ghosal, U.N. *Studies in Indian History and Culture*. Bombay: Orient Longman, 1965.

Ghosha, Nanda Lal. 'How to Make a Demon Subservient to Your Will.' *North India Notes and Queries* 5, no. 4 (July 1895).

Ghurye, G.S. *The Scheduled Tribes*. 1943. 3rd edn. Bombay: Popular Prakashan, 1963.

Glucklich, Ariel. *The Sense of Adharma*. Oxford: Oxford University Press, 1994.

Gonda, Jan. *Ancient Indian Kingship from the Religious Point of View*. Leiden: E.J. Brill, 1969.

———. *Aspects of Early Viṣṇuism*. Utrecht: A. Oosthoek, 1954.

———. *Le religioni dell'India:. Veda e antico Induismo*. Milan: Jaca Book, 1981. Originally published as *Religions de l'Inde* (Paris: Payot, 1962–66).

Goswami, Jaya. *Cultural History of Ancient India: A Socio-Economic and Religio-Cultural Survey of Kapiśa and Gandhāra*. Delhi: Agam Kala Prakashan, 1979.

Grierson, George A. 'On the *Adbhuta-Rāmāyaṇa*.' *Bulletin of the School of Oriental Studies* 4, no. 1 (1926): 11–27.

Grigson, W.V. *The Maria Gonds of Bastar*. 1938. 2nd rev. edn. London: Oxford University Press, 1949.

Gupta, Parmeshwari Lal. *Coins*. 3rd edn. Delhi: National Book Trust, 1969.

Gupta, P.L. and D.C. Sircar. 'Umā-Maheśvara Image Inscription from Skandar (Afghanistan).' *Journal of Ancient Indian History*, 6, pts. 1–2 (1972–73): 1–4.

Gupta, Sanjukta. 'The Caturvyūha and the Viśākha-yūpa in the Pāñcarātra.' *Adyar Library Bulletin* 35, pts. 3–4 (1971): 189–204.

———. 'Yoga and *Antaryāga* in Pāñcarātra'. In *Ritual and Speculation in Early Tantrism: Studies in Honor of André Padoux*, ed. Teun Goudriaan, 175–208. Albany: State University of New York Press, 1992.

Gupta, Sanjukta, and Richard Gombrich. 'Kings, Power and the Goddess.' *South Asia Research* 6, no. 2 (November 1986): 123–38.

Halbfass, Wilhelm. *Tradition and Reflection: Explorations in Indian Thought*. Albany: State University of New York Press, 1991.

Hansen, Kathryn. 'Heroic Modes of Women in Indian Myth, Ritual, and History: The *Tapasvinī* and the *Vārāṅganā*.' In *The Annual Review of Women in World Religions*, eds. Arvind Sharma and Katherine K. Young, 2: 1–62. Albany: State University of New York Press, 1992.

Haque, Enamul. *Bengal Sculptures: Hindu Iconography up to c.1250 AD*. Dacca: Bangladesh National Museum, 1992.

Harper, Katherine Anne. 'Appendix: Post-Seventh Century References on the Mātṛkās.' In id., *The Iconography of the Saptamātṛkās: Seven Hindu Goddesses of Spiritual Transformation*. Lewiston, UK: Edwin Mellen Press, 1989.

Hartel, Herbert. 'Some Results of the Excavations at Sonkh: A Preliminary Report.' In *German Scholars on India: Contributions to Indian Studies*, ed. the Cultural Department of the Embassy of the Federal Republic of Germany, New Delhi, 2: 70–99. 2 vols. Varanasi: Chowkhamba Sanskrit Series Office, 1973–76.

Hastings, James, ed., *The Encyclopedia of Religion and Ethics*, 13 vols. New York: Scribner, 1913.

Hatt, G. 'The Corn Mother in America and in Indonesia,' *Anthropos* 46 (1951): 882–89.

Hazra, R. C. *Studies in the Upapuranas*. Vol. 2: *Śākta and Non-Sectarian Upapuranas*. 2 vols. Calcutta: Sanskrit College, 1963.

Heesterman, J. C. *The Ancient Indian Royal Consecration: The Rājasūya Described According to the Yajus Texts and Annotated*. The Hague: Mouton, 1957.

———. 'The Case of the Severed Head.' *Wiener Zeitschrift für die Kunde Süd- und Ostasiens* 11 (1967): 22–43.

———.'Self-Sacrifice in Vedic Ritual.' In *Gilgul: Essays on Transformation, Revolution and Permanence in the History of Religions, Dedicated to R.J. Zwi Werblowsky*, ed. S. Shaked, D. Shulman, and G.G. Stroumsa, 91–106. Leiden: E.J. Brill, 1987.

———. 'Vrātya and Sacrifice.' *Indo-Iranian Journal* 6 (1962): 1–37.

Herrmann-Pfandt, Adelheid. 'The Good Woman's Shadow: Some Aspects of the Dark Nature of Ḍākinīs and Śākinīs in Hinduism.' In *Wild Goddesses in India and Nepal: Proceedings of an International Symposium, Bern and Zurich, November 1994*, eds. Cornelia

Vogelsanger, Axel Michaels, and Annette Wilke, 39–70. Bern: Peter Lang, 1996.

Hillebrandt, A. *Vedic Mythology*. 1927–1929. 2nd rev. edn. Delhi: Motilal Banarsidass, 1980.

Hiltebeitel, Alf. 'The Indus Valley "Proto-Śiva" Reexamined Through Reflections on the Goddess, the Buffalo, and the Symbolism of Vāhanas.' *Anthropos* 73, nos. 5–6 (1978): 767–97.

______. 'Rāma and Gilgamesh: The Sacrifices of the Water Buffalo and the Bull of Heaven.' *History of Religions* 19 (1980): 187–223.

______. 'Religious Studies and Indian Epic Texts.' *Religious Studies Review* 21, no. 1 (January 1995): 26–32.

______, ed. *Popular Hinduism*. Albany: State University of New York Press, 1989.

Homans, Peter. 'Once Again, Psychoanalysis, East and West: A Psychoanalytic Essay on Religion, Mourning, and Healing.' *History of Religions* 24, no. 2 (1984): 133–54.

Hopkins, Jeffrey. 'The Compatibility of Reason and Orgasm in Tibetan Buddhism: Reflections on Sexual Violence and Homophobia.' In *Que(e)rying Religion: A Critical Anthology*, ed. Gary David Comstock and Susan E. Henking, 372–83. New York: Continuum, 1997.

———. *Sex, Orgasm, and the Mind of Clear Light: The Sixty-four Arts of Gay Male Love*. Berkeley, Calif.: North Atlantic Books, 1998.

———. trans. *Tibetan Arts of Love*. New York: Snow Lion, 1992.

Hota, N. R. 'Human Sacrifice Among the Khonds of Orissa.' *Orissa Historical Research Journal* 8 (1959–60): 158–63.

Humes, Cynthia Ann. 'Becoming Male: Salvation Through Gender Modification in Hinduism and Buddhism.' In *Gender Reversals and Gender Cultures: Anthropological and Historical Perspectives*, ed. Sabrina Petra Ramet, 123–37. New York: Routledge, 1996.

———. 'Is the *Devi Mahatmya* a Feminist Scripture?' In *Is the Goddess a Feminist? The Politics of South Asian Goddesses*, eds. Alf Hiltebeitel and Kathleen M. Erndl, 123–50. Sheffield: Sheffield Academic Press, 2000.

———. 'Wrestling with Kālī: South Asian and British Constructions of the Dark Goddess.' In *Encountering Kālī: At the Margins, at the Center, in the West*, eds. Rachel Fell McDermott and Jeffrey J. Kripal, 145–68. Berkeley: University of California Press, 2003.

Huntington, Susan L. *The 'Pala-Sena' Schools of Sculpture*. Leiden: E.J. Brill, 1984.

Hutton, J.H. *Census of India 1931*. Vol. 1. 32 vols. Delhi: Government of India Press, 1933.

———. 'Head Hunting.' *Man in India* 10 (1930): 207–15.

———. 'Lycanthropy.' *Man in India* 11 (1931): 208–16.

———. *The Sema Nagas*. 2nd edn. 1921. London: Oxford University Press, 1968.

Jacobs, J. *Les Nagas*. Geneva: Oligane, 1991.

Jayakar, Pupul. *The Earthen Drum*. New Delhi: National Museum, 1980.

———. *The Earth Mother*. New Delhi: Penguin Books (India), 1989. Revised, updated edition of *The Earthen Drum*.

Joshi, N. P. 'Sasthi in Literature and Art.' In *Ajaya-Sri: Recent Studies in Indology: Prof. Ajay Mitra Shastri Felicitation Volume*, ed. Devendra Handa. Vol. 2: 391–95. 2 vols. Delhi: Sundeep Prakashan, 1989.

Jurewicz, Joanna. 'Playing with Fire: The *Pratītyasamutpāda* from the Perspective of Vedic Thought.' *Journal of the Pali Text Society* 26 (2000): 77–103.

Kakar, Sudhir. *The Inner World*. Delhi: Oxford University Press, 1981.

———. *Intimate Relations: Exploring Indian Sexuality*. Chicago: University of Chicago Press, 1989.

———. *Shamans, Mystics and Doctors: A Psychological Inquiry into India and Its Healing Traditions*. New Delhi: Oxford University Press, 1982.

Keynes, Geoffrey, ed. *William Blake's The Marriage of Heaven and Hell*. With an introduction and commentary. New York: Oxford University Press, 1975.

Kinsley, David R. '"The Death that Conquers Death": Dying to the World in Medieval Hinduism.' In *Religious Encounters with Death: Insights from the History and Anthropology of Religions*, ed. Frank E. Reynolds and Earle H. Waugh, 97–108. University Park: Pennsylvania State University Press, 1977.

———. *Hindu Goddesses: Visions of the Divine Feminine in the Hindu Religious Tradition*. Berkeley: University of California Press, 1986.

———. *Tantric Visions of the Divine Feminine: The Ten Mahāvidyās*. Berkeley: University of California Press, 1997.

Kirschner, Suzanne R. *The Religious and Romantic Origins of Psychoanalysis: Individuation and Integration in Post-Freudian Theory*. Cambridge, Mass.: Harvard University Press, 1996.

Kishwar, Madhu, and Ruth Vanita. *In Search of Answers: Indian Women's Voices from Manushi*. London: Zed Books, 1984.

Kramrisch, Stella. *The Presence of Śiva*. Princeton: Princeton University Press, 1981.

Kripal, Jeffrey J. *Kālī's Child: The Mystical and the Erotic in the Life and Teachings of Rāmakrishna.* 1995. 2nd edn. Chicago: University of Chicago Press, 1998.

———. 'Why the Tāntrika Is a Hero: Kālī in the Psychoanalytic Tradition.' In *Encountering Kālī: In the Margins, at the Center, in the West*, ed. Rachel Fell McDermott and Jeffrey J. Kripal, 196–222. Berkeley: University of California Press, 2002.

———. 'Psychoanalysis and Hinduism: Thinking Through Each Other.' Afterword to *Vishnu on Freud's Desk: A Reader in Psychoanalysis and Hinduism*, ed. T.G. Vaidyanathan and Jeffrey J. Kripal, 438–52. New Delhi: Oxford University Press, 1999.

———. *Roads of Excess, Palaces of Wisdom: Eroticism and Reflexivity in the Study of Mysticism.* Chicago: University of Chicago Press, 2001.

Kruglikova, Irina Timofeevna. *Dil'berdzhin: Materialy sovetsko-afganskoi arkeologicheskoi ekspeditsii.* 3 vols. Moscow: Nauka, 1986.

Kumar, P. Pratap. *The Goddess Lakṣmī: The Divine Consort in South Indian Vaiṣṇava Tradition.* American Academy of Religion, Academy Series no. 95. Atlanta: Scholars Press, 1997.

Kvaerne, Per. *An Anthology of Buddhist Tantric Songs: A Study of the Caryāgīti.* Oslo: Universitetsforlaget, 1977.

La Barre, Weston. *They Shall Take Up Serpents: Psychology of the Southern Snake-Handling Cult.* Minneapolis: University of Minnesota Press, 1962.

Lalou, Marcelle. *Iconographie des étoffes peintes (pata) dans le Mañjuśrīmūlakalpa.* Paris: P. Geuthner, 1930.

Lorenzen, David N. *The Kāpālikas and Kālamukhas: Two Lost Śaivite Sects.* Berkeley: University of California Press, 1972.

Lutgendorf, Philip. *The Life of a Text: Performing the Rāmcaritmānas of Tulsidas.* Berkeley: University of California Press, 1991.

MacDonald, Ariane, ed. and trans. *Le Maṇḍala du Mañjuśrīmūlakalpa.* Paris: Adrien-Maisonneuve, 1962.

Macdonell, Arthur Anthony. *A Practical Sanskrit Dictionary.* 1924. Reprint. Oxford: Oxford University Press, 1965. Delhi: Munshiram Manoharlal, 1996.

Macdonnell, Arthur Anthony, and Arthur Berriedale Keith. *Vedic Index of Names and Subjects.* 1912. Reprint. Varanasi: Motilal Banarsidass, 1958.

Mackay, E.J.H. *Further Excavations at Mohenjo-daro*. Delhi: Government of India Press, 1938.

Macpherson, Samuel Charters. 'An Account of the Religion of the Khonds of Orissa.' *Journal of the Royal Asiatic Society of Great Britain* 13 (1852): 216–74.

———. *Memorials of Service in India: From the correspondence of the late Major Samuel Charters Macpherson, C.B. Political Agent at Gwalior during the mutiny and formerly employed in the Suppression of Human Sacrifice in Orissa*. Edited by William Macpherson. London: John Murray, 1865.

Mahalingam, T.V. 'The Cult of Śakti in Tamilnad.' In *The Śakti Cult and Tārā*, ed. D.C. Sircar, 17–33. Calcutta: University of Calcutta, 1967.

Majumdar, R.C. *The History of Bengal*. Vol. 1. 2 vols. Dacca: University of Dacca, 1943.

Mallmann, Marie-Thérèse de. *Les Enseignements iconographiques de L'Agni-Purana*. Paris: Presses universitaires de France, 1963.

Marshall, John H., ed. *Mohenjo-Daro and the Indus Civilization*. 3 vols. London: Arthur Probshtan, 1931.

Maxwell, T.S. *Viśvarūpa*. Bombay: Oxford University Press, 1988.

Mazumdar, B.C. 'The Kui or Kondh People.' *Man in India* 12 (1932): 245–52.

McCutchion, David. *Brick Temples of Bengal: From the Archives of David McCutchion*. Edited by George Michell. Princeton: Princeton University Press, 1983.

McDaniel, June. *The Madness of the Saints: Ecstatic Religion in Bengal*. Chicago: University of Chicago Press, 1989.

McDermott, Rachel Fell. *Of Fortunes and Festivals: Money, Power, and the Goddess of Bengal*. New York: Columbia University Press, forthcoming.

———. *Singing to the Goddess: Poems to Kālī and Umā from Bengal*. New York: Oxford University Press, 2001.

Misra, Ram Nath. *Yaksha Cult and Iconography*. New Delhi: Munshiram Manoharlal, 1981.

Mitra, Sudhīrkumār. *Huglī Jelār Debideul*. Kalikaṭa: Aparna Book Distributers, 1991.

Mitterwallner, Gritli von. 'The Kuṣāṇa Type of the Goddess Mahiṣāsuramardinī as Compared to the Gupta and Mediaeval Types.' In *German Scholars on India: Contributions to Indian Studies*, ed. the Cultural Department of the Embassy of the Federal Republic of Germany, New Delhi, 2: 196–213. 2 vols. Varanasi: Chowkhamba Sanskrit Series Office, 1973–76.

Mode, H. *Das frühe Indien*. Stuttgart: Gustav Kilpper, 1959.

Mookerjee, Ajit, and Madhu Khanna. *The Tantric Way: Art, Science, Ritual*. London: Thames & Hudson, 1977.

Mukherjea, C. *The Santals*. 1939. 2nd edn. Calcutta: A. Mukherjee, 1962.

Mukherjee, B.N. 'Foreign Elements in Iconography of Mahishāsuramardinī—The War Goddess of India.' In *Zeitschrift der Deutschen Morgenländischen Gesellschaft*, suppl. 6, 402–14. Stuttgart: Franz Steiner, 1985.

———. *Mathura and Its Society—the Śaka-Pahlava Phase*. Calcutta: Firma K.L. Mukhopadhyay, 1981.

———. *Nanā on Lion: A Study in Kushāṇa Numismatic Art*. Calcutta: Asiatic Society, 1969.

———. 'Pictures from Woodcut Blocks: An Iconological Analysis.' In *Woodcut Prints of Nineteenth-Century Calcutta*, ed. Ashit Paul, 108–21. Calcutta: Seagull, 1983.

———. *Śaktir Rūp Bhārate o Madhya Eśiyāy*. Calcutta: Ānanda, 1990.

Mukherjee, P. 'Human Sacrifices Among the Khonds of Orissa—A Note.' *Orissa Historical Research Journal* 8 (1959–60): 164–67.

Mukhopadhyay, Ajit Kumar, and Kalyan Chakrabortty. *Discover Chandernagore*. Chandannagar, Hooghly: Kumar, 1999.

Nagaswami, R. *Tantric Cult of South India*. Delhi: Agam Kala Prakashan, 1982.

Narasimhachary, M. *Contribution of Yāmunācārya to Viśiṣṭādvaita*. Hyderabad: Sri Jayalakshmi, 1998.

Narayan, Kirin. *Storytellers, Saints, and Scoundrels: Folk Narrative in Hindu Religious Teaching*. Philadelphia: University of Pennsylvania Press, 1989.

Narayanan, Vasudha. 'Śrī: Giver of Fortune, Bestower of Grace.' In *Devī: Goddesses of India*, eds. John Stratton Hawley and Donna Marie Wulff, 87–108. Berkeley: University of California Press, 1996.

O'Flaherty, Wendy Doniger. *Asceticism and Eroticism in the Mythology of Śiva*. London: Oxford University Press, 1973.

———. *Hindu Myths: A Sourcebook Translated from Sanskrit*. New York: Penguin Books, 1975.

———. *The Origins of Evil in Hindu Mythology*. Berkeley: University of California Press, 1976.

———. *Sexual Metaphors and Animal Symbols in Indian Mythology*. Delhi: Motilal Banarsidass, 1981.

———. *Women, Androgynes, and Other Mythical Beasts*. Chicago: University of Chicago Press, 1980.

Olivelle, Patrick. 'Orgasmic Rapture and Divine Ecstasy: The Semantic History of "Ānanda".' *Journal of Indian Philosophy* 25 (1997): 153–80.

Padoux, André. 'Hindu Tantrism.' In *The Encyclopedia of Religion*, ed. Mircea Eliade, 14: 274–80. 16 vols. New York: Macmillan, 1987.

Pal, Pratapaditya. *Hindu Religion and Iconology According to the Tantrasāra*. Los Angeles: Vichitra Press, 1981.

Pandharipande, Rajeshwari. 'Spiritual Dimension of Fertility Cult and Power in Woman.' *Journal of Dharma* (Bangalore) 13 (July–September 1988): 267–81.

Parpola, Asko. *Deciphering the Indus Script*. Cambridge: Cambridge University Press, 1994.

______. 'The Harappan "Priest King's" Robe and the Vedic Tārpya Garment: Their Interrelation and Symbolism (Astral and Procreative).' In *South Asian Archaeology 1983*, ed. Janine Schotsmans and Maurizio Taddei, 1: 385–403. 2 vols. Naples: Istituto universitario orientale, Dipartimento di studi asiatici, 1985.

———. 'The Pre-Vedic Indian Background of the Śrauta Rituals.' In *Agni: The Vedic Ritual of the Fire Altar*, ed. Frits Staal, in collaboration with C.V. Somayajipad and M. Itti Ravi Nambudiri, 2: 41–75. 2 vols. Berkeley, Calif.: Asian Humanities Press, 1983.

Parry, Jonathan. 'Sacrificial Death and Necrophagous Ascetic.' In *Death and the Regeneration of Life*, ed. Maurice Bloch and Jonathan Parry, 74–110. New York: Cambridge University Press, 1982.

Parsons, William B. *The Enigma of the Oceanic Feeling: The Freud-Rolland Correspondence and the Revisioning of the Psychoanalytic Theory of Mysticism*. New York: Oxford University Press, 1999.

Pathak, S.K. 'The Language of the Ārya Mañjuśrīmūlakalpa (-tantra).' In *Aspects of Buddhist Sanskrit: Proceedings of the International Symposium on the Language of Sanskrit Buddhist Texts, Oct. 1–5, 1991*, ed. Kameshwar Nath Mishra, 278–306. Samyagvāk series 6. Sarnath: Central Institute of Higher Tibetan Studies, 1993.

Pintchman, Tracy. *The Rise of the Goddess in the Hindu Tradition*. Albany: State University of New York Press, 1994.

Pott, P.H. *Yoga and Yantra: Their Interrelation and Their Significance for Indian Archaeology*. The Hague: Martinus Nijhoff, 1966.

Powers, John. *Introduction to Tibetan Buddhism*. Ithaca, N.Y.: Snow Lion, 1995.

Prasad, R.R. and Sachchidananda, eds. *Encyclopaedic Profile of Indian Tribes*. 4 vols. New Delhi: Discovery, 1996.

Pratap, P. 'The Development of Ego Ideal in Indian Children.' Ph.D. thesis, Banaras Hindu University, 1960.

Pugachenkova, Galina Anatol'evna, and L.I. Rempel'. *Ocherki iskusstva Srednei Azii: Drevnosti srednevekove*. Moscow: Iskusstvo, 1982.

Raghavan,V., ed. *The Rāmāyaṇa Tradition in Asia*. New Delhi: Sahitya Akademi, 1980.

Rahmann, R. 'Shamanistic and Related Phenomena in Northern and Middle India.' *Anthropos* 54 (1959): 681–760.

———. 'The Ritual Spring Hunt of Northeastern and Middle India.' *Anthropos* 47 (1952): 871–90.

Ramanujan, A. K. 'Three Hundred *Rāmāyaṇas*: Five Examples and Three Thoughts on Translation.' In *Many Rāmāyaṇas: The Diversity of a Narrative Tradition in South Asia*, ed. Paula Richman, 22–49. Berkeley: University of California Press, 1991.

———. 'Toward a Counter-System: Women's Tales.' In *Gender, Genre, and Power in South Asian Expressive Traditions*, ed. Arjun Appadurai, Frank J. Korom, and Margaret A. Mills, 33–55. Philadelphia: University of Pennsylvania Press, 1991.

Rao, T. Gopinath. *Elements of Hindu Iconography*. Madras: Law Printing House, 1914.

Rao, Velchuru Narayan. 'A *Rāmāyaṇa* of Their Own: Women's Oral Tradition in Telugu.' In *Many Rāmāyaṇas: The Diversity of a Narrative Tradition in South Asia*, ed. Paula Richman, 114–36. Berkeley: University of California Press, 1991.

Rawson, Philip. *Oriental Erotic Art*. New York: A & W, 1981.

Raychaudhuri, Hemchandra. *Materials for the Study of the Early History of the Vaishnava Sect*. Calcutta: University of Calcutta, 1936.

Richman, Paula. *Questioning Rāmāyaṇas: A South Asian Tradition*. Berkeley: University of California Press, 2001.

Rocher, Ludo. *The Purāṇas*. Vol. 2, fasc. 3 of *A History of Indian Literature*, ed. Jan Gonda. Wiesbaden: Otto Harrassowitz, 1986.

Roxburgh,William. *Flora Indica; or, Descriptions of Indian Plants*. Vol. 3. 3 vols. Serampore: W. Thacker, 1832.

Roy, Kumkum. *The Emergence of Monarchy in North India, Eighth–Fourth Centuries B.C., as Reflected in the Brāhmaṇical Tradition*. New Delhi: Oxford University Press, 1994.

———. 'Perceptions of Power: An Analysis of the *Paryāya Sūkta* (8.10) of the *Atharva Veda.*' In *Proceedings of the Indian History Congress,* 1992: 56–62.

Roy, S. C. *The Orāons of Chotā Nāgpur: Their History, Economic Life, and Social Organization.* 1915. Reprint. Ranchi: Man in India Office, 1984.

———. *Orāon Religion and Customs.* Ranchi: Man in India Office, 1928.

———. *The Mundas and Their Country.* 1912. Reprint. Bombay: Asia Publishing House, 1970.

Sahay, K.N. 'Oraon.' In *Encyclopaedic Profile of Indian Tribes*, ed. Sachchidananda and R.R. Prasad. Vol. 3: 771–73. 4 vols. New Delhi: Discovery, 1996.

Saletore, R.N. *Indian Witchcraft.* New Delhi: Abhinav, 1981.

Sarkar, Benoy Kumar. *The Folk Element in Hindu Culture: A Contribution to Socio-Religious Studies in Hindu Folk-Institutions.* 1917. Reprint. New Delhi: Cosmo, 1972.

Schefold, Karl. *Myth and Legend in Early Greek Art.* New York: Harry N. Abrams, 1966.

Sen Gupta, Nilima. *Cultural History of Kapiśa and Gandhara.* Delhi: Sundeep, 1984.

Sengupta, Gautam. *Treasures of the State Archaeological Museum, West Bengal.* Vol. 2: *Sculptures.* 3 vols. Calcutta: Directorate of Archaeology, Government of West Bengal, 1991.

Sentapau, H. *Common Trees.* New Delhi: National Book Trust, 1966.

Shabad, Peter. 'The Most Intimate of Creations: Symptoms as Memorials to One's Lonely Suffering.' In *Symbolic Loss: The Ambiguity of Mourning and Memory at Century's End*, ed. Peter Homans, 197–212. Charlottesville: University Press of Virginia, 2000.

Sharma, Ursala. 'Foreword.' In Joanna Liddle and Rāma Joshi, *Daughters of Independence: Gender, Caste and Class in India*, 1–2. London: Zed Books, 1986.

Shaw, Miranda. *Buddhist Goddesses of India, Tibet, and Nepal.* Princeton: Princeton University Press, forthcoming.

———. *Passionate Enlightenment: Women in Tantric Buddhism.* Princeton: Princeton University Press, 1994.

Shukla, H.L. *History of the People of Bastar.* Delhi: Sharada, 1992.

———. *Tribal History: A New Interpretation.* Delhi: B.R., 1988.

Shulman, David. 'Battle as Metaphor in Tamil Folk Narrative.' In *Another Harmony: New Essays on the Folklore of India*, ed. Stuart H.

Blackburn and A.K. Ramanujan, 105–30. Berkeley: University of California Press, 1986.

———. 'The Murderous Bride: Tamil Versions of the Myth of the Devī and the Buffalo-Demon.' *History of Religions* 16 (1976): 120–46.

———. 'Sītā and Satakantharāvaṇa in a Tamil Folk Narrative.' *Journal of Indian Folkloristics* 2, nos. 3–4 (1979): 1–26.

Sinha, Jadunath. *The Cult of Divine Power: Saktisadhana*. Calcutta: Sinha, 1977.

Sinha, Kāliprasanna. *Hutom Pyāṇcār Nakśā*. 2nd edn. Calcutta: Bose, 1862.

Sircar, D. C. 'Jaynagar Image Inscription of Year 35.' *Journal of the Bihar Research Society* 41, pt. 2 (June 1955): 143–53.

———. *The Śākta Pīṭhas*. 2nd rev. ed. Delhi: Motilal Banarsidass, 1973.

———. 'Three Inscriptions from Valgudar.' *Epigraphia Indica* 28, pt. 3 (July 1949).

Skilling, Peter. 'The Rakṣā Literature of the Śrāvakayāna.' *Journal of the Pali Text Society* 16 (1992): 109–82.

Slusser, Mary Shepherd. *Nepal Mandala: A Cultural Study of the Kathmandu Valley*. 2 vols. Princeton: University Press, 1982.

Smith, Brian K. *Reflections on Resemblance, Ritual, and Religion*. Delhi: Motilal Banarsidass, 1988.

Smith, Brian K., and Wendy Doniger. 'Sacrifice and Substitution: Ritual Mystification and Mythical Demystification.' *Numen: International Review for the History of Religions* 36, no. 2 (1989): 189–224.

Smith, W.C. *The Ao Naga Tribe of Assam: A Study in Ethnology and Sociology*. London: Macmillan, 1925.

Smith, W.L. *Rāmāyaṇa Traditions in Eastern India*. Stockholm: University of Stockholm Department of Indology, 1988.

Snellgrove, David L. *The Hevajra Tantra: A Critical Study*. 2 vols. London Oriental Series 6. London: Oxford University Press, 1959.

———. *Indo-Tibetan Buddhism: Indian Buddhists and Their Tibetan Successors*. London: Serindia, 1987.

Srinivasan, Doris. 'The So-Called Proto-Śiva Seal from Mohenjo Daro: An Iconological Assessment.' *Archives of Asian Art* 29 (1975–76): 47–58.

Staal, Frits, in collaboration with C.V. Somayajipad and M. Itti Ravi Nambudiri. *Agni: The Vedic Ritual of the Fire Altar*. 2 vols. Berkeley, Calif.: Asian Humanities Press, 1983.

Steinberg, Leo. *The Sexuality of Christ in Renaissance Art and Modern Oblivion*. 1983. 2nd edn. Chicago: University of Chicago Press, 1996.

Stietencron, Heinrich von. 'Die Gottin Durgā Mahiṣāsuramārdini: Mythos, Darstellung und geschichtliche Rolle bei der Hinduiseirung Indiens.' In *Visible Religion: Annual for Religious Iconography*, 118–66. Leiden: E.J. Brill, 1983.

Stirn, Aglaja, and Peter Van Ham. *The Seven Sisters of India: Tribal Worlds Between Tibet and Burma*. New York: Prestel, 2000.

Stutley, Margaret, and James Stutley. *A Dictionary of Hinduism: Its Mythology, Folklore and Development, 1500 B.C.–A.D. 1500*. London: Routledge & Kegan Paul, 1977.

Sutherland, Gail Hinich. *The Disguises of the Demon: The Development of the Yakṣa in Hinduism and Buddhism*. Albany: State University of New York Press, 1991.

Sutherland, Sally. 'Sītā and Draupadī: Aggressive Behavior and Female Role-Models in the Sanskrit Epics.' *Journal of the American Oriental Society* 109, no. 1 (1989): 63–79.

Svoboda, Robert. *Aghora: At the Left Hand of God*. Albuquerque, N.M.: Brotherhood of Life, 1986.

———. *Aghora II: Kundalini*. Albuquerque, N.M.: Brotherhood of Life, 1993.

Tattwananda, Swami. *The Saints of India*. Calcutta: Nirmalendu Bikash Sen, n.d.

Thiel-Horstmann, Monika, ed. *Rāmāyaṇa and Rāmāyaṇas*. Wiesbaden: Otto Harrassowitz, 1991.

Thurston, Edgar. *Castes and Tribes of Southern India*. Madras: Government Press, 1909.

Troisi, J. *Tribal Religion: Religious Beliefs and Practices Among the Santals*. New Delhi: Manohar, 1978.

Turner, Victor. *The Ritual Process: Structure and Anti-Structure*. Harmondsworth, U.K.: Penguin Books, 1969.

Venkatachari, K.K.A. *The Maṇipravāḷa Literature of the Śrīvaiṣṇava Ācāryas, 12th to 15th Century A.D.* Bombay: Ananthacharya Research Institute, 1978.

Vogel, J.P. 'The Head-Offering to the Goddess in Pallava Sculpture.' *Bulletin of the School of Oriental Studies* (London) 6, no. 2 (1931): 539–43.

Ward, William. *The History, Literature, and Mythology of the Hindoos*. 1817–20. 4 vols. Reprint. Delhi: Low Price, 1990.

Watts, N.A. *The Half-Clad Tribals of Eastern India*. Bombay: Orient Longmans, 1970.

Whaling, Frank. *The Rise of the Religious Significance of Rāma*. Delhi: Motilal Banarsidass, 1980.

White, David Gordon. *The Alchemical Body: Siddha Traditions in Medieval India*. Chicago: University of Chicago Press, 1996.

______. 'Introduction.' In *Tantra in Practice*, ed. David Gordon White, 3–38. Princeton: Princeton University Press, 2000.

Wolfson, Elliot. *Through a Speculum That Shines: Vision and Imagination in Medieval Kabbalah*. Princeton: Princeton University Press, 1994.

Woodroffe, Sir John, ed. *The Garland of Letters (Varnamalā)*. Madras: Ganesh, 1922.

Wulff, David H. *Psychology of Religion: Classic & Contemporary*. New York: Wiley, 1997.

Zimmer, Heinrich. *Myths and Symbols in Indian Art and Civilization*. Edited by Joseph Campbell. 1946. Reprint. New York: Harper & Brothers, 1962.

Index

Page numbers accompanied by the letter F refer to figures; page numbers accompanied by the letter M refer to maps; page numbers accompanied by the letter n refer to notes.

Contributors

FRANCESCO BRIGHENTI, Independent Researcher, Italy.

THOMAS B. COBURN, President and Professor of Religious Studies Naropa University, Boulder, Colorado.

SANJUKTA GUPTA, Professor, Oriental Institute, Oxford University, Oxford, United Kingdom.

CYNTHIA ANN HUMES, CTO and Associate Professor of Religious Studies, Claremont McKenna College, Claremont, California.

DAVID R. KINSLEY, Professor (deceased), Department of Religion, McMaster University, Hamilton, Ontario, Canada.

JEFFREY J. KRIPAL, J. Newton Rayzor Professor and Chair of Religious Studies, Rice University, Houston, Texas.

JUNE MCDANIEL, Professor, Dept. of Religious Studies, College of Charleston, Charleston, South Carolina.

RACHEL FELL MCDERMOTT, Associate Professor, Asian and Middle Eastern Cultures, Barnard College, New York, New York.

B.N. MUKHERJEE, Carmichael Professor Emeritus, Department of Ancient Indian History and Culture, University of Calcutta, Kolkata, West Bengal, India.

KUMKUM ROY, Associate Professor, Centre for Historical Studies, School of Social Sciences, Jawaharlal Nehru University, New Delhi, India.

GAUTAM SENGUPTA, Director, Directorate of Archaeology and Museums, Government of West Bengal; Member-Secretary, Centre for Archaeological Studies and Training, Eastern India, Kolkata, West Bengal, India.

MIRANDA SHAW, Professor, Department of Religion, University of Richmond, Richmond, Virginia.